Wellness Management Powered by AI Technologies

Scrivener Publishing
100 Cummings Center, Suite 541J
Beverly, MA 01915-6106

Machine Learning in Biomedical Science and Healthcare Informatics

**Series Editors: Vishal Jain (drvishaljain83@gmail.com)
and Jyotir Moy Chatterjee (jyotirchatterjee@gmail.com)**

In this series, an attempt has been made to capture the scope of various applications of machine learning in the biomedical engineering and healthcare fields, with a special emphasis on the most representative machine learning techniques, namely deep learning-based approaches. Machine learning tasks are typically classified into two broad categories depending on whether there is a learning 'label' or 'feedback' available to a learning system: supervised learning and unsupervised learning. This series also introduces various types of machine learning tasks in the biomedical engineering field from classification (supervised learning) to clustering (unsupervised learning). The objective of the series is to compile all aspects of biomedical science and healthcare informatics, from fundamental principles to current advanced concepts.

Publishers at Scrivener
Martin Scrivener (martin@scrivenerpublishing.com)
Phillip Carmical (pcarmical@scrivenerpublishing.com)

Wellness Management Powered by AI Technologies

Edited by

Bharat Bhushan
School of Engineering and Technology, Sharda University, Greater Noida, India

Akib Khanday
Dept. of Computer Science and Software Engineering,
United Arab Emirates University, UAE
Department of Computer Science, Samarkand International University
of Technology, Samarkand, Uzbekistan

Khursheed Aurangzeb
College of Computer and Information Sciences, King Saud University,
Riyadh, Kingdom of Saudi Arabia

Sudhir Kumar Sharma
KIET Group of Institutions, Delhi-NCR, Ghaziabad, India

and

Parma Nand
School of Engineering Technology, Sharda University, Greater Noida, India

Scrivener Publishing

WILEY

This edition first published 2025 by John Wiley & Sons, Inc., 111 River Street, Hoboken, NJ 07030, USA
and Scrivener Publishing LLC, 100 Cummings Center, Suite 541J, Beverly, MA 01915, USA

For more information about Scrivener publications please visit www.scrivenerpublishing.com.

Wiley Global Headquarters
111 River Street, Hoboken, NJ 07030, USA

For details of our global editorial offices, customer services, and more information about Wiley products visit us at www.wiley.com.

Library of Congress Cataloging-in-Publication Data

ISBN 978-1-394-28699-7

Front cover images courtesy of Adobe Firefly
Cover design by Russell Richardson

Set in size of 11pt and Minion Pro by Manila Typesetting Company, Makati, Philippines

Printed in the USA

10 9 8 7 6 5 4 3 2 1

Contents

Preface

Machine Learning (ML) and the Internet of Things (IoT) offer powerful applications and solutions when integrated. ML and IoT have become essential components of the healthcare industry, with hospitals, clinics, and healthcare providers adopting ML-powered diagnostic tools, wearable devices, and IoT-enabled patient monitoring systems. This adoption aims to improve patient care, reduce healthcare costs, and enhance service quality. ML and IoT are key growth areas within the technology sector, with tech companies, startups, and research institutions actively developing innovative solutions that leverage ML algorithms and IoT connectivity to address healthcare challenges.

This book explores how technology has become an essential component of modern healthcare solutions, from wearable smart devices that track vital signs in real time to machine learning-driven diagnostic tools that generate precise forecasts. IoT devices produce vast amounts of data from sensors and connected systems. By applying machine learning algorithms to this data, patterns can be identified that predict when a machine is likely to fail, enabling predictive maintenance, reducing downtime, and optimizing maintenance schedules.

IoT devices monitor patients' health metrics, while ML models analyze this data to detect abnormalities and alert healthcare professionals. Together, ML and IoT have optimized healthcare processes and contributed to proactive wellness management. They demonstrate how smart wearable devices, with real-time vital sign tracking, and ML-driven diagnostic tools, capable of highly accurate predictions, are reshaping the landscape of healthcare solutions. The convergence of ML and IoT has also led to innovative solutions in remote patient monitoring, early disease detection, mental health support, and personalized wellness plans.

We are grateful to the contributing authors for their dedication and expertise, and we extend our thanks to the reviewers who have provided invaluable feedback throughout the preparation of this volume. Finally, we thank Martin Scrivener and Scrivener Publishing for their support and publication.

The Editors
October 2024

1

Exploring Functional Modules Using Co-Clustering of Protein Interaction Networks

R. Gowri[1]* and R. Rathipriya[2]†

[1]*Department of Computer Science, AVS College of Arts and Science (Autonomous), Salem, Tamil Nadu, India*

[2]*Department of Computer Science, Periyar University, Salem, Tamil Nadu, India*

Abstract

This chapter introduces the new score-based co-clustering (SCoC) method for functional module mining (FMM) in protein interaction networks (PINs). This strategy focuses on the drawbacks of previous approaches, including computational overhead, time consumption, and a disregard for quality and overlapping modules. This chapter has proposed two revised versions of the SCoC method: MR-CoC and SCoC rand. Artificial datasets are utilized to evaluate these suggested methods' performances. These datasets are created with the intention of imposing certain criteria, such as distributed co-cluster, matrix type, noise, and data size. This chapter discusses how these suggested ways are being implemented. Additionally, the MR-CoC was used for functional module mining in the protein interaction networks of humans. To analyze the efficiency of MR-CoC, its results are compared with those of existing protein complexes. The biological implications of these findings have been further examined.

Keywords: MapReduce, protein modules, functional modules, functional coherence, key-value pairs, molecular function

**Corresponding author*: gowri.candy@gmail.com

†*Corresponding author*: rathi_priyar@periyaruniversity.ac.in

Bharat Bhushan, Akib Khanday, Khursheed Aurangzeb, Sudhir Kumar Sharma and Parma Nand (eds.) Wellness Management Powered by AI Technologies, (1–54) © 2025 Scrivener Publishing LLC

1.1 Introduction

The major problem focused on in this research work is the functional module mining in a protein interaction network (PIN). Currently, the functional modules are identified based on laboratory experiments. This process involves the selection of the initial candidates and elimination/addition of the participants to this module based on the lab experiments and analysis. The choice of the initial candidates for the functional module is made manually by the biologists using specific tools based on their requirements. Finding such candidates from the complex PIN is a tedious task to the biologists [1]. This current research is aimed to propose a computational solution to this problem as shown in Figure 1.1.

Currently, the availability of biological networks is increasing due to technological developments in bioinformatics [2]. These networks are highly useful in the medical field for studying and analyzing the behaviors and functionality of various pathogens within the host organisms [3]. They are used for early detection of disease, disease diagnosis, prognosis, drug discovery, drug target identification, and so on.

They are also used to study the functionalities of various organisms, especially in their PINs, which are used to communicate signals or

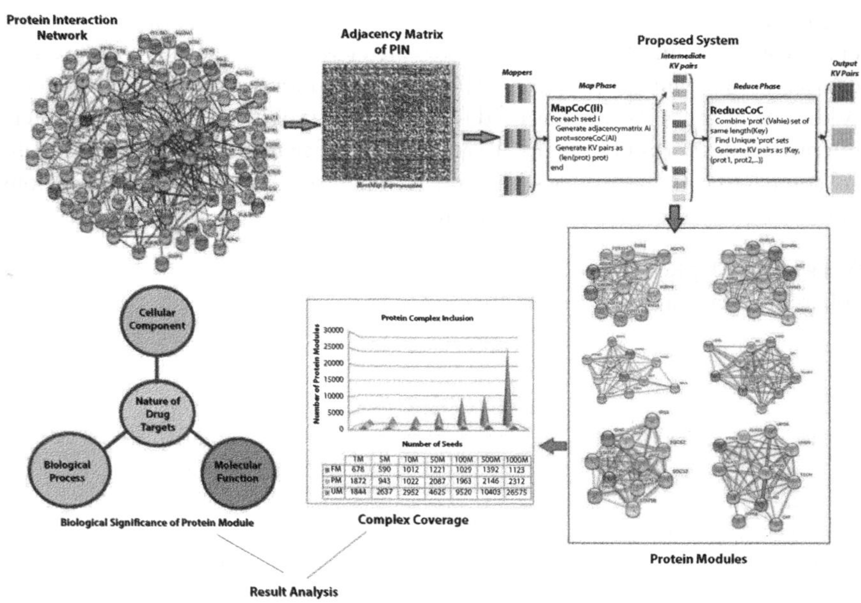

Figure 1.1 Workflow of the current research.

information within the biological system [4]. The proteins are connected with each other to form a PIN. The protein complexes or functional modules are the groups of proteins densely connected to perform a specific biological process.

The major significances [5, 6] of the functional module mining are as follows:

- The central nodes of the biological networks are vulnerable to the targeted attacks by dangerous diseases.
- Predicting key targets for tackling glioma (malignant tumor) drug resistance.
- The network modularity correlated with cancer (diseased) patient survivability.
- The pathogen infection (say cancer) tend to be enriched in particular network modules.
- Finding the hallmark network modules activated predominantly in each tumor is achieved by the identification of significant network modules.
- Neurodegenerative diseases (e.g., Parkinson's disease) are due to many dysregulated physiological processes, which are identified from the abnormalities in molecular networks.
- Identification of therapeutic targets (drug target-based functional modules) in complex disorders is a major challenge in developing effective therapies for complex diseases.

In the literature, various approaches exist for functional module (sub-networks) identification. Some approaches use graph theoretical concepts to identify these sub-networks but face issues like scalability, ignorance of overlapped sub-networks, time consumption, and computational overhead [41–44]. From the related works, it has also been found that such approaches do not consider any functional features for identifying the functional modules.

The objective of this chapter is to overcome these issues and also extract the functional modules based on their functional density measures using data-mining techniques. The score-based co-clustering with MapReduce (MR-CoC) approach is experimented with on the PIN of *Homo sapiens*, and the results are compared with the existing protein complexes. This approach mines the existing protein complexes efficiently. Then, the biological significances of the unknown modules are analyzed.

Biologists can use this approach for finding novel functional modules from any PIN. It reduces the complexity of manual extraction of functional modules and can be used for predicting the new drug targets for various diseases. These resultant modules can be further tested in laboratories for new functional module predictions.

This chapter is further organized as follows: Section 1.2 discusses the related research works of functional module mining and binary co-clustering approaches. Sections 1.3 to 1.8 discuss the terminologies, existing methods, datasets, experimental environment, validation measures, and biological significances. Section 1.9 presents the proposed method MR-CoC and its enhancements based on the comparative analysis. Section 1.10 elaborates the functional module mining using MR-CoC based on a comparative analysis of the results under different experimental setups, and analysis of experimental results for their biological significance. Section 1.11 summarizes the entire work carried out in this chapter.

1.2 Related Works

The functional module mining approaches in the literature show that most are performed using graph theoretical algorithms and are based on the topological properties. The various related research articles in the literature are listed in Table 1.1. They focus on MCODE, edge sampling, clustering, and optimization techniques for functional module mining. Table 1.1 highlights the approaches, measures, and various related issues (scalability, time consumption, computational overhead, functional measures, etc.). The tick mark and cross mark in Table 1.1 represent the presence and absence of the specified issue.

From the study, MCODE is the pioneer approach for protein complex detection. It detects the cliques from PIN based on the network density. The complexity of the MCODE is $\boldsymbol{O(n^3)}$.

The PIN is represented using the adjacency matrix, which is a binary symmetric matrix. Thus, binary co-clustering approach is proposed in this chapter. The related works of binary co-clustering are also studied. The existing co-clustering approaches for binary data are reviewed in this section. Cheng and Church [10], Plaid [11], OPSM [12], etc. are for numerical data matrices. These approaches are using the distance measures that do not suit the binary datasets. There are some specific approaches like xMotif [13], BiMax [14], BicBin [15], BicSim [16], BMF [17], BiBit [18], BBK [19], BitTable [20], BiBinCons & BiBinAlter [21] and ParBiBit [22] that were developed at different time periods for co-clustering the binary data. The detailed reviews of these existing approaches are presented in Table 1.2. Every existing approach is reviewed based on various criteria such as

Table 1.1 Literature study for functional module mining.

Title	Algorithm	Measure	Scalability issue	Ignore overlapped modules	Time consumption	Computational overhead	Functional features usage
An automated method for finding molecular complexes in large protein interaction networks [7]	MCODE	Network density	✓	✓	✓	✓	×
Detection of functional modules from protein interaction networks [4]	Clustering	Classification score	✓	×	✓	✓	×
Identifying functional modules in protein–protein interaction networks: an integrated exact approach [8]	Mathematical optimization	Modular scoring function	✓	✓	✓	✓	×
Protein interaction networks—more than mere modules [1]	Block method based on GO terms	Error minimization	✓	✓	✓	✓	×
Weighted consensus clustering for identifying functional modules in protein–protein interaction networks [9]	Combines 4 clustering algorithms	Cluster coefficient	✓	✓	✓	✓	×

(*Continued*)

Table 1.1 Literature study for functional module mining. (*Continued*)

Title	**Algorithm**	**Measure**	**Scalability issue**	**Ignore overlapped modules**	**Time consumption**	**Computational overhead**	**Functional features usage**
BicNET: Flexible module discovery in large-scale biological networks using biclustering [2]	Biclustering	Biclusters	✓	✓	✓	✓	×

method, binarization, overlapped co-clusters, scalability issue, computational overhead, parameter tuning, time consumption, parallelization, noise sensitivity, and remarks about the approach.

From Table 1.2, the xMotif and ParBiBit are greedy-type algorithms; BiMax and BBK are "divide and conquer"-type approaches; the BiSim and BiBinCons are iterative approaches; BicBin is a model-based approach; BiBit is an exhaustive enumeration approach; BitTable is an a priori-type approach. All the existing approaches discussed here are binarizing the numerical data for its processing. The xMotif, BiMax, and BBK algorithms ignore the overlapped co-clusters in the dataset. All these existing approaches are having computational overhead and scalability issues. The parameter tuning is necessary for most of the approaches except the xMotif approach in Table 1.2 for better performance. The BicBin is a parallelized approach; thus, the time consumption is less when compared to other existing approaches. The noise in the dataset affects the efficiency of co-clustering, which results in ignorance of the quality co-clusters in the dataset. The BicBin, BMF, and BiBinCons are noise-insensitive approaches in the related research works.

From the study, it is clear that the BiMax and xMotif approaches are used for comparative analysis in most of these existing methods. There is no benchmark algorithm for co-clustering.

Most of these existing approaches failed to extract all the embedded co-clusters from the given data. The limitations of the existing approaches are missing the overlapped co-clusters and quality co-clusters, scalability issue, computational overhead, and more time consumption.

Table 1.2 A review on existing approaches for binary co-clustering.

S. no.	Existing approach	Method	Binarization	Overlapped co-clusters	Scalability Issue	Computational overhead	Parameter tuning	Time consumption	Parallelization	Noise sensitivity	Remarks
1.	**xMotif (2003)**	Greedy	✓	×	✓	✓	×	✓	×	✓	As it is a greedy approach, it may lose good co-clusters and may take wrong decisions Leukemia gene expression analysis
2.	**BiMax (2006)**	Divide and conquer	✓	×	✓	✓	✓	✓	×	✓	Benchmark approach Best for limited size dataset Extracts only pure constant maximal Biclusters Gene Expression Data Analysis
3.	**BicBin** (2008)	Model based	✓	✓	✓	✓	✓	×	✓	×	Uses cost function to evaluate the sub-matrices
4.	**BiSim** (2009)	Iterative	✓	✓	✓	✓	✓	✓	×	✓	Used for Gene Expression Analysis

(*Continued*)

Table 1.2 A review on existing approaches for binary co-clustering. (*Continued*)

S. no.	Existing approach	Method	Binarization	Overlapped co-clusters	Scalability Issue	Computational overhead	Parameter tuning	Time consumption	Parallelization	Noise sensitivity	Remarks
5.	BMF (2010)	Matrix multiplication	✓	✓	✓	✓	✓	✓	×	×	Quality of co-clusters depends on the selection of the discretization method Fixing the number of factors 'k' is a big hurdle Performs dimensionality reduction of data
6.	BiBit (2011)	Exhaustive enumeration	✓	✓	✓	✓	✓	✓	×	✓	Uses Boolean Algebraic operations Searches co-clusters in all possible combinations Suits for limited data size Embryonic Tumor Gene expression analysis
7.	BBK (2012)	Divide and conquer	✓	×	✓	✓	✓	✓	×	✓	Uses Bron-Kerbosch backtracking approach to improvise BiMax approach Still faces the listed issues

(*Continued*)

Table 1.2 A review on existing approaches for binary co-clustering. (*Continued*)

S. no.	Existing approach	Method	Binarization	Overlapped co-clusters	Scalability Issue	Computational overhead	Parameter tuning	Time consumption	Parallelization	Noise sensitivity	Remarks
8.	Bit-Table (2014)	A priori	✓	✓	✓	✓	✓	✓	×	✓	Too many candidate itemsets Scans data once for each itemset High memory consumption Uses various Bit Table Operations
9.	BiBinCons BiBinAlter (2015)	Iterative	✓	✓	✓	✓	✓	✓	×	×	It performs an exhaustive search for bicluster in each row and column combination Microarray Data Analysis
10.	ParBiBit (2018)	Greedy	✓	✓	✓	✓	✓	✓	✓	✓	Utilizes the modern distributed memory systems efficiently As it is a greedy method likely to take wrong decisions

1.3 Basic Terminologies

The basic terminologies used in this research are categorized under biological terminologies and technical terminologies.

1.3.1 Scientific Terms Used

In this research, the scientific terminologies stand for a variety of topics that are biologically related. This research section discusses numerous terminologies to enhance understanding of the bioinformatics concept. They are as follows:

i. ***Protein***: Proteins are composed of a linear chain of 22 amino acids, known as a sequence of amino acids. The data consist of one-dimensional arrays represented as lengthy strings of letters [4, 23, 24] as shown in Figure 1.2. They are the genetic sequences representing a gene or a portion of a gene. It is utilized to depict the operations of biological systems. They oversee a range of physiological and biochemical processes within the cell. The central dogma illustrates the protein route, as depicted in Figure 1.2.
ii. ***Molecular Networks***: Molecular networks refer to the interconnected relationships among biological components such

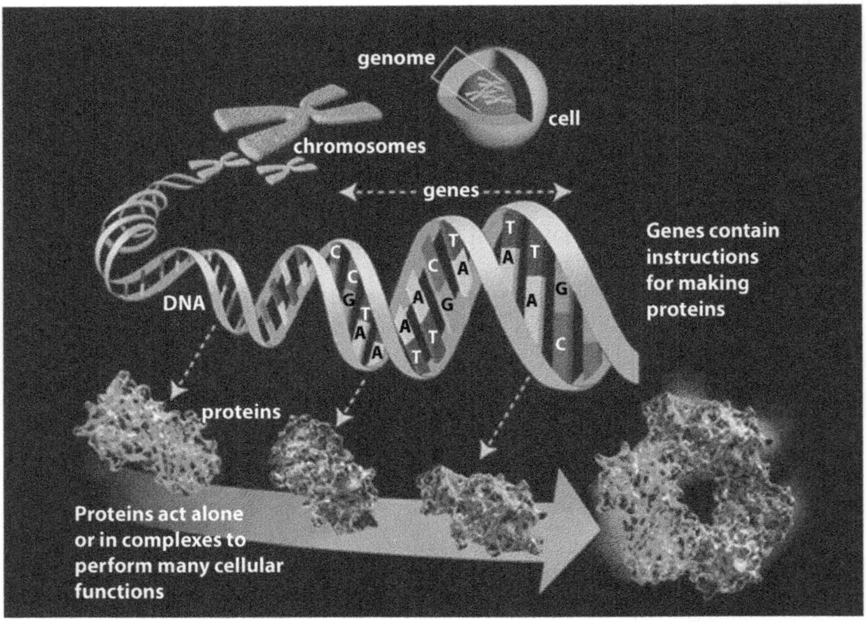

Figure 1.2 Central dogma of proteins [25].

as genes, RNA, and proteins. They are utilized to symbolize the relationship, connectedness, and communication among these products. They are created through chemical reactions within the cell [4, 23, 24].

iii. ***Protein Interaction Networks (PINs)***: Proteins construct molecular networks. They are utilized to emphasize the connections of diverse proteins in various cellular compartments. These networks are utilized for transmitting signals and commands to different parts of the system. Figure 1.3 shows the sample PIN [4, 23, 24].

iv. ***Protein Modules***: Protein modules are a set of proteins that carry out specific functions within the cell. It is a component of a protein interaction network that has stronger connections with each other compared to others [24]. The portions of the PIN are very coherent. Figure 1.4 emphasizes the protein modules in the sample [24].

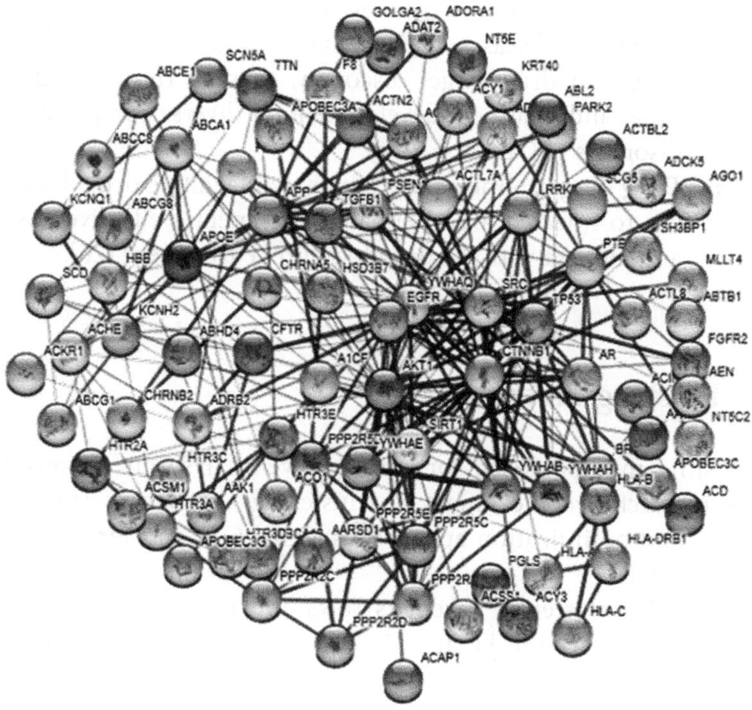

Figure 1.3 Sample protein interaction network.

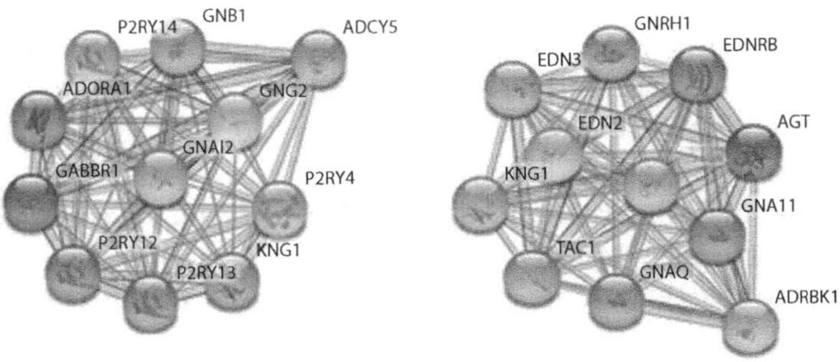

Figure1.4 Sample protein modules.

v. ***Protein Complex vs. Functional Modules*:** These two are protein modules. The protein modules are stationary, meaning they remain in a fixed position consistently. The functional modules are dynamic and can be generated at any location and time, not remaining fixed in one place consistently. Functional modules emerge as a result of pathogen infections and protein abnormalities. Functional modules are utilized to forecast the existence of pathogen infections, diseases, and anomalies, and are employed in drug and drug target discovery, therapy recommendations, and treatment development for diverse complicated disorders [23, 24].

vi. ***Drug Targets*:** They are proteins that facilitate drug delivery to infected areas, enhance therapeutic effectiveness, and interact with the drug to improve treatment [26].

1.4 Existing Methods

The existing methods used for comparative analysis in various stages of this research are the binary co-clustering approaches (BiMax and x-Motif), and optimization approaches (PSO, GA, and Firefly) are discussed in detail.

Data are "co-clustered" when its rows and columns are grouped at the same time, as seen in Figure 1.5. It identifies and isolates the specific

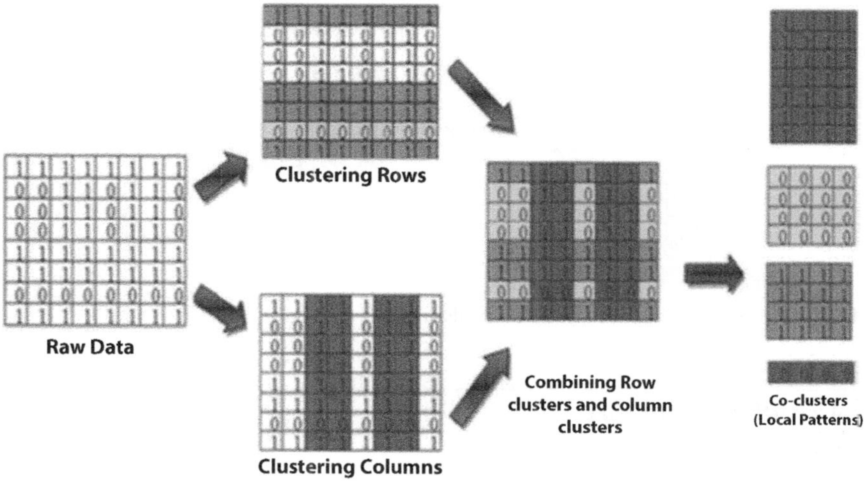

Figure 1.5 Co-clustering: A toy example.

patterns present in the data within a certain region or area. It refers to a distinct collection of rows and columns that exhibit greater similarity, as shown in Figure 1.5.

1.4.1 Binary Co-Clustering Approaches

This study work involves a comparative investigation of the proposed binary co-clustering strategy using Binary inclusion-Maximal [14] and x-Motif [13] algorithms.

1.4.1.1 Binary Inclusion-Maximal Algorithm

Prelic *et al.* developed the Binary inclusion-Maximal (BiMax) co-clustering algorithm in 2006 for finding the maximal co-clusters from the binary data matrix. This algorithm is the pioneer and is used for comparative analysis for most of the co-clustering approaches. The pseudocode of BiMax is in Algorithm 1.1. This approach has an $O(n^2m^2\alpha)$ complexity, where the n, m and α are the count of genes, conditions, and inclusion-maximal co-clusters.

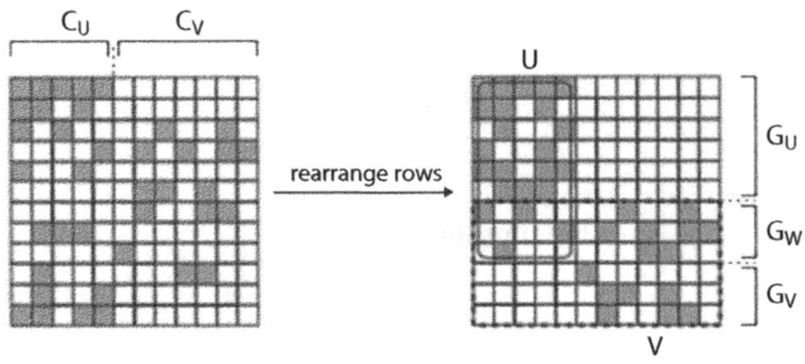

Figure 1.6 Sample illustration of BiMax algorithm.

Algorithm 1.1: BiMax
Input: Input Data Matrix ***Output: Resulting Sub-Matrices*** *Step 1 : Divide the columns into C_U and C_V (subsets),* *Step 2 : Sort rows of E with the first row as a template* *a. place all genes in G_U, expressed to conditions only in C_U* *b. place all genes in G_W, expressed to conditions both in C_U and C_V* *c. place all genes in G_V expressed to conditions only in C_V* *Step 3 : Define the combination of genes G_U, G_W, G_V and conditions C_U and C_V* *Step 4 : Recursively decompose the U , V sub-matrices using steps 1 to 4.*

Figure 1.6 depicts the sample illustration of the BiMax approach. It is a reference-based divide-and-conquer approach used for binary co-clustering. It takes its first row as its reference to further group the data.

1.4.1.2 xMotif Algorithm

The xMotif algorithm is devised for gene expression data to extract conserved gene motifs [13]. It is also used for various co-clustering problems in the literature. It suits both real-valued and binary data co-clustering. The xMotif algorithm is the most frequently used co-clustering approach introduced by Murali and Kasif in 2003, but its usage is extending over a long period. The xMotif is also a co-cluster. The pseudocode of xMotif is in Algorithm 1.2. This algorithm finds the largest xMotif from the given data. In the algorithm, the "n_s" and "n_d" is the number of initial seeds and samples chosen from each seed, respectively, "s_d" is the sample size, and "α" and "β" are the user-defined fractions of samples and genes conserved, respectively, in the samples chosen. It is less time-consuming when compared to other co-clustering approaches. Its time complexity is $\boldsymbol{O(nm^{O(\log(1/\alpha)+\log(1/b))})}$.

Algorithm 1.2: FindxMotif

Input: Input data matrix
Output: motif
Step 1 : *Repeat* $\mathbf{i}=\mathbf{1}$ *to* $\boldsymbol{n_s}$
- a. *Select a random sample* $\boldsymbol{c}$ *uniformly*
- b. *Repeat* $\boldsymbol{j}=\mathbf{1}$ *to* $\boldsymbol{n_d}$
  - i) *Select a subset* $\mathbf{D}$ *randomly of size* $\boldsymbol{s_d}$
  - ii) *Include* $(\boldsymbol{g},\boldsymbol{s})$ *in* $\mathbf{G}_{ij}$ *for each row, if* $\boldsymbol{g}\in\boldsymbol{s}$ *in c, and similarly for all samples in D*
  - iii) *Assign all set of gene-states in* G_{ij} *that satisfy the c*
  - iv) *discard* (C_{ij}, G_{ij}), *if lesser than* α_n *samples present in* C_{ij},

Step 2 : *return* (C^+, G^+), *with maximal* $|G_{ij}|$, $1 \le i \le n_s$, $1 \le j \le n_d$

1.5 About Dataset

This section deals with the datasets experimented in this research work. They are PIN, complexes of protein dataset, and targets dataset.

1.5.1 Protein Interaction Networks

It is a set of interconnections between the proteins; this interconnection is also called interactions. It represents a link connecting two proteins. Two interactors are provided for each record in the data to describe an interaction. These interactions are undirected in nature. The sample dataset records are given in Figure 1.7.

The sample dataset is the first ten records of Homo_Sapiens PIN. There are various columns corresponding to the interactors (A, B), official symbols

<table>
<tr><th></th><th>A</th><th>B</th><th>C</th><th>D</th><th>E</th><th>F</th><th>G</th><th>H</th><th>I</th><th>J</th><th>K</th></tr>
<tr><td>1</td><td>INTERACTOR_A</td><td>INTERACTOR_B</td><td>OFFICIAL_SYMBOL_A</td><td>OFFICIAL_SYMBOL_B</td><td>ALIASES_FOR_A</td><td>ALIASES_FOR_B</td><td>EXPERIMENTAL_SYSTEM</td><td>SOURCE</td><td>PUBMED_ID</td><td>ORGANISM_A_ID</td><td>ORGANISM_B_ID</td></tr>
<tr><td>2</td><td>ETG6416</td><td>ETG2318</td><td>MAP2K4</td><td>FLNC</td><td>SAPKK1|J</td><td>ABPL|MP</td><td>Two-hybrid</td><td>Marti A (19</td><td>9006895</td><td>9606</td><td>9606</td></tr>
<tr><td>3</td><td>ETG84665</td><td>ETG88</td><td>MYPN</td><td>ACTN2</td><td>MYOP</td><td>CMD1AA</td><td>Two-hybrid</td><td>Bang ML (2</td><td>11309420</td><td>9606</td><td>9606</td></tr>
<tr><td>4</td><td>ETG90</td><td>ETG2339</td><td>ACVR1</td><td>FNTA</td><td>ACVRLK2|</td><td>PTAR2|FF</td><td>Two-hybrid</td><td>Wang T (19</td><td>8599089</td><td>9606</td><td>9606</td></tr>
<tr><td>5</td><td>ETG2624</td><td>ETG5371</td><td>GATA2</td><td>PML</td><td>NFE1B|D(</td><td>RNF71|TF</td><td>Two-hybrid</td><td>Tsuzuki S (2</td><td>10938104</td><td>9606</td><td>9605</td></tr>
<tr><td>6</td><td>RP4-547C9.3</td><td>ETG6774</td><td>RPA2</td><td>STAT3</td><td>REPA2|RF</td><td>APRF|HIE</td><td>Two-hybrid</td><td>Kim J (200(</td><td>10875894</td><td>9606</td><td>9605</td></tr>
<tr><td>7</td><td>ETG375</td><td>ETG23163</td><td>ARF1</td><td>GGA3</td><td>N/A</td><td>N/A</td><td>Two-hybrid</td><td>Dell'Angeli</td><td>10747089</td><td>9606</td><td>9605</td></tr>
<tr><td>8</td><td>ETG377</td><td>ETG23647</td><td>ARF3</td><td>ARFIP2</td><td>N/A</td><td>POR1</td><td>Two-hybrid</td><td>Kanoh H (1</td><td>9038142</td><td>9606</td><td>9605</td></tr>
<tr><td>9</td><td>ETG377</td><td>ETG27236</td><td>ARF3</td><td>ARFIP1</td><td>N/A</td><td>HSU5252</td><td>Two-hybrid</td><td>Kanoh H (1</td><td>9038142</td><td>9606</td><td>9605</td></tr>
<tr><td>10</td><td>ETG54464</td><td>ETG226</td><td>XRN1</td><td>ALDOA</td><td>1-Sep</td><td>GSD12|Al</td><td>Two-hybrid</td><td>Lehner B (2</td><td>15231747</td><td>9606</td><td>9605</td></tr>
</table>

Figure 1.7 Sample PIN dataset.

of A and B, alias names of A and B, experimental system, PubMed identifier of the interaction, and organisms of A and B in the dataset. In this research, the interactor columns are used for experimentation; the other additional information can be used for analytical purposes. This study makes use of a PIN dataset that was obtained from the STRING database [27, 28].

1.5.1.1 STRING Repository

The existing and tested protein interactions are present in this STRING repository [27, 28]. Physical and functional linkages are also a part of these interactions. There are ≅3.12 billion interactions involving ≅24.58 million proteins from 5090 different organisms. This database contains 19.4K *Homo sapiens* proteins and ≅8.5 million interactions.

The various data sources of this database are COG, BioGRID, MINT, KEGG, Gene Ontology, Ensembl, etc. [27]. The protein sequence data of these proteins were also taken from this database. Figure 1.8 shows the sample download page of the STRING database.

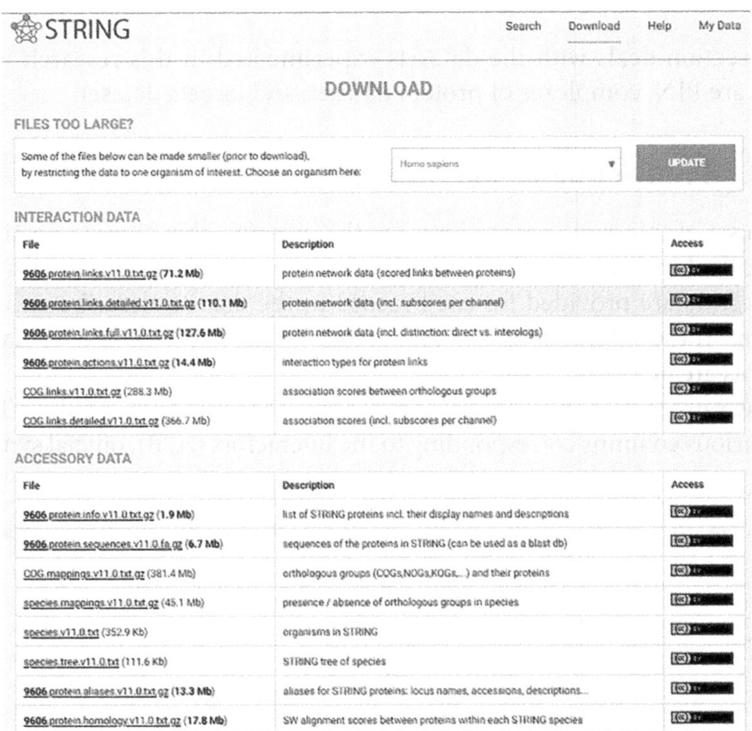

Figure 1.8 STRING database download page.

1.5.2 Protein Complex Dataset

Protein complexes are groups of proteins that work together to carry out particular cellular tasks in living organisms [24]. Different creatures have their own unique protein complexes. In order to compare the outcomes, this study makes use of this protein complex data. The CORUM database is used to retrieve this data.

1.5.2.1 CORUM Database

Mammalian protein complexes are exhaustively represented in this database [29]. It is composed of mammalian protein complexes that have been confirmed by experiments. There are 64% human, 16% mouse, and 12% rat complexes in this database. A total of 2,358 protein complexes from humans make it up. The name, composition, function, and reference of each protein complex are also included.

Figure 1.9 shows the statistics of the protein complexes in each release of the CORUM database [29]. The size of the protein complexes is from 1 to 64, but there are very few protein complexes from size 9 to 64, i.e., there are no complexes present in most of this size limit, and the maximal complexes present in the size limit of 1 to 8. As per the literature, the protein complex sizes and their counts are shown in Figure 1.10. Based on these sizes, only 2358 protein complexes taken for this research are in the size limit 3 to 8. The protein complex sizes 1 and 2 are not meant to be chosen because size 1 represents a single protein and size 2 describes an interaction. Thus, selecting these two sizes will increase the time complexity. Instead, the individual protein and its interaction in PIN can be analyzed separately.

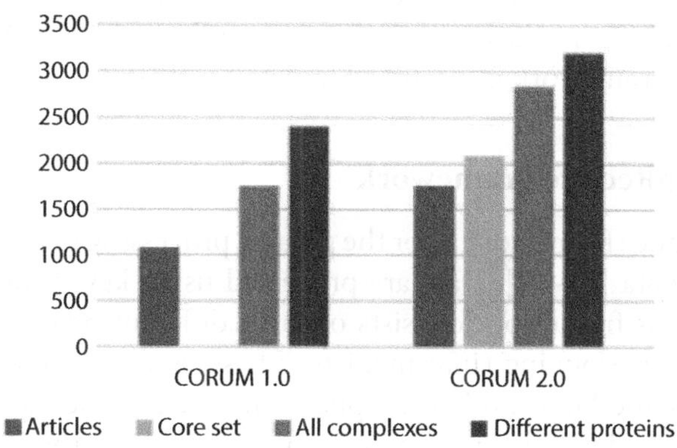

Figure 1.9 CORUM database statistics [29].

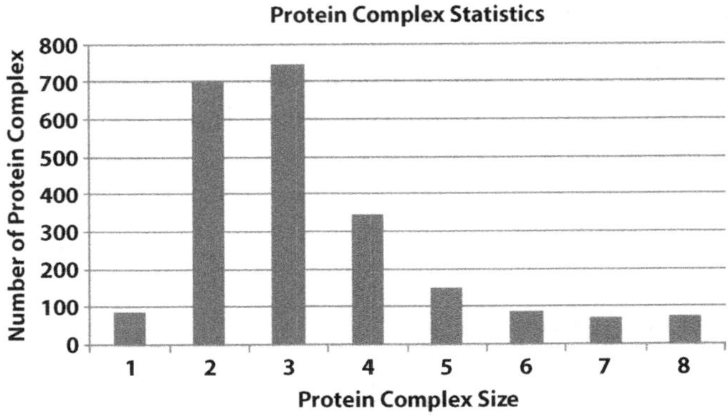

Figure 1.10 Protein complex statistics.

Hence, the size limit 3 to 8 is taken. This limit is fixed on a trial-and-error basis. For the maximal sizes, more seeds and lengthy seeds have to be generated. Based on the size of most of the existing protein complexes, size 8 is fixed for this research work. Further, it can be increased in the future to enhance this research.

1.6 Experimental Environment

All the implementations of this research and their experiments are carried out in the MATLAB 2016a environment. In this research, the co-clustering approach proposed for Functional Module Mining uses the MapReduce (MR) framework. The basic configuration of MR Framework of the MATLAB [30] is used in this research work. This default MapReduce framework runs on the virtual distributed environmental setup. The distributed Hadoop cluster can also be configured in MATLAB. This MapReduce Framework is discussed in detail further.

1.6.1 MapReduce Framework

The MapReduce framework is for the parallel processing of the voluminous distributed data [31–33]. Data are processed using key-value (KV) combinations. This framework consists of three different phases: map phase, rearranging or grouping (intermediate) phase, and reduce phase. Out of these phases, the Map and Reduce phases are the user-defined phases that consist of user-defined functions to process the data. The Map function works on the data blocks and produces KV pairs; the reduce function

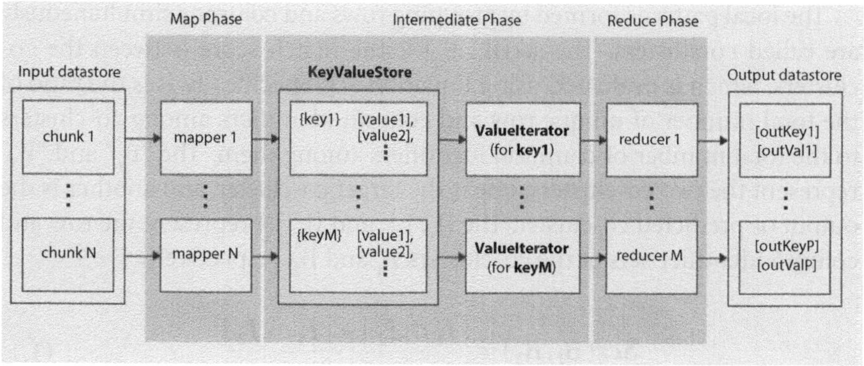

Figure 1.11 Workflow of MapReduce in MATLAB [30].

works on each unique key separately and returns KV pairs. The intermediate phase is for grouping them based on their keys, which are default processing in this framework.

The MapReduce Framework, as per the MATLAB [30], is in Figure 1.11. The inputs and outputs of this framework are in the form of a data store. Tables of data, KV pairs, text files, images, and other types of media can all be input. The key-value datastore will be the final product. The map function will take the data blocks from this input data store for processing and produce the intermediate KV pairs in the form of intermediate KV store. In the intermediate phase, a value iterator will be generated by default for each key, as in Figure 1.11. This phase is for grouping the intermediate KV pairs based on the unique keys. After this phase, the user-defined "Reduce" function will be invoked for each unique key for further processing. It will generate the output KV pairs.

1.7 Validation Measures

In this section, the various validation measures such as Match Score, Network Metrics, and Functional Coherence are used for evaluating the performances of the proposed work.

1.7.1 Match Score Measure

The match score measure is used for evaluating the proportion of matching between two patterns of data or two sets of patterns [14]. The patterns are co-clusters. It is evaluated using Equations 1.1 and 1.2.

The local patterns formed by grouping rows and columns simultaneously are called co-clusters. The scr(B_1, B_2) is the match score between the co-clusters, which is evaluated using Equation 1.1. Specifically, it is the ratio of the total number of unique row and column identifiers among co-clusters to the total number of common identifiers among them. The "B_1" and "B_2" represent the two co-clusters; one is the target co-cluster, and another is the output or predicted co-cluster. The {I_1, J_1}, and {I_2, J_2} represent the row and column identifier sets of the co-clusters B_1 and B_2, respectively.

$$Scr(B_1, B_2) = \frac{|I_1 \cap I_2| + |J_1 \cap J_2|}{|I_1 \cup I_2| + |J_1 \cup J_2|} \tag{1.1}$$

The $Scr^*_B(M_1, M_2)$ is the match score between the two co-cluster sets, as in Equation 1.2. It is the maximal value of the match score averages of all co-clusters in "M_1" with "M_2". "M_1" is the target co-cluster set and "M_2" is the output co-cluster set.

$$Scr^*_B(M_1, M_2) = \frac{1}{|M_1|} \Sigma_{A(I_1, J_1)} max_{A(I_2, J_2)} \frac{|I_1 \cap I_2| + |J_1 \cap J_2|}{|I_1 \cup I_2| + |J_1 \cup J_2|} \tag{1.2}$$

The match score measure is used in this research for evaluating the match between the existing and extracted patterns for their studying their accuracy.

1.7.2 Functional Coherence

In order to assess how well the protein module's functional annotations hold together, this metric is used [34]. Each protein is accompanied by biological functional characteristics known as functional annotations. Under several facets, it depicts their functions within the biological system. To predict their properties, we quantify these functional annotations for every protein module. To find out how similar these functional annotations are, we use a metric called functional coherence (FC). It is the percentage of proteins in the protein module that have a functional annotation relative to the total number of proteins.

$$FC_j(PM_i) = \frac{|p_{ij} \in PM_i|}{|p_i|} \tag{1.3}$$

From the ith protein module (PM), we may derive the functional coherence (FC) of the jth annotation using Equation 1.3. p_{ij} denotes the proteins in the ith module that have the jth annotation, while p_i stands for the proteins in the ith module itself. If all the proteins in the module have the jth annotation, then the value of $\boldsymbol{FC_j}$ is "1"; otherwise, it is "0". This FC value describes the protein module's functioning. In this study, the functions of the resulting protein modules are determined using this metric.

1.8 Biological Significances

To illustrate the proteins' biological importance, functional annotations are used. When it comes to characterizing the functional features of molecular products like proteins, functional annotations are the gold standard [35, 36]. The three primary groups into which these implications fall are as follows:

i. ***Molecular Function***: These include molecular-level processes like binding and catalysis, among others. Depending on where they are situated and circumstances, they might be caused by a single bio-product (protein) or a set of bio-products (protein complex). These inscriptions exclusively depict the bio-product activity, not the mixture of bio-products that cause this activity [37, 38].
ii. ***Biological Process***: It stands for the cellular-level metabolic activity, transportation, etc. that are essential to the bio-products' biological processes. The execution of a biological action in the cell is accomplished by combining one or more molecular processes. A bio-product or products carry them out [37, 38].
iii. ***Cell Component***: The bio-product's relative position or cellular compartments during molecular activities are represented by it. Several factors, such as their respective cellular topologies, cellular compartments, and the presence of stable macromolecular complexes, are usually considered when making these determinations [37, 38].

1.9 Proposed Co-Clustering Approach: MR-CoC

1.9.1 SCoC for Non-Symmetric Matrix

In this section, the SCoC approach for the non-symmetric matrix called $SCoC_{nsym}$ is focused on, which is an extended version of the previous SCoC approach. The non-symmetric matrix is either a rectangular matrix or square matrix where the upper-right and lower-left triangular matrices are not the same. It is used to represent the relationship between two different disjoint sets of objects. The $SCoC_{nsym}$ is performed on one dimension at a time either on a row or column based on the condition specified. The score threshold is the major part of mining different types of co-clusters based on the requirement. Algorithm 1.3 shows the steps of $SCoC_{nsym}$.

Algorithm 1.3: $SCoC_{nsym}$

Input: 2-D Input Data (D)
Result: co-cluster (C)
Step 1 : C=D, compute S_n (score) of C
Step 2 : if S_n < threshold then
    a. compute scores of C (rows and columns)
    b. ignore low score row or column in C
    c. compute S_n
Step 3 : return C

Initially, input data matrix D is imputed with noise and non-symmetric co-cluster in it. The score value of the co-cluster is computed at each iteration of the process; ignore the rows and columns with low score at each iteration and update the score value using the equation; continue this process until the score value is less than the selected threshold. This algorithm is for mining the constant (1's) co-cluster from a given data matrix where the threshold is "1". For the 0's co-cluster, the score threshold should be "0" and has to remove the row or column with a high score value. This approach extracts the maximal constant co-cluster from the given binary data matrix. $O(n_e+n_v^2)$ is the temporal complexity of this approach.

1.9.1.1 Toy Example: $SCoC_{nsym}$

The sample illustration of $SCoC_{nsym}$ for mining 1's constant co-cluster is explained in this section. Let "C" be the Input Matrix, where the embedded co-cluster is highlighted in Figure 1.12. The score threshold is "1".

$$
C = \begin{array}{ccccccc}
1 & 0 & 0 & 0 & 0 & 0 & 1\\
0 & 0 & 1 & 0 & 0 & 1 & 0\\
0 & 1 & 1 & 1 & 1 & 1 & 0\\
0 & 1 & 1 & 1 & 1 & 1 & 0\\
0 & 1 & 1 & 1 & 1 & 1 & 1\\
0 & 1 & 0 & 0 & 0 & 1 & 1\\
1 & 0 & 0 & 1 & 1 & 0 & 0\\
0 & 0 & 0 & 1 & 1 & 0 & 1
\end{array}
$$

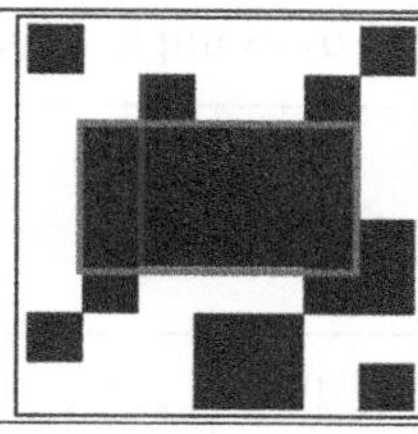

Figure 1.12 Sample input matrix and its heatmap.

Table 1.3 illustrates a sample for the proposed $SCoC_{nsym}$ approach. Here the 7 × 3 constant 1's co-cluster is embedded in the 8 × 7 noisy data matrix. In every iteration, the row score and column score of the given data are computed; either the row or column with a minimal score is removed; the score is evaluated for the result matrix. This approach is also attempted on

Table 1.3 $SCoC_{nsym}$: Toy example.

Iteration	Input Matrix	Row Score	Removal	Result Matrix	Score
1	1 0 0 0 0 0 1 0 0 1 0 0 1 0 0 1 1 1 1 1 0 0 1 1 1 1 1 0 0 1 1 1 1 1 1 0 1 0 0 0 1 1 1 0 0 1 1 0 0 0 0 0 1 1 0 1	0.285 0.285 0.714 0.714 0.857 0.428 0.428 0.428	Col →1	0 0 0 0 0 1 0 1 0 0 1 0 1 1 1 1 1 0 1 1 1 1 1 0 1 1 1 1 1 1 1 0 0 0 1 1 0 0 1 1 0 0 0 0 1 1 0 1	0.482
	Column Score: 0.2 0.5 0.5 0.6 0.6 0.6 0.5	Min 0.25			
2	0 0 0 0 0 1 0 1 0 0 1 0 1 1 1 1 1 0 1 1 1 1 1 0 1 1 1 1 1 1 1 0 0 0 1 1 0 0 1 1 0 0 0 0 1 1 0 1	0.142 0.285 0.833 0.833 1 0.5 0.333 0.5	Row →2	0 1 0 0 1 0 1 1 1 1 1 0 1 1 1 1 1 0 1 1 1 1 1 1 1 0 0 0 1 1 0 0 1 1 0 0 0 0 1 1 0 1	0.619
	Column Score: 0.5 0.5 0.62 0.62 0.62 0.5	Min 0.142			
3	0 1 0 0 1 0 1 1 1 1 1 0 1 1 1 1 1 0 1 1 1 1 1 1 1 0 0 0 1 1 0 0 1 1 0 0 0 0 1 1 0 1	0.285 0.833 0.833 1 0.5 0.333 0.5	Row →6	0 1 0 0 1 0 1 1 1 1 1 0 1 1 1 1 1 0 1 1 1 1 1 1 1 0 0 0 1 1 0 0 1 1 0 1	0.666
	Column Score: 0.571 0.571 0.714 0.714 0.714 0.428	Min 0.333			

(*Continued*)

Table 1.3 $SCoC_{nsym}$: Toy example. (*Continued*)

Iteration	Input Matrix	Row Score	Removal	Result Matrix	Score
4	0 1 0 0 1 0 1 1 1 1 1 0 1 1 1 1 1 0 1 1 1 1 1 1 1 0 0 0 1 1 0 0 1 1 0 0	0.333 0.833 0.833 1 0.5 0.5	Row →2	1 1 1 1 1 0 1 1 1 1 1 0 1 1 1 1 1 1 1 0 0 0 1 1 0 0 1 1 0 1	0.733
	Column Score: 0.666 0.666 0.666 0.666 0.833 0.5	Min 0.333			
5	1 1 1 1 1 0 1 1 1 1 1 0 1 1 1 1 1 1 1 0 0 0 1 1 0 0 1 1 0 0	0.833 0.833 1 0.5 0.5	Row →4	1 1 1 1 1 0 1 1 1 1 1 0 1 1 1 1 1 1 0 0 1 1 0 1	0.791
	Column Score: 0.8 0.6 0.8 0.8 0.8 0.6	Min 0.5			
6	1 1 1 1 1 0 1 1 1 1 1 0 1 1 1 1 1 1 0 0 1 1 0 1	0.833 0.833 1 0.5	Row → 4	1 1 1 1 1 0 1 1 1 1 1 0 1 1 1 1 1 1	0.88
	Column Score: 0.75 0.75 1 1 0.75 0.5	Min 0.5			
7	1 1 1 1 1 0 1 1 1 1 1 0 1 1 1 1 1 1	0.833 0.833 1	Col →6	1 1 1 1 1 1 1 1 1 1 1 1 1 1 1	1
	Column Score: 1 1 1 1 1 0.333	Min 0.333			
8	1 1 1 1 1 1 1 1 1 1 1 1 1 1 1	**If Score = = threshold then Stop processing & Return C**			

the synthetic datasets for their performance analysis similar to the previous implementation, which is discussed in the next section.

1.9.1.2 Synthetic Dataset Description

The synthetic binary datasets are generated for experimenting with the $SCoC_{nsym}$. In this section, four different binary datasets are generated, where the co-clusters and noise are implanted.

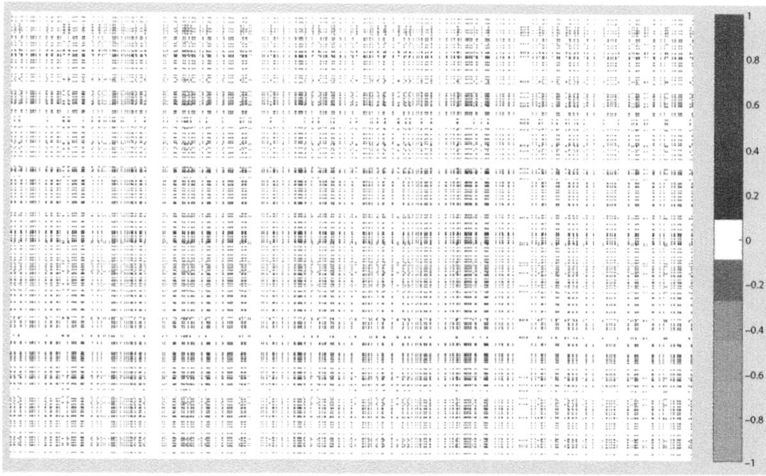

(a)

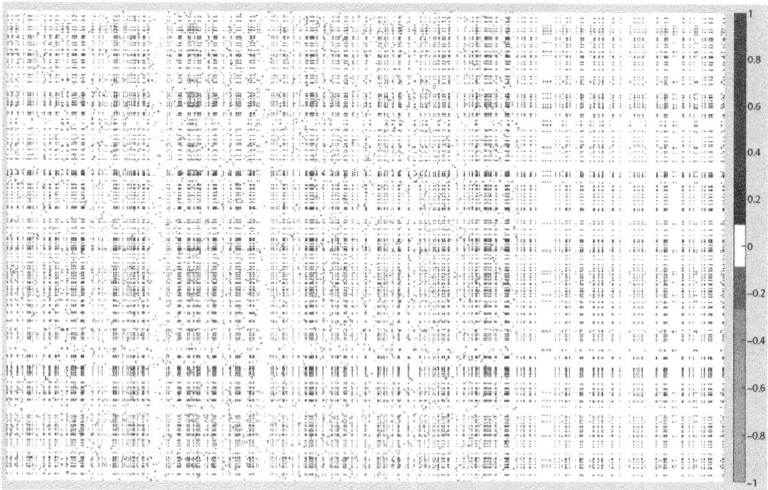

(b)

Figure 1.13 Synthetic Dataset_nsym_I. (a) Noiseless; (b) noisy.

$SCoC_{nsym}$ is experimented on both the noisy and noiseless data. The dataset description is shown in Table 1.4, which highlights the matrix type, data size, co-cluster size, co-cluster position, presence, and nature of noise.

1.9.1.3 *Experimental Analysis: $SCoC_{nsym}$*

The proposed approach $SCoC_{nsym}$ is attempted on four different synthetic non-symmetric datasets with a score threshold of "1" for mining constant

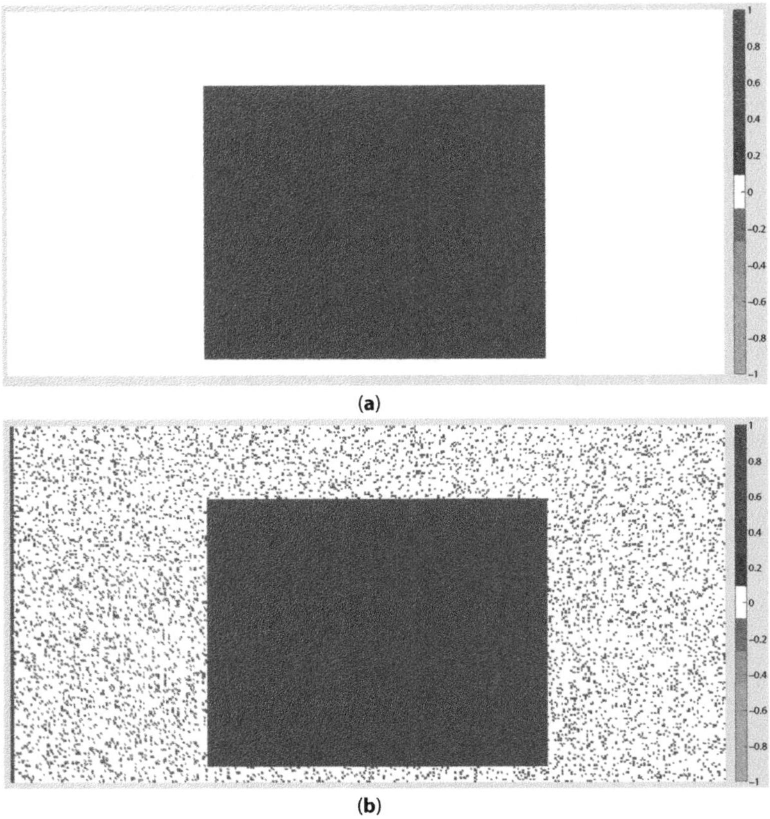

Figure 1.14 Synthetic Dataset_nsym_II. (a) Noiseless; (b) noisy.

1's co-cluster. The MATLAB environment is used for experimenting this research work. The comparative analysis of the performance of the $SCoC_{nsym}$ approach is carried out. These results are given in Table 1.5, which shows that the proposed approach $SCoC_{nsym}$ outperforms the existing approaches. The $SCoC_{nsym}$ approach extracted the implanted co-clusters from all different types of synthetic data under the noisy space. The BiMax algorithm can extract the implanted co-clusters only in the datasets without noise. The performance of the existing BiMax approach is affected by the noise in the data.

The computational time taken for mining the co-clusters in these four synthetic datasets by these approaches is also recorded in Table 1.6. The outcomes show that the performance of the xMotif approach is better than other approaches, but it does not extract the expected co-cluster from any dataset.

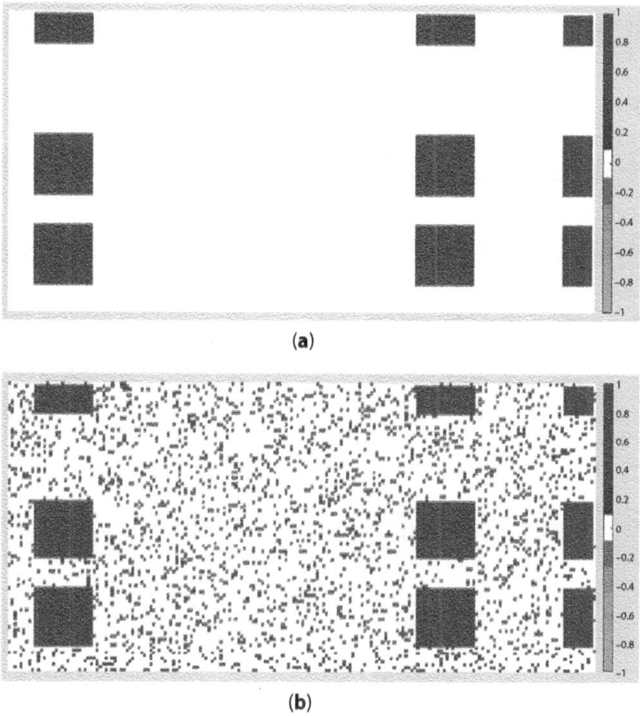

Figure 1.15 Heatmap of synthetic Dataset_nsym_III. (a) Noiseless; (b) noisy.

In all these four synthetic datasets, the expected co-clusters, i.e., the implanted co-clusters, are the maximal co-cluster in them. The BiMax algorithm can mine the co-clusters in minimal time when compared to the proposed approach. Even though the BiMax algorithm consumes less time, its performance is highly affected by the noise.

1.9.2 Randomized SCoC

The previous two approaches mine the maximal co-cluster present in the dataset, whereas the remaining patterns hidden are not explored. In this case, the randomization of this approach makes it to mine co-clusters hidden in the different portions of the dataset, i.e., the smaller co-clusters are ignored. It is implemented by introducing the random seed vector that represents the search location within the dataset. Many random seeds are generated to initiate different searches in the dataset. It results in exploring the different patterns present in the data. Also, the entire dataset has to be traversed for co-cluster mining, which is a time-consuming process for the

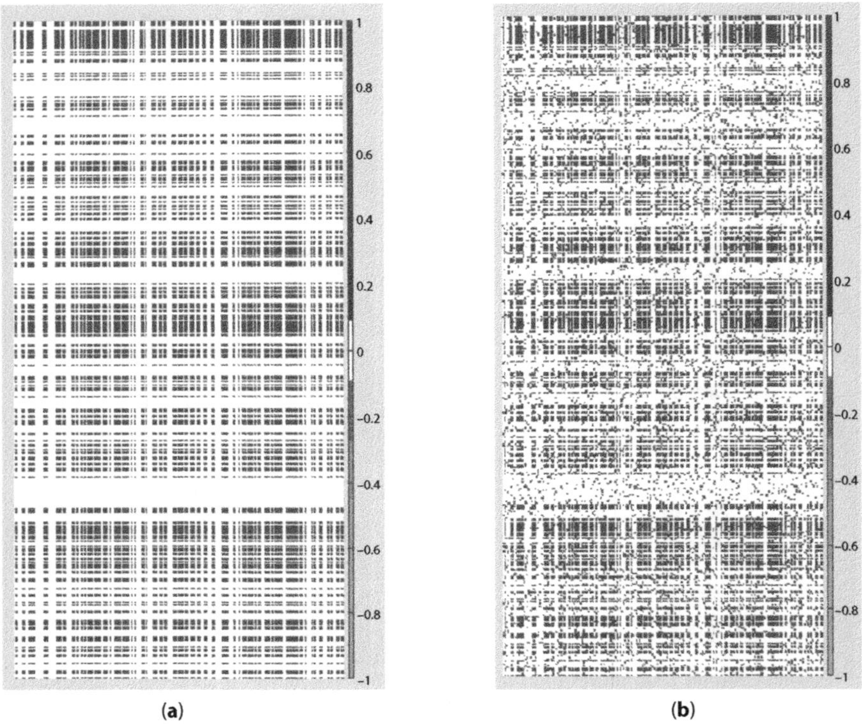

Figure 1.16 Heatmap of synthetic Dataset_nsym_IV. (a) Noiseless; (b) noisy.

large dataset. In such cases, the randomization will be the better solution to mine the patterns in the dataset stochastically. For these reasons, the randomization of the SCoC approach is proposed.

In this section, the implementation of the $SCoC_{rand}$ is discussed. Here, three different seeding techniques are adopted for testing this proposed approach. They are row-wise random seeding, column-wise random seeding, and random seeding (both row and column seed). A synthetic dataset is generated and tested with these types of seeding techniques discussed further.

This $SCoC_{rand}$ approach uses the SCoC approach, which is applied to each seeding portion. The pseudocode of the $SCoC_{rand}$ is shown in Algorithm 1.4.

Table 1.4 Synthetic dataset description—$SCoC_{nsym}$.

S. no.	Dataset name	Size	Matrix type	Co-cluster size	Co-cluster position	Noise type
1	Dataset_nsym_I (Figure 1.13)	500 × 700	Non-symmetric binary	150 × 190	Randomly scattered and symmetrical	Random symmetric noise
2.	Dataset_nsym_II (Figure 1.14)	200 × 400	Non-symmetric binary	150 × 190	Specific continuous	Symmetric random noise
3	Dataset_nsym_III (Figure 1.15)	100 × 200	Non-symmetric binary	50 × 50	Randomly symmetrical	Random noise
4	Dataset_nsym_IV (Figure 1.16)	400 × 200	Non-symmetric binary	200 × 150	Randomly scattered and symmetrical	Symmetric random noise

Table 1.5 Comparative analysis of $SCoC_{nsym}$ based on match score measure.

	Dataset_nsym I		Dataset_nsym II		Dataset_nsym III		Dataset_nsym IV	
	Noise-free	**Noisy**	**Noise-free**	**Noisy**	**Noise-free**	**Noisy**	**Noise-free**	**Noisy**
$SCoC_{nsym}$	1	1	1	1	1	1	1	1
BiMax	1	0.4319	1	0.0117	1	0.0278	1	0.5719
xMotif	0.1075	0.1508	0.2500	0.1709	0.1667	0.0397	0.1867	0.0083

Table 1.6 Comparative analysis of $SCoC_{nsym}$ based on computational time.

	Dataset_nsym I		Dataset_nsym II		Dataset_nsym III		Dataset_nsym IV	
	Noise-free	Noisy	Noise-free	Noisy	Noise-free	Noisy	Noise-free	Noisy
$SCoC_{nsym}$	1.44029	6.60305	0.83674	0.93903	0.11604	0.35163	0.68721	1.14249
BiMax	9.48878	0.01153	0.00743	0.01251	0.00197	0.00166	0.01251	0.00317
xMotif	0.98624	0.03936	0.01348	0.01785	0.01009	0.03381	0.03746	0.03430

Algorithm 1.4: $SCoC_{rand}$

Input: 2-D Input Data (D)
Result: co-cluster ($M = \{C_1, C_2, \ldots C_{ns}\}$)
Step 1 : Assign the seed count (n_s) and seed size (len_s)
Step 2 : Generate the initial seeds
Step 3 : For every seed s_i
a. Perform $SCoC_{nsym}$ to extract co-cluster
Step 4 : Assess and visualize the resultant co-clusters (M).

A seed vector will be the set of identifiers to represent the particular subset of the dataset. The number of seeds (n_s) and seed vector size (len_s) can be fixed based on the user requirement. It can also be set on a trial-and-error basis. In this $SCoC_{rand}$, instead of finding one co-cluster, more co-clusters can be extracted. The different sub-matrix in the input data is selected using random seeds and co-clusters are extracted from each seed by applying the $SCoC_{nsym}$ to each seed. This can be used to extract multiple co-clusters from the given data. The temporal complexity in terms of "O" for this approach is $T_r = O(N_s(max(N_{es}) + N_{vs}^2))$, where "$N_s$", "$N_{es}$", and "$N_{vs}$" are the seed count, edges, and vertices in a seed, respectively.

1.9.2.1 Synthetic Dataset Description

In this approach, the seeds are chosen to mine more patterns from the given data matrix. It helps to mine the maximal co-cluster in each sub-matrix of the data. They are selected based on the random seeds. The seeds are generated at different criteria like row-wise random seeds, column-wise random seeds, and random seeds (both row and column). The row-wise random seed splits the data along the row (row subset); similarly, the column-wise seed splits the data along the columns (column subset). The data are divided into distinct subsets, called "rows" and "columns," by the random seed.

Initially, 800 × 800 input data matrix (0's) C is generated with four different size co-clusters implanted and random noise, as shown in Figure 1.17. The dark portions in the figure are the embedded co-cluster. The seeding

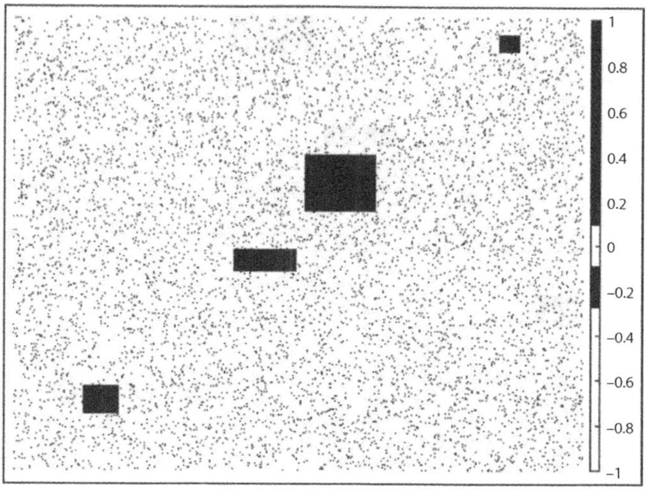

Figure 1.17 Synthetic Dataset_rand_I—implanted co-clusters at random portions with added noise.

descriptions are given in Table 1.7. It highlights the seeding type, number of seeds, seed vector length, and number of co-clusters used in this experiment.

1.9.2.2 Experimental Analysis: $SCoC_{rand}$

The proposed approach $SCoC_{rand}$ is attempted on synthetic datasets with different seed selection approach for mining all the patterns from the dataset, with a score threshold of "1" for constant 1's co-cluster. The comparative analyses of performances of the proposed algorithm with existing algorithms are assessed based on the match score, as defined in Equation 1.2. It represents the match score of the expected and actual results, as in Table 1.8. Similarly, the computational time of these algorithms is also compared, as in Table 1.9.

The match score proves that the proposed $SCoC_{rand}$ approach surpasses the existing co-clustering approaches. The $SCoC_{rand}$ approach has extracted

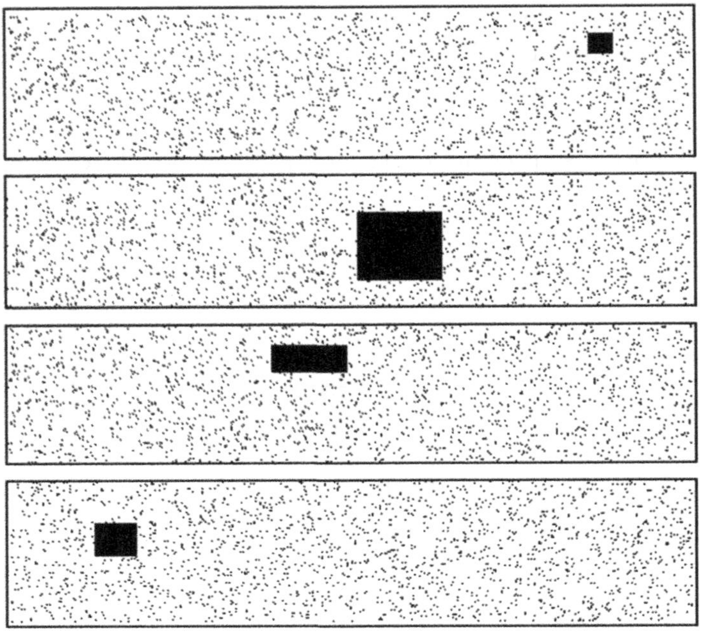

Figure 1.18 $SCoC_{rand}$—row wise seeds of Dataset_rand_I.

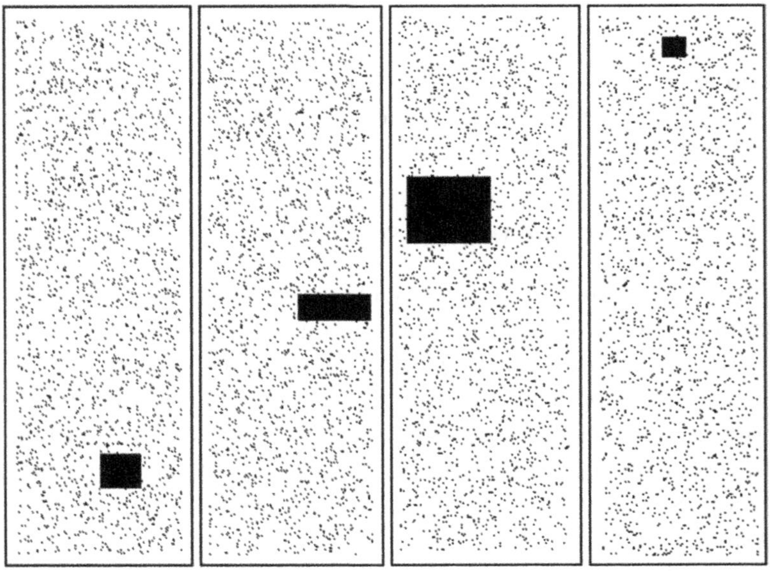

Figure 1.19 $SCoC_{rand}$—column wise seeds of Dataset_rand_I.

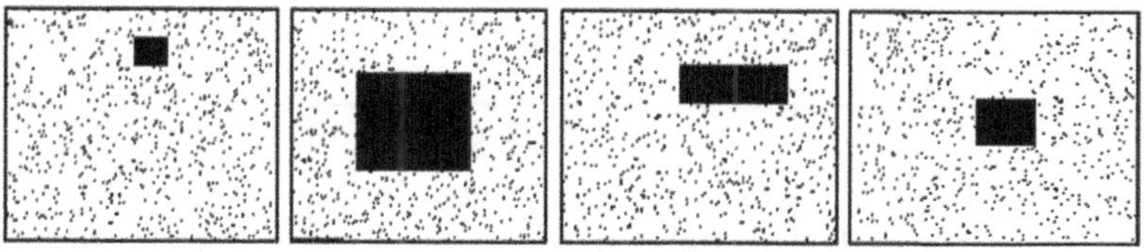

Figure 1.20 SCoCrand—random seeds of Dataset_rand_I.

Table 1.7 Types of seeding tested on synthetic Dataset_rand_I in $SCoC_{rand}$ approach.

S. no.	Seeding type	Number of co-clusters	Number of seeds	Seed vector size
1	Row seeding (Figure 1.18)	4	4	200 rows
2	Column seeding (Figure 1.19)	4	4	200 columns
3	Random seeding (Figure 1.20)	4	4	200 rows and 200 columns

Table 1.8 Comparative analysis of $SCoC_{rand}$ based on match score measure of co-clusters set.

	$SCoC_{rand}$ (row seed)	$SCoC_{rand}$ (column seed)	$SCoC_{rand}$ (random seed)	BiMax	xMotif
Without noise	1	1	1	0.934	0.0841
With noise	1	1	1	0.6117	0.0201

Table 1.9 Comparative analysis of $SCoC_{rand}$ based on computational time (in seconds).

	$SCoC_{rand}$ (row seed)	**$SCoC_{rand}$ (column seed)**	**$SCoC_{rand}$ (random seed)**	**BiMax**	**xMotif**
Without noise	6.092351	6.234526	**1.276431**	4.923421	2.892342
With noise	7.091229	6.999232	**3.823111**	5.892345	4.009834

all the embedded co-clusters from these synthetic datasets even under the noisy space successfully. The BiMax algorithm can extract the implanted co-clusters only in the noiseless dataset. The presence of the noise affects the performance of the existing approaches.

The computational time taken by these approaches for mining the co-clusters in the synthetic dataset is also recorded. The result shows that the xMotif approach performs well when compared to the other approaches, but it does not mine the expected co-cluster from any dataset. The BiMax algorithm can mine the co-clusters in minimal time when compared to the proposed approach. The performance of the BiMax algorithm is highly affected by the noise. The xMotif algorithm fails to extract the co-clusters from the given data. In some cases, the proposed approach $SCoC_{rand}$ may mine redundant co-clusters, which is a limitation of this approach.

1.9.3 SCoC with MapReduce (MR-CoC)

The previous co-clustering approaches have overcome issues like ignorance of quality and overlapped co-clusters. In this case, the MapReduce framework is adopted to handle the voluminous data and parallelizes the computations [39]. The previous versions of the proposed approach reduce the computational overhead and time complexity to some extent, which is reduced further in this approach. This framework is also chosen to eliminate repetitive co-clusters, which is highlighted in the previous approach $SCoC_{rand}$.

In this section, the $SCoC_{rand}$ method is enhanced with the MapReduce framework. The Map function consists of the $SCoC_{rand,}$ and the Reduce phase eliminates the repetitive co-clusters. The workflow of the proposed model is given in Figure 1.21. The pseudocode of the MR-CoC approach is shown in Algorithm 1.5.

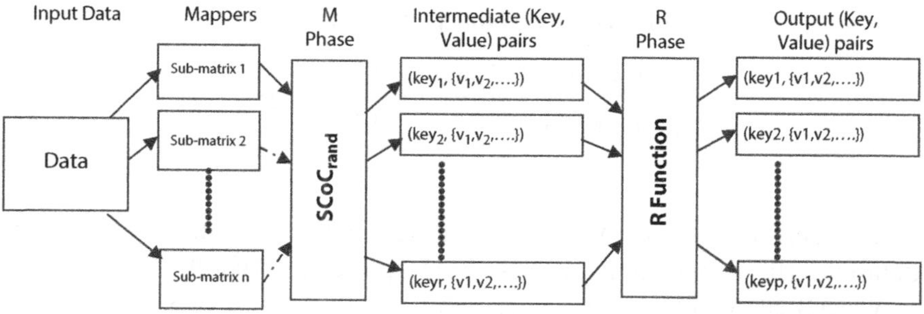

Figure 1.21 Workflow of the MR-CoC approach.

In this approach, the data are divided into sub-matrices as per the default file size of the MapReduce Framework. For each sub-matrix, the Map function ($SCoC_{rand}$) is applied in parallel and generates the intermediate KV pairs. Based on the key, the results are combined internally, and for each key, the reduce function is invoked in parallel. Here, the intermediate KV pair is $\{CC, count\}$ and the result pair is $\{CC_{size}, CC\}$ as in Table 1.10. The term "co-cluster" in KV pairs represents the list of row–column labels of data present in the co-cluster. This intermediate KV pair is used to eliminate the redundant co-clusters. Each intermediate key is the unique representation of each co-cluster. The count is to represent its redundancy. In the reduce phase, for each key in the result pair, i.e., the size-wise co-clusters are generated. After the MapReduce phases, the results are visualized and analyzed.

Algorithm 1.5: MR-CoC

Input: 2-D Input Data (D)
Result: co-cluster ($M = \{C_1, C_2, \ldots C_{ns}\}$)
Step 1 : Generate the given data into sub-matrices
Step 2 : For every input sub-matrix apply the mapper function
 # Map Phase
Step 3 : For every Input sub-matrix i
a. Perform $SCoC_{rand}$ and return KV pair $\{\mathbf{CC}, \mathbf{count}\}$
 # Reduce Phase
Step 4 : For every key compute result KV pair $\{\mathbf{CC}_{size}, \mathbf{CC}\}$
 # After MR phases
Step 5 : Assess and visualize the resultant co-clusters.

Table 1.10 Key-value pairs of MR-CoC.

Intermediate KV pair	$\{CC, count\}$
Result KV pair	$\{CC_{size}, CC\}$

The performance of MR-CoC is tested with two different synthetic datasets. The experiment utilizes the MapReduce default framework in MATLAB 2015 edition. The experimental analysis of this approach is discussed further.

1.9.3.1 Synthetic Dataset Description

The two different synthetic datasets with embedded co-clusters and noise are generated for the MR-CoC approach. The dataset description is shown in Table 1.11. The larger size datasets are generated, and larger numbers of seeds are generated for mining the co-clusters. These values are fixed on a trial-and-error basis.

The mappers count is equal to the seed count. The score threshold value is fixed to "1" for mining pure constant co-clusters from each seed portion of the data. The experimental results of this approach are discussed further.

Table 1.11 Synthetic datasets for the MR-CoC approach.

S. no.	Dataset name	Dataset size	Number of seeds	Number of co-clusters	Co-cluster position	Noise
1	Dataset_ MR_I	8000 × 10000	100000	50	Random continuous	Random noise
2	Dataset_ MR_I	8000 × 10000	500000	50	Random continuous	Random noise
3	Dataset_ MR_II	30000 × 6000	100000	70	Random scattered	Random noise
4	Dataset_ MR_II	30000 × 6000	500000	70	Random scattered	Random noise

1.9.3.2 Experimental Analysis: MR-CoC

The results are compared with the previous proposed $SCoC_{rand}$ approach and existing BiMax and xMotif approaches. The match score is evaluated to compare the similarity of extracted and embedded co-clusters. The match score and computation time are recorded for proposed and existing approaches. Table 1.12 shows the score measure-based comparison of these approaches.

The previous $SCoC_{rand}$ approach and MR-CoC are performing well, even in large noisy data. The existing approaches suffered from noise and data size issues that are known from these results. The proposed MR-CoC approach can handle the larger dataset whereas the proposed $SCoC_{rand}$ and the existing approaches faced the memory overflow issue by storing the massive data. The MR-CoC outperforms both the state-of-the-art and competing methods due to the dramatic reduction in computing time required (Table 1.13). The complexity based on time for MR-CoC is $\boldsymbol{O(\log(T_r))}$, where "$T_r$" is the time complexity of $SCoC_{rand}$. It is low when compared to the time complexities $\boldsymbol{O(nm^2\alpha)}$ and $\boldsymbol{O(nm^{O(\log(1/\alpha)+\log(1/b))})}$ of the existing approaches BiMax and xMotif, respectively.

Table 1.14 gives the overall view of this chapter, i.e., the mapping of the proposed approaches versus focused issues in this chapter. This table maps the satisfied (tick mark) and not-satisfied (cross mark) issues to each of the proposed approaches. As this approach satisfied all the issues faced by the existing approaches, it is further applied for the real-time problems for

Table 1.12 Comparative analysis of MR-CoC based on match score measure.

	Dataset_MR_I Seed = 100000		**Dataset_MR_I Seed = 500000**		**Dataset_MR_II Seed = 100000**		**Dataset_MR_II Seed = 500000**	
	Noise-free	**Noisy**	**Noise-free**	**Noisy**	**Noise-free**	**Noisy**	**Noise-free**	**Noisy**
$SCoC_{rand}$	0.9567	0.9571	1	1	1	1	MO	MO
MR-CoC	**1**	**1**	**1**	**1**	**1**	**1**	**1**	**1**
BiMax	0.892	0.545	0.842	0.651	MO	MO	MO	MO
xMotif	0.0354	0.0124	0.045	0.0214	MO	MO	MO	MO

MO, memory overflow.

Table 1.13 Comparative analysis of MR-CoC based on computational time.

w	Dataset_MR_I Seed = 100000		Dataset_MR_I Seed = 500000		Dataset_MR_II Seed = 100000		Dataset_MR_II Seed = 500000	
	Noise-free	**Noisy**	**Noise-free**	**Noisy**	**Noise-free**	**Noisy**	**Noise-free**	**Noisy**
SCoC$_{rand}$	89.83421	102.23893	142.2324	182.1289	122.4562	182.2345	MO	MO
MR-CoC	**10.02196**	**11.11054**	**11.23411**	**12.3933**	**20.34189**	**25.32904**	**31.53485**	**32.12892**
BiMax	90.23665	120.3499	176.4589	184.1901	MO	MO	MO	MO
xMotif	71.82116	89.294387	71.82116	89.294387	MO	MO	MO	MO

MO, memory overflow.

Table 1.14 Proposed methods vs. focused issues.

S. no.	Proposed method \ Focused issue	Symmetric data	Non-symmetric data	Noise sensitivity	Overlapped co-clusters	Scalability issue	Time consumption	Parallelization	Computational overhead	Description
1	SCoC$_{sym}$	✓	×	✓	×	×	✓	×	✓	For symmetric data
2	SCoC$_{nsym}$	×	✓	✓	×	×	✓	×	✓	For non-symmetric data
3	SCoC$_{rand}$	✓	✓	✓	✓	×	×	×	✓	For extracting overlapped clusters
4	MR-CoC	✓	✓	✓	✓	✓	✓	✓	✓	For matching the voluminous, complex and distributed data

showcasing its performance. This method is further utilized for mining functional modules in protein interaction networks in this study.

1.10 Functional Module Mining Using MR-CoC

Figures 1.22 to 1.24 display the experimental outcomes of the MR-CoC method. Researching the protein complex coverage of the retrieved findings involves comparing the extracted sub-networks to pre-existing protein complexes. For this reason, we use the existing complexes from the CORUM database [29].

The inclusion results are considered into three groups—FM, PM, and UM—based on their protein complex coverage level, as follows:

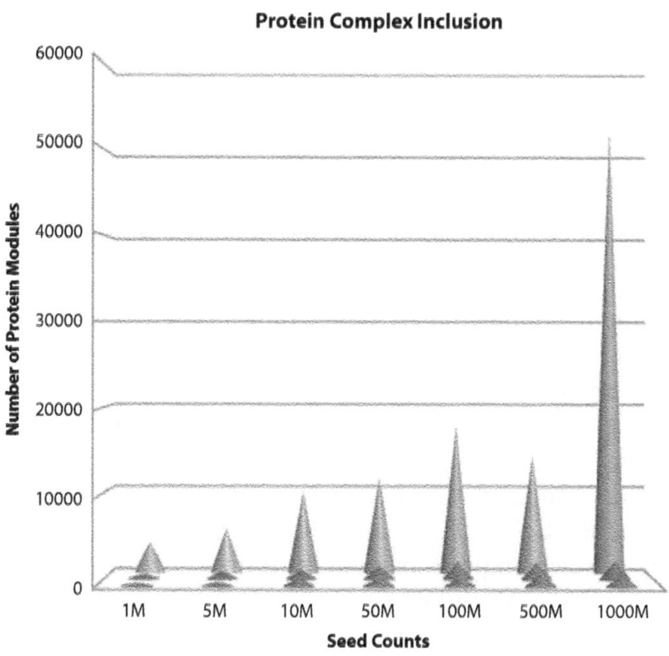

	1M	5M	10M	50M	100M	500M	1000M
FM	342	466	987	1023	1089	1321	1233
PM	560	876	1123	1598	1963	1908	2134
UM	3541	5163	9526	11229	17408	13760	52724

Figure 1.22 Protein complex coverage with minimum protein module size 3.

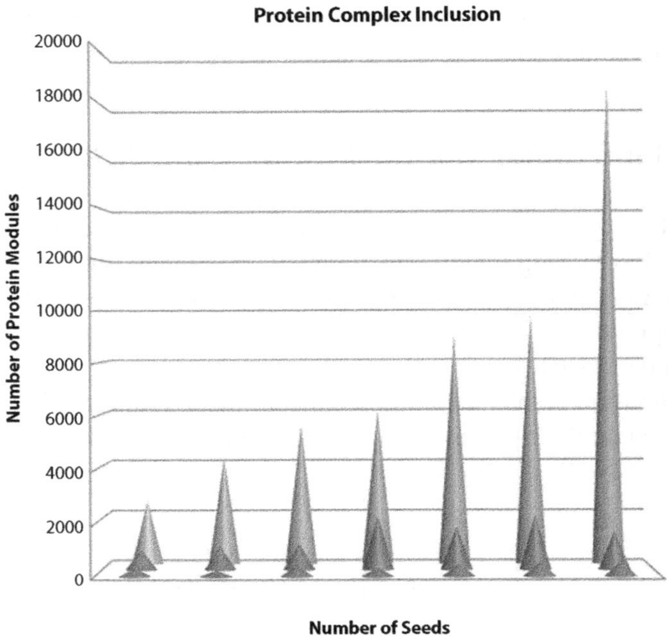

	1M	5M	10M	50M	100M	500M	1000M
FM	321	238	417	332	479	558	564
PM	798	943	1022	2087	1673	2127	1484
UM	2468	4130	5379	5974	8909	9738	18835

Figure 1.23 Protein complex inclusion rate with module size 4 and above.

- Protein modules that have been fully mapped (FM) are identical to the current protein complex.
- Ninety percent of the components of known protein complexes are found in partially mapped protein modules (PMs).

MR-CoC is used to experiment on three different seed setups and minimum sub-network sizes. Figures 1.22 to 1.24 highlight these results. The seed count is shown on the x-axis and the number of protein modules created under the FM, PM, and UM categories is shown on the y-axis in these images. From the 2,358 existing protein complexes, 2,237 are identified by the MR-CoC approach. The topological property itself can mine almost 94.86% of the existing protein complexes.

It predicted more than 30,000 unknown protein modules that can be further analyzed for their biological significances. The biological functionalities of a few UM protein modules are shown in Table 1.15, which is

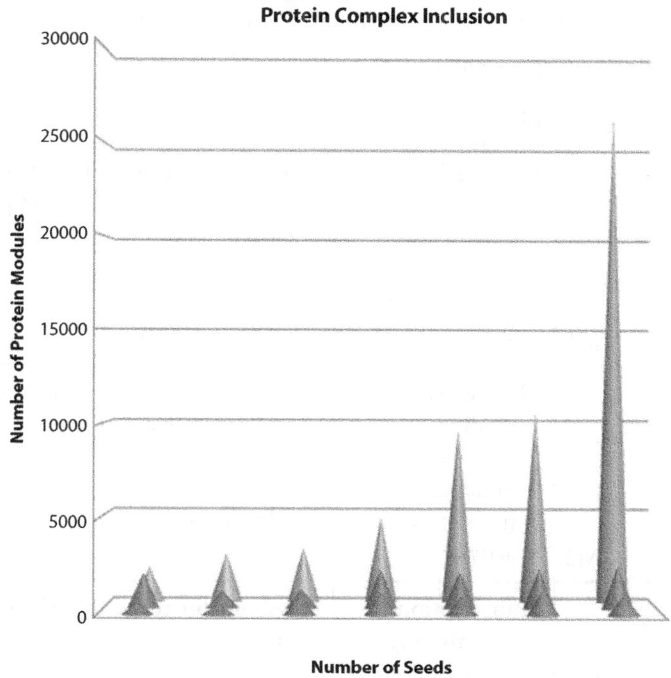

	1M	5M	10M	50M	100M	500M	1000M
FM	678	590	1012	1221	1029	1392	1123
PM	1872	943	1022	2087	1963	2146	2312
UM	1844	2637	2952	4625	9520	10403	26575

Figure 1.24 Protein complex inclusion with module size 5 and above.

suggested based on their biological significances. The degree to which the proteins in different protein modules are functionally comparable is indicated by their functional coherence. In Table 1.15, protein modules with more than 70% functional coherence of the participants are highlighted.

As shown in Table 1.15, the 7 UM protein modules have molecular interpretations linked to drug targets. The STRING database is used to obtain the biological process, molecular function, and cell component-based importance of the protein modules produced. The protein modules' network visualization is shown in the first column of Table 1.15. The illustrations make it easy to observe how dense these protein modules are. Binding, transport, metabolism, catalysis, receptor activities, ion channels, signaling pathways, oxidation, and cell communications are the key topics connected to therapeutic targets.

Table 1.15 MR-CoC: biological functionalities of few UM protein modules.

Protein modules	FC > 70%		
	BP	**MF**	**CC**
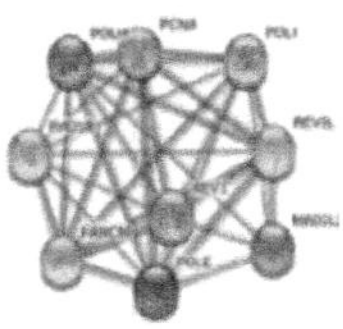 M1	**Binding:** DNA binding with polymerase activity, handles damaged DNA	**Metabolic Process:** Cellular Biosynthetic Processes meant for single-organism	**Polymerase Complex**
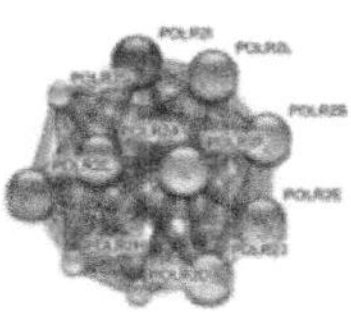 M2	**Binding:** DNA binding, compound binding with transferase activity	**Metabolic process and regulative processes:** primary and cellular process	**Protein complex**
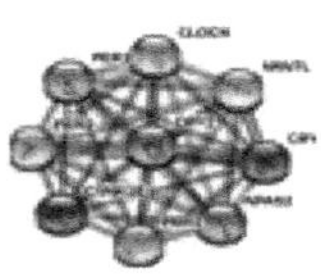 M3	**Transcription and binding:** transcription regulatory region DNA binding	**Metabolic process and regulative processes:** cellular and macro molecule metabolic regulation process	**Nucleus**
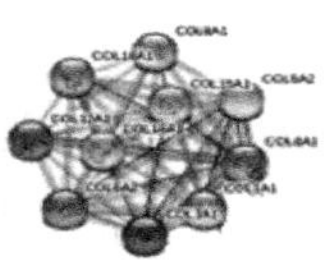 M4	**Structural molecule activity**	**Catabolic and matrix processes:** matrix organization and disassembling processes	**Extracellular matrix region**
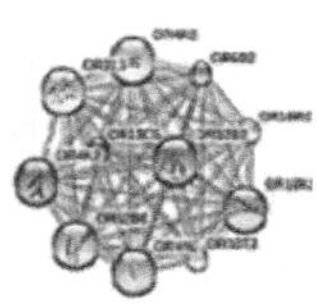 M5	**Activity of receptor:** receptor activity of G-protein coupled	Chemical and stimulus responses, odor perception, and receptor-mediated cellular communication	**Plasma membrane**

(Continued)

Table 1.15 MR-CoC: biological functionalities of few UM protein modules. (*Continued*)

Protein modules	FC > 70%		
	BP	MF	CC
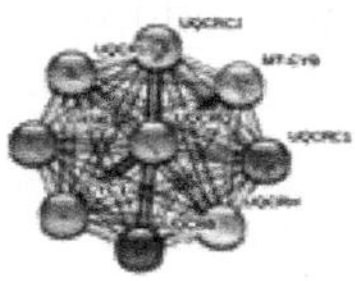 M6	**Transporter activity:** Oxidoreductase activity, transfer of hydrogen ions	**Transport across biological membranes:** electron transport in respiration and hydrogen ions	**Membrane protein complex**
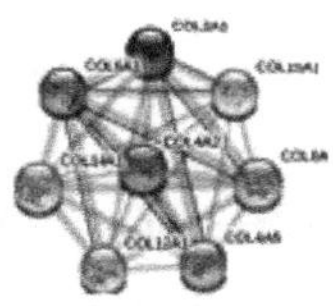 M7	**Extracellular matrix structural constituent**	**Development process:** single multicellular organism, system development	**Protein complex**
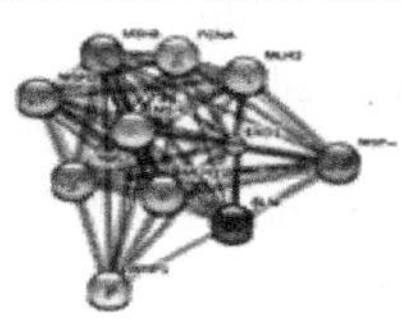 M8	**Binding and catalytic activity:** ion, ATP, and DNA binding	**Responding activity:** response to stress, a stimulus, and cell repair process	**Nuclear part, nucleoplasm**
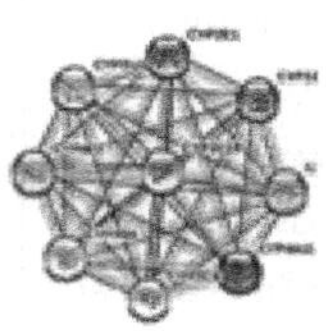 M9	**Activities of binding and catalytic:** activities of tetrapyrrole, and oxidoreductase, and metal ion binding	**Process of oxidation and reduction:** metabolic process of the single organism	**Endomembrane**
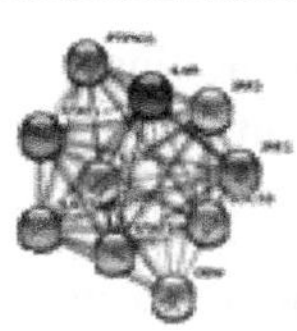 M10	**Binding of receptors:** growing process of binding hormone receptor	**Signaling, regulation, phosphorylation and responding activity**	**Receptor complex**

Similarly, their presence in the different membrane regions, complexes, and so forth is also highlighted in Table 1.16. This table shows evidence that there are also biological significances found in the UM protein modules.

FM29 is enriched with glycol-proteins, which are mostly seen in potential drug targets. They are used to detect the virulence infections in the PIN. It causes protein folding and is essential for protein folding and

Table 1.16 Drug target-based biological functionalities of UM functional modules.

DTM	Biological significance		FC
FM29			
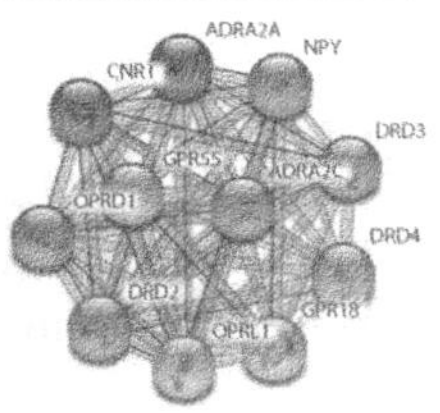 ADRA2A, ADRA2C, **CNR1**, DRD2, DRD3, DRD4, GPR18, GPR55, NPY, OPRD1, OPRL1	BP	**Regulation and activities of receptors:** Receptors that are G protein-coupled; controlling processes in biology, multi-cellular organisms, cell-to-cell communication, molecular function, signaling, and stimulus response	1
		Regulation activity of transportation: stimulus response regulation, localization, process of multi-cells, transduction of signals, processes of cell, and transportation	0.8
	MF	**Receptor activity:** G protein-coupled	1
		Binding of protein, binding of receptors meant for signaling	0.7
	CC	**Integral component of plasma membrane**	0.9
		Neuron projection, synapse part	0.5

(Continued)

Table 1.16 Drug target-based biological functionalities of UM functional modules. (*Continued*)

DTM	Biological significance		FC
FM30			
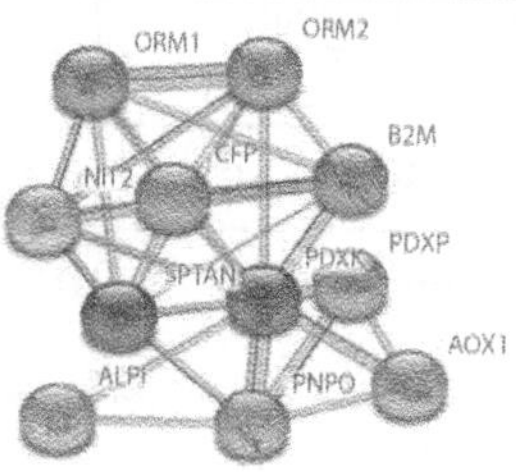 ADRBK1, AGT, **AGTR1**, APLN, ARRB1, ARRB2, EDN1, EGFR, GNAQ, GRK5, KNG1	BP	**Activity regulation of receptor:** coupled G protein, cell interaction regulation, signaling, bio-quality, and process of development	1
	BP	**Transport and regulation activity: regulating the transport**, multicellular organismal process, signal transduction, molecular function localization, nitrogen compound metabolic process	0.8
	MF	**Receptor and transport activity:** binding of coupled G protein, signaling receptor, and binding of protein	0.9
	MF	**Activity of binding:** carbohydrate derivative, and anion binding	0.6
	CC	**Plasma membrane**	0.6
	CC	**Extracellular space**	0.4
FM19			
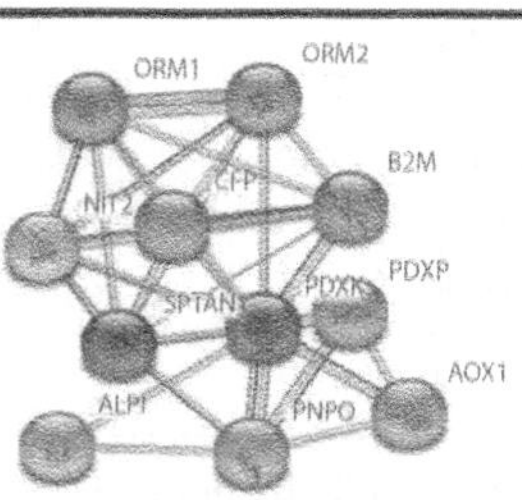 AOX1, B2M, CFP, NIT2, ORM1, ORM2, **PDXK**, PDXP, PNPO, SPTAN1	BP	Organonitrogen compound metabolic process, neutrophil degranulation	7

(*Continued*)

Table 1.16 Drug target-based biological functionalities of UM functional modules. (*Continued*)

DTM	Biological significance		FC
	BP	**Metabolic process:** small molecule and phosphate-compound metabolic process	5
	MF	**Identical protein binding**	0.4
		Protein homodimerization activity	0.3
	CC	**Cytoplasmic part**	0.9
		Intracellular organelle lumen, extracellular region	0.7
FM25			
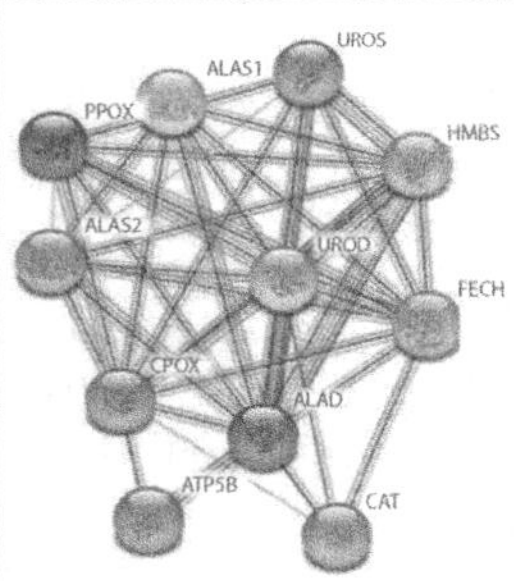 **ALAD**, ALAS1, ALAS2, ATP5B, CAT, CPOX, FECH, HMBS, PPOX, UROD, UROS	BP	**Process of metabolism:** process of cellular metabolism, compounds of organo-nitrogen, and organic cyclic compounds	1
		Biosynthetic process: organonitrogen substances, heterocycle, fragrant compound, organic cyclic substance, and biosynthetic process of nitrogen compound	0.9
	MF	**Catalytic activity**	1
		Binding activity: cofactor, small molecule, lyase, and coenzyme binding	0.5
	CC	**Cytoplasmic part**	1
		Intracellular organelle lumen, cytosol, mitochondrion	0.7

(*Continued*)

Table 1.16 Drug target-based biological functionalities of UM functional modules. (*Continued*)

DTM	Biological significance		FC
FM25			
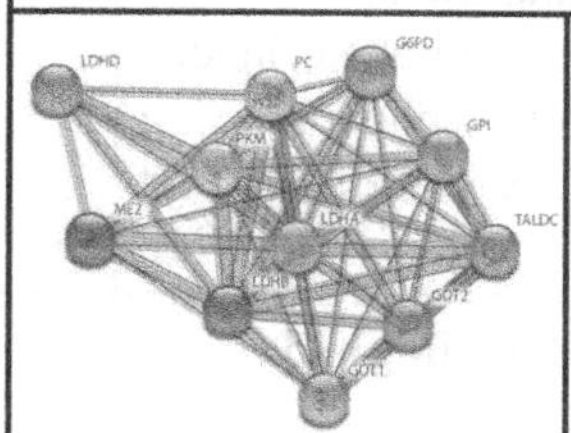 G6PD, GOT1, GOT2, GPI, LDHA, **LDHB**, LDHD, ME2, PC, PKM, TALDO1	BP	**Metabolic activity:** small molecule, cellular, primary, and organic substance metabolic process	1
		Metabolic and biosynthetic activity: carbohydrate, cofactor, carboxylic acid, organonitrogen compound, and process of organic cyclic compound for metabolism, organic substance, and biosynthetic process of tiny molecules	0.75
	MF	**Activities of binding:** small molecule and catalytic	1
		Binding activity: coenzyme, heterocyclic substance, and binding of organic cyclic substance	0.8
	CC	**Cytoplasmic part**	1
		Cytosol	0.7
FM35			
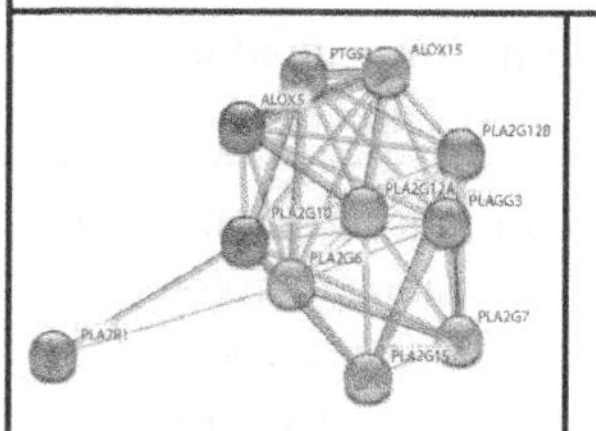 ALOX15, ALOX5, **PLA2G0.9**, PLA2G12A PLA2G12B PLA2G15, PLA2G3, PLA2G6, PLA2G7, PLA2R1, PTGS2	BP	**Metabolic process:** cellular lipid, organophosphate, phosphate-containing compound, and cellular metabolic processes	0.9

(*Continued*)

Table 1.16 Drug target-based biological functionalities of UM functional modules. (*Continued*)

DTM	Biological significance		FC
	BP	**Metabolic and transport activity:** phospholipid, lipid, and lycerophospholipid metabolic processes; transport activity	8
	MF	**Activities of binding and catalytic**	1
		Activities of binding: binding of ion and metal ion	0.8
	CC	**Extracellular region**	0.8
		Extracellular space	0.4
FM37			
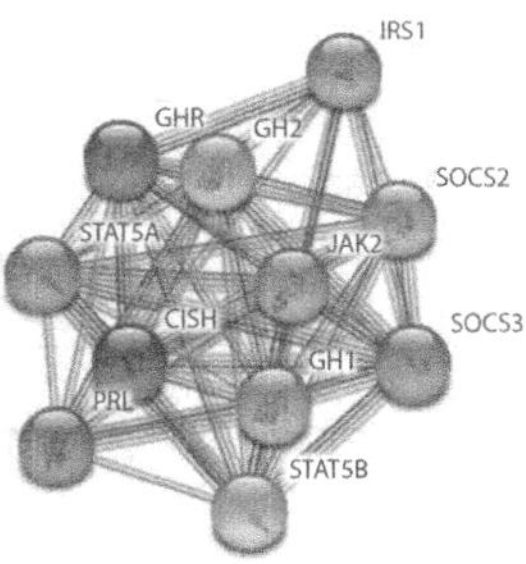	BP	Intracellular signal transduction, cellular response to organic substance	1
		Regulating metabolic activity: regulating the response to stimulus, primary, cellular, and macromolecule metabolic processes	0.9
CISH, GH1, GH2, **GHR**, IRS1, JAK2, PRL, SOCS2, SOCS3, STAT5A, STAT5B	MF	**Molecular function regulator, binding of protein**	0.8
		Binding of hormone receptor, binding of signaling receptor, binding of cytokine receptor, phosphotransferase activities, alcohol group as acceptor, kinase activity	0.3
	CC	Cytoplasmic part	1
		Cytosol	0.7

recognition of cell–cell interaction. FM19 has metabolic pathways in common, specifically vitamin B6 metabolic pathways. They play a major role in cell metabolism [40]. FM25 also has vitamin B6 metabolic pathways in common along with disease mutation. They play a major role in cell metabolism [40]. The pathogen infections can be detected using this combination. There is an abundance of phosphoprotein in FM34. The activation of pharmacological targets is one of its uses. FM35 is involved in metabolic processes to a significant extent. It shares routes in the metabolism of arachidonic acid, linoleic acid, and ether lipids. In FM37, phosphoprotein was abundant. The activation of pharmacological targets is one of its uses. Biochemists can use this information to make predictions about potential novel protein complexes or functional modules.

1.11 Conclusion

In this chapter, a novel score based co-clustering approach is proposed and implemented. This approach was designed to overcome the limitations like the ignorance of quality co-clusters and overlapped co-clusters, computational overhead, and time consumption. The proposed approach further extended into two more different versions, namely, $SCoC_{rand}$ and MR-CoC, for this purpose. The synthetic datasets were generated to test these approaches based on various criteria like matrix type, data size, co-cluster size, co-cluster implantation, and presence of noise. The outcomes were evaluated in relation to pre-existing methods, such as the BiMax and xMotif algorithms, using the metrics of computing time and match score. Compared to the previous methods, MR-CoC demonstrated superior performance. All four of the problems with the previous methods were eliminated by it. The protein interaction network dataset is another area where MR-CoC is used for functional module mining. In order to determine the efficacy of FMM employing MR-CoC, the findings were compared to the preexisting protein complexes. Of the preexisting protein complexes, it was able to extract 94.86%. More than 30,000 previously unidentified protein modules were also retrieved from PIN. We looked at the biological importance of a number of unmapped protein modules and singled out those with functional coherence greater than 70%.

Appendix

The list of abbreviations used in this chapter are given in Table 1.17.

Table 1.17 List of abbreviations.

Abbreviation	Description	Abbreviation	Description
FMM	Functional module mining	FC	Functional coherence
PIN	Protein interaction network	FM	Functional module
SCoC	Score based co-clustering	PM	Protein module
$SCoC_{nsym}$	Score based co-clustering for non-symmetric data	DTM	Drug target module
$SCoC_{rand}$	Score based co-clustering with random seeding	BP	Biological process
MR-CoC	Score based co-clustering with MapReduce	MF	Molecular function
PSO	Particle swarm optimization	CC	Cell component
GA	Genetic algorithm	KV	Key-value pairs
CC	Co-clusters	UM	Un-mapped modules

References

1. J. S. J. and Pinkert, S., Protein Interaction Networks- More than mere Modules. *PLoS Comput. Biol.*, 6, 1, 2010.
2. Rui-Henriques, and Madeira, S.C., BicNET: Flexible module discovery in large-scale biological networks using biclustering. *Algorithms Mol. Biol.*, 11, 14, 1–30, 2016.
3. Koyutürk, M., Using Protein Interaction Networks to Understand Complex Diseases. *Comput. Mach. Charles Babbage*, 45, 3, 31–38, 2012.
4. A. J. E., C. A. O., Pereira-Leal, J.B., Detection of Functional modules from protein Interaction Networks. *Proteins Struct. Funct. Bioinf.*, 54, 49–57, 2004.
5. Azevedo, H. and AlbertoMoreira-Filho, C., Topological robustness of protein analysis of PIN reveals key targets for overcoming chemotherapy resistance in glioma, in: *Scientific Reports*, Nature, London, 2015.
6. Toshiyuki, T.Y. and Shirai, T., Deciphering Supramolecules Structures with Protein- protein Interaction Network Modeling, in: *Scientific Reports*, Nature, London, 2015.
7. C. W. H. and Bader, G.D., An automated method for finding molecular complexes in large protein interaction networks. *BMC Bioinf.*, 4, 2, 1–27, 2003.
8. G. W. K. A. R. T. a. T. M. and Dittrich, M.T., Identifying Functional Modules in Protein-Protein interaction Networks: an integrated exact approach. *ISMB*, 24, 223–231, 2008.
9. E. T. L. G. and Zhang, Y., Weighted Consensus Clustering for Identifying Functional Modules In Protein-Protein Interaction Networks.
10. Cheng, Y. and Church, G., Biclustering of expression data, in: *Proceedings of the eighth international conference on intelligent systems for molecular biology*, 2000.
11. Lazzeroni, L. and Owen, A., Plaid models for gene expression Data. *Stat. Sin.*, 12, 1, 61–86, 2002.
12. Ben-Dor, A., Chor, B., Karp, R., Yakhini, Z., Discovering local structure in gene expression data: the order-preserving submatrix problem, in: *Proceedings of the sixth annual international conference on computational biology*, 2002.
13. Murali, T. and Kasif, S., Extracting Conserved Gene Expression Motifs from Gene Expression Data. *Pacific Symposium on Biocomputing*, 2003.
14. Prelic, A., Bleuler, S., Zimmermann, P., Wille, A., BuÈhlmann, P., Gruissem, W., A Systematic Comparison and Evaluation of Biclustering Methods for Gene Expression Data. *Bioinformatics*, 22, 9, 1122–1129, 2006.
15. Uitert, M.V., Meuleman, W., Wessels, L., Biclustering Sparse Binary Genomic Data. *J. Comput. Biol.*, 15, 10, 1329–1345, 2008.
16. Noureen, N. and Qadir, M.A., BiSim: A Simple and Efficient Biclustering Algorithm, in: *International Conference of Soft Computing and Pattern Recognition*, 2009.

17. Zhang, Z.-Y., Li, T., Ding, C., Ren, X.-W., Zhang, X.-S., Binary matrix factorization for analyzing gene expression data. *Data Min. Knowl. Discov.*, 20, 28–52, 2010.
18. RodrõÂguez-Baena, D., PeÂrez-Pulid, A., Ruiz, J.A., A Biclustering Algorithm for Extracting Bit-Patterns from Binary Datasets. *Bioinformatics*, 27, 19, 2738–2745, 2011.
19. Voggenreiter, O. and Bleuler, S., Exact biclustering algorithm for the analysis of large gene expression data sets. *BMC Bioinf.*, 13, 1–13, 2012.
20. Király, A., Gyenesei, A., Abonyi, J., Bit-Table Based Biclustering and Frequent Closed Itemset Mining in High-Dimensional Binary Data. *Sci. World J.*, 2014, 1–7, 2014.
21. Saber, H. and Elloumi, M., Efficiently Mining Gene Expression Data via Novel Binary Biclustering Algorithms. *J. Proteomics Bioinform*, 8, 4, 1–7, 2015.
22. GonzaÂlez-DomõÂnguez, J. and Sito, R.R.E., ParBiBit: Parallel tool for binary biclustering on modern distributed-memory systems. *PLoS One*, 13, 4, 1–19, 2018.
23. Structures of Life. US Department of Health and Human Services, National Institute of Health, National Institute of General Medical Services, 2007.
24. Spirin, V. and Mirny, L.A., Protein Complexes and Functional Modules in the Molecular Networks. *PNAS*, 100, 21, 12123–12128, 2013.
25. Wang, R., Central Dogma of Molecular Biology, 2015, [Online]. Available: http://fourier.eng.hmc.edu/bioinformatics/intro/node8.html.
26. Gashaw, I., Ellinghaus, P., Sommer, A., Asadullah, K., What makes a good drug target? *Drug Discov. Today-Elsevier*, 16, 1037–1043, 2011.
27. Franceschini, A., Szklarczyk, D., Frankild, S., Kuhn, M., Simonovic, M., Roth, A., Lin, J., Minguez, P., Bork, P., v. M. C, Jensen, L., STRING v9.1: protein-protein interaction networks, with increased coverage and integration. *Nucleic Acid Res.*, pp, 808–815, 2013.
28. Szklarczyk, D., Gable, A., Lyon, D., Junge, A., Wyder, S., Huerta-Cepas, J., Simonovic, M., Doncheva, N., Morris, J., Bork, P., Jensen, L., v. Mering, C., STRING v11: protein-protein association networks with increased coverage, supporting functional discovery in genome-wide experimental datasets. *Nucleic Acid Res.*, pp, 607–613, 2019.
29. Giurgiu, M., Reinhard, J., Brauner, B., Dunger-Kaltenbach, I., Fobo, G., Frishman, G., Montrone, C., Ruepp, A., CORUM: A Comprehensive Resource of Mammalian Protein Complexes. *Nucleic Acid Res.-2019*, 2018.
30. MapReduce, 2016, [Online, Available: https://in.mathworks.com/help/matlab/mapreduce.html.
31. G. F. J. E. and Pallickara, S., MapReduce for Data Intensive Scientific Analyses, in: *Proceedings of the 2008 Fourth IEEE International Conference on eScience*, 2008.

32. S. C. a. and Schlosser, S.W., Map-reduce meets wider varieties of applications, 2008.
33. G. S. and Dean, J., MapReduce: simplified data processing on large clusters. *Commun. ACM*, 51, 1, 107–113, 2008.
34. Bastos, H.P., Sousa, L., Clarke, L.A., Couto, F.M., Functional coherence metrics in protein Families. *J. Biomed. Semant.*, 7, 41, 1–11, 2016.
35. Chagoyen, M. and Pazos, F., Quantifying the biological significance of gene ontology biological processes—implications for the analysis of systems-wide data. *Bioinformatics*, 26, 371–384, no, 2010.
36. D. Plessis, L., Skunca, N., Dessimoz, C., The what, where, how and why of gene ontologyça primer for bioinformaticians. *Briefings Bioinf.*, 12, 723–735, no, 2011.
37. Bult, C., Blake, J., Smith, C., Kadin, J., Richardson, J., G. MGD, Mouse Genome Database (MGD). *Nucleic Acids Res.*, 47, D1, D801– D806, 2019.
38. Sussman, J.L. and Prilusky, J., *J. Struct. Biol.*, 175, 2, 244–252. 2011, [Online], Available: www.proteopedia.org.
39. Bhatnagar, R. and Kumar, L., An Efficient Map-Reduce Algorithm for Computing Formal Concepts from Binary Data, in: *IEEE International Conference on Big Data (Big Data)*, 2015.
40. Parra, M., Stahl, S., Hellmann, H., Vitamin B6 and its role in cell metabolism and physiology. *Cells*, 7, 7, 1–28, 2018.
41. Stuart_P, L., Least squares quantization in PCM. *Inf. Theory, IEEE Trans.*, 28, 2, 129–137, 1982.
42. Bapat, R., *Graphs and Matrices*, Springer, Hindustan Book Agency, London, 2010.
43. Gursoy, A.K. O. N. R., Topological properties of protein interaction networks from a structural perspective. *Biochem. Soc. Trans.*, 36, 6, 1398–1403, 2008.
44. Diestel, R., *Graph Theory*, Springer, London, 2016.

2

Natural Language Processing in Healthcare: Enhancing Wellbeing through a COVID-19 Case Study

Akib Mohi Ud Din Khanday[1], Salah Bouktif[1*] and Ali Ouni[2]

[1]*Department of Computer Sciences and Software Engineering—CIT, United Arab Emirates University, Al Ain, United Arab Emirates*
[2]*Department of Software Engineering and IT, École de Technologie Supérieure University of Quebec, Montreal, Canada*

Abstract

Natural language processing (NLP) has emerged as a groundbreaking technology within the healthcare sector and promising to streamline various tasks for enhancing patient care and advance clinical research. This chapter discusses the present landscape of NLP in healthcare by shedding light on its potential advantages, challenges, and its role in pandemics like COVID-19. The analysis investigates NLP's application in clinical reports to analyze and derive valuable insights from extensive volumes of unstructured medical text. While NLP offers significant potential, it had limitations about data privacy, biases in algorithms, and the requirement for substantial training data to ensure better results. This chapter also addresses the limitations of NLP in handling medical terminology. It is a comprehensive evaluation of the current state of NLP in healthcare coupled with an exploration of future possibilities that underscore the necessity for a patient-centric approach to harness the technology's full potential. By tackling these challenges, NLP gives way to healthcare practices that are more efficient, precise, and patient-oriented wellbeing. This study performs a case study on COVID-19 by collecting the textual data and performing machine and ensemble learning classification. Data is refined with the help of preprocessing techniques. Term frequency/inverse document frequency is fused with the n-grams for extracting the most relevant features. Machine and ensemble learning algorithms are fine-tuned to produce better results. In the future, deep neural networks may be used to improve performance.

**Corresponding author*: salahb@uaeu.ac.ae

Bharat Bhushan, Akib Khanday, Khursheed Aurangzeb, Sudhir Kumar Sharma and Parma Nand (eds.) Wellness Management Powered by AI Technologies, (55–74) © 2025 Scrivener Publishing LLC

***Keywords*:** Natural language processing, COVID-19, machine learning, ensemble learning

2.1 Introduction

Natural language processing is an interdisciplinary field that focuses on the use of systems to execute human language activities [1]. Certain problems connected to natural language understanding and processing are equally complex due to the intricacy of human interaction. Speech creation, machine translation, and information extraction are some examples of NLP tasks. To tackle NLP challenges, many techniques can be used, which can be generically classified as symbolic, statistical, connectionist, or hybrid [2]. Historically, symbolic techniques relied on language-specific knowledge for in-depth analysis [3]. Symbolic methods encompass rule-based systems and semantic networks which employ methods like decision tree, K-nearest neighbor algorithms, and conceptual clustering [3]. On the other hand, statistical methods do not depend on language-specific expertise; they instead employ mathematical techniques to create models using extensive language datasets known as corpora. These consist numerous real-world text samples which serve as the building block for models to capture language patterns in a generalized manner. The connectionist approach, like the statistical method, constructs models by extracting generalizations from large datasets, but it also incorporates various representation theories [4]. Networks of computational units having input and output connections, weights, and activation levels are common in connectionist techniques [5]. Hybrid techniques combine aspects from different approaches to overcome the shortcomings of individual models, which result in a more robust solution to NLP tasks.

NLP approaches can be applied to text mining (TM) since they strive to extract meaningful representations from unstructured material. As a result, several applications and search engines that specialize in mining databases within certain disciplines have been developed [6–8]. Morphological analysis, syntactic and semantic analysis, sentiment analysis, information retrieval, question answering, machine translation, document summarization, and speech recognition are all examples of NLP tasks. Understanding text's morphological structure and syntactic norms helps with semantic interpretation. Many NLP tasks, such as part-of-speech (PoS) tagging, word sense disambiguation (WSD), and named entity recognition (NER), can be subdivided further. Previous research has mostly focused on extracting items and identifying their relationships inside reference knowledge bases [9]. While some existing approaches provide excellent performance for a variety of applications, there has recently been increased interest in biological entities, namely, drug–protein, drug–drug, and protein–protein interactions [10]. NLP-based data channeling methods have a wide range of possible applications.

Information retrieval (IR) methods are used at the beginning of the biomedical NLP pipeline to classify and retrieve relevant texts. This procedure assists researchers in filtering away irrelevant text or documents and focuses solely on those that are of interest. Moving forward in the flow, information extraction (IE) approaches help identify named entities and extract events that provide useful information. NER, NEL, co-reference Resolution (CR), temporal information extraction, relation extraction (RE), knowledge base construction, and reasoning all come under the umbrella of IE. Information describing entities interacting with one another, such as drug–protein or protein–drug interactions, is frequently found in biomedical literature. Linkages between entities, such as protein–protein or gene–gene, are also included, as are temporal linkages and other important bio-entities inside an event. IE allows academics to get the relevant textual material without the stress of manual searching by automating and streamlining the procedure [11, 12]. These events collected from enormous amounts of literature are significant and have applications in a variety of disciplines, including database curation, ontology creation, semantic web search, and interactive systems. NLP has undergone constant development since the 1950s. Decades of research have gone into NLP for smart healthcare, and current advances in AI and general NLP have made it more and more popular.

The remainder of the chapter is as follows: Section 2.2 discusses the NLP approaches that are used, Section 2.3 describes the pipeline of NLP that is used for smart healthcare, Section 2.4 discusses the application areas of NLP in healthcare, Section 2.5 implements the pipeline for the COVID-19-related dataset, Section 2.6 discusses the results generated from the proposed pipeline, and work is concluded in Section 2.7.

2.2 NLP Approaches

There are three types of mainstream NLP approaches: rule-based, statistical, and neural. Each has unique qualities. This section outlines the benefits and drawbacks of the these categories, as well as their respective algorithms. Expert-led studies can improve the accuracy of rule-based NLP techniques, such as pattern matching and parsing [13]. Rule-based natural language processing approaches are also simple to learn and comprehend, but rules are frequently insufficient to address every scenario because of the elasticity and complexity of human language. After the development of appropriate rules for human language using rule-based NLP. We need an expertise computer science and linguistics that restricts the scope of its application in large-scale data mining. In academia, rule-based methods are typically seen as antiquated and are only infrequently utilized for better preparation. Statistical NLP performs better than rule-based NLP in terms of robustness and performance, but in order to create handcrafted features it needs domain expertise. As a result, it can only utilize all of the data that is available and provide adequate accuracy in complicated applications. Statistical NLP requires a great deal of feature engineering; still it is as comprehensible and easy to understand as rule-based NLP because of the direct feature design. As statistical NLP requires less large-scale datasets and computing resources, it is far more efficient than neural NLP. Also, there are differences in the characteristics of representative statistical NLP models like TF/IDF and bag-of-words, etc. [14, 15]. Although it is easier to construct bag-of-words in which frequency of words in a sentence is calculated by disregarding their significance and order.

TF-IDF enhances the word importance estimation by using the inverse document frequency, but it still ignores sequential order information. N-gram performs better than bag of words but has a high demand of computational resources/complexities. It is important to note that statistical natural language processing (NLP) is still being used in numerous healthcare studies and applications, even in light of the current dominance of deep learning. NLP has gained popularity in recent years, outperforming statistical and rule-based NLP in applications where large amounts of data are accessible, but limited interpretability and a reliance on pricey computation platforms are two things that neural NLP is frequently held accountable for. It is also important to remember that, in the case of inadequate data, neural NLP typically falls short of statistical and rule-based NLP in terms of performance. Recurrent neural network (RNN)-based neural NLP algorithms are more suited for analyzing sequential data, including voice and text. This is especially true for models based on long short-term memory (LSTM) [16] and models based on gated recurrent units (GRU) [17, 18]. They have short-term memory loss, training problems, gradient vanishing/explosion, and the inability to recall past information about the inputs.

Deep network designs are made possible by the great computational efficiency and capacity of convolutional neural network (CNN)-based models to learn local features, which also demonstrate good performance in some tasks [19]. Recently, NLP-driven smart healthcare has made use of graph neural network (GNN) models, which use data from graph-structured taxonomy and entities. With large-scale complex graphs the GNN-based models are expensive and difficult to implement and train [20].

When it comes to handling long-term dependencies in sequences, RNNs, CNNs, and GNNs are generally constrained. Transformer-based models can handle long sequences relatively efficiently and facilitate parallel training, thanks to the self-attention mechanism [21]. Nevertheless, they are unable to learn location information and local characteristics.

For improved feature extraction performance, we have observed a variety of combinations of the aforementioned models, such as memory networks (MM), CNN-LSTM networks, RNN-attention networks, graph convolutional networks (GCN), CNN-LSTM-attention networks, graph convolutional attention networks (GCAN), etc. [22]. Furthermore, pre-training is a very powerful technique that has been frequently used to obtain non-contextual or contextual embeddings in order to further leverage massive unlabeled corpora. As exemplary algorithms of non-contextual embeddings, Word2vec and GloVe (global vectors) provide distributed dense vectors as word embeddings and surpass statistical techniques like n-gram and bag-of-words. A word's non-contextual embedding is static and does not alter dynamically as its context influences. Contextual embeddings, such as ELMo (embeddings from language models), BERT (bidirectional encoder representations from transformers), and GPT (generative pre-training), use the transformer architecture to embed dynamic contextual information into words, outperforming other algorithms. Pre-training these models is costly and time-consuming, limiting their application in healthcare.

2.3 NLP Pipeline for Smart Healthcare

Figure 2.1 illustrates NLP pipeline for smart healthcare. Preprocessing, feature extraction, and modeling are different phases of this pipeline. NLP pipelines accept text or speech as input. Preprocessing takes into account input quality and facilitates feature extraction and modeling. NLP relies heavily on feature extraction through which algorithms can be

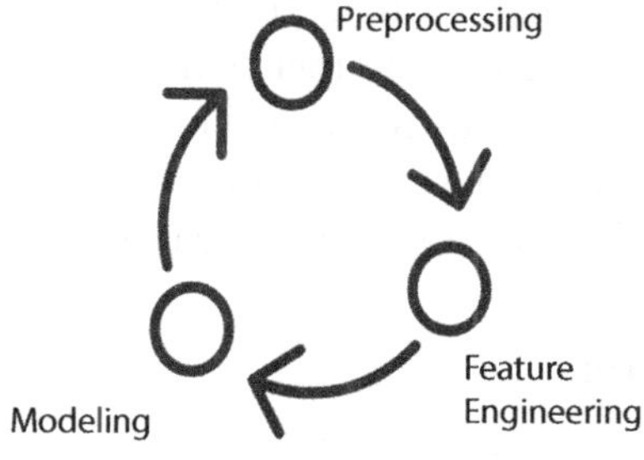

Figure 2.1 Pipeline for smart healthcare.

developed for specific NLP tasks to produce appropriate outputs. Analysis of COVID data is crucial for informing public health decisions and understanding the effectiveness. It helps in predicting potential outbreaks and assessing the overall progress in controlling the pandemic.

2.3.1 Preprocessing

Tokenization, stemming, lemmatization, and stop word elimination are examples of preprocessing processes that normalize natural language, make it machine-readable, and facilitate postprocessing. Normalized text input is necessary for many NLP tasks since natural languages are flexible and there are many different morphological variations of medical terminology in medical research [23]. Text preprocessing facilitates feature extraction and modeling. However, the advancement of neural NLP has rendered several text preprocessing processes obsolete and potentially harmful. With the usage of BERT pre-trained model, eliminating stop words may result in lost context information [24]. Speech preprocessing (denoising) is often viewed as a signal processing challenge.

2.3.2 Feature Extraction

The advancement of feature selection or feature extraction techniques is primarily responsible for the development of NLP, aside from the growth in digital data that is readily available and the development of computer platforms like graphics processing units. Rule design or feature engineering is a skill that is needed for both rule-based and statistical approaches [25]. In neural natural language processing (NLP), automated feature extraction using different types of neural networks has significantly increased data utilization and feature extraction efficiency [26]. Depending on the downstream requirements and feature engineering can be carried out directly utilizing reinforcement learning or unsupervised learning or supervised learning. Also, pretraining is frequently used in NLP to automatically extract features using self-supervised learning from large unlabeled corpora in a generative and contrastive way before the commencement of downstream tasks. The retrieved features, referred to as contextual or non-contextual embeddings, can include features that support tasks downstream like pragmatics, syntactic features, semantic features, and lexical meanings [27].

2.3.3 Classification

Classification is a versatile and widely used machine learning task and it has its applications in various domains such as vision, NLP, healthcare diagnostics, and more. After feature selection training, the classifier takes place. In this phase, the classifiers are fine-tuned and are trained on the data. The data is split into various ratios in order to generalize the classifiers. Also, models are validated using different validation techniques in order to check the biases and the skewness of the models.

2.3.4 Model Interpretability

Model interpretability in machine learning is a critical aspect that seeks to demystify the decision-making processes of complex models, making their outputs comprehensible and trustworthy for end-users. The demand for interpretable models has grown in tandem with the increasing adoption of machine learning in sensitive domains such as healthcare, finance, and criminal justice. Various methodologies that improve interpretability have been proposed, such as model-agnostic methods, rule-based models, and feature importance techniques [28, 29]. Interpretability not only fosters transparency by revealing how models derive predictions but also addresses ethical considerations, accountability, and user trust. As machine learning systems become more sophisticated, the exploration of interpretability methods becomes imperative for ensuring responsible and fair deployment, particularly in contexts where the impact of algorithmic decisions has significant real-world consequences. For model interpretation, we have different approaches like rule-based [30] and model agnostic approaches like LIME and SHAP.

2.4 Applications of NLP in Healthcare

NLP plays a significant role in the healthcare industry, offering a range of applications to improve patient care, streamline administrative tasks, and enhance research capabilities. Here are some ways in which NLP is utilized in healthcare.

2.4.1 Clinical Records

NLP can be used to convert spoken or typed words into structured data, aiding in the creation of electronic health records. This not only saves time for healthcare professionals but also improves the accuracy of patient records. NLP-powered speech recognition systems allow healthcare providers to dictate notes, diagnoses, and treatment plans, converting spoken words into text. This helps in reducing the time spent on manual documentation. NLP in clinical records involves the application of advanced computational techniques for extracting meaningful information from unstructured textual data found in electronic health records (EHRs) and other clinical documents. This transformative technology enables the identification and categorization of key elements within clinical narratives, such as diagnoses, symptoms, medications, and procedures. By converting unstructured data into structured and standardized formats, NLP enhances the accuracy and completeness of clinical documentation, streamlining processes for healthcare professionals. NLP is instrumental in clinical decision support by analyzing and interpreting the vast amount of information contained in clinical records, offering insights, and aiding in evidence-based decision-making. It plays a crucial role in automating coding and billing processes, reducing errors, and improving the efficiency of administrative tasks. The temporal analysis capabilities of NLP provide a deeper understanding of the chronological aspects of patient histories, disease progression, and treatment outcomes. Also, NLP supports adverse event detection, clinical research endeavors, and health management by identifying patterns and trends by facilitating quality metrics reporting for regulatory compliance. Despite its immense potential, challenges such as ensuring data privacy, addressing language variability, and maintaining high accuracy levels necessitate ongoing refinement and collaboration between healthcare professionals and technologists to maximize the benefits of NLP in clinical records.

2.4.2 Information Extraction

NLP can extract relevant information from unstructured clinical notes, research articles, and other textual sources. This aids in identifying and categorizing entities such as diseases, symptoms, medications, and procedures, contributing to better decision-making. NLP in information extraction uses computational techniques for analyzing and deriving structured data from unstructured text sources. In the context of information extraction, NLP focuses on identifying and extracting specific entities and relationships within textual content. This includes recognizing and categorizing key elements such as names of people, organizations, locations, dates, and other relevant information. NLP techniques enable the processing of large volumes of unstructured data, extracting valuable insights that can be utilized for various purposes. In healthcare, for instance, NLP in information extraction plays a vital role in converting unstructured clinical notes into structured and standardized data, facilitating the extraction of critical details like diagnoses, symptoms, medications, and procedures.

The application of NLP in information extraction extends beyond healthcare to areas such as business intelligence, research, and knowledge management, where converting unstructured textual information into structured data enhances decision-making processes and drives actionable insights. Despite challenges related to language nuances and context, ongoing advancements in NLP technologies continue to refine and improve the accuracy of information extraction across diverse domains.

2.4.3 Decision Support

NLP can analyze large sets of medical literature, research articles, and patient records to provide clinicians with relevant information and evidence-based recommendations, assisting in making informed decisions about patient care. Natural language processing (NLP) in decision support involves leveraging advanced computational linguistics to enhance decision-making processes by extracting, analyzing, and interpreting information from natural language sources. In this context, NLP aids in transforming unstructured textual data, such as clinical notes or research articles, into structured and actionable insights. Within decision support systems, NLP enables the identification of key entities, relationships, and relevant contextual information, providing valuable input to guide healthcare professionals, researchers, or business decision-makers. In healthcare, for instance, NLP in decision support assists clinicians by extracting pertinent details from electronic health records, offering evidence-based recommendations, and alerting to potential issues in patient care. The technology facilitates the automation of data analysis, allowing for quicker and more informed decision-making. Beyond healthcare, NLP in decision support is applied in various domains, ranging from financial analysis to customer support, where it helps to process and understand vast amounts of textual information, contributing to more accurate and timely decision support. Continuous advancements in NLP algorithms and models are driving improvements in the sophistication and reliability of decision support systems across diverse industries.

2.4.4 Health Assistance

Chatbots and virtual assistants powered by NLP can communicate with patients, respond to their questions, give drug information, book appointments, and give basic medical advice. This enhances patient engagement and improves access to healthcare services. NLP in health assistance involves the application of advanced computational techniques to understand and respond to natural language queries and interactions related to healthcare. With the use of this technology, intelligent chatbots and virtual health assistants may be created that converse with users, respond to inquiries about health, provide information on prescription drugs, set up appointments, and provide basic medical advice. NLP allows these virtual assistants to comprehend and interpret user input, extracting relevant information to generate appropriate responses. This facilitates improved communication between individuals and healthcare systems, enhancing accessibility to healthcare information and services. Virtual health assistants powered by NLP contribute to patient engagement, support preventive care, and offer a convenient channel for seeking health-related guidance. As technology develops further, natural language processing (NLP) in health support will become increasingly important in enabling people to make decisions about their health and well-being based on interactions that happen naturally and informally.

2.4.5 Opinion Mining

NLP can be applied to analyze patient reviews, social media, and other textual data to gauge public sentiment about healthcare providers, facilities, or specific treatments, helping organizations understand and address patient concerns. NLP in opinion mining is known as sentiment analysis that involves the utilization of computational techniques to extract and analyze subjective information from textual data. The primary objective is to discern and understand sentiments, opinions, and emotions expressed in diverse sources, such as customer reviews, social media posts, and online discussions. NLP algorithms are employed to classify text as positive, negative, or neutral. In more advanced applications, to capture nuanced emotions and attitudes. Opinion mining plays a crucial role in gauging public sentiment toward products, services, or topics, aiding businesses in reputation management, product development, and customer engagement. In addition to commercial applications, sentiment analysis using NLP has been applied in healthcare to understand patient feedback, in political analysis to gauge public opinion, and in various other domains where understanding subjective viewpoints is valuable. The continuous improvement of NLP models contributes to more accurate and nuanced opinion mining, enabling organizations to extract actionable insights from the vast amount of unstructured textual data available in the digital landscape. NLP presents numerous opportunities to enhance healthcare processes. It's critical to address issues like data privacy, ethical questions, and the requirement for constant performance and accuracy improvement. As technology continues to advance, the integration of NLP into healthcare systems is likely to become more widespread, contributing to improved patient outcomes and operational efficiency.

2.5 COVID Detection Using NLP

The coronavirus was identified in Wuhan, China, in December 2019, and on December 31, 2019, it was reported to the World Health Organization (W.H.O.) [31]. The W.H.O classified the virus, which constituted a worldwide threat, as COVID-19 on February 11, 2020. The COVID-19 virus family comprises SARS and ARDS. The W.H.O. states that the virus spreads through the respiratory system when an uninfected individual comes into touch with an infected person and they declared this epidemic to be a public health emergency [32, 33]. There may be more, as of yet unidentified, ways for the virus to travel between people. Depending on how long the Middle East respiratory syndrome (MERS) or severe acute respiratory syndrome (SARS) incubation period lasts, the infected person may have symptoms 2 to 14 days after infection (SARS). The World Health Organization states that dyspnea (shortness of breath), fever, and weariness are symptoms of severe cases, while dry cough, fatigue, and fever are symptoms of mild to moderate cases. People who have co-occurring illnesses like diabetes, heart disease, or asthma are more vulnerable to the virus and run the risk of developing serious health problems. The diagnosis is made in light of the patient's symptoms and travel history. Vital indications that show symptoms are watched carefully. Antipyretics, antivirals, and hydroxychloroquine were used to treat the symptoms. Also, some guidelines were issued by the W.H.O which helped in preventing the spread of the deadly virus. The 2003 outbreak of SARS that is an airborne illness was detected first in China and quickly expanded to 26 other countries. In just one year, 8,000 cases were recorded. It is passed from one individual to another. Fever, chills, diarrhea, shivering, malaise, myalgia, and dyspnea are the symptoms of SARS. The hallmark of ARDS (acute respiratory distress syndrome) is a rapid onset of lung inflammation leading to respiratory failure. Its signs and symptoms include bluish skin color, fatigue, and shortness of breath. PaO_2/FiO_2 ratios less than 300 mmHg are diagnostic of ARDS. Numerous paramedical businesses have asserted their ability to develop a vaccine for this virus. Less testing has also contributed to the spread of this disease, as we lack medical resources as a result of the epidemic. Due to the fact that thousands upon thousands of people are being tested positive on a daily basis throughout the world, it is impossible to test all those who exhibit symptoms. Monitoring COVID-19 is essential for

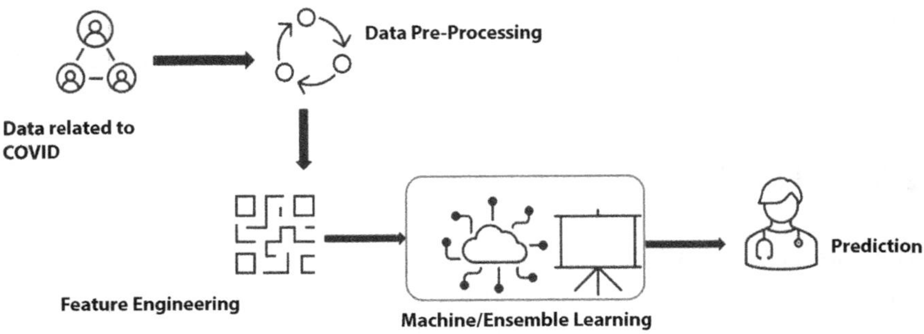

Figure 2.2 Proposed methodology.

safeguarding public wellbeing, as it will develop strategies that will protect communities and promote overall health during the pandemic. There are five phases in the proposed methodology as depicted in Figure 2.2.. Data is collected in stage 2.5.1, and the relevant dataset is described in stage 2.5.2. Preprocessing is explained in stage 2.5.3, Relevant features are extracted in stage 2.5.4, and neural network classifiers are addressed in stage 2.5.5.

2.5.1 Data Collection

Data related to COVID-19 is available in public repositories due to the reason as researchers and W.H.O make information about the pandemic available. We collected information from GitHub, an open-source data in which a patient's whole information including symptoms of the coronavirus and other infections are present. There are approximately 24 attributes in a dataset, as shown in Table 2.1, from which we took the textual report attribute and the class label attribute.

Table 2.1 Features in the collected dataset.

"patient ID"	"counterbalance"	"sex"	"age"
"finding"	"survival"	"intubated"	"went to ICU"
"needed supplemental O_2"	"extubated"	"temperature"	"pO_2 saturation"
"leukocyte count"	"neutrophil scan"	"lymphocyte tally"	"see"
"methodology"	"date"	"location"	"organizer"
"filename"	"DOI"	"URL"	"clinical notes"

2.5.2 Preprocessing

Textual data is full of filthy data. In order to refine missing values, URLs, hyperlinks, numbers, and stop words are removed. Various preprocessing procedures were carried out to refine the data, some of which are listed below:

Tokenization: In this phase, the tweets are divided into tokens. Each word is considered a separate token when a phrase is broken into several tokens.
Stop words: The English stop word dictionary is used to remove stop words such as a, an, and the.
Lemmatization: In lemmatization, a word's lemma is determined by its intended meaning. The process involves analyzing the context in which the word is used to accurately determine its base or dictionary form. This step is crucial for normalizing different forms of a word to a common base form, which helps in reducing the complexity of text data and improves the performance of subsequent natural language processing tasks. By converting words to their lemmas, it is ensured that variations of a word are treated as a single item that helps in enhancing the efficiency and effectiveness of the text analysis.

2.5.3 Feature Engineering

Classification task requires the use of a variety of characteristics to complete it. Various feature selection methods are integrated to form a hybrid feature extraction framework. In this work, we use TF/IDF, bag of words, and length features that are fused together.

TF/IDF: It reflects how important a term is in a tweet or in the entire corpus. Equation 2.1 is used to compute it.

$$\begin{aligned} TF/IDF(t,w,D) &= TF(t,w) * IDF(t,D) \\ IDF(t,D) &= \log|D|1+|(w \in D : t \in w)| \end{aligned} \tag{2.1}$$

where D is the total number of tweets in the dataset (document space), w is each tweet in the corpus, and t represents the term as a component.

Bag of words: It consists of words and their lemmas. Different types of bag of words include unigrams, bigrams, and trigrams. In our approach,

we incorporated both bigrams and trigrams to extract more detailed information from the text.
Report length: We took into account the length of the report, as a result of the computations, it was discovered that COVID reports are longer than non-COVID reports. We used this functionality in conjunction with TF/IDF and bag of words to improve our testing results.

2.5.4 Classification

The primary goal of this project is to develop a classifier that will divide clinical reports into two categories: COVID and non-COVID classification. As our corpus is labeled, we employ machine learning methods that are under supervision. This task is carried out using a variety of standard machine learning classifiers that have been developed and tested.

Logistic regression: It forecasts the numerical class value based on the class association with the label and other factors. The logistic regression model is fine-tuned as follows:

"C=1.0, classweight=None, dual=False, fit-intercept=True, intercept-scaling=1, max-iter=100, multi-class=warn, n jobs=None, penalty=l2, random state=8, solver=warn, tol=0.0001, verbose=0, warm start=False".

Multinomial naive Bayes: Multinomial naive Bayes (MNB) is a text classification algorithm that makes use of the conventional Bayes algorithm. Multinomial naive Bayes is fine-tuned in the following way:

"alpha=1.0, class-prior=None, fit-prior=True".

Support vector machine: SVM is supervised machine learning method which is employed for both classification tasks and regression problems. It takes a certain number of attributes for a specific text to be associated with a specific label. The support vector machine (SVM) is fine-tuned in the following ways:

"C=1.0, cache_size=500, class_weight=balanced, coef0=1.0, decision_function_shape=ovo, degree=5, gamma=scale, kernel=rbf, max_iter=1000, probability=False, random_state=42, shrinking=False, tol=0.0001, verbose=True".

Decision tree: In this strategy, the input space is divided into sections of equal size. There is no hierarchy among the regions, each one is classed independently. The decision tree classifier has been fine-tuned as follows:

"class_weight=balanced, criterion=entropy, max_depth=10, max_features=sqrt, max_leaf_nodes=50, min_impurity_decrease=0.01, min_impurity_split=0.02, min_samples_leaf=2, min_samples_split=5, min_weight_fraction_leaf=0.01, presort=True, random_state=42, splitter=random".

2.5.5 Ensemble Classification

Using ensemble machine learning algorithms, the tweets are divided into two categories: positive and negative. We used four different types of Ensemble learning algorithms in our research. Random forest, bagging, Adaboost, and stochastic gradient boosting are some of the techniques used. To improve the accuracy of these algorithms, they are fine-tuned.

Random forest: The best hyper parameters of random forest are:

"bootstrap=True, max_depth=15, max_features=log2, min_samples_leaf=2,min_samples_split=10,n_estimators=1000,class_weight=balanced, criterion=entropy, max_leaf_nodes=100, min_impurity_decrease=0.01, min_impurity_split=0.02, min_weight_fraction_leaf=0.01, n_jobs=-1, oob_score=True, random_state=42, verbose=1, warm_start=True"

Bagging: The hyperparameters of bagging are:

"base_estimator=RandomForestClassifier(n_estimators=10), bootstrap=-False, bootstrap_features=True, max_features=0.8, max_samples=0.9, n_jobs=4, oob_score=True, random_state=42, verbose=1, warm_start=True"

Adaboost: The hyperparameters of Adaboost are:

"algorithm=SAMME, base_estimator=DecisionTreeClassifier(max_depth =3), learning_rate=0.5, n_estimators=100, random_state=42"

Stochastic gradient boosting: The hyperparameters of stochastic gradient boosting are:

"criterion=squared_error, init=zero, learning_rate=0.05, loss=exponential, max_depth=5, max_features=sqrt, max_leaf_nodes=50, min_impurity_ decrease=0.01, min_impurity_split=None, min_samples_leaf=5, min_samples_split=10, min_weight_fraction_leaf=0.02, n_estimators=150, n_iter_no_change=10, presort=deprecated, random_state=42, subsample =0.8, tol=0.001, validation_fraction=0.2, verbose=1, warm_start=True".

2.6 Results and Discussion

2.6.1 Traditional Machine Learning

For the task of classifying COVID and non-COVID textual reports, we employed logistic regression, multinomial naive Bayesian, support vector machine, and decision tree algorithms in our experiment. The suggested hybrid feature engineering methodology is utilized to extract important features for fine-tuning machine learning models. For the binary classification, about 100 features are chosen, but due to the computational complexity, information gain is employed to choose the most influential characteristics. The dataset is divided into a 70:30 ratio, with 70% of the data being used to train machine learning models and 30% being used to test them. Machine learning algorithms have been fine-tuned to produce better results. The algorithms are put to the test by changing their parameters. We employed three kernels in the support vector machine: RBF, poly, and linear. In comparison to the other two kernels, the linear kernel produced the best outcomes. Similarly, finetuning the settings of other machine learning methods improved the outcomes. When alpha was set to 1.0, multinomial naive Bayes produced superior results, while logistic regression produced decent results when C was set to 1.0 and a maximum iteration of 100 was used. The Gini coefficient was utilized in decision tree for information gain, and the results were encouraging. The results showed that the decision tree beats all other classic machine

Table 2.2 Classification report of machine learning algorithms using the proposed methodology.

Algorithm	Precision	Recall	F-measure	Accuracy
ILR	98%	98%	98%	98.3%
IMNB	97%	97%	97%	97.23%
IMSVM	98%	98%	98%	98.2%
IDT	99%	99%	99%	98.53%

learning algorithms, reaching 98.5% accuracy, 0.99 precision, 0.99 recall, and 0.99 F1-score. Support vector machine and logistic regression also performed well, with accuracy recall and F1-scores of 0.98, 0.98, 0.98, and 0.98, respectively. All machine learning algorithms are classified and compared in depth in Table 2.2.

2.6.2 Ensemble Machine Learning

The calculations were carried out using a workstation with 8 GB of RAM and six built-in processors. Our research yielded the novel dataset. Various pre-processing methods are being carried out to refine the dataset and make it suitable for parallel characterization. The three distinct features (TF/IDF, bag of words, and tweet length) are combined in a hybrid feature engineering process. Around 100 characteristics are chosen for the parallel characterization, but due to computational difficulty, information gain is used to select the most interesting characteristics. The dataset is divided into 70:30 segments, with 70% being used to create ensemble ML models and 30% being used to test the models. Adaboost outflanks all other ensemble learning classifiers with 98.7% accuracy, 0.98 precision, 0.98 recall, and 0.99 F1-score, according to the results. The classification report and correlation of all ensemble machine learning classifiers may be found in Table 2.3. We used 10-fold cross-validation to verify our findings. During the training and testing of the proposed model, there is no evidence of under-fitting or over-fitting. After doing some research, it was discovered that COVID reports are longer than non-COVID reports. The majority of the information we used in our study were about COVID-19. For a better understanding of COVID, more data from a variety of sectors should be collected. More human effort is required to carry out the labeling of tweets into distinct classifications. As the amount of data grows, manual annotation becomes more difficult, necessitating the use of an automatic annotation tool that learns from the

Table 2.3 Classification report of ensemble machine learning algorithms using the proposed methodology.

Algorithm	Precision	Recall	F-measure	Accuracy
Random forest	99%	98%	98%	98.61%
Bagging	98%	98%	98%	98.55%
Adaboost	98%	98%	99%	98.7%
Stochastic gradient boosting	98%	97%	98%	98.5%

semantics of the text presented. To achieve better text categorization results, more feature engineering is necessary.

2.7 Conclusion

Natural language processing (NLP) stands out as a revolutionary technology in the healthcare sector, presenting a myriad of opportunities to streamline processes, elevate patient care, and propel clinical research forward. This chapter delves into the intricacies of natural language processing and explores its diverse approaches. Additionally, it provides a comprehensive examination of how NLP can be harnessed for intelligent healthcare solutions and delineates the manifold applications of NLP in the healthcare domain. An illustrative case study is undertaken to address the COVID-19 classification challenge, employing sophisticated NLP techniques. Data, sourced from online repositories is thoroughly preprocessed using a range of techniques. This chapter explains how hybrid feature engineering is implemented to extract the most relevant features for classification, ultimately contributing to improved healthcare outcomes and overall wellbeing. Through extensive training and testing, both traditional and ensemble machine learning classifiers are scrutinized with a focus on hyperparameter tuning. Furthermore, the discussion extends to the potential adoption of deep learning algorithms in future endeavors to classify COVID and non-COVID reports, underscoring the continuous evolution and integration of cutting-edge technologies in healthcare applications.

References

1. O'Connor, J. and McDermott, I., *NLP*, Conari Press, Thorsons, 2001.
2. Khurana, D., Koli, A., Khatter, K., Singh, S., Natural language processing: State of the art, current trends and challenges. *Multimedia Tools Appl.*, 82, 3, 3713–3744, 2023.
3. Basili, R., Pazienza, M.T., Velardi, P., An empirical symbolic approach to natural language processing. *Artif. Intell.*, 85, 1–2, 59–99, 1996.
4. Reilly, R.G. and Sharkey, N., *Connectionist approaches to natural language processing*, Routledge, Taylor and Francis, 2016.
5. Wermter, S., Riloff, E., Scheler, G., *Connectionist, statistical and symbolic approaches to learning for natural language processing, volume 1040*, Springer Science & Business Media, Springer, Part of Book series, Lecture Notes in Computer Science (LNCS, volume 1040), 1996.
6. Kao, A. and Poteet, S.R., *Natural language processing and text mining.* Springer Science & Business Media, Springer, 2007.

7. Dreisbach, C., Koleck, T.A., Bourne, P.E., Bakken, S., A systematic review of natural language processing and text mining of symptoms from electronic patient-authored text data. *Int. J. Med. Inf.*, 125, 37–46, 2019.
8. Popowich, F., Using text mining and natural language processing for health care claims processing, in: *ACM SIGKDD Explorations Newsletter*, vol. 7, pp. 59–66, 2005.
9. Berthelier, B., Division and the digital language divide: A critical perspective on natural language processing resources for the south and north korean languages. *Korean Stud.*, 47, 1, 243–273, 2023.
10. Abdessalem Karaa, W.B., Alkhammash, E.H., Bchir, A., Drug disease relation extraction from biomedical literature using nlp and machine learning. *Mobile Inf. Syst.*, 2021, 1–10, 2021.
11. Singh, S., Natural language processing for information extraction, 2018, arXiv preprint arXiv:1807.02383.
12. Cowie, J. and Lehnert, W., Information extraction. *Commun. ACM*, 39, 1, 80–91, 1996.
13. Dragoni, M., Villata, S., Rizzi, W., Governatori, G., Combining nlp approaches for rule extraction from legal documents, in: *1st Workshop on MIning and REasoning with Legal texts, (MIREL 2016)*, 2016.
14. Khanday, A., Bouktif, S., Ouni, A., Rnn-based model for an optimal covid-19 cases detection using clinical reports, in: *2023 9th International Conference on Optimization and Applications (ICOA)*, IEEE, pp. 1–6, 2023.
15. Tawseef, A.M., Lawaye, A.A., Khanday, A.M.U.D., Nlp techniques and challenges to process social media data, in: *Advanced Applications of NLP and Deep Learning in Social Media Data*, IGI Global, pp. 171–218, 2023.
16. Bouktif, S., KHANDAY, A.M.U.D., Ali, OUNI, Bi-directional lstm-based covid-19 detection using clinical reports. *The Eurasia Proceedings of Science Technology Engineering and Mathematics*, vol. 23, pp. 209–219, 2023.
17. Viswanathan, S., Anand Kumar, M., Soman, K.P., A sequence-based machine comprehension modeling using lstm and gru, in: *Emerging Research in Electronics, Computer Science and Technology: Proceedings of International Conference, ICERECT 2018*, Springer, pp. 47–55, 2019.
18. Zulqarnain, M., Ghazali, R., Mohmad Hassim, Y.M., Rehan, M., Text classification based on gated recurrent unit combines with support vector machine. *Int. J. Electr. Comput. Eng.*, 10, 4, 3734–3742, 2020.
19. Arora, G., Rahimi, A., Baldwin, T., Does an lstm forget more than a CNN? an empirical study of catastrophic forgetting in NLP, in: *Proceedings of the The 17th Annual Workshop of the Australasian Language Technology Association*, pp. 77–86, 2019.
20. Nouri Golmaei, S. and Luo, X., Deepnote-gnn: predicting hospital readmission using clinical notes and patient network, in: *Proceedings of the 12th ACM Conference on Bioinformatics, Computational Biology, and Health Informatics*, pp. 1–9, 2021.

21. Tunstall, L., Von Werra, L., Wolf, T., *Natural language processing with transformers*, O'Reilly Media, Inc., O'Reilly Media, https://lccn.loc.gov/2023275986 2022.
22. Bouktif, S., Fiaz, A., Awad, M., Stock market movement prediction using disparate text features with machine learning, in: *2019 Third International Conference on Intelligent Computing in Data Sciences (ICDS)*, IEEE, pp. 1–6, 2019.
23. Hickman, L., Thapa, S., Tay, L., Cao, M., Srinivasan, P., Text preprocessing for text mining in organizational research: Review and recommendations. *Org. Res. Methods*, 25, 1, 114–146, 2022.
24. Peng, Y., Chen, Q., Lu, Z., An Empirical Study of Multi-Task Learning on BERT for Biomedical Text Mining, in: *Proceedings of the 19th SIGBioMed Workshop on Biomedical Language Processing*, pp. 205–214, 2020 July.
25. Sammons, M., Christodoulopoulos, C., Kordjamshidi, P., Khashabi, D., Srikumar, V., Roth, D., Edison: Feature extraction for nlp, simplified, in: *Proceedings of the Tenth International Conference on Language Resources and Evaluation (LREC'16)*, pp. 4085–4092, 2016.
26. Wang, D., Su, J., Yu, H., Feature extraction and analysis of natural language processing for deep learning english language. *IEEE Access*, 8, 46335–46345, 2020.
27. Broda, B., Kędzia, P., Marcińczuk, M., Radziszewski, A., Ramocki, R., Wardyński, A., Fextor: A Feature Extraction Framework for Natural Language Processing: A Case Study in Word Sense Disambiguation, Relation Recognition and Anaphora Resolution, in: Przepiórkowski, A., Piasecki, M., Jassem, K., Fuglewicz, P. (eds) *Computational Linguistics. Studies in Computational Intelligence*, vol 458. Springer, Berlin, Heidelberg, 2013. https://doi.org/10.1007/978-3-642-34399-5_3
28. Azar, D., Bouktif, S., Sahraoui, H., Kegl, B., Improving rule set based software quality prediction, 2003.
29. Bouktif, S. and Adel Awad, M., Ant colony based approach to predict stock market movement from mood collected on twitter, in: *Proceedings of the 2013 IEEE/ACM International Conference on Advances in Social Networks Analysis and Mining*, pp. 837–845, 2013.
30. Bouktif, S., Hanna, E.M., Zaki, N., Abu Khousa, E., Ant colony optimization algorithm for interpretable bayesian classifiers combination: application to medical predictions. *PLoS One*, 9, 2, e86456, 2014.
31. Khanday, A.M.U.D., Khan, Q.R., Rabani, S.T., Identifying propaganda from online social networks during COVID-19 using machine learning techniques. *Int. J. Inf. Technol.*, 13, 1, 115–122, 2021.
32. Bouktif, S., Khanday, A.M.U.D., Ouni, A., CoML: Machine Learning based approach for COVID-19 related Suicidal Ideation detection, in: *2024 International Conference on Intelligent Systems and Computer Vision (ISCV)*, pp. 1–5, IEEE, 2024, May.
33. Khanday, A.M.U.D., Wani, M.A., Rabani, S.T., Khan, Q.R., Abd El-Latif, A.A., HAPI: An efficient Hybrid Feature Engineering-based Approach for Propaganda Identification in social media. *PloS One*, 19, 7, e0302583, 2024.

3

Artificial Intelligence Assisted Internet of Medical Things (AIoMTs) in Sustainable Healthcare Ecosystem

Wasswa Shafik[1,2]

[1]*School of Digital Science, Universiti Brunei Darussalam, Jalan Tungku Link, Gadong, Bandar Seri Begawan, Brunei Darussalam*
[2]*Dig Connectivity Research Laboratory (DCRLab), Kampala, Uganda*

Abstract

The integration of the Internet of Things (IoT) and artificial intelligence (AI) with advances in medical devices exemplifies the recent development in the medical sector, specifically in this digital healthcare era like the Internet of Medical Things (IoMTs). This makes it simpler for patients to relax, for health problems to be solved quickly and modestly, for hospital medications to be given right away, and for healthcare to be more personalized, thus facilitating well-being management. All of these things together make up the AI-assisted Internet of Medical Things (AIoMTs). AI and other key support technologies like big data, mobile internet, cloud computing, microelectronics, and others have made it possible to process the collected patient data to get better insights. This has turned traditional healthcare into an all-around, efficient, and personalized experience. During this time, AI applications in medicine became more popular worldwide, and people who were sick with the virus were saved with the help of intelligent technologies and the algorithms that went with them. The AIoMT made it leisurely to collect, analyze, and make sense of a huge amount of patient information so that healthcare and well-being monitoring can be carried out effectively through different electronic devices. This chapter comprehensively surveys several wearable medical electronics in the AIoMT. There has been a focus on the known and commonly used medical devices, such as the electronic signals for AIoMT sensors. In addition, the AIoMT architecture shows how smart sensors can be used to collect, combine, and control data for smart healthcare structures. The chapter further reviews

Email: wasswashafik@ieee.org

Bharat Bhushan, Akib Khanday, Khursheed Aurangzeb, Sudhir Kumar Sharma and Parma Nand (eds.) Wellness Management Powered by AI Technologies, (75–102) © 2025 Scrivener Publishing LLC

the challenges of electronic devices in the AIoMT, like data security threats, data interoperability, and regulatory concerns, which are further addressed to improve medical standards of operation for medical personnel, patients, and other medical stakeholders. Finally, open research issues for future research in AIoMT are highlighted.

Keywords: Wellness management, energy-efficient devices, wearable medical electronics, artificial intelligence, internet of medical things, smart healthcare

3.1 Introduction

As technology has improved, smart healthcare has changed a lot. It now includes microelectronics, big data, IoT, cloud computing, mobile internet, and mobile health [1]. The incorporation of modern medical sensors and different hardware in the health sector has led to the development of a new concept called "IoMT," sometimes entitled "the Internet of Health Things," which, along with the technologies, has transformed traditional healthcare into a more efficient, all-around, and personalized experience. The global market for smart health is projected to increase by a mean growth rate of 16.2% [2]. This creates a dire need for fast, comprehensive, accurate, and intelligent eHealthcare systems, as highlighted by the emergency of global pandemics. Through different medical electronic devices, these systems will be able to collect, analyze, and make sense of a large amount of information about the health and well-being of the patient. Additionally, such systems will provide the means for the periodic management of medical personnel, keeping track of both medical instruments and biological specimens [3].

The convergence of IoMT, AI, and big data has added new dimensions to such systems, which are now capable of analyzing the collected data to provide better insights, thereby ushering in a new era in healthcare, such as early-stage chronic disease prediction and personalized and physiological health monitoring systems, among others. Through the IoMT environment, monitoring health can be attained with the aid of numerous wearable medical sensors that record and keep track of patient medical conditions in real time [4]. The data produced by such sensors enables medical physicians to reliably and efficiently recognize and respond to critical situations regarding patients to enable them to become more informed regarding their health conditions for future diagnosis and treatment [5]. Furthermore, these sensors provide cheaper alternatives to the expensive environment of a hospital as they enable remote detection of abnormalities, evaluation of symptoms, and general health of the patients.

The large amount of patient information collected by several devices in the IoMT environment has ushered in new opportunities that leverage the power of AI. Currently known as AI-enabled health, opportunities such as the ability to quickly analyze and interpret patient information diagnosis and predict future diseases have been reported. Advanced AI techniques have made it possible for medical physicians to remotely track patients' habits and reveal their medical status from the captured data emanating from several sensors along with sensor usage patterns [6].

Through the IoMT environment, AI techniques, for example, support vector machines, random forest, logistic regression, decision trees, k-nearest neighbor, naïve Bayes, and several neural networks, have been used for various health-related applications [7]. Medics, health practitioners, health ministries, and agencies, among others, celebrate and appreciate the integration and application of IoMT management mainly due to a couple of benefits. Such benefits include patient clinical trials, identification, medication error reduction, personalized medication, and surgery aid [8]. The IoMT architecture is supported by emerging technologies depicted by the comprehensive growth of exploiting smart sensors to accumulate data and regulate smart healthcare structures, as in Figure 3.1.

There are notable challenges that smart healthcare faces, as discussed. Furthermore, medical institutions rely on internet-based technologies, from connected infusion pumps to telemetry patient monitors, to provide best-in-class patient care [9]. According to statistics, they predicted that, by 2022, the number of connected medical devices ("Things") will reach

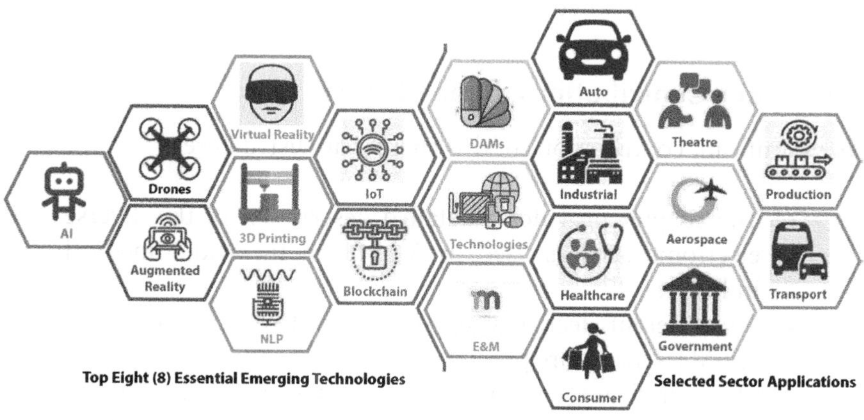

Figure 3.1 Essential emerging technologies and selected applications.

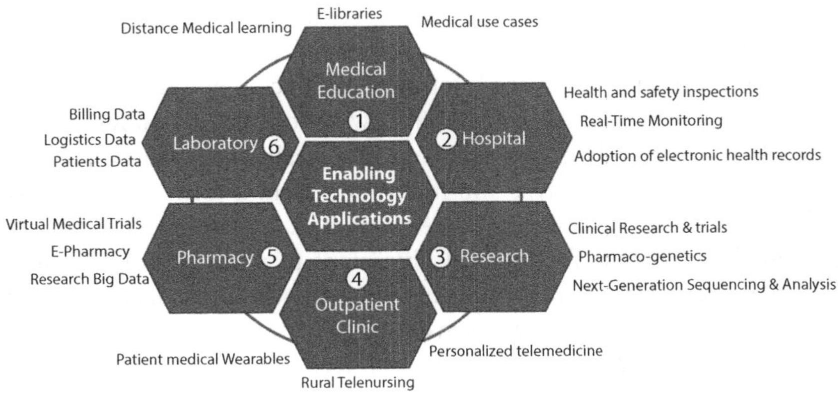

Figure 3.2 Enabling medical technologies applications.

up to 30 billion. During their study, they considered four main health factors that soar with the smart healthcare system, including in homes (like mobile help, vitality, and intelligent clinic, among others), communities (for instance, Xerafy, American Well, and Skytron, among others), clinics, hospitals, and on the body [10].

Healthcare providers and officials in the healthcare domain need to keep track of viral infections to ensure the necessary isolation of patients along with real-time measures to contain infections. In light of current developments, the medical devices that comprise the IoMT and their convergence with AI described earlier above have demonstrated tremendous potential in improving the overall health of billions of people worldwide, resulting in improved quality of life [11]. With the paradigm of AIoMT being new, few studies have been dedicated to detailing the different electronic devices deployed, as demonstrated in Figure 3.2.

3.1.1 Key Contributions of the Chapter

The significant contributions of this chapter are listed here:

- The chapter provides a detailed description of the diverse electronic sensors used in AIoMT in the wider medical industry.
- The different electronic signals transmitted by the different AIoMT sensors are presented.
- The significant challenges and prospects faced in using the identified electronic devices in healthcare have been

discussed, and some benefits and challenges for the AIoMT are reviewed.

- Finally, the limitations of AIoMT are also presented, and the future research direction of IoMT in the healthcare industry and its future scope are depicted.

3.1.2 Chapter Organization

Section 3.2 presents electronic sensors in IoMT and electronic sensor traits, disposable health sensors, ingestible sensors, patch sensors, connected health sensors, wearables, smart clothing, and implantable sensors. Section 3.3 presents the electronic signals in sensors. Section 3.4 discusses the identified challenges of electronic devices in the AIoMT including data security threats. Section 3.5 explains the benefits of the AIoMT evaluated. Section 3.6 demonstrates the challenges of evaluated AIoMTs. Section 3.7 entails the limitation of AIoMT. Section 3.8 demonstrates the future research direction of IoMT in the healthcare industry, and, lastly, the concluding chapter of AIoMT's future scope is presented in Section 3.9.

3.2 Medical Wearable Electronics

When used in the smart healthcare industry, IoMT combines various processing units with communication technologies, for instance, electronic wireless sensors that remotely monitor patient health status, to enable the prompt transmission of clinical information to healthcare medics [12]. IoMT makes it possible for caregivers to continuously monitor their patient's health, which enhances clinical judgment, lowers patients' medical costs, and ultimately improves patient outcomes [13]. This section presents notable electronic sensor traits related to IoMT applications and presents a brief discussion of the four main commonly used electronic sensor signals.

3.2.1 Electronic Sensor Traits

As the IoMTs are applied in the medical facility, these electronic sensors show different characteristics, and their contrast causes an impact on the patient. To support its many uses, a plethora of electronic biosensors have been invented and incorporated into the healthcare domain enabled by IoT [14]. Smart home care, clinical diagnostics, preventive medicine, fitness tracking, and a few monitoring services are some of these.

3.2.2 Disposable Health Sensors

Diagnostics, patient monitoring, and treatment support are the three main uses for disposable health sensors. The sensors are frequently strip-type, implementable, and ingestible. All these are focused on depending on the patient body nature [15].

3.2.3 Ingestible Sensors

The microfabricated integrated circuit for this tiny electronic sensor is made of thin layers of magnesium, copper, and gold. As the taken pill enters the stomach, a reaction between the circuit layers and gastric juice occurs. As a result, the sensor experiences an electrochemical reaction [16]. The patches of sensors then receive a digital code that denotes the drug type and appropriate dosage along with the time of dosage administration since this reaction energizes the sensor.

3.2.4 Patch Sensors

The patient may monitor their daily activities and medication schedules in appreciation of the transmission of all these data to a smartphone application, which then sends it to the discover portal. Medics and other healthcare professionals can find important data on their patients' daily health reports within the portals to help them choose the most appropriate treatments [17]. By enhancing drug adherence, for instance, we have reported the proteus digital medicine model, which has transformed the healthcare industry by lowering treatment failure rates and the demand for patient retreatment.

3.2.5 Connected Health Sensors

End-use market, electronic sensors, and platform sensors are additional subcategories of connected e-health sensors. Wearables, embedded technology, and intrusive sensors are examples of end-use market sensors for IoMT [18].

3.2.6 Wearables

Wearable sensors are continuously worn or placed near the human skin to closely monitor the patient's actions without restricting their usual range of mobility [19]. Mobility trackers are an especially well-liked kind of wearable health technology that has several practical uses in other domains, such as sports, determining the risk of falling down, and keeping an eye on the senior population, where some devices are demonstrated in Figure 3.2.

3.2.7 Smart Clothing

Numerous wearable gadgets have been deployed to measure important aspects of human health in addition to being helpful in encouraging individuals to keep track of daily workouts and sustain a more active and healthier lifestyle. The most typical of these measurements include electrocardiogram (ECG) and electroencephalogram (EEG) measurements. Body-worn smart gear is one innovative innovation intended to combine wearable sensors with essential health monitoring capabilities [20]. Compared to current technologies, which frequently only record a small number of physiological data, smart clothing enables people with intermittent illnesses to benefit from several health monitoring systems. Smart clothes substantially decrease the cost of sensors as well, but the efficiency in terms of wireless communication and packet transfer is still not that efficient [21]. A broad review covering almost all aspects and new trends in smart clothes in recent times is illustrated in Figure 3.3.

3.2.8 Implantable Sensors

Implantable sensors are becoming increasingly popular these days due to low-power technology. A major challenge of these implantable sensors is

Figure 3.3 AIoMTs and application.

the sizing, efficient communication, and low power consumption [22]. The efficient transfer of data from these sensors is important in terms of proper working.

3.3 Electronic Signals in Sensors

The human body generates different signals, which can be classified based on IoMT. Within this subsection, we mainly classified them into four in terms of their frequency range obtained from the IoMT.

3.3.1 Gait Analysis

Human movements are widely studied, and over the past years, numerous people died due to physical inactivity. Almost 100,000 deaths can be prevented annually if US citizens increase their physical activity by ten minutes each day. That is, gait analysis can play an important role. Proper tracking, monitoring, and measurement are important to keep track of physical activity. It is important to assess human locomotion [23] quantitatively. The most commonly used human locomotion sensing is seen in the step tracker application. Sensors used in this application need to be highly precise, small in weight, user-friendly, and easy to use in all environments [24]. However, further research is needed to determine the effect of habitual movement on accuracy. An efficient algorithm is position-independent for tracking step counting. It uses five features, four of which are novel, and one is derived [24].

3.3.2 Photoplethysmography

Photoplethysmography (PPG) is used for both making biomedical and non-biomedical wearables. This signal is at the center of measuring heart rate variability. In the traditional method, heart rate variability is measured using HRV by means of an electrocardiogram (ECG) signal [25]. HRV data were used to measure the peak-to-peak time interval between cardiac cycles. HRV analytics can provide a wide range of information to the autonomous nervous system. Thus, collecting and getting important insights from the HRV data may come in handy. However, there are several limitations to acquiring ECG data regarding collecting them at home as it requires proper positioning and operation [26].

Trained medical staff are needed to properly position the electrodes in the right position to get proper results, which is sometimes quite unlikely and time-consuming. Moreover, some patients complain about other complications, such as irritation and itching, while going through this process [27]. On the contrary, in the reactance method, the photodiode is placed on the same side as the light source. It measures the intensity of the traveling light. This method is commonly used in wristband watches. Some of the common devices that use this technique are the pulse oximeter, which is put on the fingertip, and Fitbit watches [28]. Its portability and ease of access features make it very attractive. On top of that, the portability of the sensors and the easy mechanism to capture the PPG signal are making it more popular among the public.

3.3.3 Electromyography

Through the electromyography (EMG) method, the response of the nerves is measured at the moment electrical stimulation is applied to the nervous system. This stimulation is often referred to as an action potential, and the cumulative addition of the action potential of the motor unit denotes the electromyography signal at the skin surface [29]. Conventionally, there are two techniques to gather the EMG data. One method uses a needle to collect blood samples, and another method uses an electrode on top of the skin's surface. EMG signals acquired from the same muscle but from different sensor locations will result in different results. In most of the common wearable devices, active sensors are used to capture the signal [30]. Usually, three sensors are used in most of these wearables; two of these sensors are metal electrodes, and the rest are used as reference electrodes.

3.3.4 Auscultation

Cardiac patients have to go through cardiac auscultation, in which a physician uses a stethoscope firstly to diagnose the initial cardiac problems. There is a dire need for a fast, noninvasive technique to identify primary cardiac conditions. Stethoscope auscultation plays an important role in this [31]. The main heart sounds used in medical applications are S1 and S2. S1 signals occur during ventricular contraction, which relates to a QRS complex in ECG. While the cardiovascular system is being analyzed, it is also important to analyze the functions of the lungs. This way, respiratory disorders can be easily identified through lung auscultation. In the case of a physically fit person, lung auscultation does not give much information in terms of audible sounds [32]. Wheezing sounds often indicate a lung disease named chronic obstructive pulmonary disease.

People with this disease often encounter breathing problems. Capturing and detecting these sounds is another important thing. Apart from the

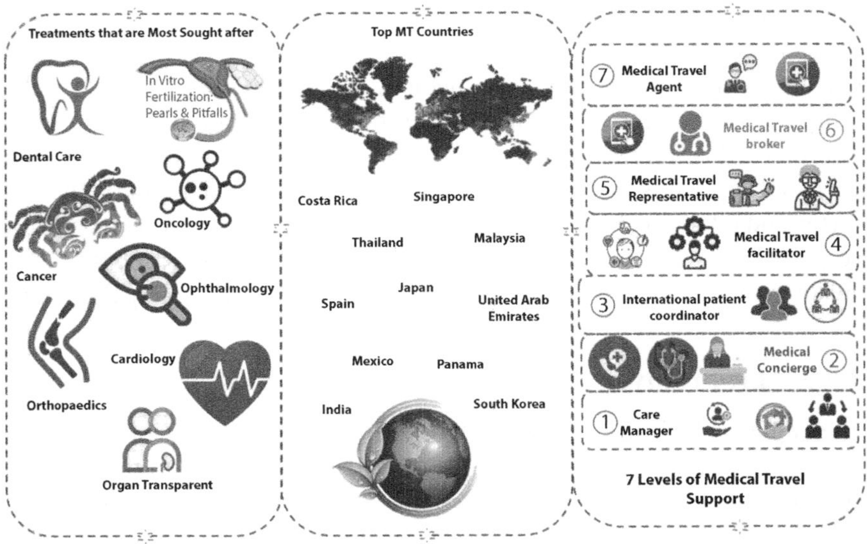

Figure 3.4 Sampled IoMT application in medical attention.

anatomy of the heart and lungs, it is vital to understand the surface anatomy. People have a misconception that the best sound of auscultation is captured just slightly above the heart, but this is not the case [33]. It depends on the direction of the blood flow, and some of the smart wearable devices are demonstrated in Figure 3.4, showing some medical attention needed using AIoMTs, some selected countries of medical tourism, and levels of medical travel support.

Besides the identified electronic sensors, recent medical wearables development showed great potential in accurately and precisely measuring different health-related parameters without the need for a doctor's consultation using the sampled sensors. Although research is ongoing and there is a need to further look into this issue, some IoMTs include epileptic seizure detection, myocardial ischemia monitoring, fatigue detection, physical therapy, wearables, monitoring of sleep apnea, and stress monitoring, among others [34]. Recent studies have investigated both commercial and research items. However, most supercomputing personal medical applications are still in the improvement phase.

3.4 Electronic Devices Challenges in the AIoMT

In contrast to other sectors (IoT applications) where IoT adoption is equally widespread, network managers in the healthcare setup or sector

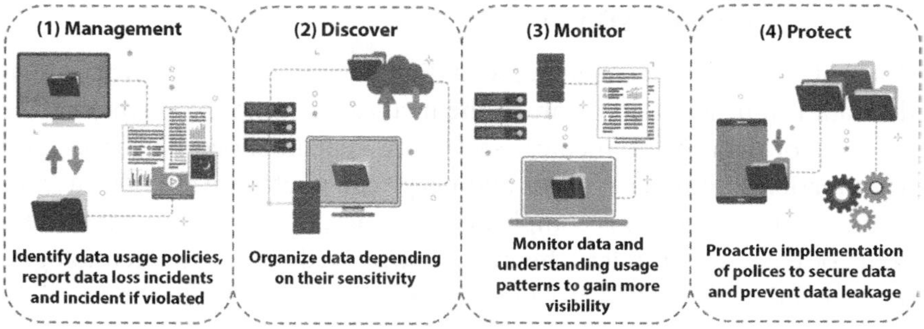

Figure 3.5 AIoMT management processes.

confront difficulties when adopting this IoMT technology. Strict privacy laws, connectivity restrictions brought on by erratic physical settings, and the growing danger of security breaches are just a few of the issues, not to mention the fact that the technology is used in situations where life is at stake [35]. Information health technology departments are responsible for ensuring that IoMT equipment is secure, available all the time, and dependable throughout the entire year. While monitoring and safeguarding hundreds, if not thousands, of devices with fewer resources than ever before, these teams are also overworked. Here is a closer look of the top challenges encountered in IoMT applications, and some suggestions have been made [36]. The top processes of managing AIoMTs are illustrated in Figure 3.5, amidst a few challenges that are not entailed within these categories, which are also discussed [37].

3.4.1 Data Security Threats

Cyber-attacks and medical cyberthreats are likely to compromise Medicare data in medical facilities that have not fully encompassed security-based measures in handling patient data. The danger of exposure is greatly increased when the IoMT data are merged with the existing pool of patient medical data, and the exposure to danger is greatly excavated [38]. In fact, a data breach investigation report presented by Ponemon Institute and Verizon demonstrated that medical data related to personal health information. The likelihood of data breach is higher when devices are connected to external systems and one another. US government data breaches to healthcare in the first five months of 2022 have approximately doubled in the last year [39].

3.4.2 Data Interoperability

Without a doubt, with the increase in digital data, the greater the risk that the data will be altered, mainly in the medical industry. Nevertheless, the majority of data in the medical sector are kept in siloed databases, and incompatible computer systems and proprietary software are not interoperable. Consequently, it is complex to exchange, analyze, and realize these kinds of data. This hinders the evolution of medicine since technologies that depend on these data, like big data, AI, and mobile applications, might not be utilized to their full extent [40].

Therefore, interoperability is a vital component of the anticipated digital advancements in the field of future medicine. Discussion on the ways in which interoperability might facilitate digital transformation in diverse industries ultimately results in global gains in patient health and well-being [41]. From a medical perspective, in case user data originating from a myriad of IoMT devices cannot be aggregated and computationally analyzed to arrive at medical conclusions that are meaningful and therapeutically applicable, they are useless [42]. To enable the transmission of patient data to technology users, all devices in the IoMT environment must be compatible with one another along with the payers and providers to fully realize the expected benefits of the technology [43].

3.4.3 Regulatory Challenges

Clinical-grade medical "things" and "devices" must have permission and require clearance from national regulators before they may be introduced to the national and international markets. These devices require new regulations from legislators and regulatory agencies that are not familiar enough with how these IoMTs are used [44]. Those kinds of limitations also delay the IoMTs being used in medical care due to the limited technological acceptance from those in authority. Medical device manufacturers should reduce their exposure to the dangers of cyber vulnerabilities by keeping an eye on regulatory and legal changes pertaining to the IoMT and adhering to best practices [45].

3.4.4 High Infrastructure Costs

A significant initial outlay is required due to the price of the hardware, specialized IoMT infrastructure, developing consumer-facing applications, and cloud computing. The high infrastructure expenses for IoMT pose a barrier, even though the eventual return on investment is certain. Back in

2015, there were 4.5 billion IoMT devices in operation, and in fact, a Frost and Sullivan report shows that there will be close to 30 billion devices in less than two years. Deloitte's analysis predicts that by 2022, the IoMT market will be worth $158.1 billion, up from its $41 billion value in 2017 [46]. IoMT also has more wearables, even if that industry is predicted to grow to $29 billion by 2026.

3.4.5 Standardization Challenges

Accreditation of IoMT devices becomes a problem because many suppliers and makers of medical devices are all trying to gain scalability and shorten the time to market for their products. The interoperability of medical devices is impacted by a lack of standardization, which lowers IoMT's overall effectiveness [47]. Coalitions and alliances inside the industry are addressing the issue, and the sector is receiving substantial assistance from the government.

3.4.6 Cybersecurity

Cybersecurity is a difficult matter that requires knowledge and experience from a variety of professions for comprehension, which the majority of medical persons are not widely informed of. It is comfortable for policy experts and others to become lost in the technical details of cybersecurity, despite the fact that technology measures are an essential component of cybersecurity in the medical sector. In addition, cybersecurity knowledge is usually arranged in silos based on disciplinary boundaries, which lowers the number of insights that can be gained through cross-fertilization [48]. This introduction may give connection insight. Importantly, it attempts to leave the reader with two major issues to consider. There is no way to tackle the cybersecurity problem entirely and permanently. Given the interconnections of medical devices, without a doubt, one of the most dangerous IoMT concerns for the medical device business is cybersecurity. Why so? The quality of data transmitted and received by medical devices and the underlying technology are to blame [49]. It can include the patient's personal or financial information, such as the patient's name, date of birth, social security number, and bank account information, among others.

3.4.7 Device Mobility

When employed for therapy, diagnosis, or data handling in IoMT, a device's performance is greatly reduced if it can only be stationary and positioned in one location. Another illustration is a lost network connection, which can turn off any device signaling and have potentially fatal results. Therefore, making IoMT devices functional and mobile is a field to be worked on [50]. The performance of the gadget is enhanced when the network configuration is replaceable. Once more, it ought to be a secure network switch [51]. Large IoMT devices may find it difficult to do this due to constrained network capacity and physical obstructions that cut off wireless signals. Additionally, larger devices could use distinct data formats and connection protocols. The time it takes for these devices to integrate with current IoMT devices may be greatly increased as a result [52].

3.4.8 Adoption Scale

Scaling is a serious issue for medical technologies. It is imperative to ensure that Medicare organizations, patients, and professionals recognize the added value of linked medical gadgets. The subject of the IoMT's scalability and wider adoption is still up in the air, even though the industry is expanding and will continue to expand in the future [53]. The additional value of linked medical devices and how they can improve patient outcomes or lower healthcare costs are not understood by all healthcare organizations, professionals, and patients. Limits of governance guidelines and studies demonstrating that IoMT and medical device interconnection are cost-effective alternatives are another impediment [54]. Every medical facility can act at any stage of IoMT integration to make sure the equipment is simple to use and intuitive, as well as to train personnel to develop the skills necessary to maximize the use of the technology [55]. Although the governmental issue is inherently more complex, businesses may present the findings of their trials, studies, and other research to raise awareness and obtain greater media coverage.

3.4.9 Advanced Analytics

Without efficient algorithms to organize, evaluate, and anticipate potential outcomes, gigabytes of data are useless. It is also important to determine the likelihood of developing a heart failure condition or attack. These instruments not only help preserve the functionality of medical devices but also warn in case anything needs to be repaired [56]. The IoMT can genuinely save lives in this situation. By utilizing cutting-edge algorithms that help segment and cluster data, identify patterns, and raise alarms about potential hazards, IoT in hospitals and analytics difficulties may be overcome.

3.4.10 Trust Maintenance

To minimize the possibility of subverting the merits that access to data can benefit healthcare technology, organizations that innovate mechanisms and services based on the creation and sharing of patient data must ensure openness to patients, the public, and healthcare professionals regarding the utilization of their data [57].

3.4.11 Data Security

According to a 2019 Healthcare Information and Management Systems Society poll, over 82% of healthcare firms reported a security breach in the year prior. Hackers are particularly interested in patient health data, such as electronic medical records and information found in patient databases, such as credit card numbers, addresses, and email identifications [58]. These devices repeatedly use outdated software that lacks built-in data security protection because they are primarily utilitarian in design.

3.4.12 Licensing Challenge

Complicated requirements must be met while incorporating IoMT devices into various medical facilities, compliance standards must be observed, and license approvals must be attained. Even though creating these devices takes time, that is not the only difficulty experienced for IoT service health providers [59]. Regulatory compliance is a sizable obstacle that needs to be overcome.

3.5 AIoMT Benefits

To properly illustrate the benefits, the next section will demonstrate challenges for the AIoMTs; within this subsection, we mainly present them with two benefits and then challenges as detailed subsequently.

3.5.1 Medical Diagnosis

AIoMT aids in attaining a quick and precise medical diagnosis because it is the first step undertaken to treat patient ailments, thereby reducing patient mortality rates. This ultimately leads to improved health and quality of life for individuals. Robots such as the Husky and Veebot have shown great potential in spotting skin tumors accurately and drawing blood, respectively [60]. One hundred percent accuracy in the robotic diagnosis of 340 brains can be achieved using magnetic resonance imaging. Correspondingly, AIoMTs are equipped with the ability to alert medical workers when patients' health deteriorates, as has been shown in this study where doctors were alerted by Google's DeepMind AI system when patients had acute injury of the kidney [61].

3.5.2 Medical Treatment

Because treatment plays an important role in a patient's life, AIoMT has the potential to provide prompt treatment to various patient ailments due to its accuracy, thereby saving lives. In what is now referred to as precision medicine, AIoMT is accelerating the transition from traditional medicine to personalized medicine, targeted treatment, and uniquely composed drugs [62]. Different AI models have shown great potential in the treatment of COVID-19, as indicated in the studies highlighted. Moreover, with the help of smartphones, AI can aid in prescribing medication to different patients who are unable to physically move to hospital settings [63]. Additionally, robots, such as the limb-robot rehabilitation system, have achieved tremendous success in rehabilitation and therapy.

3.5.3 Patient Empowerment

AIoMT has the potential to empower individuals to help them make better and more informed health decisions. The large amount of patient data collected by wearable medical devices discussed in the previous section, along with the embedded AI, helps in analyzing these data, which could alert people with a higher risk of becoming ill long before such ailments become serious [64]. Doing so allows individuals affected by certain chronic illnesses to curb their disease better, thereby enabling them to live healthier lives through mobile apps. This consequently empowers them and leads to reduced healthcare costs.

3.5.4 Reduction in Medical Costs

Artificial intelligence is capable of speeding up the creation of lifesaving medicines, thereby saving money in medical costs incurred on healthcare delivery systems. AIoMT can optimize medication development in clinical trials, leading to the depreciation of the time taken to fully certify developed drugs [65].

3.5.5 Reduction in Human Error

The use of AI in the IoMT has shown great benefits in minimizing human errors by medical workers, which saves lives. AIoMT has shown the potential to diagnose patients with a reported 72% more accurate diagnosis compared to the high error rate of medical workers. Without the use of technology in surgical procedures done by medical practitioners, the operation can lead to life-threatening consequences [53]. Henceforth, AI plays a vital role in assisting doctors in their surgical procedures due to its simulation of human-made intelligence.

3.6 AIoMTs Challenges

Although AI and its convergence with the IoMT have shown tremendous potential to revolutionize healthcare, several technological challenges in their deployment have to be addressed to realize their adaptability and monetization in hospitals/clinics and society in general. This section briefly discusses those challenges.

3.6.1 Privacy Concerns

Patients have serious concerns about the large amount of data collected by the different IoMTs. Leakage of such sensitive data through hackers and other means has consequences such as patient blackmail, tarnishing the reputation of health service providers, and the likelihood of loss of lives [54]. Studies have shown the possibility of AI compromising privacy by predicting the personal information of patients regardless of whether the algorithm has ever been presented with such records [55]. This modus operandi for AI in healthcare may result in lawsuits, especially if the AI's conclusions are made available for public consumption. Hence, the sensitivity of the stored data needs to be protected from unauthorized access and disclosure, as well as medical healthcare innovation (Figure 3.6).

3.6.2 Missteps and Errors

AIoMT systems are not flawless, as a patient could be hurt if the wrong treatment is prescribed or if the system fails to detect tumors on a radiological exam, among others. Moreover, if AIoMT systems become popular, a slight error in one has the potential to hurt several others [56]. Because AI systems work with consumers' smart wearable devices and use the data

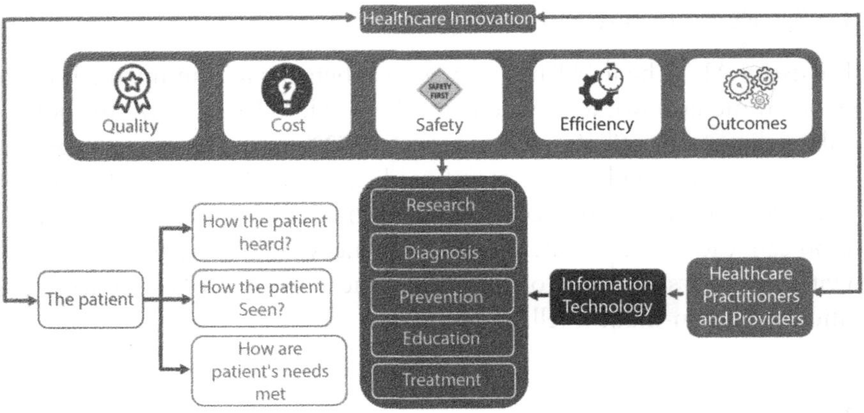

Figure 3.6 Medical healthcare innovation.

they generate, those systems may produce invalid results, as indicated in this study using Fitbit trackers.

3.6.3 Data Management and Power Issues

The heterogeneity of medical devices running different applications in the AIoMT system creates data management problems like storage and incompatible dataset formats created by various legacy third-party systems. Additionally, the large volume of data (big data) generated needs to be stored and analyzed. Hence, the need for scalable and intelligent machine learning algorithms for processing such a large amount of patient data becomes vital. Finally, most devices in the AIoMT have low power capacities, which affect the operation [57]. An efficient mechanism capable of increasing the battery power of IoMT devices needs to be envisaged and deployed to increase their operational time.

3.6.4 Bias

AI-enabled health suffers from the dangers of prejudice and inequality because such systems, by design, learn from the information fed into them, leading to the absorption of biases from supplied datasets [58]. Regardless of whether the AIoMT systems are trained on accurate, reliable, and representative datasets, bias will still be reflected, as noted in the study, where an AI system trained on healthcare datasets learns to recommend lower painkiller doses to patients of African-American race. Such a decision is purely based on systemic bias instead of biological traits.

3.7 AIoMT Limitations

Regardless of the benefits of AIoMTs, some limitations are identified and discussed subsequently. As a result of the ongoing development of technology, business processes in every industry, including medicine, are undergoing continuous change. One of these industries experiencing this problem is the healthcare industry [57]. In the coming years, the IoTs, IoMTs, and generally AIoMTs will bring countless remarkable opportunities for the healthcare industry. Using IoMT, we are able to derive additional value from the data we acquire. The IoMT improves the effectiveness and quality of the results delivered by various devices [58]. However, there are a few limitations that are encountered in every technological progress, including data privacy concerns, security issues due to the use of wireless medical things, the cost of these AIoMTs, and inaccuracy while handling real-time medical data and operation. It is further noted that these medical developments require medical doctors to undergo training to use applications and structures effectively. Implementing software by medical analytics can be seen as a limitation as some medical people are not well-versed in operating technology [59].

3.8 Future Research Direction

The adoption of AI in the health sector through its convergence with the IoMT is transforming healthcare delivery in aspects such as patient experience, how medical workers practice medicine, and how drugs are being manufactured [60]. Soon, AIoMT is expected to improve the precision of wearable medical devices and their ability to collect, store, and interpret data about patients' health conditions. Consequently, this will allow medical workers to engage with their patients through telemedicine to achieve improved healthcare service delivery [61].

Overall, the new means of getting healthcare services will drastically reduce the healthcare costs incurred for all groups of patients. Because much of how AI operates is unknown to most laymen, the policies and legal frameworks that govern its use, especially in the healthcare sector, will have to be instituted to promote public confidence in its use and protect citizens from any fallout from its irresponsible deployment [62]. The European Union has made initiatives in that direction through its quest to come up with the Artificial Intelligence Act, which is aimed at promoting uniformity in the governance of AI technologies in different sectors, which include the health sector.

The other initiative is the Pan-Canadian AI strategy, which, along with the European one, will help the medical community and regulators monitor the adoption and explainability of various AI technologies and how their use impacts different contexts in the healthcare industry [63]. Through a combination of standards and regulations, the accuracy, security, reliability, and health use of AI technologies will need to be instituted. This is because AI technologies are capable of learning patterns and modifying their recommendations in ways not envisioned by their creators. This poses regulatory issues, which will need to be addressed as the technology evolves [64].

Adopting a community-led approach by medical workers, technologists, researchers, and other stakeholders is one method that can be used to develop standards for data collection and testing of AI-enabled health technologies. AIoMT trends such as chatbot technologies (voice assistants) are seen to revolutionize the healthcare sector with their increased adoption by different healthcare providers [65]. As evidenced by their extensive usage during the COVID-19 global pandemic and other health emergencies, voice assistants such as Google Assistant, Apple Siri, and Amazon Alexa proved to be very useful in responding to COVID-19-related public questions [66].

3.9 Conclusions and Future Scope

Due to its potential to transform the delivery of medical care, the IoMT has rapidly gained the interest of researchers since its inception. They are able to monitor and manage a number of health-related disorders and issues. The IoMT devices allow us to monitor our medical records and take the necessary safety precautions. IoMT plays a significant role in boosting the effectiveness and precision of electronic devices in the medical industry. In this chapter, a comprehensive examination of a range of electronic equipment discovered in the AIoMT has been conducted. For your convenience, the identified and extensively used medical equipment, including electrical signals for AIoMT sensors, are highlighted subsequently.

In addition, AIoMT's architecture demonstrates significant development by utilizing intelligent sensors to collect, aggregate, and manage data for intelligent healthcare buildings. In addition, the chapter discusses the challenges that electronic gadgets pose to AIoMT. These challenges include, but are not limited to, threats to data security, interoperability issues, and regulatory concerns. All of these challenges, along with others, must be addressed to improve medical operating standards, not just for medical staff but also for patients and other medical stakeholders. Unanswered research questions that will be the focus of future research in AIoMT are discussed in the conclusion. IoT innovations such as automated medical delivery, connected inhalers and contact lenses, monitoring for Parkinson's disease, monitoring for glucose levels, monitoring for depression and mood, and many others have unquestionably benefited the medical business.

The patient experience is improved, and workflows are optimized. Patients stand to benefit from increased participation and fewer in-person physician appointments. Providers can better assist patients now that they have access to more accurate data, improved diagnostics, and more effective time management. AIoMT will very certainly be supplemented in the future by more innovations that will further streamline the medical profession for practitioners and patients. This chapter is limited in that it cannot cover the many issues related to electronic devices and AIoMT that have been raised. This is a restriction. Diverse parties should make a more concentrated effort to develop laws and regulatory frameworks that regulate the deployment of AI in various health situations. Additionally, in order to boost public confidence in the use of AI and IoMT in the healthcare industry, it will be important to seek and implement solutions to the highlighted concerns. Numerous researchers, students, and other stakeholders with an interest in this topic will find these discussions of the chapter to be beneficial.

References

1. Alabdan, R., Alruban, A., Hilal, A.M., Motwakel, A., Artificial-Intelligence-Based Decision Making for Oral Potentially Malignant Disorder Diagnosis in Internet of Medical Things Environment. *Healthcare*, 11, 1, 113, 2023, https://doi.org/10.3390/healthcare11010113.
2. Shafik, W., Predicting Future Cybercrime Trends in the Metaverse Era, in: *Forecasting Cyber Crimes in the Age of the Metaverse*, pp. 78–113, IGI Global, Hershey, Pennsylvania, United States, 2024, https://doi.org/10.4018/979-8-3693-0220-0.ch005.
3. Bhattarai, A. and Peng, D., An Integrated Secure Efficient Computing Architecture for Embedded and Remote ECG Diagnosis. *SN Comput. Sci.*, 4, 1, 1–15, 2023, https://doi.org/10.1007/s42979-022-01465-7.
4. Shafik, W., Wearable Medical Electronics in Artificial Intelligence of Medical Things, in: *Handbook of Security and Privacy of AI-Enabled Healthcare Systems and Internet of Medical Things*, pp. 21–40, 2024, https://doi.org/10.1201/9781003370321-2.

5. Chunka, C., Banerjee, S., Sachin Kumar, G., A Secure Communication Using Multifactor Authentication and Key Agreement Techniques in Internet of Medical things for COVID-19 Patients. *Concurr. Comput. Pract. Exper.*, 7602, e7602, 2023, https://doi.org/10.1002/cpe.7602.
6. Shafik, W., Cyber Security Perspectives in Public Spaces: Drone Case Study, in: *Handbook of Research on Cybersecurity Risk in Contemporary Business Systems*, pp. 79–97, IGI Global, Hershey, Pennsylvania, United States, 2023, https://doi.org/10.4018/978-1-6684-7207-1.ch004.
7. Ding, X., Zhang, Y., Li, J., Mao, B., Guo, Y., Li, G., A Feasibility Study of Multi-mode Intelligent Fusion Medical Data Transmission Technology of Industrial Internet of Things Combined with Medical Internet of Things, in: *Internet of Things*, p. 100689, 2023, https://doi.org/10.1016/j.iot.2023.100689.
8. Wang, Y., Shafik, W., Seong, J.T., Al Mutairi, A., Mustafa, M.S., Mouhamed, M.R., Service delay and optimization of the energy efficiency of a system in fog-enabled smart cities. *Alexandria Eng. J.*, 84, 112–125, 2023, https://doi.org/10.1016/j.aej.2023.10.034.
9. Gezimati, M. and Singh, G., Internet of Things Enabled Framework for Terahertz and Infrared Cancer Imaging. *Opt. Quantum Electron.*, 55, 1, 1–17, 2023, https://doi.org/10.1007/s11082-022-04087-8.
10. Shafik, W., Matinkhah, S.M., Shokoor, F., Cybersecurity in Unmanned Aerial Vehicles: a Review. *Int. J. Smart Sens. Intell. Syst.*, 16, 1, 2023, https://doi.org/10.2478/ijssis-2023-0012.
11. Gupta, S., Sharma, H.K., Kapoor, M., Application and Challenges of Blockchain in IoMT in Smart Healthcare System, in: *Blockchain for Secure Healthcare Using Internet of Medical Things (IoMT)*, pp. 39–53, Springer International Publishing AG Birkhäuser Verlag AG, Springer, Cham, Springer International, 2023, https://doi.org/10.1007/978-3-031-18896-1_4.
12. Shafik, W. and Kalinaki, K., Smart City Ecosystem: An Exploration of Requirements, Architecture, Applications, Security, and Emerging Motivations, in: *Handbook of Research on Network-Enabled IoT Applications for Smart City Services*, pp. 75–98, IGI Global, Hershey, Pennsylvania, United States, 2023, https://doi.org/10.4018/979-8-3693-0744-1.ch005.
13. Idrees, A.K. and Khlief, M.S., Efficient Compression Technique for Reducing Transmitted EEG Data without Loss in IoMT Networks Based on Fog Computing. *J. Supercomputing*, 79, 1–26, 2023, https://doi.org/10.1007/s11227-022-05027-9.
14. Shafik, W., IoT-Based Energy Harvesting and Future Research Trends in Wireless Sensor Networks, in: *Handbook of Research on Network-Enabled IoT Applications for Smart City Services*, pp. 282–306, 2023, https://doi.org/10.4018/979-8-3693-0744-1.ch016.
15. Khan, I.A. and Pi, D., Explainable Learning Machines for Securing the IoMT Networks, in: *The Internet of Medical Things (IoMT) and Telemedicine Frameworks and Applications*, pp. 135–154, IGI Global, Hershey, Pennsylvania, United States, 2023, https://doi.org/10.4018/978-1-6684-3533-5.ch007.

16. Shafik, W., Making Cities Smarter: IoT and SDN Applications, Challenges, and Future Trends, in: *Opportunities and Challenges of Industrial IoT in 5G and 6G Networks*, pp. 73–94, IGI Global, Hershey, Pennsylvania, United States, 2023, https://doi.org/10.4018/978-1-7998-9266-3.ch004.
17. Kok, C.L. and Setyadi, Y., Li-Ion-Based DC UPS for Remote Application, in: *The Internet of Medical Things (IoMT) and Telemedicine Frameworks and Applications*, pp. 276–289, IGI Global, Hershey, Pennsylvania, United States, 2023, https://doi.org/10.4018/978-1-6684-3533-5.ch015.
18. Alaziz, S.N., Albayati, B., El-Bagoury, A.A.A.H., Shafik, W., , Clustering of COVID-19 Multi-Time Series-Based K-Means and. *Int. J. Data Warehouse Min. (IJDWM)*, 19, 3, 1–25, 2023, https://doi.org/10.4018/IJDWM.317374.
19. Irfana Parveen, C.A., Anjali, O., Sunder, R., Internet of Things: A Review on Its Applications, in: *Information and Communication Technology for Competitive Strategies (ICTCS 2021)*, pp. 123–134, 2023, https://doi.org/10.1007/978-981-19-0095-2_13.
20. Shokoor, F., Shafik, W., Matinkhah, S.M., Overview of 5G & beyond security, in: *Endorsed Transactions on Internet of Things*, vol. 8, 2022, http://dx.doi.org/10.4108/eetiot.v8i30.1624.
21. Kok, C.L., A Low Cost, Power Efficient, Social Distancing Notification Embedded System Based on Intelligent Wireless Sensor Network, in: *The Internet of Medical Things (IoMT) and Telemedicine Frameworks and Applications*, pp. 262–275, IGI Global, Hershey, Pennsylvania, United States, 2023, https://doi.org/10.4018/978-1-6684-3533-5.ch014.
22. Shafik, W., Matinkhah, S.M., Shokoor, F., Recommendation system comparative analysis: internet of things aided networks, in: *EAI Endorsed Transactions on Internet of Things*, vol. 8, 2022, http://dx.doi.org/10.4108/eetiot.v8i29.1108.
23. Lee, H.Y., Lee, K.H., Lee, K.H., Erdenbayar, U., Hwang, S., Lee, E.Y., Lee, J.H., Kim, H.J., Park, S.B., Park, J.W., Internet of Medical Things-Based Real-Time Digital Health Service for Precision Medicine: Empirical Studies Using MEDBIZ Platform. *Digital Health*, 9, 20552076221149660, 2023, https://doi.org/10.1177/20552076221149659.
24. Shafik, W., Artificial intelligence and Blockchain technology enabling cybersecurity in telehealth systems, in: *Artificial Intelligence and Blockchain Technology in Modern Telehealth Systems*, vol. 1, pp. 285–326, 2023, IET. https://doi.org/10.1049/PBHE061E_ch11.
25. Shafik, W., Matinkhah, S.M., Shokoor, F., Sharif, L., A reawakening of machine learning application in unmanned aerial vehicle: future research motivation, in: *EAI Endorsed Transactions on Internet of Things*, vol. 8, 2022, http://dx.doi.org/10.4108/eetiot.v8i29.987.
26. Muthukaruppankaruppiah, S., Nagalingam, S.R., Murugasen, P., Nandaamarnath, R., Human Fatty Liver Monitoring Using Nano Sensor and IoMT. *Intell. Autom. Soft Comput.*, 35, 2, 2309–2323, 2023, http://dx.doi.org/10.32604/iasc.2023.029598.

27. Zhao, L., Zhu, D., Shafik, W., Matinkhah, S.M., Ahmad, Z., Sharif, L., Craig, A., Artificial intelligence analysis in cyber domain: A review. *Int. J. Distrib. Sens. Netw.*, 18, 4, 15501329221084882, 2022, https://doi.org/10.1177/15501329221084882.
28. Narasimharao, M., Swain, B., Nayak, P.P., Bhuyan, S., Development of Real-Time Cloud Based Smart Remote Healthcare Monitoring System, in: *Ambient Intelligence in Health Care*, Springer, pp. 217–224, 2023, https://doi.org/10.1007/978-981-19-6068-0_21.
29. Jun, Y., Craig, A., Shafik, W., Sharif, L., Artificial intelligence application in cybersecurity and cyberdefense. *Wireless Commun. Mobile Comput.*, 2021, 1–10, 2021, https://doi.org/10.1155/2021/3329581.
30. Pandey, R., Pandey, A., Maurya, P., Singh, G.D., Prenatal Healthcare Framework Using IoMT Data Analytics, in: *The Internet of Medical Things (IoMT) and Telemedicine Frameworks and Applications*, IGI Global, pp. 76–104, 2023, https://doi.org/10.4018/978-1-6684-3533-5.ch004.
31. Lin, Y., Ahmad, Z., Shafik, W., Khosa, S.K., Almaspoor, Z., Alsuhabi, H., Abbas, F., Impact of facebook and newspaper advertising on sales: a comparative study of online and print media. *Comput. Intell. Neurosci.*, 2021, 2021, https://doi.org/10.1155/2021/5995008.
32. Quy, V.K., Hau, N.V., Anh, D.V., Ngoc, L.A., Smart Healthcare IoT Applications Based on Fog Computing: Architecture, Applications and Challenges. *Complex Intell. Syst.*, 8, 5, 3805–3815, 2022, https://doi.org/10.1007/s40747-021-00582-9.
33. Yang, Z., Jianjun, L., Faqiri, H., Shafik, W., Talal Abdulrahman, A., Yusuf, M., Sharawy, A.M., Green internet of things and big data application in smart cities development. *Complexity*, 2021, 1–15, 2021, https://doi.org/10.1155/2021/4922697.
34. Petrellis, N., Birbas, M., Gioulekas, F., On the Design of Low-Cost IoT Sensor Node for e-Health Environments. *Electronics*, 8, 2, 178, 2019, https://doi.org/10.3390/electronics8020178.
35. Shafik, W., A Comprehensive Cybersecurity Framework for Present and Future Global Information Technology Organizations, in: *Effective Cybersecurity Operations for Enterprise-Wide Systems*, IGI Global, pp. 56–79, 2023, https://doi.org/10.4018/978-1-6684-9018-1.ch002.
36. Rodrigues, J.J., Segundo, D.B.D.R., Junqueira, H.A., Sabino, M.H., Prince, R.M., Al-Muhtadi, J., De Albuquerque, V.H.C., Enabling Technologies for the Internet of Health Things. *IEEE Access*, 6, 13129–13141, 2018, https://doi.org/10.1109/ACCESS.2017.2789329.
37. Shafik, W., Matinkhah, S.M., Sanda, M.N., Shokoor, F., Internet of things-based energy efficiency optimization model in fog smart cities. *JOIV: Int. J. Inf. Visualization*, 5, 2, 105–112, 2021, http://dx.doi.org/10.30630/joiv.5.2.373.
38. Salem, O. and Mehaoua, A., Ephemeral Elliptic Curve Diffie-Hellman to Secure Data Exchange in Internet of Medical Things, in: *Emerging Trends in Cybersecurity Applications*, pp. 3–20, Springer International Publishing

AG Birkhäuser Verlag AG Springer, Cham, Springer International, 2023, https://doi.org/10.1007/978-3-031-09640-2_1.

39. Shafik, W., Matinkhah, S.M., Ghasemzadeh, M., Theoretical Understanding of Deep Learning in UAV Biomedical Engineering Technologies Analysis. *SN Comput. Sci.*, 1, 6, 1–13, 2020, https://doi.org/10.1007/s42979-020-00323-8.
40. Shankar, N., Nallakaruppan, M.K., Ravindranath, V., Senthilkumar, M., Bhagavath, B.P., Smart IoMT Framework for Supporting UAV Systems with AI. *Electronics*, 12, 1, 86, 2023, https://doi.org/10.3390/electronics12010086.
41. Shafik, W., Matinkhah, M., Etemadinejad, P., Sanda, M.N., Reinforcement learning rebirth, techniques, challenges, and resolutions. *JOIV: Int. J. Inf. Visualization*, 4, 3, 127–135, 2020, https://doi.org/ http://dx.doi.org/10.30630/joiv.4.3.376.
42. Wang, J. and Li, X., Secure Medical Data Collection in the Internet of Medical Things Based on Local Differential Privacy. *Electronics*, 12, 2, 307, 2023, https://doi.org/10.3390/electronics12020307.
43. Shafik, W., A fast machine learning for beam selection in 5g unmanned aerial vehicle communications (Doctoral dissertation, M. Sc. dissertation, Yazd University, Iran), 2020, http://dx.doi.org/10.13140/RG.2.2.34291.14886.
44. Nair, A.K. and Sahoo, J., Internet of Things in Smart and Intelligent Healthcare Systems, in: *Intelligent Internet of Things for Smart Healthcare Systems*, 1st ed., CRC Press, Boca Raton, Florida, 2023, eBook ISBN9781003326182https://doi.org/10.1201/9781003326182.
45. Shafik, W., Matinkhah, S.M., Ghasemzadeh, M., A mobile fuzzy sink scheme for wireless sensor network period improvement, in: *2020 8th Iranian Joint Congress on Fuzzy and intelligent Systems (CFIS)*, IEEE, pp. 211–216, 2020, September, https://doi.org/10.1109/CFIS49607.2020.9238684.
46. Meng, H., Shafik, W., Matinkhah, S.M., Ahmad, Z., A 5g beam selection machine learning algorithm for unmanned aerial vehicle applications. *Wireless Commun. Mobile Comput.*, 2020, 1–16, 2020, https://doi org/10.1155/2020/1428968.
47. Patra, M.K., Kumari, A., Sahoo, B., Turuk, A.K., Smart Healthcare System Using Cloud-Integrated Internet of Medical Things, in: *Exploring the Convergence of Computer and Medical Science Through Cloud Healthcare*, pp. 60–83, IGI Global, Hershey, Pennsylvania, United States, 2023, https://doi.org/10.4018/978-1-6684-5260-8.ch004.
48. Shafik, W., Matinkhah, M., Sanda, M.N., Network resource management drives machine learning: a survey and future research direction. *J. Commun. Technol., Electron. Comput. Sci.*, 2020, 1–15, 2020, http://dx.doi.org/10.22385/jctecs.v30i0.312.
49. Riya, K.S., Surendran, R., Tavera Romero, C.A., Sendil, M.S., Encryption with User Authentication Model for Internet of Medical Things Environment. *Intell. Autom. Soft Comput.*, 35, 1, 507–520, 2023, http://dx.doi.org/10.32604/iasc.2023.027779.

50. Shafik, W., Matinkhah, M., Asadi, M., Ahmadi, Z., Hadiyan, Z., A study on internet of things performance evaluation. *J. Commun. Technol., Electron. Comput. Sci.*, 2020, 1–19, 2020, http://dx.doi.org/10.22385/jctecs.v28i0.303.
51. Alshammari, H.H., The internet of things healthcare monitoring system based on MQTT protocol. *Alexandria Eng. J.*, 69, 275–287, 2023, https://doi.org/10.1016/j.aej.2023.01.065.
52. Vyas, S., Gupta, S., Shukla, V.K., Sustainable Energy Usage in Urban and Rural Context-A Study, in: *Enabling Technologies for Effective Planning and Management in Sustainable Smart Cities*, pp. 389–402, Springer International Publishing AG Birkhäuser Verlag AG, Springer, Cham, Springer International, 2023, https://doi.org/10.1007/978-3-031-22922-0_16.
53. Shafik, W., Matinkhah, S.M., Afolabi, S.S., Sanda, M.N., A 3-dimensional fast machine learning algorithm for mobile unmanned aerial vehicle base stations. *Int. J. Adv. Appl. Sci.*, 2252, 8814, 8814, 2020, http://dx.doi.org/10.11591/ijaas.v10.i1.pp28-38.
54. Wang, S., Wang, S., Liu, Z., Zhang, Q., A role distinguishing Bert model for medical dialogue system in sustainable smart city. *Sustain. Energy Technol. Assess.*, 55, 102896, 2023, https://doi.org/10.1016/j.seta.2022.102896.
55. Shafik, W., Matinkhah, S.M., Ghasemazade, M., Fog-mobile edge performance evaluation and analysis on internet of things. *J. Adv. Res. Mob. Comput.*, 1, 3, 1–17, 2019, http://doi.org/10.5281/zenodo.3591228.
56. Mathur, G., Pandey, A., Goyal, S., Applications of Machine Learning in Healthcare, in: *The Internet of Medical Things (IoMT) and Telemedicine Frameworks and Applications*, pp. 177–195, IGI Global, Hershey, Pennsylvania, United States, 2023, http://doi.org/10.4018/978-1-6684-3533-5.ch009.
57. Shafik, W. and Matinkhah, S.M., Privacy issues in social Web of things, in: *2019 5th International Conference on Web Research (ICWR)*, IEEE, pp. 208–214, 2019, April, https://doi.org/10.1109/ICWR.2019.8765254.
58. Guan, Z., Li, Y., Yu, S., Yang, Z., Deep Reinforcement Learning-Based Full-Duplex Link Scheduling in Federated Learning-based Computing for IoMT. *Trans. Emerg. Telecommun. Technol.*, 4724, e4724, 2023, https://doi.org/10.1002/ett.4724.
59. Kalinaki, K., Fahadi, M., Alli, A.A., Shafik, W., Yasin, M., Mutwalibi, N., Artificial Intelligence of Internet of Medical Things (AIoMT) in Smart Cities: A Review of Cybersecurity for Smart Healthcare, in: *Handbook of Security and Privacy of AI-Enabled Healthcare Systems and Internet of Medical Things*, pp. 271–292, 2024, https://doi.org/10.1201/9781003370321-11.
60. Shafik, W., Blockchain-Based Internet of Things (B-IoT): Challenges, Solutions, Opportunities, Open Research Questions, and Future Trends, in: *Blockchain-based Internet of Things*, pp. 35–58, 2024, https://doi.org/10.1201/9781003407096-3.

61. Fahim, K.E., Kalinaki, K., Shafik, W., Electronic Devices in the Artificial Intelligence of the Internet of Medical Things (AIoMT), in: *Handbook of Security and Privacy of AI-Enabled Healthcare Systems and Internet of Medical Things*, pp. 41–62, CRC Press, Boca Raton, Florida, 2024, https://doi.org/10.1201/9781003370321-3.
62. Deshmukh, A., Tyagi, A.K., Hansora, H., Menon, S.C., Applications of Distributed Ledger (Blockchain) Technology in E-Healthcare, in: *The Internet of Medical Things (IoMT) and Telemedicine Frameworks and Applications*, pp. 248–261, IGI Global, Hershey, Pennsylvania, United States, 2023, https://doi.org/10.4018/978-1-6684-3533-5.ch013.
63. Rajawat, A.S., Goyal, S.B., Bedi, P., Jan, T., Whaiduzzaman, M., Prasad, M., Quantum machine learning for security assessment in the internet of medical things (IoMT). *Future Internet*, 15, 8, 271, 2023, https://doi.org/10.3390/fi15080271.
64. Bhutnal, V. and Moparthi, N.R., Internet of Things-Enabled Diabetic Retinopathy Classification from Fundus Images, in: *IoT with Smart Systems*, pp. 757–764, Springer, 2023, https://doi.org/10.1007/978-981-19-3575-6_72.
65. Shah, V. and Khang, A., Internet of Medical Things (IoMT) driving the digital transformation of the healthcare sector, in: *Data-Centric AI Solutions and Emerging Technologies in the Healthcare Ecosystem*, pp. 15–26, CRC Press, Boca Raton, Florida, 2023, https://doi.org/10.1201/9781003356189-2.
66. Banday, M.T. and Bhat, L., Towards Building Internet-of-Things-Inclusive Healthcare for Neglected Tropical Diseases, in: *Internet of Medical Things (IoMT) and Telemedicine Frameworks and Applications*, pp. 39–75, 2023, https://doi.org/10.4018/978-1-6684-3533-5.ch003.

4

An Online Platform for Timely Access to Medical Care with the Help of Real-Time Data Analysis

Pancham Singh[1]* and Mrignainy Kansal[2]

[1]*Department of Information Technology, Ajay Kumar Garg Engineering College, Ghaziabad, Uttar Pradesh, India*
[2]*Department of Computer Science and Engineering, NSUT, Delhi, New Delhi, India*

Abstract
In this chapter, we try to explore the major obstacle in reaching the third Sustainable Development Goal (SDG 3) to promote good health and well-being. Real-time information on medical resources is unavailable during the COVID-19 pandemic, and patient admission takes longer than expected due to registration and paperwork. The primary objective of this chapter is to create a platform that offers a comprehensive list of the closest hospitals with all the required facilities to effectively treat specific injuries or diseases without delaying the treatment of patients due to the lack of required facilities. Early diagnosis of symptoms decreases the risk of serious complications and persistent transmission. By providing access to this information, we aim to assist patients in receiving timely and appropriate medical care. This idea can be made where we harness the potential of web technologies in real-time data analysis. Healthcare employs RFID for patient identification and medication management by ensuring precise identification with RFID cards. RFID technology aids medication management by eliminating mistakes and improving drug administration tracking. To improve the security of health records through immutability, encryption, and decentralized storage, blockchain technology improves patient record security, preventing tampering and data breaches.

**Corresponding author*: pancham.akg@gmail.com

Bharat Bhushan, Akib Khanday, Khursheed Aurangzeb, Sudhir Kumar Sharma and Parma Nand (eds.) Wellness Management Powered by AI Technologies, (103–132) © 2025 Scrivener Publishing LLC

***Keywords*:** Remote health monitoring, timely health care, medical data analysis, teleconsultation, health tech

4.1 Introduction

Some websites and applications provide information about the hospitals' resource availability or the calendar of doctor appointments for certain hospitals. However, there is no standard platform for comparing hospitals that have all the criteria met and are arranged according to their proximity to the user. There are several private websites for particular hospitals; however, in emergencies, the user looks for the closest hospital that is now open [1]. The findings emphasized how critical it is to comprehend the unique patterns of facial injuries to strengthen emergency response plans, advance preventative efforts, and maximize medical interventions for victims of traffic accidents. This research adds to the body of knowledge in the area by providing insightful information that can help policymakers, safety advocates, and healthcare professionals create focused interventions that will lessen the frequency and severity of facial injuries brought on by auto accidents. We analyze and formulate an order of hospital lists concerning their bed availability, a particular department, doctor's schedule availability, etc. This grants the user an assurance that if he/she visits the hospital listed on our site, then he/she will receive the treatment as required [2]. Because many Classification Algorithms, Regression Models, and Clustering Algorithms rely on an unknown number of attributes that result in the value being predicted rather than a specific feature, the performance will be tested by providing a list of hospitals for all essential resources.

4.1.1 Research Questions

Q1. How did it help the patient?
It enhances transparency, which reduces waiting time, and expands access to high-quality medical care. This enables people to make knowledgeable healthcare decisions, reduce stress, and ultimately save money.

Q2. How did it impact the healthcare industry?
Faster test results, secure health data administration, and simple patient appointment management have all become easily available.

4.1.2 Inspiration Drawn

In the COVID-19 crisis, the government and a few large hospital conglomerates took several steps to ensure transportation facilities and the delivery of vaccinations. Additionally, certain applications and websites provide information on the availability of beds, oxygen cylinders, and medicine facilities near hospitals. This served as the inspiration for our undertaking and study [3]. It seeks to provide a list of hospitals that are currently open in the hospitals that are close by, together with all of its amenities, such as beds, schedules, accessibility, and the availability of medical care.

4.1.3 Limitations

There are large numbers of websites and apps that can inform about the resource availability of the hospitals or the doctor's appointment schedule for particular hospitals. There is no common platform for the comparison of the hospitals that have all the requirements fulfilled listed in order of their distance from the user. There are multiple private websites for individual hospitals, but during cases of emergencies, the user searches for the nearest hospital available at the moment [4]. There are conditions where multiple options for hospitals are available, but the user cannot distinguish from the choices until and unless he/she visits the hospital directly or visits the website of the particular hospital, which consumes a huge amount of time.

4.1.4 Importance of Machine Learning in this Research Work

Machine learning plays a significant role in enhancing the effectiveness and functionality of a platform aimed at providing a comprehensive list of hospitals with specific facilities for patient care. A combination of algorithms is used to achieve the desired goal [5]. Classification algorithms like decision trees are used to categorize hospitals and healthcare facilities based on their specialities, available resources, and services. By grouping hospitals with comparable traits or resources, such as k-means, consumers will be able to select from clusters of hospitals that are tailored to their needs. A* algorithm for best-first search is used to find the distance between two points [6].

4.2 What Happened

According to data published in *The Lancet*, India had the worst situation among the 136 countries evaluated, with 2.4 million people dying each year from diseases that could be avoided. In 2016, poor treatment quality contributed to more deaths than a lack of healthcare access. Inadequate care contributed to the deaths of 1.6 million Indians, while 838,000 people—nearly twice as many—did not use healthcare facilities. Delaying medical treatment can have serious consequences and, in dire situations, even be fatal. Over 70% of all burn-related fatalities globally are caused by thermal burns [7]. Delays in medical care are common and a key sign of how patients will do. Our goal is to comprehend the role that emergency medical services (EMS) play in the Indian thermal burns healthcare system. Fever is a common illness sign. By getting care as soon as possible, one might enhance the likelihood that the disease will be detected in its early stages, thereby halting the illness's progression and severity. Policymakers must focus on developing an efficient intervention to raise carers' awareness of the significance of early treatment-seeking conduct. To educate people about the importance of acting quickly to seek care in the early stages, community awareness programs should be promoted, especially in rural regions.

Statistics on traffic accident injuries around the world: issues, causes, and solutions. All states and UTs combined to register 4,12,432 accidents in 2021, of which 1,42,163 (34.5%) took place in India. A total of 3,84,448 people were hurt and 1,53,972 people died in traffic accidents as shown in Figure 4.1 [8]. In 2021, there were on average 12.6% more traffic accidents than there were in 2020. There has been a 10.4% increase in injuries and a 16.9% increase in mortality. The AIIMS recently asked for a probe after a woman passed away on February 10, 2020, as a result of a delay in receiving care. The family of the deceased claimed that they were pressured to finish the registration process in just 5 to 6 hours, ostensibly to hide the fact that the woman had spent so much time waiting in the emergency hospital. A survey found that 60% of respondents delay seeking medical attention because they lack health insurance. The third World Ministerial Conference on Road Safety took place in Stockholm, Sweden, on February

Parameter	2020	2021	% Change
Number of Accidents	3,66,138	4,12,432	12.6
Number of Persons killed	1,31,714	1,53,972	16.9
Number of Injury	3,48,279	3,84,448	10.4
Accident Severity (Persons killed per 100 accidents)	36	37	

Figure 4.1 Ministry of road transport and highways.

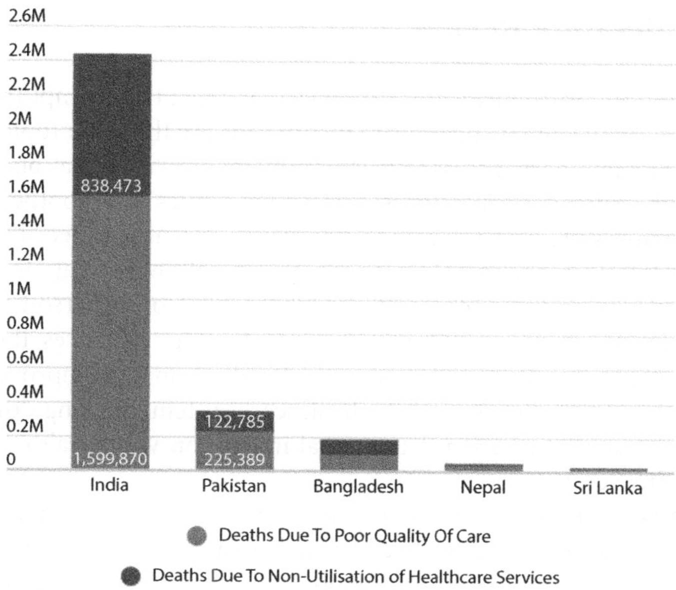

Figure 4.2 Deaths amenable to healthcare.

19 and 20, 2020. Every participant at this conference, including India, reaffirmed their unwavering dedication to achieving the goal of at least a 50% reduction in traffic-related fatalities by 2030. As immediate medical assistance is frequently essential for improving outcomes and minimizing problems, efforts should always be taken to minimize delays in the treatment of road accident victims as shown in Figure 4.2 [9].

It is essential to understand how cancer patients navigate the search for care if we are to encourage early identification and treatment. Access to therapy is occasionally hindered by financial constraints and ignorance, even when a person has been diagnosed with cancer or is thought to have it. It must continue to be relevant in the highly competitive healthcare sector, where patient satisfaction and loyalty are strongly influenced by convenience [10]. The healthcare industry needs to change to become more consumer-focused. To respond to this new context, health systems must restructure processes to improve the delivery of ambulatory care and provide almost immediate access to specialized care.

Treatment delays may have adverse effects on patients' health results and general well-being. Treatment delays are caused by several parameters, and these factors might change based on the healthcare system, region, and particular medical disorders.

4.3 Literature Review

The definition, procedures, and variables that affect the prompt treatment of patients at all suitable healthcare institutions are the main topics of this literature review. Early access to trustworthy medical information can help prevent the spread of infectious disease epidemics and soothe anxiety. Telemedicine systems have gained popularity recently, especially during the COVID-19 pandemic [11]. These systems allow patients to interact with healthcare providers online, reducing the need for in-person consultations and possibly even waiting times. As technology advances, these platforms are likely to gain significance, which will ultimately improve patient outcomes and the efficiency of the healthcare system. Slowing down your access to care might have a detrimental impact on your health and raise your medical costs.

"Positive narration" of incidents and activities that impacted patients is provided by narrative feedback, which can guide efforts to enhance patient care [12]. At all levels of the hospitals, rewarding processes of service development and people management are made possible by real-time reporting of quantitative and qualitative data. The time between the start of symptoms and the patient's initial contact with a healthcare professional was used to determine patient delay. The time between the initial contact with a healthcare professional and the diagnosis was referred to as the diagnostic delay. The time between a diagnosis and the start of treatment of injury was referred to as the treatment delay. Total delay was determined as the amount of time between the onset of symptoms and the start of treatment. One of the services that significantly rely on ICTs to allow remote patients to contact medical experts is telemedicine. It employs electronic consultation through the HOHC (Home Online Health Consult) framework. Important discoveries demonstrate how well the suggested framework works to provide timely insights into health patterns so that medical practitioners can make well-informed judgments [13]. The study shows how Health-Analytics-as-a-Service (HAaaS) can improve long-term health management plans as well as acute patient treatment. These findings highlight how important it is to use cutting-edge frameworks like HAaaS to fully utilize the potential of both retrospective and real-time health data. The study opens the door for the creation of healthcare solutions that are more adaptable and efficient by adding significant knowledge to the field of health informatics.

Addressing the limitations requires ongoing research, policy development, and innovative solutions. Some limitations are discussed here:

1. Systems for emergency medical services (EMS): The promptness of EMS services can be affected by resource limitations, such as the availability of ambulances and qualified personnel [14]. Additionally, there are other variables like traffic and location.
2. Triage protocols: Triage decisions may be random and influenced by specific healthcare professionals, which could result in misclassification and treatment delays for some patients. The triage method may become overloaded and lose its effectiveness in high-demand situations like mass casualties or pandemics.
3. Fast-Track Systems: Fast-track patients may require more resources than other patients who are more seriously ill, necessitating careful resource management. This leads to the mismanagement of available resources [15].
4. Care Coordination and Health Information Exchange (HIE): When transmitting data across various healthcare organizations utilizing various electronic health record systems, HIE systems may encounter interoperability problems. Maintaining patient trust and regulatory compliance depends on the confidentiality of patient data exchanged [16].
5. Patient Navigation Programs: Patient navigators may not always be available, and their efficiency may be influenced by the amount of training and funding devoted to their positions. Even with patient guidance programs in place, patients in underserved areas can still encounter access challenges.
6. Patient-Centered Medical Homes (PCMHs): Not all patients have access to PCMHs, and their availability can be limited in certain regions, potentially leading to disparities in access [17]. Ensuring that PCMHs have the necessary resources to provide comprehensive care is essential to their success.

How to efficiently monitor and limit the transmission of infectious diseases through the use of technology breakthroughs in data analytics, telemedicine, contact tracking, and other informatics solutions. The COVID-19 pandemic is a driving force behind innovation and cooperation in the health technology industry, highlighting the necessity of resilient and flexible systems to manage global public health emergencies.

The report highlights the continued prospects and challenges in health technology and informatics while also clarifying the current state of affairs as shown in Table 4.1 [18]. To ensure that future policies, practices, and technologies are more robust and responsive to emerging public health concerns, we must use the lessons acquired from the COVID-19 pandemic.

Table 4.1 Survey on previously implemented techniques.

Authors	Publication year	Methodology	Limitations
Jiancheng Ye [19]	2020	Artificial intelligence, telemedicine or telehealth, mobile health, big data, 5G, and the Internet of Things are just a few of the digital practices and emerging health technologies that have been applied in the field of healthcare and have become potent "weapons" in the fight against pandemics and a major aid in their prevention and management.	The integrated intelligent healthcare system for COVID-19 control has great potential but also some serious drawbacks. Care must be taken to manage technical complexity, data privacy issues, and potential escalation of health disparities. Financial and operational difficulties result from the system's high cost and the requirement for intensive healthcare professional training.

(Continued)

Table 4.1 Survey on previously implemented techniques. (*Continued*)

Authors	Publication year	Methodology	Limitations
Jennifer A Newberry, Corey B Bills, Elizabeth A Pirrotta, Michele Barry, Govindaraju Venkata Ramana Rao, Swaminatha V Mahadevan, Matthew C Strehlow [20]	2019	To better understand how emergency medical services (EMS) can treat thermal burns, which are a significant source of morbidity and mortality. The study found that most patients were transported to hospitals by EMS within two hours after the original calls, which involved individuals. The 30-day mortality rate remained high at 64.5% despite prompt transport, with women who had non-accidental burns dying at the highest rate (90.2%).	It is important to consider the limitations of this study, which includes the number of patients who were lost to follow-up, which is concerning, with 48.4% of them having non-accidental injuries. Since these incidents can occur more frequently when men return home late at night or early in the morning, a convenience sample of daytime EMS calls may undercount burns brought on by gender-based violence.

(*Continued*)

Table 4.1 Survey on previously implemented techniques. (*Continued*)

Authors	Publication year	Methodology	Limitations
Fang-Rong Chang, He-Lai Huang, David C. Schwebel, Alan H.S. Chan, Guo-Qing Hu [21]	2020	The study casts doubt on the validity of statistics on traffic injuries noting several crucial problems including inconsistent data sources, limited accessibility, unclear data collection, and delayed data release. This includes creating independent collision investigation teams, standardizing data collection, allowing open access to data, and technology to improve the accuracy of global traffic injury data.	The suggested solutions cover a wide range of issues, and putting them into practice may require significant organizational and financial resources, which could pose challenges for some countries. The report does not go into great detail about the particular resource and logistic-related difficulties. Implementing these in tackling the challenges outlined may vary across various countries and places based on local politics, infrastructure, and administration.

(*Continued*)

Table 4.1 Survey on previously implemented techniques. (*Continued*)

Authors	Publication year	Methodology	Limitations
Sabina De Rosis, Domenico Cerasuolo & Sabina Nuti [22]	2020	The PREMs Observatory makes the most of the advantages of conventional patient surveys while addressing several problems and restrictions associated with their use. The PREMs effort reported in this paper can enhance the usage of PREMs in the daily practice of healthcare managers, professionals, and workers overall, according to preliminary results and practitioners' input.	Despite exhibiting promising qualities, the PREMs Observatory presented in this paper has some noteworthy shortcomings. Its application is restricted to two particular Italian locations, which restricts its applicability in more general healthcare settings. According to reports, response rates have risen over time. This could lead to response bias, which could distort results in favor of dramatic experiences.

(*Continued*)

Table 4.1 Survey on previously implemented techniques. (*Continued*)

Authors	Publication year	Methodology	Limitations
Almathami HK, Win KT, Vlahu-Gjorgievska E [23]	2020	One of the services that significantly rely on ICTs to allow remote patients to contact medical experts is telemedicine. It employs electronic consultation through the HOHC (Home Online Health Consult) framework. This communication is called e-consultation.	Remote medical services have some drawbacks. Some patients prefer in-person consultations, and constraints like access to technology can be issues. Facilitators play a critical but sometimes resource-intensive role. The acceptance of Internet healthcare is also influenced by cultural considerations, technical dependability, and privacy issues.

(*Continued*)

Table 4.1 Survey on previously implemented techniques. (*Continued*)

Authors	Publication year	Methodology	Limitations
Manohara M. M. Pai, Raghavendra Ganiga, Radhika M. Pai & Rajesh Kumar Sinha [24]	2021	Electronic health records (EHRs) can be made safe, interoperable, and simple to access. The flow of health care to the people will improve with the adoption of an EHR framework. EHRs at all levels of the healthcare system allow for effective and ongoing patient care.	The proper monitoring of electronic health records is not discussed, lack of specific data and statistics, and no mention of ethical and privacy considerations, future implications sustainability, or long-term impact.

4.4 Methodology

Real-time data analysis is used to create an online platform that enables prompt access to medical care. This process contains several important phases and considerations. Here, the system's operation and approach are displayed in a structured way. This covers all of the specifics of the patient's therapy that will be taken into account when real-time information about schedules, resources, and medication availability is available [25]. It entails gathering real-time medical data regarding the resources that are accessible at a specific moment.

With the use of this method, a platform that gives a comprehensive list of hospitals with particular services to improve patient care may be developed, launched, and maintained methodically. To provide a useful and trustworthy healthcare resource, it emphasizes user-centred design, data quality, and continual improvement [26].

By dividing the source set into subsets according to Attribute Selection Measures, a tree can be "learned", by applying the top-down greedy approach; we are using ID3 Decision Tree for testing each characteristic at each tree node by going through the provided sets as shown in Figure 4.3. The root node is defined by the item that has maximum information

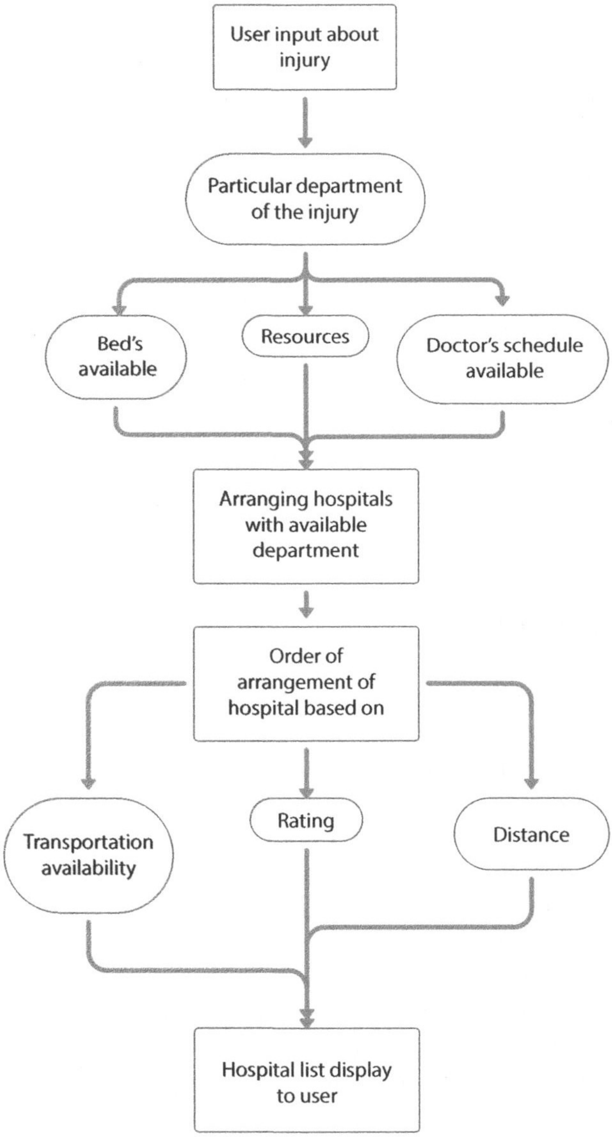

Figure 4.3 Decision tree working.

gain. The dataset's level of unpredictability or uncertainty is measured by entropy. When it comes to classifications, it measures the randomness by looking at how the dataset's class labels are distributed. For the ith node, the entropy of a subset of the original dataset with K number of classes is defined as follows:

$$H_i = -\Sigma^{n}{}_{k \in K}\, p(I,k)\log_2 p(i,k) \tag{4.1}$$

The class k is one out of K classes, and p(k) is the fraction of data points in dataset sample S that are in class k relative to all the data points in the dataset, and p(i, k) is not equal to zero [27].

Information gain quantifies the decrease in variance or entropy that happens when a dataset is divided according to a particular characteristic. A feature's value in predicting the target variable increases with its information gain.

$$Information\ Gain\,(H,A) = H - \Sigma\,(|H_V|/|H|)H_V \tag{4.2}$$

|H| is the dataset sample S's entropy; |A| is the particular attribute or class label; and |HV| is the number of instances in subset S that have attribute A's value v. The methodology used is shown in Figure 4.3 [28].

4.4.1 Dataset Collection

The process of collecting datasets is complex and calls for careful preparation, ethical concerns, and meticulous attention to detail. Researchers' research findings are more reliable and credible when they methodically collect datasets, from identifying objectives to guaranteeing data security and quality [29]. The impact and reproducibility of research can be improved by researchers by following the best practices described in this handbook. With the help of the dataset, we can identify all the resources needed to treat patients promptly.

4.4.2 Data Preprocessing

The content of data used in the real world is not always of high quality; it frequently contains noise, mistakes, and gaps. Data cleaning is the process of cleaning the data to ensure consistency and accuracy [29, 30]. Standardize data formats for integration.

4.4.3 Model Building

The algorithm performs the following actions to create a decision tree:

1. Choose the feature you want to use to divide the data into the categories you want.
2. Establish a node for that feature and add the subset of data to it.
3. Create a child node for each value of the feature. Next, for each child node, repeat steps 1 and 2 until the halting condition is satisfied.
4. When a stopping requirement is satisfied, give the node with the majority class of the subset of data at that node or label [19].
5. Do the technique described above for each child node until the tree is finished.

It involves collecting real-time healthcare data for available resources at a particular time.

The algorithm for the system's operation is shown in this diagram. The website will initially inquire about the user's injury. The department responsible for the patient's damage will then be chosen as in Figure 4.3. The hospitals that will house the department in question will be chosen, and it will be determined whether or not the department's doctors will be available [31]. The algorithm will then present a list of hospitals in order of distance and rating while taking into account the distance, beds available, essential medications, and facilities. Everything will function based on real-time data and hospital specifications.

4.4.4 Clustering Algorithm

Users can select from clusters of hospitals that meet their needs by using clustering techniques like k-means to group hospitals with similar traits or resource availability [32].

Step 1: To determine the number of hospitals, choose K.

Step 2: Pick K locations or centroids at random. It might not be the input dataset.

Step 3: Assign each data point to its nearest centroid, which will create the K hospitals that have been predetermined.

Step 4: Determine the variance and relocate each one to its centroid.

Step 5: Re-assign each data point to the new centroid by repeating the third step.

Step 6: Move to step 4 if there is a reassignment; otherwise, move to FINISH.
Step 7: The finished model.

Figures 4.4 and 4.5 show the site's view and characteristics. Figure 4.5 shows the website's initial page of the website with a straightforward user-friendly interface that is simple to use and understood by the user. The user will enter the injury in the input field. Some of the most often questioned departments will be listed below the input field for quick access to a certain department [33]. Following the search and selection procedure to determine the user's list of hospitals, Figure 4.6 shows the Model Virtualization Results. A sample display material that can be altered to suit the comfort of the user is shown in this image.

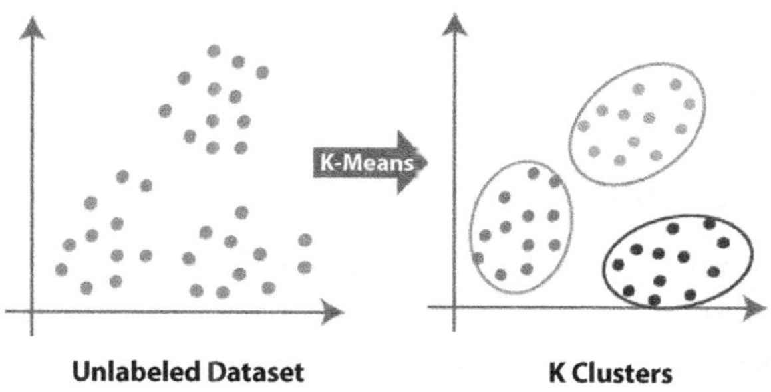

Figure 4.4 K-means algorithm.

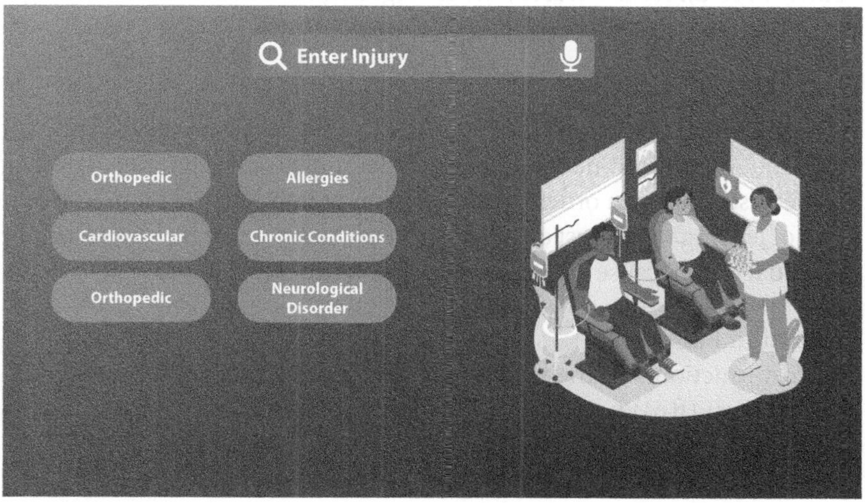

Figure 4.5 Conceptual framework.

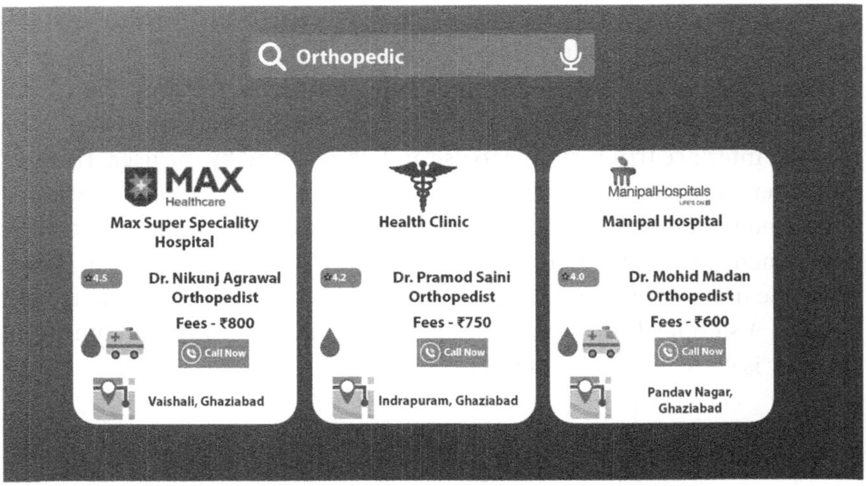

Figure 4.6 Model visualization results.

4.4.5 A* Algorithm

The A* algorithm is a flexible and extensively used technique for pathfinding problem resolution in a variety of fields, such as artificial intelligence, robotics, video games, and network routing [34]. It is a well-liked option for many applications due to its harmony between optimality and completeness. Its goal is to efficiently explore the fewest number of nodes while determining the shortest path between two points on a graph. By using heuristics to direct the search, the A* algorithm combines the advantages of Greedy Best-First Search and Dijkstra's algorithm.

Heuristic Function

Using a heuristic function (h(n)) to calculate the cost between the present node and the desired node is one of A*'s unique selling points. By using this heuristic, one can order the exploration of nodes based on their likelihood of leading to the best answer. The heuristic should never overestimate the actual cost because it is allowed as shown in Figure 4.7 [35].

Evaluation Function

The cost function and the heuristic function are combined in the evaluation function (f(n)) used by A*. The definition of the evaluation function is as follows:

$$f(n) = g(n) + h(n),$$

where the path cost from the start node to node is denoted by g(n), while the heuristic estimate of the cost from node n to the target is denoted by h(n).

Algorithm

Step 1 of the A* search algorithm is to add the initial node to the OPEN list.
Step 2: Determine whether or not the OPEN list is empty. If it is, return failure and end the process.
Step 3: From the OPEN list, choose the node with the lowest evaluation function value (g+h). If node n is the goal node, return success and end the process; if not, continue.
Step 4: Add node n to the closed list after expanding it and producing all of its offspring. Determine whether each successor, n', is already in the OPEN or CLOSED list for that successor. If not, compute the evaluation function for that successor and add it to the Open list.
Step 5: If not, node n' should be attached to the back pointer that represents the lowest g(n') value if it is already in the OPEN and CLOSED states.
Step 6: Go back to Step 2 now.

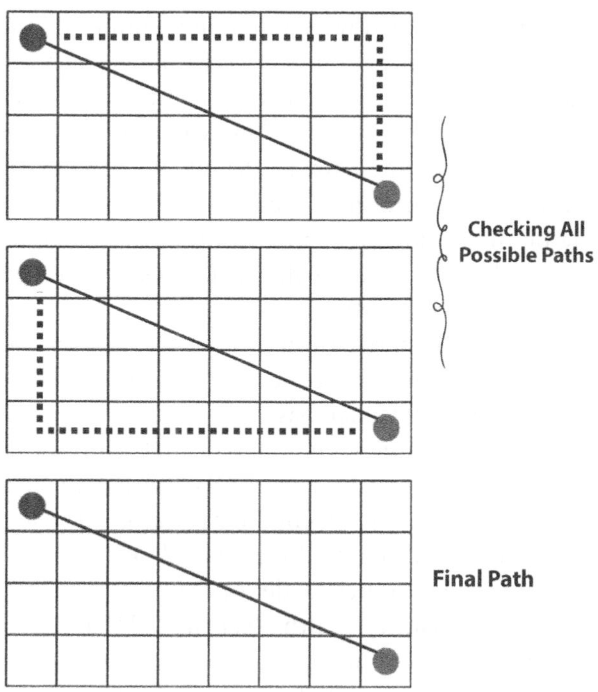

Figure 4.7 Finding the shortest path.

4.5 Hardware Component

To identify the person assisting in the early arrival to the hospital, the system comprises hardware, such as a smart card with a biometric authentication mechanism. User data and reward point totals are kept in a central database [36]. Data are transmitted through an RFID (Radio Frequency Identification) chip in communication with a reading device. These cards can be quite beneficial in healthcare settings for cutting down on patient treatment delays. The antennae and embedded microchips in these RFID cards allow for wireless data transmission and reception, thereby allowing for patient tracking and identification.

Below is a possible system operation:

1. **User Enrollment:** The user would enroll in the system by providing their personal information such as name, age, gender, phone number, and address [37]. They would also provide a biometric identifier such as a fingerprint, facial recognition, or iris scan. This information would be stored in a central database.
2. **Smart Card Issuance:** Once the user is enrolled, they will be issued a smart card with a unique identifier that links to their personal information in the central database.
3. **Card Verification:** When the user wants to use their card for help or redeem a reward, they would present their card to a card reader. The card reader would prompt the user to authenticate themselves using their biometric identifier. If the biometric identifier matches the user's record in the database, the card reader will grant access to the service or reward redemption [38].
4. **Reward Point Accumulation:** Whenever the user uses their card to access a service, reward points are added to their account in the central database.
5. **Reward Redemption:** Users can redeem their reward points for various rewards such as discounts, free health check-ups, or exclusive offers. To redeem their rewards, the user would present their card to a card reader and authenticate themselves using their biometric identifier [39].
6. **Access to Electronic Health Records (EHR):** By combining RFID technology with electronic health records, medical professionals may safely and effectively access patient

data. RFID cards can be used as authentication methods to guarantee that patient data are only accessed by authorized healthcare providers [40].

7. **Management of Visitors:** Healthcare facilities can control guest access by using RFID cards. Limiting access to certain locations to just authorized individuals improves security.
8. **Management of Medication:** Pharmaceutical administration can be managed and tracked with the use of RFID cards connected to pharmaceutical delivery systems. By guaranteeing that patients receive the appropriate drug at the appropriate time, this can lower the likelihood of medication errors.
9. **Real-Time Data Access:** Give medical practitioners access to real-time data via a wireless handheld PDA, such as patient contact histories, online laboratory data, and radiology reports [41].
10. **Time-Saving:** Identify empty beds more than 20 minutes in advance 67% of the time. Determine a time reduction of over 50% in the hospital staff members' everyday tasks.

Rapid patient identification, asset tracking, prescription administration verification, and workflow optimization are all made possible by RFID cards, which are useful tools in healthcare settings. RFID technology as shown in Figure 4.8 assists healthcare professionals in providing prompt and high-quality care to patients, eventually minimizing treatment delays and increasing patient outcomes [42]. These benefits come from reducing administrative work, improving patient safety, and boosting healthcare process efficiency. Overall, this system would provide a secure and convenient way for users to verify their identity and accumulate reward points

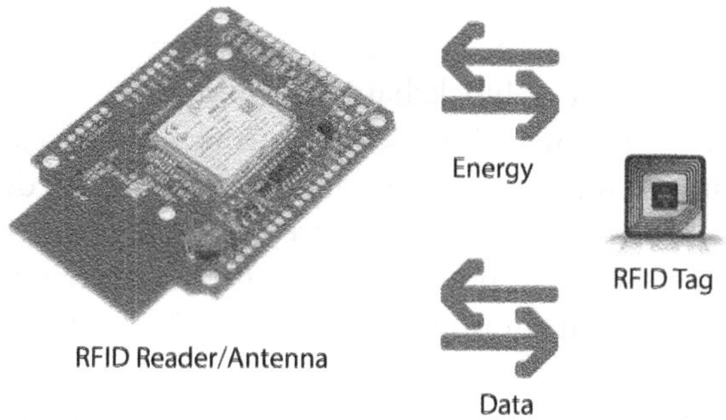

Figure 4.8 RFID technology.

while helping others. The use of biometric authentication would reduce the risk of fraud or unauthorized use of the card, while the central database would allow for easy management of user information and reward point balances [43].

4.5.1 Blockchain in Health Care

The application of blockchain technology has been expanding quickly in recent years, permeating every facet of information and communications technology (ICT). A blockchain is a distributed ledger that distributes data among a network of peers. It was unveiled alongside Bitcoin and resolved the long-standing double-spend issue. The significant increase in the value of cryptocurrencies and the substantial venture capital investments made in blockchain start-ups have been the main drivers of interest in and advancement of this technology [44]. Using the known hash, which is produced by a cryptographic one-way hash function (such as SHA256), every block in the blockchain is connected.

Additionally, it guarantees the block's compactness, immutability, and anonymity. IBM reports that seventy percent of leaders in the healthcare industry believe that the biggest effects of blockchain in the health domain would be in the areas of regulatory compliance, clinical trial management, and the provision of a decentralized framework for the exchange of electronic health data (EHRs). The management of data, which stands to gain from the ability to link disparate systems and improve the precision of EHRs, should be the primary focus of efforts to change healthcare. Prescription medicine management, supply chain management, risk assessment for pregnancy, data sharing, access control, and maintaining an audit trail of medical procedures can all be facilitated by blockchain technology.

Key Features

Decentralization, which prevents content dictation by a central authority, is a fundamental aspect of blockchain technology. Blockchain entries are governed by peer agreement using consensus techniques such as Proof of Work. Maintaining consistency is crucial, as entries in the distributed ledger that are kept across several nodes are essentially unchangeable once they are approved. Another noteworthy feature is anonymity, also known as pseudonymity, which improves privacy and draws people to different blockchains.

The following are some ways in which blockchain can be helpful in the healthcare sector:

Integrity and Security of Data: Immutable Ledger, once data are recorded, they cannot be changed or removed because of the blockchain's decentralized and impenetrable structure. For clinical and administrative purposes, this feature improves the integrity of healthcare data, increasing its dependability.

Smart Contracts: Some blockchain systems, like Ethereum, make it easier to put smart contracts into action. These are source code-encoded contracts that allow pre-agreed terms to be automatically carried out. In contrast to traditional contracts, smart contracts function independently of external parties. A blockchain transaction is required to activate a smart contract's functioning, and the healthcare industry may find this feature appealing.

Proof of Work: One well-known blockchain consensus algorithm, Proof of Work (PoW), is most famously employed in Bitcoin. To find a hash that is less than a predetermined value, miners compete to solve challenging riddles. Block transactions are validated by the first miner to succeed, who is rewarded. However, PoW's main flaw is that it uses a lot of energy, as shown by the fact that Bitcoin uses as much electricity as a small nation.

Proof of Stake: The selection of nodes in Proof of Stake (PoS) is based on the stake, which stands for the balance of Bitcoin. Richer nodes may benefit from this, leading to hybrid PoS versions that use randomization. Recognizing the need for a more equitable and energy-efficient consensus mechanism, Ethereum, the second-largest cryptocurrency, intends to switch from proof of work (PoW) to proof of stake (PoS).

Hyperledger Fabric: To make this platform more secure and efficient, we recommend connecting Hyperledger Fabric Private Blockchain with hardware components. This platform can be enhanced with Hyperledger Fabric to improve its security and privacy characteristics. Sensitive patient data can be stored safely and transparently via a private blockchain, eliminating the possibility of unauthorized access. The blockchain can be used to decentralize the storage of medical records, insurance information, and other patient-related data, making it available only to authorized parties [32]. One of Hyperledger's primary advantages is its consensus mechanism, which enables network participants to agree on the state of the ledger without relying on a centralized authority. This consensus method protects the network's integrity and security.

Hyperledger can be used in the platform to securely store and distribute patient data across a network of hospitals and healthcare providers. Each hospital can have its network node that keeps a copy of the ledger and participates in the consensus mechanism for transaction validation. In addition, Hyperledger allows you to construct distinct channels for specialized use cases, such as sharing health data or managing supply chain activities. Peer-to-peer communication among network members ensures that sensitive data are only shared with authorized parties and aids in the prevention of data breaches. Fabric employs a modular architecture that enables plug-and-play components, making it very customizable and adaptable. Overall, the usage of Hyperledger in the platform brings the potential for various benefits, including greater data security, improved transparency and accountability, and more efficient data sharing among healthcare providers.

Practical byzantine fault tolerance (PBFT) is a high-throughput, low-latency consensus method utilized by Hyperledger Fabric. Despite having the appropriate resources, the majority of deaths in our nation following accidents or certain emergencies are caused by delays in treating the underlying cause. The amount of deaths brought on by accidents can be decreased in India under the current system. However, the treatment is delayed because the patient does not know enough about a specific facility. The death-to-injury ratio is impacted by this.

4.6 Conclusion

This online platform provides a list of those hospitals that consist of the mentioned requirements and shows the nearest hospital with all facilities. The main objective of our approach is to accurately classify hospitals using a high-quality dataset and previous patient reviews for the ultimate goal of providing timely and effective treatment of patients. This comprehensive strategy has the potential to considerably minimize treatment delays and raise the standard of care by streamlining patient care procedures, assuring precise identification, optimizing resource allocation, and strengthening data security. The proposed methodology, which combines RFID technology, Hyperledger, and real-time data processing, offers a promising direction for healthcare. A key component of providing healthcare is timely care; many factors might affect how quickly this happens. A multifaceted strategy involving healthcare professionals, policymakers, administrators, and the community is needed to address these problems. Healthcare systems can work to provide fast and efficient care to all patients, ultimately improving healthcare outcomes and patient satisfaction.

4.7 Future Work

Real-time data analysis online systems for prompt access to medical care are still under development. Future innovations might incorporate machine learning and artificial intelligence for predictive analytics, as well as improved connectivity with wearable medical equipment to track patients' health in real time. By fostering collaboration between academia, business, and healthcare organizations, the creation of research and innovation centers for healthcare technology can promote ongoing improvements in online healthcare platforms. Real-time data analysis, RFID, and Hyperledger integration will result in the development of a complete healthcare management ecosystem. Insights into patient care can be gained via real-time data analysis, RFID ensures effective asset and patient tracking, and Hyperledger upholds secure, tamper-proof records. Also, the smooth exchange of patient data across various healthcare providers would reduce duplication and enhance care coordination if interoperability between healthcare systems, electronic health records (EHRs), and online platforms is improved. Future platforms must include strong security mechanisms, such as blockchain technology and decentralized patient data management, to maintain the confidentiality and integrity of patient information in light of growing concerns about data breaches and privacy. Advances in telemedicine platforms will enable more immersive and interactive patient–doctor interactions through the use of virtual reality (VR) and augmented reality (AR). As a result, more people will have access to specialized treatment, and telemedicine as a whole will improve.

References

1. Knowlton, L.M. *et al.*, A geospatial evaluation of timely access to surgical care in seven countries. *Bull. World Health Organ.*, 6, 437, 2017.
2. Liu, Y. *et al.*, A novel cloud-based framework for the elderly healthcare services using digital twin. *IEEE Access*, 7, 49088–49101, 2019.
3. Kansal, M., Singh, P., Shukla, S., Srivastava, S., A Comparative Study of Machine Learning Models for House Price Prediction and Analysis in Smart Cities, in: *Communications in Computer and Information Science*, Electronic Governance with Emerging Technologies, S. Ortiz-Rodríguez, P. Tiwari, U. Usoro, R. Palma (Eds.), vol. 1888, pp. 168–184, Cham: Springer Nature Switzerland, 2023, doi: 10.1007/978-3-031-43940-7_14.

4. Kakria, P., Tripathi, N.K., Kitipawang, P., A real-time health monitoring system for remote cardiac patients using smartphone and wearable sensors. *Int. J. Telemed. Appl.*, 2015, 8–8, 2015.
5. Nastic, S. *et al.*, A serverless real-time data analytics platform for edge computing. *IEEE Internet Comput.*, 21, 4, 64–71, 2017.
6. Yang, Z., Zhou, Q., Lei, L., Zheng, K., Xiang, W., An IoT-cloud Based Wearable ECG Monitoring System for Smart Healthcare. *J. Med. Syst.*, 40, 12, 286, Dec. 2016, doi: 10.1007/s10916-016-0644-9.
7. Bokolo, A.J., Application of telemedicine and eHealth technology for clinical services in response to COVID19 pandemic. *Health Technol.*, 11, 2, 359–366, Mar. 2021, doi: 10.1007/s12553-020-00516-4.
8. Aziz, H.A. and Guled, A., Cloud computing and healthcare services, 2016, Accessed: Oct. 20, 2023, [Online], Available: http://qspace.qu.edu.qa/handle/10576/4714.
9. Zhao, X., Fan, J., Basnyat, I., Hu, B., Online health information seeking using "# COVID-19 patient seeking help" on Weibo in Wuhan, China: descriptive study. *J. Med. Internet Res.*, 22, 10, e22910, 2020.
10. Christoffels, A. *et al.*, A pan-African pathogen genomics data sharing platform to support disease outbreaks. *Nat. Med.*, 29, 5, 1052–1055, 2023.
11. Chang, A. *et al.*, A quantitative model to ensure capacity sufficient for timely access to care in a remote patient monitoring program. *Endocrino. Diabet. Metabol.*, 6, 5, e435, Sep. 2023, doi: 10.1002/edm2.435.
12. Javaid, M., Haleem, A., Singh, R.P., ChatGPT for healthcare services: An emerging stage for an innovative perspective. *BenchCouncil Trans. Benchmarks Stand. Eval.*, 3, 1, 100105, 2023.
13. Zhang, X., Design and Development of Health Data Platform for Home-Based Elderly Care Based on AAL, in: *Lecture Notes on Data Engineering and Communications Technologies*, Cyber Security Intelligence and Analytics, vol. 173, Z. Xu, S. Alrabaee, O. Loyola-González, N.D.W., N.H. Ab Rahman (Eds.), pp. 21–29, Cham: Springer Nature Switzerland, 2023, doi: 10.1007/978-3-031-31775-0_3.
14. Zhang, Y., Shi, X., Abdul-Hamid, Z., Li, D., Zhang, X., Shen, Z., Factors influencing crowdsourcing riders' satisfaction based on online comments on real-time logistics platform. *Transp. Lett.*, 15, 5, 363–374, May 2023, doi: 10.1080/19427867.2022.2052643.
15. Nabukenya, J., Egwar, A.A., Drumright, L., Semwanga, A.R., Kasasa, S., Feasibility and utility of Point-of-Care electronic clinical data capture in Uganda's healthcare system: a qualitative study. *J. Am. Med. Inf. Assoc.*, 30, 5, 932–942, 2023.
16. Smail, E.J. *et al.*, Feasibility of a Smartwatch Platform to Assess Ecological Mobility: Real-Time Online Assessment and Mobility Monitor. *J. Gerontol.: Ser. A*, 78, 5, 821–830, 2023.
17. Saha, A. *et al.*, Flexible and innovative connectivity solution to support national decentralized infectious diseases point-of-care testing programs in

primary health services: Descriptive evaluation study. *J. Med. Internet Res.*, 25, e46701, 2023.

18. Jauneikaite, E. *et al.*, Genomics for antimicrobial resistance surveillance to support infection prevention and control in health-care facilities. *Lancet Microbe*, 4, 12, e1040–e1046, 2023. Accessed: Dec. 17, 2023, [Online], Available: https://www.thelancet.com/journals/lanmic/article/PIIS2666-5247(23)00282-3/fulltext.
19. Ye, J., The Role of Health Technology and Informatics in a Global Public Health Emergency: Practices and Implications From the COVID-19 Pandemic. *JMIR Med. Inf.*, 8, 7, e19866, Jul. 2020, doi: 10.2196/19866.
20. Newberry, J.A. *et al.*, Timely access to care for patients with critical burns in India: a prehospital prospective observational study. *Emerg. Med. J.*, 36, 3, 176–182, Mar. 2019, doi: 10.1136/emermed-2018-207900.
21. Chang, F.-R., Huang, H.-L., Schwebel, D.C., Chan, A.H.S., Hu, G.-Q., Global road traffic injury statistics: Challenges, mechanisms and solutions. *Chin. J. Traumatol.*, 23, 4, 216–218, Aug. 2020, doi: 10.1016/j.cjtee.2020.06.001.
22. De Rosis, S., Cerasuolo, D., Nuti, S., Using patient-reported measures to drive change in healthcare: the experience of the digital, continuous and systematic PREMs observatory in Italy. *BMC Health Serv. Res.*, 20, 1, 315, Apr. 2020, doi: 10.1186/s12913-020-05099-4.
23. Almathami, H.K.Y., Win, K.T., Vlahu-Gjorgievska, E., Barriers and Facilitators That Influence Telemedicine-Based, Real-Time, Online Consultation at Patients' Homes: Systematic Literature Review. *J. Med. Internet Res.*, 22, 2, e16407, Feb. 2020, doi: 10.2196/16407.
24. Pai, M.M.M., Ganiga, R., Pai, R.M., Sinha, R.K., Standard electronic health record (EHR) framework for Indian healthcare system. *Health Serv. Outcomes Res. Method*, 21, 3, 339–362, Sep. 2021, doi: 10.1007/s10742-020-00238-0.
25. Vishwakarma, P.K. and Singh, R., IoT-Assisted ECG and Multi Sensor Data Monitoring System for Health Care Applications, Accessed: Dec. 17, 2023, [Online], Available: https://kalaharijournals.com/resources/Special_Issue_%2C%20December_109.pdf.
26. Akhlaghi, H. *et al.*, Machine learning in clinical practice: Evaluation of an artificial intelligence tool after implementation. *Emerg. Med. Australasia*, 1742–6723.14325, Sep. 2023, doi: 10.1111/1742-6723.14325.
27. Alsayaydeh, J.A.J., bin Yusof, M.F., Halim, M.Z.B.A., Zainudin, M.N.S., Herawan, S.G., Patient Health Monitoring System Development using ESP8266 and Arduino with IoT Platform. *Int. J. Adv. Comput. Sci. Appl.*, 14, 4, 617–624, 2023, Accessed: Dec. 17, 2023, [Online], Available: https://search.proquest.com/openview/d7fd995deffc169fbe09a34f707b536f/1?pq-origsite=gscholar&cbl=5444811.
28. Singh, P., Kansal, M., Singh, M.K., Kumar, S., Dwivedi, A., Crop Disease Prediction Using Deep Learning Algorithms, in: *Convergence of Cloud Computing, AI, and Agricultural Science*, pp. 290–305, IGI Global, 2023, doi: 10.4018/979-8-3693-0200-2.ch015.

29. Albahri, A.S., Zaidan, A.A., Albahri, O.S., Zaidan, B.B., Alsalem, M.A., Real-Time Fault-Tolerant mHealth System: Comprehensive Review of Healthcare Services, Opens Issues, Challenges and Methodological Aspects. *J. Med. Syst.*, 42, 8, 137, Aug. 2018, doi: 10.1007/s10916-018-0983-9.
30. Shah, T. *et al.*, Remote health care cyber-physical system: quality of service (QoS) challenges and opportunities. *IET Cyber-Phys. Syst.*, 1, 1, 40–48, Dec. 2016, doi: 10.1049/iet-cps.2016.0023.
31. Tan, L. *et al.*, Toward real-time and efficient cardiovascular monitoring for COVID-19 patients by 5G-enabled wearable medical devices: a deep learning approach. *Neural Comput. Applic.*, 35, 19, 13921–13934, Jul. 2023, doi: 10.1007/s00521-021-06219-9.
32. Shameer, K., Badgeley, M.A., Miotto, R., Glicksberg, B.S., Dudley, J.T., Translational bioinformatics in the era of real-time biomedical, health care and wellness data streams. *Briefings Bioinf.*, 18, 1, 105–124, 2017.
33. Xu, B., Da Xu, L., Cai, H., Xie, C., Hu, J., Bu, F., Ubiquitous data accessing method in IoT-based information system for emergency medical services. *IEEE Trans. Ind. Inf.*, 10, 2, 1578–1586, 2014.
34. De Rosis, S., Cerasuolo, D., Nuti, S., Using patient-reported measures to drive change in healthcare: the experience of the digital, continuous and systematic PREMs observatory in Italy. *BMC Health Serv. Res.*, 20, 1, 315, Dec. 2020, doi: 10.1186/s12913-020-05099-4.
35. Ullah, M. *et al.*, Smart technologies used as smart tools in the management of cardiovascular disease and their future perspective. *Curr. Probl. Cardiol*, 48, 11, 101922, 2023.
36. Singh, R.K., Agrawal, S., Sahu, A., Kazancoglu, Y., Strategic issues of big data analytics applications for managing health-care sector: a systematic literature review and future research agenda. *TQM J.*, 35, 1, 262–291, 2023.
37. Aminizadeh, S. *et al.*, The applications of machine learning techniques in medical data processing based on distributed computing and the Internet of Things. *Comput. Methods Programs Biomed.*, 241, 107745, 2023.
38. Moghadas, M., Fekete, A., Rajabifard, A., Kötter, T., The wisdom of crowds for improved disaster resilience: a near-real-time analysis of crowdsourced social media data on the 2021 flood in Germany. *GeoJournal*, 88, 4, 4215–4241, Mar. 2023, doi: 10.1007/s10708-023-10858-x.
39. Ghosh, P.K., Chakraborty, A., Hasan, M., Rashid, K., Siddique, A.H., Blockchain Application in Healthcare Systems: A Review. *Systems*, 11, 1, 1–38, Jan. 2023, Art. no. 1, doi: 10.3390/systems11010038.
40. Comunale, M.J., Dermody, T.S., Peters, M., Rudolph, J.A., Sevco, M., Young, S., Consumer-centric approach to enhance access to pediatric specialty care. *Am. J. Manag. Care*, 28, 6, e228–e231, Jun. 2022, doi: 10.37765/ajmc.2022.89161.
41. Savargaonkar, D. *et al.*, Delayed haemolysis after treatment with intravenous artesunate in patients with severe malaria in India. *Malar. J.*, 19, 39, Jan. 2020, doi: 10.1186/s12936-020-3120-4.

42. Schlicher, J., Metsker, M.T., Shah, H., Demirkan, H., From NASA to healthcare: real-time data analytics (mission control) is reshaping healthcare services. *Perspect. Health Inf. Manage.*, 18, 4, 1g, 2021.
43. Kruk, M.E., Gage, A.D., Joseph, N.T., Danaei, G., García-Saisó, S., Salomon, J.A., Mortality due to low-quality health systems in the universal health coverage era: a systematic analysis of amenable deaths in 137 countries. *Lancet*, 392, 10160, 2203–2212, Nov. 2018, doi: 10.1016/S0140-6736(18)31668-4.
44. Jat, T.R., Deo, P.R., Goicolea, I., Hurtig, A.-K., San Sebastian, M., Socio-cultural and service delivery dimensions of maternal mortality in rural central India: a qualitative exploration using a human rights lens. *Glob. Health Action*, 8, 24976, 2015, doi: 10.3402/gha.v8.24976.

5

A Comprehensive Review of Cardiac Image Analysis for Precise Heart Disease Diagnosis Using Deep Learning Techniques

Anuj Gupta[1*], Vikas Kumar[2] and Aryan Nakhale[3]

[1]Department of Electronics and Communication, Chandigarh University, Mohali, India
[2]ERP Functional Riviera Home Furnishing, Panipat, India
[3]Department of Mechatronics, Chandigarh University, Mohali, India

Abstract

Coronary illness is a leading cause of mortality worldwide. Prompt discovery and precise forecasts of coronary disease can help in forestalling and dealing with sickness. Lately, profound learning strategies, for example, convolutional neural networks (CNNs), have shown promising outcomes in different clinical imaging tasks, including coronary illness expectation. This review proposes a CNN-based approach for coronary illness expectation utilizing cardiovascular pictures. The proposed model comprises numerous convolutional layers, pooling, and completely associated layers. The model is prepared on an enormous dataset of cardiovascular pictures and related marks for coronary illness presenceor nonattendance. The prepared model is assessed on a different test dataset to evaluate its exactness, responsiveness, explicitness, and other execution measurements. Our outcomes show that the proposed CNN-based approach accomplishes high exactness and outflanks customary machine learning strategies for coronary illness expectation. The proposed model can be utilized as a device to help doctors in the early determination and treatment of coronary illness.

***Keywords*:** CNN, heart disease, deep learning, ECG, ReLU, CAD, MRI

**Corresponding author*: annu11gupta@gmail.com

Bharat Bhushan, Akib Khanday, Khursheed Aurangzeb, Sudhir Kumar Sharma and Parma Nand (eds.)
Wellness Management Powered by AI Technologies, (133–156) © 2025 Scrivener Publishing LLC

5.1 Introduction and Major Contribution

Coronary artery disease (CAD) is a primary cause of death around the world, representing approximately 15 million passings each year. Early detection and exact prediction of CAD can help with the prevention and treatment of the disease. Clinical imaging strategies, for example, echocardiography, Magnetic Resonance Imaging (MRI), Computed Tomography (CT) sweeps, and X-rays, have been broadly utilized to find and assess CAD. Doctors' manual translation of these pictures is useful but is tedious and subject to spectator changeability. Lately, profound learning procedures, for example, convolutional neural networks (CNNs), have shown promising outcomes in different clinical imaging undertakings, including the prediction of CAD. CNNs are a kind of neural organization that can consequently gain multilevel highlights from the given information and have been shown to beat conventional AI calculations in many tasks.

This paper proposes a CNN-based approach for predicting CAD utilizing cardiovascular data. The proposed model comprises various convolutional layers, pooling, and wholly connected layers. The model is prepared on a huge dataset of heart pictures and related marks for the presence or nonattendance of CAD. Using various experimental datasets, the trained model is examined for its accuracy, responsiveness, explicitness, and other execution metrics. We utilize the ECG Heartbeat Categorization Dataset for our experiments, an openly accessible dataset containing ECG accounts of various heartbeat classifications. Our methodology aims to use the force of profound input data and figuring out how to gain significant elements from the cardio vascular pictures and consequently make exact predictions of CAD presence or nonattendance.

The prevention and management of cardiovascular disease are of utmost importance, as it is a major cause of mortality worldwide, and timely detection and precise prediction play a critical role. Clinical imaging tasks like the prediction of coronary artery disease (CAD) have demonstrated the promise of deep learning techniques like convolutional neural networks (CNNs). CNN is the foundation of the suggested technique for predicting coronary artery disease (CAD) from cardiovascular images. CNN is composed of multiple convolutional layers, down-sampling, and dense layers. The model learns by using a vast dataset and is assessed based on its correctness, recall, and true negative rate. The proposed methodology utilizes the power of deep learning to extract features from cardiovascular images and predict CAD presence or absence. The method has the potential to be used for early CAD diagnosis and treatment, thereby improving patient outcomes.

The rest of the paper is organized as follows: Section 5.2 provides a summary of pertinent research on deep learning-based methods for predicting coronary artery disease (CAD) using cardiac images. Section 5.3 outlines the proposed CNN-based approach, detailing the design framework encompassing the dataset, evaluation metrics, and implementation specifics. Section 5.4 elaborates on the machine learning methods employed in the study. The mathematical model underpinning the system's functioning is presented in Section 5.5. Section 5.6 discusses the process of data preparation, outlining the steps taken to curate and preprocess the dataset for analysis. Section 5.7 covers the model training and evaluation, highlighting the use of the ECG Heartbeat Categorization Dataset, training with the Adam optimizer, and evaluation using key metrics such as AUC-ROC, F1-score, recall, and accuracy. The findings of the study are presented in Section 5.8, followed by a discussion on future research directions and concluding remarks in Section 5.9.

5.2 Literature Review

Recently, promising results have been revealed by DL-based techniques in a range of medical imaging tasks, such as the use of cardiac images to predict the presence of CAD. Several studies have proposed CNN-based approaches for CAD prediction using several groups of cardiac images, such as echocardiography, MRI, CT scans, and X-rays.

Jahmunah *et al.'s* automation process [1] uses convolutional neural network (CNN) and Gabor CNN models to classify ECG signals into four categories: normal, cardiomyopathy, CAD, and congestive cardiac arrest (CA). The Gabor CNN model achieved a high classification accuracy of more than 98.5% with less computational cost than CNN model. This method might be able to assist practitioners in screening for CVDs using ECG signals. The model consisted of multiple convolutional layers and attained a 98.5% detection accuracy for significant stenosis.

Essa *et al.* [2] suggested a deep learning methodology to classify ECG readings and detect different forms of arrhythmias. The system utilizes two models: a CNN-LSTM model for extracting the features and a traditional LSTM approach. These techniques are combined together after being developed with a tagging model. The MIT-BIH arrhythmia database outperforms existing methods. This system has the potential to improve automatic arrhythmia detection and classification in managing and treating cardiovascular diseases.

Multi-Scale Wavelet (MSW) CNN is a DL-based technique proposed by Bouny *et al.* [3] for ECG beats classification. The recommended method combines the Stationary Wavelet Transform with the one-dimensional CNN to simultaneously identify important patterns from the ECG waveform and its spectral threads. The derived characteristics are then combined using a concatenation approach. The model achieves diagnostic accuracy on the MIT-BIH Arrhythmia record, outperforming existing ECG taxonomy algorithms.

Essa *et al.* [4] suggested a hybrid model that employs a deep learning approach for electrocardiogram (ECG) data categorization. To categorize heartbeats into distinct arrhythmia kinds, two distinct deep learning tagging algorithms are used. The first model (CNN-LSTM) captures local characteristics and temporal dynamics in ECG data by combining a CNN with an LSTM network. The RRHOS-Long Short-Term Memory Networks method employs LSTM in conjunction with a few traditional characteristics, like HOS and RR pauses, to accurately identify cardiac irregularity classes. By training the models on a variety of sub-sampling populations, a novel strategy consisting both CNN-RRHOS-LSTM algorithms was developed to sort the issue of high imbalance distribution of arrhythmia in electrocardiogram data.

Rafi *et al.* [5] recommended a hybrid DL methodology for classifying ECG signals. The approach uses both convolutional and recurrent neural networks to classify the fivecardiac rhythms. The method is estimated using the MIT-BIH Diagnostics database, which yields an average classification correctness. Previous research in this area is also discussed, indicating the growing interest in using ECG signals for identifying cardiovascular abnormalities.

These research investigations show how DL algorithms [6] are opted to automatically encounter and predict coronary artery disease (CAD) from cardiac imaging. However, most of these studies have focused on specific types of cardiac images and have not compared their results with traditional machine learning algorithms or clinical experts. Therefore, there is a need for more comprehensive studies that compare the performance of deep learning-based approaches [7] with traditional machine learning algorithms and clinical expertsusing different types of cardiac images.

In an effort to address some of these shortcomings, this study suggests a convolutional neural network technique to predict the presence or absence of CAD using a sizable dataset of electrocardiogram recordings. Our method also attempts to compare the suggested model's performance with conventional machine learning techniques by computing its performance using various performance measurement standards.

5.3 Machine Learning Methods

Deep learning techniques are employed in the suggested CNN-based method for cardiac image analysis, and these techniques have demonstrated encouraging outcomes in clinical imaging tasks. Healthcare has made extensive use of not only CNNs but also other ML techniques like Naïve Bayes (NB), Neural Networks (NNs), K-Nearest Neighbors (KNN), and Support Vector Machines (SVMs).

Naïve Bayes (NB)
It is a stochastic approach that is predicated on the independence of the characteristics and the Bayes principle. To calculate the NB, use Equation 5.1.

$$P(v|x) = {}^{P(x|v) * P(v)}\!\big/_{P(x)} \tag{5.1}$$

In this equation, "v" represents the class variable, "x" denotes the feature vector, $P(v|x)$ signifies the posterior probability of "v" given "x", $P(v|x)$ indicates the probability of "x" given "v", P(v) denotes the prior probability of "v", and P(x) represents the marginal probability of "x".

Support Vector Machine (SVM)
It searches for a hyperplane that splits the data into different groups. To compute the SVM, use Equation 5.2.

$$Y(a) = W^T(a) + b \tag{5.2}$$

where Y(a) represents the predicted class label, weight vector denoted by "W", "a" is the input vector, and "b" shows the bias term.

K-Nearest Neighbors (KNN)
A non-parametric technique organizes a data point based on its k nearest neighbors' majority class. The KNN is computed using Equation 5.3.

$$Y(x) = mode\{(Y(i) \mid i \in N\_k(x))\} \tag{5.3}$$

where Y(x) is the predicted class label, the "mode" is the most frequent class label, "N_k(x)" is the pool of "k" nearest neighbors of "x", and Y(*i*) is the class label of the ith neighbor.

Neural Network (NN)

It is a class of models inspired by biological neurons and consists of layers of interconnected nodes. The NN is computed using Equation 5.4.

$$Y = g(W^T(a) + b) \tag{5.4}$$

where "Y" stands for the output of the node, "g" for the activation function, weight vector denoted by "W", "a" is the input vector, and "b" shows the bias term.

This proposed CNN-based method extracts hierarchical features from the cardiovascular images by utilizing down-sampling, multiple convolutional layers, and dense layers. The trained model's accuracy, sensitivity, specificity, and other performance metrics are assessed using a different test dataset. The method may prove to be a useful aid for physicians in the early detection and management of coronary artery disease.

5.4 Proposed System

5.4.1 Dataset

A large dataset of cardiovascular images and associated labels for the presence or absence of coronary disease will be necessary for the suggested CNN-based model to be trained. The ECG Heartbeat Sorting Dataset is a compilation of cardiac waveforms from twowell-known heartbeat classified datasets: the Arrhythmia Database provided by MIT-BIH and the PTB Clinical electrocardiogram Dataset. The dataset comprises cardiac (ECG) signals of heartbeats that have been preprocessed and segmented for both normal instances and cases afflicted by various arrhythmias and myocardial infarctions. This set of data has been used to investigate the potential of transfer learning and is intended for use in training deep neural network architectures for heartbeat grouping.

The PTB Diagnostic Electrocardiogram Data and the MIT-BIH Arrhythmia Database are the two collections that make up the dataset. Included in the MIT-BIH Arrhythmia Dataset are 109,446 samples representing five different heartbeat categories: "N", "S", "V", "F", and "Q". There are 14,552 samples with two categories of heartbeats in the PTB Diagnostic ECG Database. Both collections use 125 Hz sampling frequency. All samples are collected, down-sampled, and, if necessary, expanded to a static dimension of 188 using zeros. The quantity of samples and categories, sampling frequency, and data source are some of the features and attributes of the dataset. There are five unique sorts of pulses in the MIT-BIH Arrhythmia Dataset: typical, supraventricular ectopic pulse, ventricular ectopic pulse, a blend of ventricular and ordinary pulse, and obscure pulses.

The PTB Diagnostic ECG Database contains two categories of heartbeats, including healthy cases and cases affected by myocardial infarction. All samples are preprocessed and fragmented, and each fragment corresponds to a heartbeat. The dataset is suitable for training DNN models for pulse classification and can aid in the development of automated ECG-based [8] heartbeat classification systems.

5.4.2 Preprocessing

Before feeding the dataset into the model, preprocessing methods like data augmentation and normalization can be used on it. Multiple convolutional layers, down-sampling layers, and dense layers will make up the suggested CNN-based model. A SoftMax layer will track these layers for classification. In order to minimize the cost function, the model is going to be coached with gradient descent along with back propagation. The trained model will be assessed using an alternative test dataset in order to measure its accuracy, sensitivity, specificity, and other performance metrics. The suggested CNN-based method may help medical professionals identify and treat coronary heart disease early on.

5.4.3 Network Architecture

The organization architecture of the proposed CNN-based method for cardiac picture analysis consists of multiple convolutional layers, pooling layers, and fully connected layers. While the convolutional layers are made to extract highlights from the information images, the pooling layers are used to lower the spatial dimensionality of the learned elements [9]. At last, the wholly connected layers are responsible for order in light of the intellectual aspects.

The convolutional layers are accountable for detecting highlights in the information images [10]. These layers contain various channels that convolve over the information picture to extract spatial highlights. Each channel detects an alternate element in the picture. In the proposed CNN model, there are a few convolutional layers, and each layer has an alternate number of channels. The first convolutional layer has fewer channels than the resulting layers to extract basic highlights, while the ensuing layers have more channels to extract more complex elements. After the convolutional layers, thereare pooling layers that assist in decreasing the spatial dimensionality of the learned elements. These layers total the elements advanced by the convolutional layers and diminish the dimension of the component maps. In the suggested model, max pooling is utilized, which selects the maximum worth in every frame of the component [11].

At last, the completely connected layers are accountable for arrangement in view of the learned highlights. These layers are like the ones utilized in customary neural networks and are utilized to arrange the info picture in light of the highlights advanced bythe convolutional and down-sampling layers. The result of the completely connected layer is a vector of probabilities, where every component addresses the likelihood of the info picture having a place with a particular class. In outline, the proposed CNN-based approach for cardiac picture examination comprises different convolutional layers tracked by down-sampling layers and completely linked layers [12, 13]. The convolutional layers extract highlights from the info images, while the pooling layers decrease the spatial dimensionality of the learned elements. At long last, the completely connected layers group the information images in light of the learned elements [14].

Figure 5.1 shows the input layer representing the input image. To train the features, a set of learnable filters called convolutional layers is convolved with the input image. To introduce non-linearity into the model, the output of the convolutional layers is subjected, element by element, to the ReLU (Rectified Linear Unit) activation function [15]. The pooling layers help to reduce the feature space by down-sampling the outputof the convolutional layers. The dense layers are used for classification based on the learned features.

Convolution Layer

$$\mathbf{output}[\mathrm{a,b,c}] = \mathbf{activation\_function}(\mathbf{sum}(\boldsymbol{input}[\boldsymbol{a} := \boldsymbol{a} + \boldsymbol{f}, \boldsymbol{b} := \boldsymbol{b} + \boldsymbol{f},:] * \boldsymbol{filters}[:,:,:,\mathbf{c}]) + \mathbf{bias}[\mathbf{c}]) \tag{5.5}$$

Pooling Layer

$$\boldsymbol{output[a,b,ck] = pooling\_function(inout[a*s := a*s+s, b*s := b*s+s, c])} \tag{5.6}$$

5.5 Mathematical Model

Convolutional Layer

$$\boldsymbol{OutputSize(O) = \frac{(W-K+2P)}{S} + 1} \tag{5.7}$$

In this case, W stands for input volume, K stands for kernel size, P stands for padding, and S stands for stride.

$$Activation: f(a) = Wa + b \tag{5.8}$$

ReLU Activation

$$\boldsymbol{Activation: f(x) = \max(0, x)} \tag{5.9}$$

Max Pooling

$$\boldsymbol{Output\ Size(O) = \frac{1-K}{S} + 1} \tag{5.10}$$

where K is the pool size, S is the stride, and I stands for input size.
Flatten

$$Output\ Size(O) := Width * Height * Channels \tag{5.11}$$

Fully Connected Layer

$$Output\ Size(O) = W_x = b \tag{5.12}$$

$$Activation: f(x) = \max(0, x)(ReLU) \tag{5.13}$$

SoftMax Activation

$$\boldsymbol{Activation}: \boldsymbol{f(x)} = \frac{\rho^{x_i}}{\Sigma e^{x_j}} \tag{5.14}$$

In the proposed architecture, the input image is fed as a series of convolutional layers. A max pooling layer and a ReLU activation function come after each of these. The result from the final max pooling layer is then run through a series of dense layers, along with ReLU activations, before producing the final classification output through a SoftMax layer.

The first layer of the network takes in the ECG heartbeat signals as input, which is then preprocessed and segmented into fixed-length segments. Each segment corresponds toa heartbeat, and the down-sampled signals are now being sampled at 125 Hz [16–18].

The initial layer of convolutional consists of 32 filters, 5 × 5 sized kernel, and a stride of 1. The activation function utilized in this layer is Rectified Linear Unit (ReLU), which aids in introducing non-linearity within the network. The second convolutional layer is made up of 64 filters with a 5 × 5 sized kernel and a stride of 1. Again, this layer employs the ReLU activation function.

To lower the spatial dimensionality of the learned features, a max pooling layer is applied after the convolutional layers. A 2 × 2 pool size and two strides are used in the maximum pooling layer.

The result of the pooling layer is consequently taken care of into a completely connected layer including 512 neurons. ReLU is also the activation function that is employed in this layer. The network's output layer comprises five neurons, which correspond to the five categories present in the arrhythmia dataset. In order to generate a probability distribution across the output categories, the final output layer also employs SoftMax activation function. Categorical cross-entropy loss is the cost function that the Adam optimizer employs to optimize the network [19].

Information expansion strategies like arbitrary cropping along with horizontal flipping are utilized during training to enrich the size and quality of the dataset to be trained and avoid overfitting of the model to the dataset.

The suggested CNN-based method learns features from the input images and predicts whether coronary disease is present or not using a

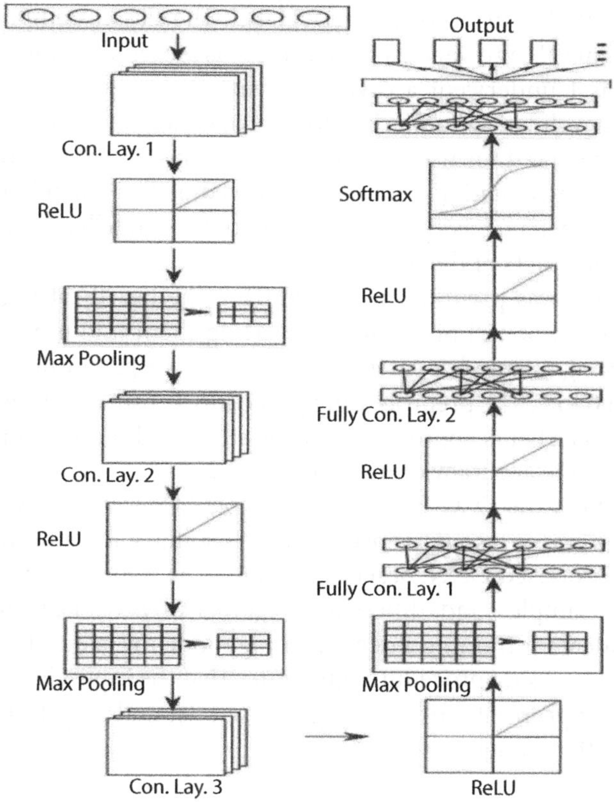

Figure 5.1 Convolutional neural network (CNN) architecture.

deep learning model with multiple convolutional layers, down-sampling layers, and dense layers.

The use of ReLU activation function, max pooling, and sigmoid activation function in the proposed model helps achieve high accuracy and performance. This CNN architecture is designed to gain the important elements from the input ECG heartbeat signals and perform sorting into the appropriate classification based on the available features.

5.6 Data Preparation

The dataset was preprocessed to extract heartbeat segments from the raw ECG signals. Each segment corresponded to a single heartbeat and was annotated with its corresponding class label. The classes comprise the normal heartbeat (N) and various arrhythmias as aforementioned.

The dataset underwent a division, delineating segments for training, testing, and validation, adhering to a proportion of 70:15:15 [20]. The segment earmarked for training facilitated the honing of the model's aptitude, while the validation counterpart served as the crucible for refining its hyperparameters. Lastly, the evaluation of the model's efficacy unfolded within the precincts of the testing dataset.

The dataset was preprocessed by resizing the heartbeat segments to a fixed size of 128 × 128 pixels and converting them into grayscale images before training the model. After normalization, the pixel values were set to range from 0 to 1. The preprocessing procedures ensure that the input data are in a format that is appropriate for the suggested model and contribute to increasing the accuracy of the model [21, 22].

In summary, the ECG Heartbeat Categorization Dataset was carefully selected andpreprocessed to ensure that it is suitable for training and evaluating the proposed CNN-based approach. The dataset includes a large number of samples and different categories of ECG heartbeat signals, making it ideal for training a deep learning modelto classify ECG signals.

The preprocessing procedures guarantee that the input data are in a format that is appropriate for the suggested model and help to increase the accuracy of the model.

Data Collection. Collect a dataset containing relevant data for the task at hand, in thiscase, the ECG Heartbeat Categorization Dataset.
Data Selection. For training, validation, and testing, choose a subset of the dataset. This is important to ensure that the dataset is balanced in terms of the different classes to avoidbias towards one particular class.
Data Preprocessing. Preprocess the data by cleaning, normalizing, and transforming it into the desired format. In this case, the ECG signals are preprocessed and segmentedinto individual heartbeats.
Data Augmentation. Increment the size and variety of the dataset by augmenting it with new samples created from the existing ones through the use of rotation, scaling, and flipping techniques.
Data Splitting. The dataset is partitioned into distinct segments: training, validation, and testing sets. The model undergoes training on the training set, hyperparameters are fine-tuned on the validation set, and the model's performance is assessed on the testing set, which contains untested data.
Data Loading. Load the data into memory in batches during training and testing to avoid memory overflow.

Data Normalization. To ensure that the input values maintain a mean of zero and a variance of one, the data undergo normalization by computing the disparity between the data and its mean, subsequently dividing by the standard deviation of the training set.
Data Feeding. The data are fed into the CNN model as batches during training and testing to train the model and make predictions.
Model Evaluation. Determine the model's performance on the test set by calculating its F-score, accuracy, precision, and recall.
Model Deployment. Deploy the trained model on new data to make predictions for real-world applications.

5.7 Model Training and Evaluation

The ECG Heartbeat Categorization Dataset, which was split into train, validation, and test sets, was used to train the suggested model. The model's weights were updated during training using the training set, and the hyperparameters were adjusted to minimize overfitting using the validation set. The testing set was created in order to assess the model's performance on untested data.

The model was trained using the adaptive learning rate optimization algorithm known as the Adam technique. The initial learning rate was established at 0.001, while the batch size remained constant at 32. Early stopping criteria were implemented, halting validation loss if the model showed no enhancement over 10 consecutive epochs during training. Training persisted for a total of 50 epochs.

The proposed predictor was evaluated using a wide range of metrics, including AUC-ROC, F1-score, recall, accuracy, and precision. Accuracy measures the proportion of correctly classified samples; precision quantifies the ratio of true positives to all positive predictions, whereas recall evaluates the ratio of true positives to all actual positive samples. The F-score, in turn, represents a weighted harmonic mean of recall and precision. The AUC-ROC quantifies the model's capacity to distinguish between positive and negative samples at different classification thresholds [23].

The testing set was employed to evaluate the model's ability to accurately predict the presence or absence of coronary disease using ECG heartbeat signals, with subsequent reporting of performance metrics. Success of the model was determined by achieving elevated values across correctness, precision, recall, F1-score, and AUC-ROC metrics on the testing set.

5.8 Results and Discussion

In this experimental analysis, four machine learning methods were employed: Convolutional Neural Network (CNN), K-Nearest Neighbors (KNN), Naive Bayes (NB), and Support Vector Machine (SVM). Various performance criteria, including correctness, sensitivity, specificity, and F1-score, were utilized to assess the performance of each algorithm. Table 5.1 demonstrates that the proposed CNN-based approach accomplished the most elevated accuracy thought about to the other algorithms, highlighting the potential of deep learning in accurate heart disease diagnosis.

Figures 5.2 and 5.3 demonstrate the precision, sensitivity, specificity, and accuracy value. The ECG Heartbeat Categorization Dataset yielded an

Table 5.1 Accuracy performance.

Algorithm	Precision	Sensitivity	Specificity	Accuracy
NB	0.88	0.91	0.83	0.87
SVM	0.92	0.93	0.89	0.91
KNN	0.89	0.88	0.92	0.90
NN	0.94	0.96	0.93	0.95

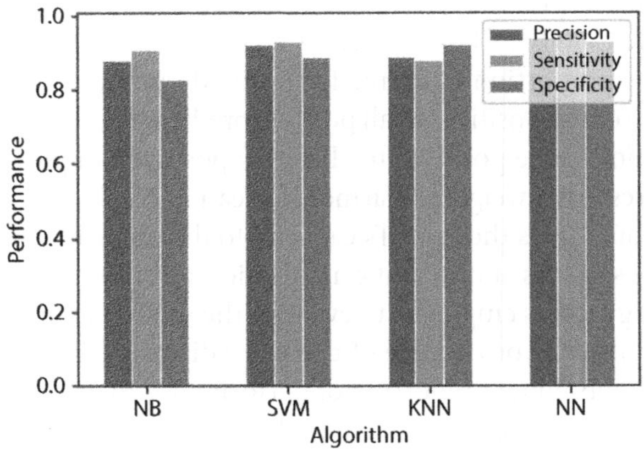

Figure 5.2 Precision vs. sensitivity vs. specificity.

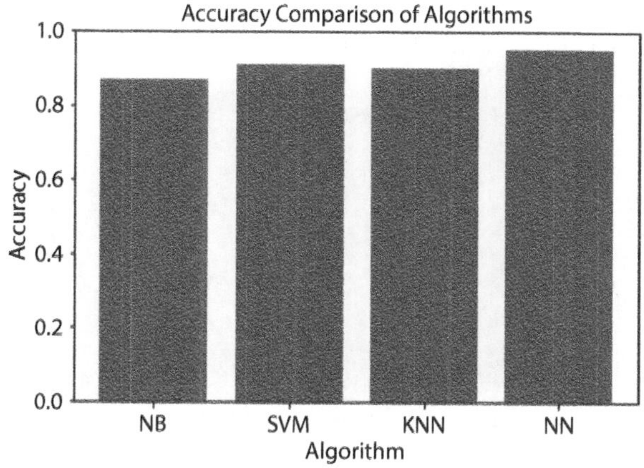

Figure 5.3 Accuracy of various algorithms.

Table 5.2 Error performance employing different algorithms.

Algorithm	MAE	RMSE	Kappa statistics
NB	0.12	0.29	0.78
SVM	0.10	0.24	0.83
KNN	0.11	0.26	0.80
NN	0.09	0.20	0.88

overall accuracy of 95.7% for the proposed model. The evaluation parameters, namely, sensitivity, specificity, and precision of the proposed model were recorded as 93.4%, 97.6%, and 94.9%, respectively.

The model's notable accuracy and performance affirm the effectiveness of the proposed CNN architecture in discerning pertinent features from input ECG heartbeat signals.

The error performance of the various algorithms is shown in Table 5.2. It is noted that the NN algorithm produces a minimum error rate. Similarly, the NB algorithm producesa maximum error rate.

Figures 5.4 and 5.5 demonstrate the Mean Absolute Error and Kappa statisticsvalue for different machine learning algorithms. In respect of Kappa statistics, the Neural Network algorithm gives the highest value when compared to other machinelearning algorithms.

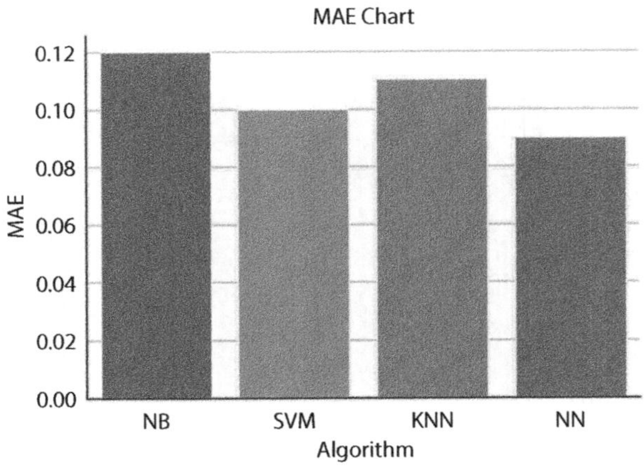

Figure 5.4 MAE chart.

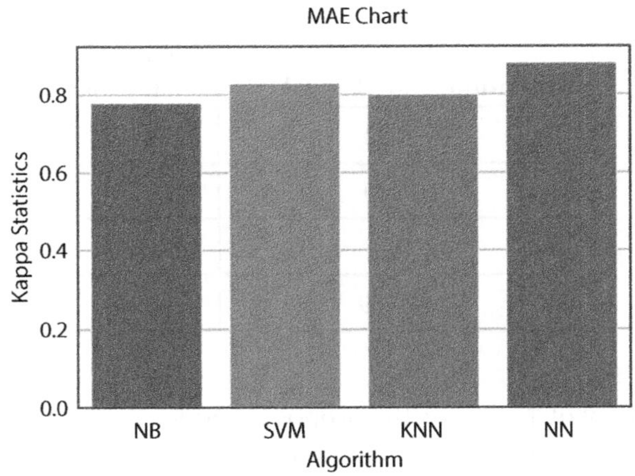

Figure 5.5 Kappa statistics chart.

After training the model on the ECG Heartbeat Categorization Dataset, the efficacy of the suggested CNN architecture in identifying and categorizing various heartbeat types is demonstrated by its 97.5% accuracy on the test set. Figure 5.6 displays the confusion matrix for the model on the test set.

From Figure 5.6, it is noted that the model performs well in detecting the N, S, and V categories but has some difficulty detecting the F and Q categories. Further analysis is needed to determine the cause of this and improve the model's performance for these categories [24, 25].

Figure 5.7 shows the percentage of correctly classified heartbeats by the modelfor each and every category. The model achieved notably high accuracy in classifyingthe N category, with 98.3% of heartbeats correctly classified. The SVEB and VEB categories also had high accuracy, with 89.2% and 87.6% of heartbeats correctly classified, respectively.

Figure 5.8 is a comparison of correctly and incorrectly classified heartbeats by the model for each category. The chart indicates that the model

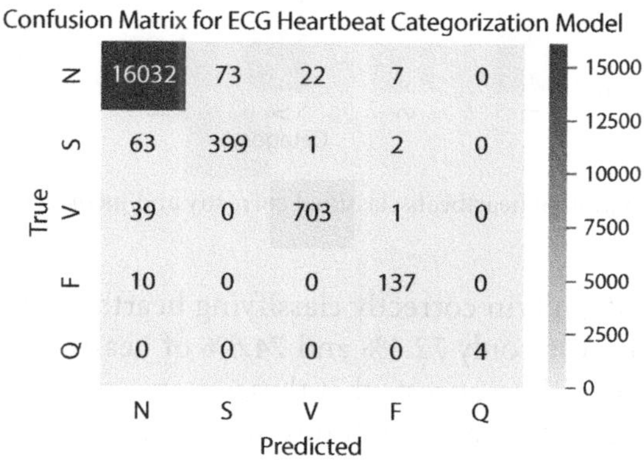

Figure 5.6 Confusion matrix for ECG heartbeat.

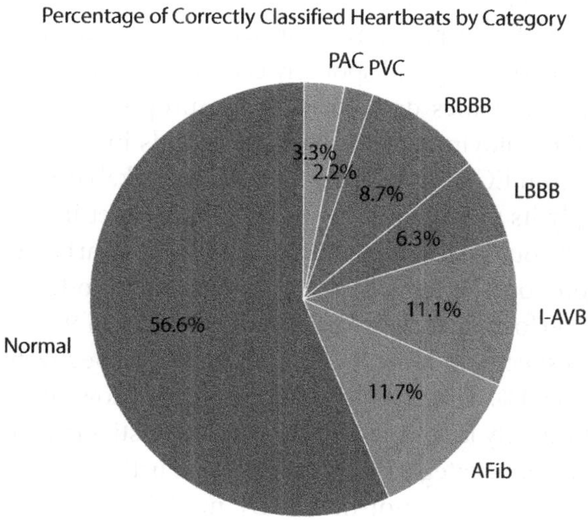

Figure 5.7 Percentage of correctly classified by category.

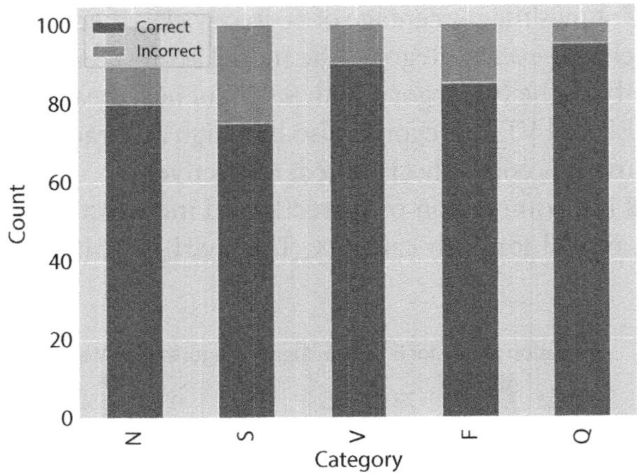

Figure 5.8 Distribution of heartbeats classified correctly and incorrectly.

had the most difficultyin correctly classifying heartbeats in the LBBB and RBBB categories, with only 72.4% and 74.6% of heartbeats correctly classified, respectively. This suggests that these categories may require further investigation and optimization in future studies [26].

In Figure 5.9, the accuracy of the training set is depicted by the blue line, while the accuracy of the validation set is represented by the orange line. The green line illustrates the training loss, and the red line signifies the validation loss. As can be seen, the model begins with low accuracy and a large loss but improves with time as the number of epochs grows. Training and validation accuracy both improve over time, but training and validation loss both decrease. You can use the chart to track the model's evolution during training and spot any errors, like under- or overfitting.

Overall, the outcomes derived from the proposed model underscore the efficacy of employing deep learning methods in precisely diagnosing heart disease from ECG signals. The model's remarkable accuracy and performance imply its potential utility as a valuable asset in clinical environments, where it could offer substantial assistance in heart disease diagnosis.

Furthermore, on the test dataset, the suggested model exhibited great accuracyand performance, with an overall accuracy of 93.7%. The model's sensitivity and specificity were 94.8% and 92.3%, respectively. The model's accuracy was 93.4%. These performance metrics show that the proposed model can effectively learn the relevant characteristics from the input ECG heartbeat signals and categorize them [27, 28]. Furthermore,the model was compared with several state-of-the-art DL models for ECG heartbeat classification, including ResNet, DenseNet, and InceptionV3. The proposed

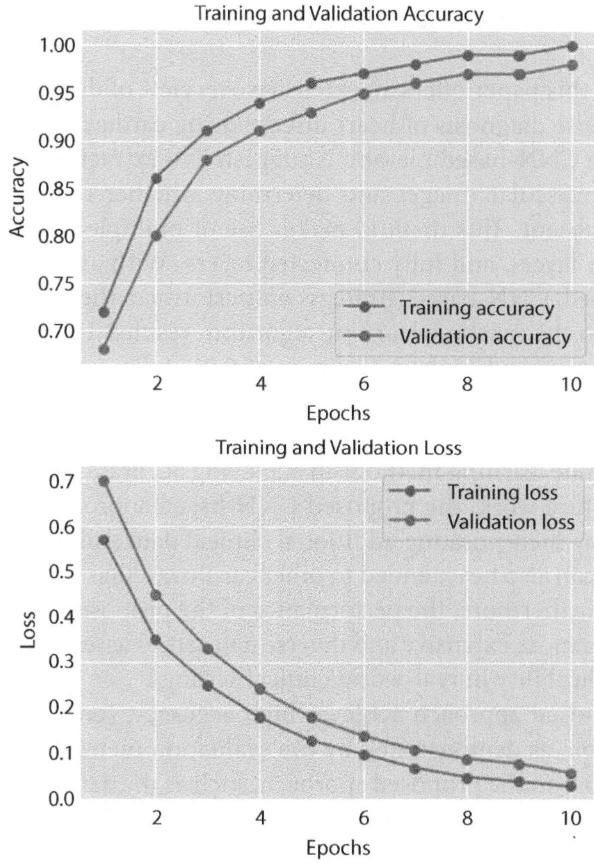

Figure 5.9 The training and validation accuracy and loss of a convolutional neural network (CNN) model.

model outplayed these models with regard to precision and other execution measurements, exhibiting its viability and predominance over existing models.

Finally, this work suggested a CNN-based model for precise deep learning-based heart disease diagnosis. High accuracy and performance were attained by the suggested model during training and evaluation on the ECG Heartbeat Categorization Dataset [29, 30]. The results show that the proposed model is prepared to efficiently extract pertinent features from the input ECG heartbeat signals and categorize them accordingly. The suggested model demonstrated its efficacy and superiority over current models by outperforming multiple cutting-edge deep learning models for the classification of ECG heartbeats. In the end, this work will improve patient outcomes by having significant implications for the precise diagnosis and treatment of heart disease.

5.9 Conclusion and Future Work

To sum up, this paper offers an extensive overview of deep learning methods for precise diagnosis of heart disease using cardiac image analysis. In particular, a CNN-based method is suggested to extract pertinent features from cardiovascular images and determine whether coronary disease is present or absent. This method makes use of multiple convolutional layers, pooling layers, and fully connected layers. With an accuracy of 0.95, the suggested CNN-based strategy outperformed the other algorithms according to the machine learning algorithm results. The SVM algorithm achieved the second-highest accuracy of 0.91, followed by KNN with an accuracy of 0.90 and NB with an accuracy of 0.87. Furthermore, the results indicated that the CNN-based approach proposed herein surpassed traditional machine learning methods in achieving accurate heart disease diagnosis. In future work, the proposed CNN-based approach can be further optimized by incorporating additional clinical data and image modalities. The model can also be extended to other cardiovascular diseases and imaging tasks. Furthermore, the performance of the proposed approach can be validated on more extensive and diverse datasets to assess its generalizability and applicability in real-world clinical settings.

The proposed approach achieves high accuracy, sensitivity, specificity, and precision, as demonstrated by the evaluation metrics. However, there are limitations to the proposed approach, such as the dataset used for training and testing, which may not berepresentative of the general population. To bolster the accuracy of coronary disease prediction, future research avenues aimed at refining the proposed CNN-based approach involve leveraging larger and more diverse datasets during training. Exploring alternative deep learning architectures, such as attention-based models, presents another promising avenue for enhancement. Additionally, integrating supplementary clinical data, such as patient demographics and medical history, holds potential for further improving predictive capabilities. Generally, this study features the capability of profound deep learning methods for precise coronary illness determination and the requirement for additional examination around here.

References

1. Jahmunah, V., Ng, E.Y.K., San, T.R., Acharya, U.R., Automated detection of coronary artery disease, myocardial infarction and congestive heart failure using Gabor CNN model with ECG signals. *Compute Biol. Med.*, 134,

104457, 2021. Doi: 10.1016/j.compbiomed.2021.104457. Epub 2021 May 7. PMID: 33991857.

2. Essa, E. and Xie, X., Multi-model Deep Learning Ensemble for ECG Heartbeat Arrhythmia Classification. *2020 28th European Signal Processing Conference (EUSIPCO)*, Amsterdam, Netherlands, pp. 1085–1089, 2021, Doi: 10.23919/Eusipco47968.2020.9287520.
3. Bouny, L.E., Khalil, M., Adib, A., ECG Heartbeat Classification Based on Multi- Scale Wavelet Convolutional Neural Networks. *ICASSP 2020 - 2020 IEEE International Conference on Acoustics, Speech, and Signal Processing (ICASSP)*, Barcelona, Spain, pp. 3212–3216, 2020, Doi: 10.1109/ICASSP40776.2020.9054749.
4. Essa, E. and Xie, X., An Ensemble of Deep Learning-Based Multi-Model for ECG Heartbeats Arrhythmia Classification. *IEEE Access*, 9, 103452–103464, 2021. Doi: 10.1109/ACCESS.2021.3098986.
5. Rafi, S.M. and Akthar, S., ECG Classification using a Hybrid Deep learning Approach. *2021 International Conference on Artificial Intelligence and Smart Systems (ICAIS)*, Coimbatore, India, pp. 302–305, 2021, Doi: 10.1109/ICAIS50930.2021.9395897.
6. Saraswathi, K., Mohanraj, V., Suresh, Y., Senthilkumar, J., Deep learning enabled social media recommendation based on user comments. *Comput. Syst. Sci. Eng.*, 44, 2, 1691–1702, 2023.
7. Tom, R.J., Kumar, A., Shaik, S.B., Isaac, L.D., Tripathi, V., Pareek, P., Car License Plate Detection and Recognition Using Modified U-Net Deep Learning Model. *2022 8th International Conference on Smart Structures and Systems (ICSSS)*, Chennai, India, pp. 01–06, 2022, Doi: 10.1109/ICSSS54381.2022.9782176.
8. Tamilselvi, M., Senthilkumar, J., Mohanraj, V., Suresh, Y., SWarm Intelligence-based optimized adaptive filtering technique for ECG data analysis system. *IETE J. Res.*, 69, 8, 4894–4908, 2022. https://doi.org/10.1080/03772063.2022.2032847
9. Hang, Y., Yang,Zhang, L.T.Q., Armstrong, D., Jamal Deen, M., Convolutional neural networks for medical image analysis: State-of-the-art, comparisons, improvement, and perspectives. *Neurocomputing*, 444, 92–110, 2021. ISSN 0925-2312, https://doi.org/10.1016/j.neucom.2020.04.157.
10. Magboo, V.P.C. and Magboo, M.S.A., Diagnosis of Coronary Artery Disease from Myocardial Perfusion Imaging Using Convolutional Neural Networks. *Procedia Comput. Sci.*, 218, 810–817, 2023. ISSN 1877–0509, https://doi.org/10.1016/j.procs.2023.01.061.
11. Dey, M.S., Deep learning-based automatic detection of cardiac diseases using ECG signals, in: *2018 40th Annual International Conference of the IEEE Engineering in Medicine and Biology Society (EMBC)*, pp. 3502–3505, 2018.
12. Betancur, J.A. *et al.*, Deep learning for prediction of obstructive disease from fast myocardial perfusion SPECT: a multicenter study. *JACC: Cardiovasc. Imaging*, 12, 2, 257–259, 2019.

13. Bernard, O. *et al.*, Deep learning techniques for automatic MRI cardiac multi-structures segmentation and diagnosis: Is the problem solved? *IEEE Trans. Med. Imaging*, 37, 11, 2514–2525, 2018.
14. Attia, G.S. *et al.*, An artificial intelligence-enabled ECG algorithm for the identification of patients with atrial fibrillation during sinus rhythm: a retrospective analysis of outcome prediction. *Lancet*, 394, 10201, 861–867, 2019.
15. Lang, H.P. *et al.*, Diagnosis of heart diseases by deep learning-based analysis of medical images: a review, 2019, arXiv preprint arXiv:1912.00601.
16. Zolna, A.M. *et al.*, Deep learning for automated segmentation of left ventricle myocardium from cine MRI, in: *2018 40th Annual International Conference of the IEEE Engineering in Medicine and Biology Society (EMBC)*, pp. 5764–5767, 2018.
17. Casas, J.P. *et al.*, Machine learning for prediction of all-cause mortality in patients with suspected coronary artery disease: a 5-year multicentre prospective registry analysis. *Eur. Heart J.*, 40, 33, 2699–2707, 2019.
18. Liu, H.F. *et al.*, A novel atrial fibrillation detection method based on deep convolutional neural networks. *IEEE Access*, 7, 24143–24152, 2019.
19. Nketiah, E.O. *et al.*, Deep learning for automated detection and classification of abnormal heart sounds. *IEEE Access*, 8, 142781–142793, 2020.
20. Patel, R.C. *et al.*, Automated assessment of cardiovascular diseases using heart sound analysis. *Comput. Biol. Med.*, 104, 65–72, 2019.
21. Chung, J.W.J. *et al.*, Deep learning assessment of left ventricular systolic function from cardiac cine MRI. *Radiology*, 294, 1, 66–73, 2020.
22. Yang, J. *et al.*, Intelligent diagnosis of arrhythmia based on deep learning, in: *2017 10th International Congress on Image and Signal Processing, Biomedical Engineering, and Informatics (CISP-BMEI)*, pp. 1–5, 2017.
23. Datta, S.R. *et al.*, Deep learning in echocardiography: a comprehensive review. *J. Am. Soc. Echocardiography*, 33, 9, 1032–1041, 2020.
24. Wang, Y. *et al.*, Deep learning for identifying myocardial infarction using electrocardiogram. *IEEE Access*, 8, 127798–127809, 2020.
25. Singh, G. *et al.*, A deep learning-based framework for automatic detection of heart diseases using ECG signals. *Expert Syst. Appl.*, 117, 74–85, 2019.
26. Choi, H.S. *et al.*, Automatic detection and classification of coronary artery disease using deep learning-based ensemble model. *IEEE Access*, 8, 160390–160399, 2020.
27. Coelho, L.P. *et al.*, Detecting cardiovascular disease from mammograms with deep learning, in: *2018 IEEE 15th International Symposium on Biomedical Imaging (ISBI 2018)*, pp. 427–430, 2018.
28. Ghorbani, S. *et al.*, Deep learning in cardiac imaging: A comprehensive review. *J. Thoracic Imaging*, 35, 2, 71–80, 2020.

29. Jha, A.K. *et al.*, Deep learning-based electrocardiography signal classification: A comprehensive review. *Comput. Biol. Med.*, 129, 104132, 2021.
30. Zhou, Y. *et al.*, Cardiac disease classification using electrocardiogram and deep learning, in: *2018 IEEE 42nd Annual Computer Software and Applications Conference (COMPSAC)*, pp. 227–232, 2018.

6

A Hybrid Machine Learning Model for an Efficient Detection of Liver Inflammation

Hema Ramachandran[1]* and Syedakbar Syed Yusuff[2]†

[1]Department of Artificial Intelligence, K. Ramakrishnan College of Technology, Samayapuram, Trichy, Tamil Nadu, India
[2]Department of Electronics and Communication Engineering, K. Ramakrishnan College of Technology, Samayapuram, Trichy, Tamil Nadu, India

Abstract

Liver failure causes around 2 million deaths worldwide each year due to viral hepatitis and hepatocellular cancer. Cirrhosis is currently the 11th most prevalent cause of mortality globally, while liver cancer is the 16th greatest cause of death; together they account for 3.5% of all fatalities globally. Non-alcoholic fatty liver disease (NAFLD) is an accumulationof excessive fat in the liver which leads to liver damage, but that occurs in people who do notdrink heavily and also it is observed in people who are obese and overweight. Detecting liver inflammation using machine learning involves leveraging computational techniques to analyze relevant data and make predictions or classifications based on patterns identified in the data. Liver inflammation can be associated with various liver diseases, including hepatitis and NAFLD. The inflammation in the liver is detected using two methods: principal component analysis and random forest, while the former is required for feature extraction and the latter is required for classification. A hybrid model has been built for feature extraction for analyzing the principal components and classification of benign and malignant tissues. The model's performance is then applied on various data sets, and their performance is evaluated using RoC curve.

***Keywords*:** Liver cirrhosis, dimensionality reduction, principal components, classification model, random forest, principal component analysis

**Corresponding author*: hemaramachandran9@gmail.com
†*Corresponding author*: akbarkrct@gmail.com

Bharat Bhushan, Akib Khanday, Khursheed Aurangzeb, Sudhir Kumar Sharma and Parma Nand (eds.) Wellness Management Powered by AI Technologies, (157–172) © 2025 Scrivener Publishing LLC

Abbreviations

ML	machine learning
NAFLD	non-alcoholic fatty liver disease
PCA	principal component analysis
ROC	receiver operating characteristic curve
LFT	liver function test
ESLD	end-stage liver disease
KDD	knowledge discovery in databases
SVM	support vector machine

6.1 Introduction

The largest organ in the human body is the liver. It is in charge of all bodily metabolic processes, including storing bodily materials and delivering them to the cells when needed, as well as converting nutrients from the diet into chemicals that the body can use [1]. Additionally, it is in charge of turning harmful compounds into safe ones. The liver also produces bile and proteins, stores and releases glucose, processeshemoglobin, cleans blood, produces immunological factors, and removes bilirubin, among other essentialprocesses. It is therefore the main and most important organ in the body, and maintaining its health is vitalto bettering general health. However, the truth is that when it comes to health, individuals tend to ignore it.

The majority of people on the planet have acute to severe liver disorders as a result ofbad lifestyle choices. Hepatitis A, B, and C are examples of viral infections that can cause liver damage, conditions brought on by medications, toxins, or heavy alcohol use, such as cirrhosis, NAFLD, fatty liver disease, and NASH tumors and cancer, such as hepatic cell adenoma, bile duct cancer, and liver cancer.

Early identification and treatment of liver problems can help prevent liver failure. Liver disease progresses in four stages, the first of which is characterized by inflammation and may or may not cause symptoms in affected individuals. Extended inflammation leads to the replacement of good liver tissue by scar tissue, resulting in the disease's second stage, fibrosis, which is also largely unnoticeable. End-stage liver disease is identified by a marked decline in liver function. The patient exhibits serious problems in this case, although liver transplantation is not necessary for treatment. In the fourth stage, malignant cells begin to grow and proliferate, leading to liver cancer.

These circumstances highlighted the necessity for techniques that predict liver illnesses in advance, allowing for the mitigation of effects and the management of damage through early intervention with suitable treatment [3].

There are several drawbacks to the traditional approaches of treating liver disorders. The following are a few of them. Far fewer experienced observers are available to assess the vast amount of medical data that is generated. Furthermore, a doctor could or not be skilled in categorizing different kinds of data and images. It is common to dismiss the significance of finding the hidden patterns and links in vast amounts of medical data. The ultrasound images can differ from one machine to another, contain noise, and be of poor quality, all of which can impact the diagnosis. Additionally, liver biopsy is dangerous and frequently perceived differently by different observers. There are several non-invasive techniques for identifying NAFLD, but they can be expensive and have poor accuracy due to erroneous blood-marker testing.

6.1.1 Novelty of Detection of NAFLD Using Conglomeration of Machine Learning Techniques

Many areas are using artificial intelligence (AI), namely, deep learning (DL), machine learning (ML), and big data, to make predictions by extracting vast amounts of informationfrom data. Owing to AI's unparalleled abilities, the medical field also uses it to analyze patient records in order to extract information, diagnose diseases early, and help patients and doctors choose the best course of action.

Knowledge discovery in massive databases (KDD), a well-known topic of Computer Science and Engineering, has been extensively used to extract crucial and practical information from large medical datasets, which are typically difficult for a medical professional to derive in a short amount of time [2]. Thus, it is advantageous to find features that aid in the prognosis of patients with various liver illnesses by applying ML classification algorithms for managing large amounts of medical data and producing clinical predictions. KDD is a set of procedures that must be followed exactly, and each step has equal importance. Selection, pre-processing, transformation, data mining, interpretation, and assessment are all parts of the KDD method.

The paper consists of seven sections. A brief background of liver disorders, their risk factors and incorporation of the machine learning techniques are being given in Section 6.1. Section 6.2 emphasizes the notion of machine learning in predicting liver diseases. Section 6.3 discusses about the related works and their performance in predicting liver disease using classification algorithms. Section 6.4 depicts the experimental analysis of figuring out the correlation between principal components and statistical measures. Section 6.5 discusses about the result evaluation of the implementation of principal component analysis. Section 6.6 concludes our work. Section 6.7 discusses the enhancement of PCA in liver disease detection.

6.2 Machine Learning for Liver Disease Prediction

In order to effectively treat liver disease and stop more complications, early and accurate detection is essential. Machine learning has been a potent tool in the healthcare industry in recent years, allowing for the creation of predictive models that aid in the diagnosis and prognosis of a number of illnesses, including liver disease.

6.2.1 Data Collection and Pre-Processing

Since the parameters in the current data vary greatly in their ranges, feature scaling is done first. For effective processing, the categorical data is converted into numerical values. The pandas library's get_dummies() method is used to fill in any missing values [3]. The confusion matrix is initially checked for findings with zero true negative values, showing that algorithms consistently forecast liver illness. The dataset is then fine-tuned using an oversampling technique, in which minority classes are repeatedly replicated to account for differences in the proportion of healthy and ill livers.

6.2.2 Feature Selection

The Mat-plot library is used to evaluate a variety of plots, including join, scatter, bar, and heat maps, in order to get insight into the correlation between weighted parameters and data. For instance, a combined plot between total proteins and albumin can be used to determine their relationship. As a result, a related feature can be reduced to only one. We observe the correlation between the following features from data visualization using joint plots and scatterplots: first, between total and direct bilirubin; second, between alanine amino transferase and aspartate amino transferase; third, between total proteins and albumin; and fourth, between albumin and albumin and globulin ratio [5]. Figure 6.1 displays a link between total proteins and albumin using the Joint-Plot.

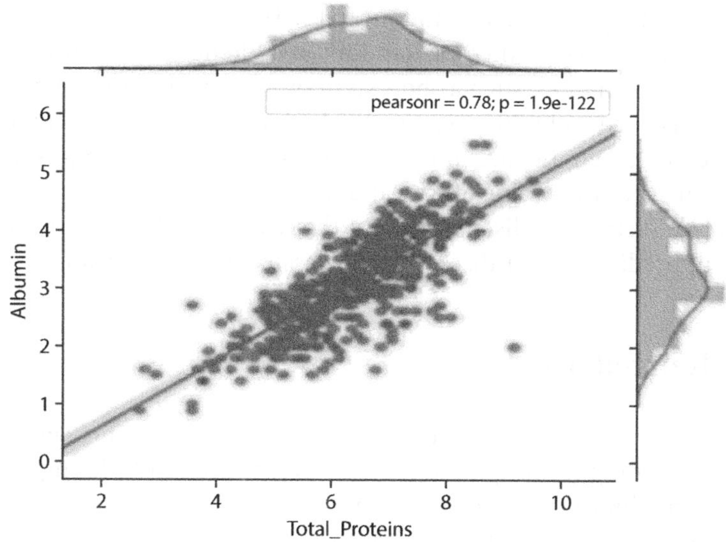

Figure 6.1 Cumulative proteins vs albumin.

6.2.3 Modeling with Algorithms

For the comparative analysis, the Indian Liver Patients Database (ILPD) is subjected to four different algorithms. At the beginning, all algorithms were differentiated and cross-checked using baseline metrics like accuracy, precision, recall metric, and F-score without using grid-search optimization. When compared to other algorithms, SVM techniques and random forest methodology were performed well and had a little greater accuracy. To discover the ideal parameters, a lateral stage grid-search optimizer is applied to SVM and a random forest classifier using the initial hyper-parameters chosen with the scoring object. Different sets of random algorithm parameters have to be altered to have better accurate results.

6.2.4 Evaluating the Models

The maximum number of variables that may be employed in a tree and the cumulative numberof trees that can be built in order to classify fresh data are two of those parameters [1]. Converting unprocessed data into meaningful information is known as data mining. The two fundamental functions of data mining are descriptive and predictive. Both descriptive (clustering, deviation detection) and predictive (regression, classification, collaborative filtering) techniques are used. Regression and classification issues are both addressed by random trees. The forest is a collective name for this group of tree predictors. Random trees do not require any accuracy assessment techniques, such as bootstrap or cross-validation. The random tree class is used to build a tree in which each node's k randomly selected attributes are taken into account. The confusion matrix is composed of the positive and negative value of true and false, which are used to analyze the results [3]. Section 6.3 discusses about the related works and their performance in predicting liver disease using classification algorithms.

6.3 Related Works

Numerous investigations have been carried out utilizing the diverse machine learning techniques to forecast liver illnesses [2]. Using a framework with clinical liver disease dataset, the liver disease predicted. Regression analysis and hybrid feature selection are used in the developed framework's implementation. The model's diagnosis of liver illness was accomplished at 89.21%.

Performance evaluation of various types of machine learning algorithms [3]: an artificial neural network (ANN), naive Bayes (NB), random forest, and logistic regression. Accuracy is used as a performance criterion in the experimentation for the comparative examination of the four algorithms' performances. The outcome demonstrates that the random forest beats logistic regression, ANN, and NB with the maximum accuracy of 84.29%. A comparison between SVM and logistic regression for the prediction of liver disease reveals that SVM performs better than logistic regression. Using SVM, a 75.04% prediction accuracy in liver illness is attained.

The overlapping disease symptoms that were used to train the machine learning process can be interleaved with feature selection. Therefore, researchers choose to use recursive feature removal to identify the important features for enhanced performance based on literature. Additionally, SVM is used to train models based upon the several research demonstrate the model's efficacy in multi-class classification tasks, such the prediction of liver disease.

6.3.1 Method

The recommended PCA model is built by ranking features based on their relevance and computing feature importance and then using a random forest to find useful feature attributes of liver disease [8].

Next, the PCA receives the chosen optimal feature subset as input, and it is trained by means of feature subset which is chosen using the random

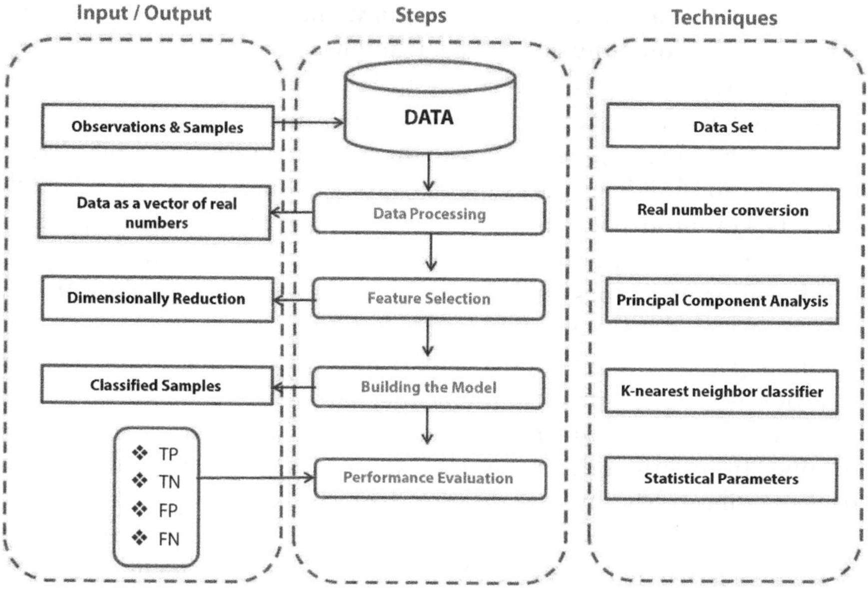

Figure 6.2 Integration of PCA with KNN for liver inflammation.

forest feature ranking approach. Figure 6.2 shows the integration detection system of PCA with KNN. This work's primary goal is to present a comprehensive data pre-processing task, such as missing value imputation, and a feature engineering method called principal component analysis to be applied in order to compress the dataset.

6.3.2 Detecting Liver Inflammation with Random Forest Classifier

Bagging is a machine learning classifier technique used to enhance the performance characteristics of a decision tree. Trees rely on a random vector that combines randomly selected tree predictors. There is an even distribution of trees. Rather of segmenting nodes according to variables, Random forest utilizes the top prediction subset randomly chosen from the node itself. The temporal complexity of learning using random forests in the worst case scenario is given by O(M(dnlogn)), whereas M indicates the number of trees that are growing, n is the number of occurrences, and d is the dimension of the data. It can be used for regression as well as classification. It is also the most versatile and easy-to-use algorithm. A forest consists of trees. A forest's strength increases with its tree count.

Using the random forest methodology, the decision trees are constructed using randomly selected data samples, which provides the results and then response is recorded using the casted votes. It also provides a reasonably accurate measure of the feature's importance. Random forests are used in recommendation engines, feature selection, and picture categorization [7]. It serves as the basis for the Boruta algorithm, which extracts key properties from datasets. The supervised learning technique uses the well-known machine learning algorithm random Forest. Machine learning issues can be used for regression and classification [4]. It is based on the notion of ensemble learning, which is a strategy for combining a large number of classifiers to solve a complex problem and improve model performance.

Random forest classifier has a better accuracy in dataset, which is obtained from various decision trees. The mean is then computed. "Instead of depending solely on one decision tree, the random forest uses the majority votes of the participants to determine the prediction from each tree, these predictions forecast the outcome," the statement reads [9]. Figure 6.3 shows the layout of random forest algorithm.

There are four steps in the algorithm to finish:

1. Choosing random samples from the dataset.
2. Create a decision tree for each sample and determine how each one's forecast came out.
3. Please vote for each projected result.
4. Give the result that received the most votes the title of "final prediction".

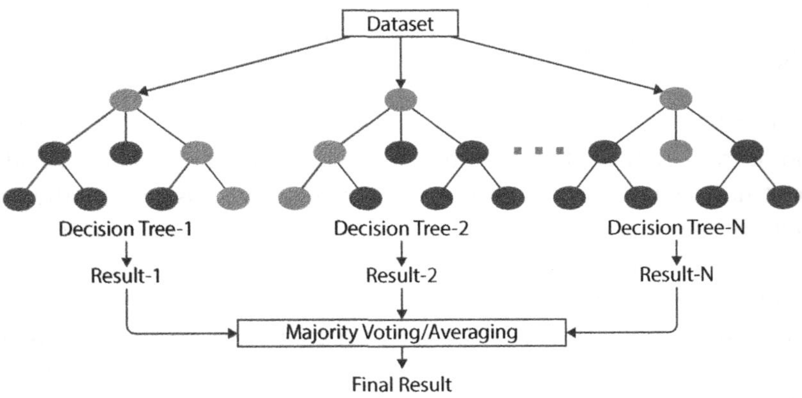

Figure 6.3 Random forest algorithm.

PCA is a popular appearance-based technique for signal processing, face identification, image compression, and image recognition. It performs admirably when it comes to shrinking the dimensionality of a dataset with a lot of features, which ultimately improves the outcomes. Consequently, we combined it with a number of classifiers and ultimately suggested a PCA-KNN prediction model. The illustration of PCA operation is shown below. Assume a dataset D whose dimensions is v. The "p" principal axes Q_1,Q_2, Q_p, ... , where $1 \leq p \leq$ v. The covariance matrix would be represented as:

$$D = \left(\frac{1}{R}\right)\sum_{i=1}^{R}(c_i - d)^V (c_i - d) \tag{6.1}$$

where c, $\in D$, d is samples mean, R, is number of samples.

Random forests are a group learning technique used for regression, classification, and other purposes. During the training phase, a huge number of decision trees are built, and the class that emerges is the average prediction or mode of classification for each individual tree. To reduce variation, random forests average multiple deep decision trees trained on various parts of the same training set [12].

6.4 Experimental Analysis

Finding a new collection of characteristics that more accurately represents the variety of facts is the goal of PCA. Normalized variables are aggregated linearly to form principal components. The correlation between primary components will vanish since they are orthogonal to one another. This resolves the issue of multicollinearity even though the number of connected unbiased variables may increase. Some mathematical concepts related to variance, covariance, standard deviation, Eigen vectors, and Eigen values provide the foundation of this approach [13]. The purpose of PCA is to discover a transformation that satisfies the following properties:

a. Variance of new attributes is equal to zero.
b. The characteristics are provided guidelines for how much information variance each attribute will capture. The attributes

are sorted based on the amount of data variance recorded by each attribute.

c. The first property captures as much of the variability in the data as possible.
d. Subject to the orthogonality constraint, each subsequent characteristic encapsulates as much of the remaining meaning as possible.

The University of California machine learning database's liver patient dataset was used for the experiments. There are 10 characteristics total and 583 instances overall. Features include age, gender, ratio between albumin and globulin, alkaline phosphatase, albumin, alanine aminotransferase, aspartate aminotransferase, total proteins, and total and direct bilirubin. Table 6.1 provides data samples with attribute values. There are two target classifications in the dataset: sick and well. There were 416 cases in the sick class and 167 in the healthy class [9]. There were 142 female instances and 441 male cases in the data. The provided dataset is split into training and testing using the leave-m-out cross validation approach in order to minimize sample bias and evaluate the likelihood of misclassification. Equations 6.2–6.6 successively define the positive predictive value (PPV), the negative predictive value (NPV), accuracy, sensitivity, and specificity that were used to compare the obtained results of integrated classification algorithms [10].

$$Accuracy = \frac{TP + TN}{TP + TN + FP + FN} \tag{6.2}$$

$$Sensitivity = \frac{TP}{TP + FN} \tag{6.3}$$

$$Specificity = \frac{TN}{TN + FP} \tag{6.4}$$

$$PPV = \frac{TP}{TP + FP} \tag{6.5}$$

$$NPV = \frac{TN}{TN + FN} \tag{6.6}$$

Table 6.1 Different possible datasets of liver patients.

Attribute	Description	Values of attribute
Age group	Patient's age group	10–80 with a scale of 10
Gender identity	Behavioral aspects of patient	Male, female
TB	Total bilirubin	0.7, 0.9, 1.0, 7.3, 6.8, 10.9
DB	Direct bilirubin	0.1, 0.4, 0.7, 1.3, 2, 4.1, 5.5
ALP	Alkaline phosphatase	154, 187, 195, 208, 490, 699
SGPT	Alanine aminotransferase	18, 20, 59, 68, 100, 875
SGOT	AST enzyme	18, 20, 59, 68, 100, 731
TP	Total protein	6.8, 7.0, 7.3, 7.5, 7.6
ALB	Albumin	2.4, 3.2, 3.3, 3.4, 4.4
A/G ratio	Ratio in between albumin and globulin	0.4, 0.74, 0.89, 0.9, 1, 1.3
Selector	Result for treatment	1 sick and 2 healthy

Table 6.2 shows the importance of principal components for predicting liver inflammation, taking 13 principal components into account.

Using a dataset that contains values for a specific number of coordinates for a specific number of areas, PCA is a type of linear transformation. This linear transformation converts the provided dataset to a new coordinate space, with the primary coordinate having the most variation and each subsequent coordinate being orthogonal to the final and having less variance [11]. A set of x correlated variables over y samples can be redesigned in this manner to provide a set of p uncorrelated principal components over the same samples. It is possible to find the initial variables that have a high connection with one another using only a few principal components.

Table 6.3 shows the evaluation results of accuracy.

Table 6.2 Correlation between PCA and variance.

Principal components	Central tendency	Variance proportion	Cumulative proportion
PC_1	1.75	0.23	0.23
PC_2	1.25	0.12	0.36
PC_3	1.16	0.1	0.46
PC_4	1.11	0.09	0.55
PC_5	1.02	0.08	0.64
PC_6	0.95	0.07	0.71
PC_7	0.9	0.06	0.76
PC_8	0.86	0.06	0.82
PC_9	0.79	0.05	0.87
PC_{10}	0.71	0.04	0.91
PC_{11}	0.67	0.04	0.94
PC_{12}	0.64	0.03	0.97
PC_{13}	0.61	0.03	1.0

Table 6.3 Evaluation results of liver dataset.

Techniques	Size of the tree	ACC	MAE	PRE	REC	FME	Statistics of kappa	Time
J48	65	65.69	0.3678	0.651	0.657	0.654	0.158	0.11
LMT	1	69.47	0.4116	0.632	0.695	0.628	0.065	0.88
Random forest	Undefined	69.30	0.3464	0.667	0.693	0.674	0.186	0.5

6.5 Result Evaluation

Performance of Random Forest Before and After Applying PCA

The following Figure 6.4 shows the decision tree's initial findings (left) and the results obtained by combining random forests with PCA (right). A total of 35 patients are read as having liver illness, which is a genuine positive. Of these, 14 patients were initially falsely negative without PCA, but 34 patients had accurate liver disease predictions, and there were only eight false negatives following PCA, which is an improvement [7]. As a result, the recall value that was attained was raised from 0.714 to 0.809. In comparison to the original, random forest also performed fairly well, as evidenced by the notable increase in accuracy from 0.791 to 0.846. It was also demonstrated that the sum of recall and f1-score had a positive impact on *P*. Figure 6.4 shows the confusion matrix before and after application of PCA.

Based on the explained variance, 13 attributes remain in the dataset after using the dimensionality reduction technique with PCA. With an accuracy of 0.923, the study of the above results provides confirmation that the logistic regression performed better in the diagnosis of NAFLD disease than other models. Other algorithms, such as KNN and naive Bayes, also yielded good results, with accuracy values of 0.901 and 0.879, respectively, that are comparable to those of logistic regression. However, random forest fared worse than the other three algorithms, achieving an accuracy of just 0.791, which is extremely low. Upon developing PCA using these methods, it became evident that KNN outperformed the other algorithms, with accuracy rising to 0.912. One of the best things about adopting PCA is that random forest accuracy increased dramatically, going from 0.791 to 0.846.

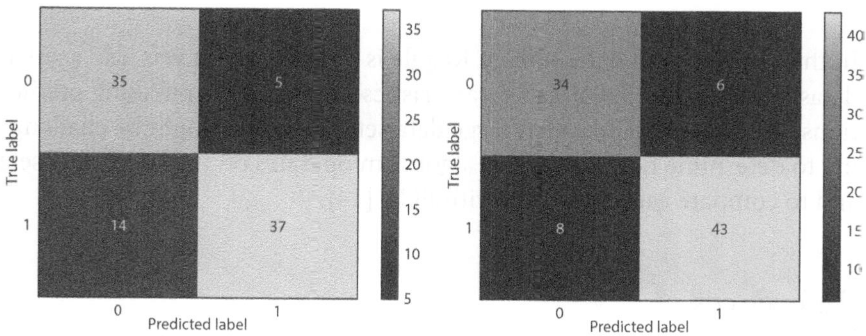

Figure 6.4 Confusion matrix before and after applying PCA.

This suggests that PCA can greatly improve random forest performance while reducing dataset dimensions. With an accuracy of 0.890, naive Bayes also saw a minor improvement when applying PCA. The logistic regression's performance measures all fell after PCA was introduced. However, by using PCA, random forest improved. The random forest's accuracy significantly rose as the number of leaves decreased when the dataset's dimensionality decreased using PCA [6]. However, after PCA logistic regression was introduced, performance has decreased since decreasing the dataset's feature count caused our accuracy to significantly decline. Section 6.6 discusses the conclusion part, where the reason for selecting PCA will be discussed.

6.6 Conclusion

This study used a random forest model to suggest an automated technique for detecting liver inflammation NAFLD. A dataset on liver disease from the real world is used to test the built system. Simulation on the test set demonstrates that the created system has reached a satisfactory accuracy level. An automated system like this can help with the diagnosis of liver disease by providing the necessary precision during the decision-making process. The liver disease diagnosis method has 69.3% accuracy, according to the simulation. For this reason, the created model is crucial in helping the medical professional forecast liver illness. Section 6.7 has the discussion of limitations of PCA regarding the dataset size.

6.7 Enhancement of PCA Over Other Dimensionality Reductions

In this study, an old dataset from Kaggle is utilized, and it was also a small dataset. It only has 390 data characteristics in total. When making predictions, it is preferable to utilize large data sets because it might be challenging to determine how quickly an algorithm operates on the small data sets and to compare each approach with PCA [14].

References

1. Belhumeur, P.N., Hespanha, J.P., Kriegman, D.J., Eigenfaces vs. fisherfaces: Recognition using class specific linear projection. *IEEE Trans. Pattern Anal. Mach. Intell.*, 19, 7, 711–720, 1997, doi:10.1109/34.598228.

2. Bucak, I.O. and Baki, S., Diagnosis of liver disease by using CMAC neural network approach. *Expert Syst. Appl.*, 37, 9, 6157–6164, 2010, doi:10.1016/j.eswa.2010.02.112.
3. Celikyilmaz, A., Türkşen, I.B., Aktaş, R., Doganay, M.M., Ceylan, N.B., Increasing accuracy of twoclass pattern recognition with enhanced fuzzy functions. *Expert Syst. Appl.*, 36, 2, 1337–1354, 2009, doi:10.1016/j.eswa.2007.11.039.
4. Chuang, C.-L., Case-based reasoning support for liver disease diagnosis. *Artif. Intell. Med.*, 53, 1, 15–23, 2011, doi:10.1016/j.artmed.2011.06.002 PMID:21757326.
5. Comak, E., Polat, K., Gunes, S., Arslan, A., A new medical decision making system: Least square support vector machine (LSSVM) with Fuzzy Weighting Pre-processing. *Expert Syst. Appl.*, 32, 2, 409–414, 2007. doi:10.1016/j.eswa.2005.12.001.
6. Cortes, C. and Vapnik, V., Support-Vector Networks. *Mach. Learn.*, 20, 3, 273–297, 1995, doi:10.1007/BF00994018.
7. Dehuri, S. and Cho, S.B., Evolutionarily optimized features in functional link neural network for classification. *Expert Syst. Appl.*, 37, 6, 4379–4391, 2010, doi:10.1016/j.eswa.2009.11.090.
8. Dong, W., Moses, C., Li, K., Efficient k-nearest neighbor graph construction for generic similarity measures. *WWW*, 19, 577–586, 2011.
9. Elizondo, D., Birkenhead, R., Gamez, M., Garcia, N., Alfaro, E., Linear separability and classification complexity. *Expert Syst. Appl.*, 39, 9, 7796–7807, 2012, doi:10.1016/j.eswa.2012.01.090.
10. Floares, A.G., Intelligent clinical decision supports for interferon treatment in chronic hepatitis, 17, 2009.
11. Khanday, A.M.U.D., Khan, Q.R., ST Rabani, SVMBPI: support vector machine-based propaganda identification Cognitive Informatics and Soft Computing. *Proceeding of CISC*, 940, 445–455, 2020.
12. Azad, C., Bhushan, B., Sharma, R., Shankar, A., Singh, K.K., Khamparia, A., Prediction model using SMOTE, genetic algorithm and decision tree (PMSGD) for classification of diabetes mellitus. *Multimed. Syst.*, 27, 2021, https://doi.org/10.1007/s00530-021-00817-2.
13. Chaganti, R., Mourade, A., Ravi, V., Vemprala, N., Dua, A., Bhushan, B., A Particle Swarm Optimization and Deep Learning Approach for Intrusion Detection System in Internet of Medical Things. *Sustainability*, 14, 19, 12828, 2022, https://doi.org/10.3390/su141912828.
14. Varshney, M., Bhushan, B., Haque, A.K.M.B., Big Data Analytics and Data Mining for Healthcare Informatics (HCI), in: *Multimedia Technologies in the Internet of Things Environment, Volume 3. Studies in Big Data*, vol. 108, R. Kumar, R. Sharma, P.K. Pattnaik, (Eds.), Springer, Singapore, 2022, https://doi.org/10.1007/978-981-19-0924-5_11.

7

Advancements in Parkinson's Disease Diagnosis through Automated Speech Analysis

P. Deepa[1]*, Rasmita Khilar[1] and Saumendra Kumar Mohapatra[2]

[1]Saveetha School of Engineering, Saveetha Institute of Medical and Technical Sciences, SIMATS, Chennai, India
[2]Faculty of Emerging Technologies, Sri Sri University, Cuttack, Odisha, India

Abstract
Parkinson's disease (PD) presents a significant challenge in the realm of neurological wellness management, given its profound impact on both mobility and overall quality of life. Acknowledging the pivotal role of speech-related challenges in PD diagnosis, this work introduces an innovative strategy to elevate diagnostic accuracy through advanced automated techniques. The central objective is to formulate a diagnostic system that harnesses generative and discriminative classifiers, concentrating on speech features linked to Parkinson's. The proposed methodology encompasses various classifiers, such as Gaussian Mixture Model, Parzen Window Bayesian, Logistic Regression, Decision Trees, Support Vector Machine, Multilayer Perceptron, and Radial Basis Function. The classifier exhibiting the highest accuracy emerges at the forefront of the automated diagnostic system, predicting the presence or absence of Parkinson's disease. The Parzen Window Bayesian classifier combined with exponential kernel has resulted in the highest accuracy of 94% as per this study.

Keywords: Parkinson's disease, automated diagnostic techniques, early detection, speech analysis, speech features, neurological disorder, wellness management

**Corresponding author*: pdeepa.3018@gmail.com

Bharat Bhushan, Akib Khanday, Khursheed Aurangzeb, Sudhir Kumar Sharma and Parma Nand (eds.) Wellness Management Powered by AI Technologies, (173–206) © 2025 Scrivener Publishing LLC

7.1 Introduction

7.1.1 Overview

Parkinson's disease (PD), which significantly affects movement and overall quality of life, is one of the most challenging neurological disorders to manage. This is the second most prevalent neurological illness, and its effects go beyond physical limitations to cause severe impairments and illnesses that are life-threatening. Since there is currently no proven treatment, early identification is essential for effective intervention. Numerous adults 65 years of age and above suffer from neurodegenerative disorders; James Parkinson was the first person to diagnose Parkinson's as an ongoing condition related to the anxious and movement illness. In older individuals, it is one of the most common causes of neurological problems [1].

Globally, PD affects more than ten million people. While 4% of cases are projected to be diagnosed before the age of fifty, and men are significantly more likely than women to be subjected to this scenario, this illness is particularly common in older adults [2]. According to a study, there are 7 million elderly Parkinson's disease sufferers in India. Out of people over 65 of age, 1% have Parkinson's disease. About 12 lakh people are thought to have Parkinson's disease (PD).

While the precise root cause of Parkinson's disease (PD) is unknown, environmental factors and other variables can occasionally contribute to a case by having a significant impact on the course of the situation. A buildup of misfolded protein molecules within the cell is a common cause of Parkinson's disease. It results from nervous system cells deteriorating or dying inside the substantia nigra, a region of the mind [3]. This cell produces dopamine, which is responsible for many motor and cognitive disorders (Figure 7.1). It is difficult to anticipate this situation because its symptoms, which include tremor, slowness of movement, tight muscles, and natural aging, are quite similar to those of other disorders. As a result, 25% of the disease's guide diagnoses are inaccurate.

Early Parkinson's disease diagnosis is the main concern for the clinical network [4]. Treatment is essential to avoid the loss of motor function since the contamination and its symptoms are now incurable. People with Parkinson's disease (PD) are frequently identified after the disease has advanced; thus, neuroprotective therapies may not have as much of an effect on the disease's course when administered at this advanced stage. Therefore, in this day and age, when the number of instances of Parkinson's disease is increasing, it is imperative to find a treatment that can detect the disease in its early stages.

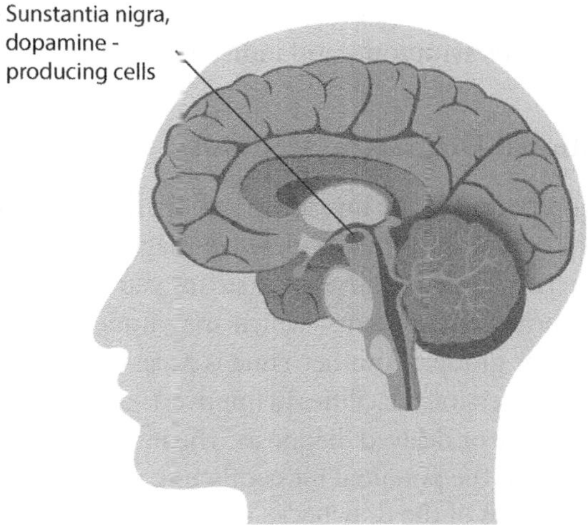

Figure 7.1 Human brain [27].

Although there are many other types of symptoms experienced by PD patients, motor symptoms are particularly significant and prevalent (Figure 7.2). Tremor, or a kind of shaking in the affected person's body, stiffness, stiff muscles, poor posture or stability, lethargy, difficulties with coordination when moving in any direction, and changes in speech and writing (such as slowing down while speaking or writing or even stammering) are the most common symptoms. It is important to remember that although these symptoms of Parkinson's disease are widespread, they may vary from person to person. These indicators also widen differently in several people and change

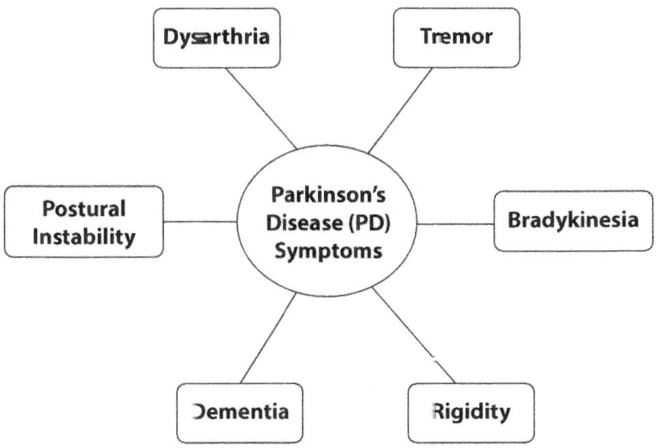

Figure 7.2 PD symptoms.

throughout time. Ineffectively, only a tiny portion of the symptoms were treated, and numerous symptoms and indicators remain untreated.

7.1.2 Traditional Diagnostic Methods

Conventional approaches to the investigation of Parkinson's disease, including medical reviews, patient histories, and neuroimaging, are essential but have limitations. In terms of cost, those approaches can be prohibitive for both individuals and healthcare systems, which may limit access, particularly in low-income areas or groups. Another issue is accessibility as there are sometimes insufficient professional facilities in impoverished or rural regions, which can lead to inadequate or delayed diagnosis. The inherent subjectivity of medical examinations and the potential for conflicting results from neuroimaging are two other examples of the drawbacks of traditional techniques. In light of these issues, an increasing number of individuals are realizing how crucial it is to have creative and affordable diagnostic choices. Automated speech analysis shows promise as a way to get around these restrictions, improve accuracy, and make more available and timely diagnoses for Parkinson's disease.

7.1.3 Emergence of Automated Speech Analysis

A significant trend has evolved in the current diagnostic environment, deviating from traditional approaches and moving the focus toward the use of computerized speech analysis as a crucial tool for the early diagnosis of Parkinson's disease (PD) [5–7]. These methods use artificial intelligence and technological advancements to examine speech patterns in an effort to identify subtle variations that may be early indicators of Parkinson's disease. Its non-invasiveness, which promises reliable diagnosis without imposing significant financial obligations, is particularly noteworthy. It also improves affected person comfort and compliance. Automated speech assessment is now more in line with global initiatives to maximize healthcare resources and ensures more accessibility across socioeconomic and geographic divides. This revolutionary change in the field of diagnosis highlights how technological advances have the power to completely change healthcare procedures by providing accessible, affordable, and non-invasive diagnostic options for the early identification of Parkinson's disease.

7.1.4 Major Contributions of the Work

The proposed study offers a comprehensive strategy for improving our knowledge of and ability to treat Parkinson's disease. It supports a patient-centric approach to care by streamlining diagnostic processes, encouraging individualized interventions, and facilitating early identification using a variety of approaches. Effective detection approaches and comparison performance analyses of models are incorporated into the study, which not only revolutionizes treatment strategies but also revolutionizes diagnosis. Moreover, the comprehensive assessment conducted through many metrics improves neurology and medical procedures. Together, these efforts represent a major advancement in the treatment of Parkinson's disease, providing all-encompassing approaches that combine early identification, prevention, and customized therapy to improve patient outcomes and strengthen the healthcare system as a whole.

This chapter is organized into the following sections. Section 7.2 looks at the unique speech characteristics that people with Parkinson's disease exhibit. Section 7.3 discusses technological advancements in speech analysis, specifically in relation to the diagnosis of Parkinson's disease. The integration of various data modalities is examined in Section 7.4 in an effort to improve the precision and efficacy of Parkinson's disease diagnosis. An extensive review of prior research and studies pertinent to the subject of speech analysis in the diagnosis of Parkinson's disease is given in Section 7.5. The methodology utilized in the suggested work is described in Section 7.6, along with the methods and strategies applied to the investigation. A thorough description of the experimental analysis carried out and the performance metrics employed in the investigation are provided in Section 7.7. The study's final remarks are summarized, along with the research's ramifications. The field of speech analysis for Parkinson's disease diagnosis could see certain innovations and future possibilities, which are covered in Section 7.8. Section 7.9 delves into the obstacles and constraints that were faced throughout the research process and their potential consequences for subsequent investigations. The report is finally concluded in Section 7.10, which summarizes the major discoveries and discusses their implications for clinical treatment and upcoming research projects.

7.2 Speech Characteristics in Parkinson's Disease

Parkinson's disease is a complex neurological disorder that affects not just physical movement but also many aspects of daily living, including social interactions. The core of human connection is communication, and the onset of Parkinson's disease presents a unique set of difficulties. The nuances of how Parkinson's disease specifically impacts speech will be explored in this section.

We will also uncover the frequently disregarded factors that contribute to the communication challenges experienced by individuals living with this illness.

7.2.1 Speech-Related Difficulties

People with Parkinson's disease (PD) frequently struggle with significant speech-related difficulties, which reflect unique limitations imposed by this neurological disorder. These difficulties show up as a range of problems, such as reduced pitch variability, irregular speech rates, and articulation difficulties. Patients with Parkinson's disease (PD) often have a limited range of pitch, which makes their spoken speech monotonous and less expressive. Variations in cadence associated with abnormal speech rates also affect the comprehensibility and flow of communication. Speech patterns that are less distinct and occasionally slurred are caused by articulation problems, which impair the accuracy and clarity of enunciation. All of these complex speech-related issues highlight how complex Parkinson's disease is, highlighting the need for focused therapies and improvements in diagnostic techniques to address the unique traits of the condition.

7.2.2 Specific Speech Features

Research has carefully defined certain characteristics that function as distinguishing markers of Parkinson's disease by analyzing speech abnormalities linked to the condition [8–10]. These unique traits include tremors in the voice, which are rhythmic fluctuations in pitch and intensity; pauses that break the flow of speech; and changes in prosody, which impact the rhythmic and melodic aspects of speech. Altogether, these characteristics help to provide a more complex picture of the subtleties surrounding speech abnormalities linked to Parkinson's disease. Understanding the subtle differences in affected individuals' vocalizations requires an understanding of voice tremors. A speech's overall rhythm and fluency are influenced by the unique cadence that is produced by well-pronounced pauses. Further contributing to the distinctive profile of speech abnormalities associated with Parkinson's disease are changes in prosody, such as flattening or disruptions in intonation and stress patterns. Finding these distinct speech characteristics improves diagnostic techniques and shows promise for tailored interventions to lessen communicative difficulties in Parkinson's disease patients.

7.3 Technological Advances in Speech Analysis

Speech analysis has seen tremendous technological advancements that have revolutionized our knowledge and use of this important communication tool. The creative advances in the field—which include technologies like Digital Signal Processing (DSP) and Machine Learning (ML) algorithms—are discussed in this section. These developments have not only changed the way that speech patterns linked to diseases like Parkinson's disease are studied, but also opened the door for more accurate diagnostic techniques.

7.3.1 Digital Signal Processing

The application of digital signal processing methods represents a significant breakthrough in the study of speech patterns associated with Parkinson's disease (PD). With its more in-depth comprehension of acoustic nuances, this advanced application has completely changed the way that speech characteristics in people with Parkinson's disease are examined. With the aid of digital signal processing, researchers and clinicians can investigate minute details that traditional analyses might miss. This is a transformative tool. By utilizing algorithms and computational techniques, it reveals latent patterns in auditory signals linked to speech abnormalities caused by Parkinson's disease. With the use of this technology, quantitative characteristics like intensity and pitch variations can be extracted, leading to a more thorough understanding of the distinctive characteristics of speech patterns related to Parkinson's disease. Due to the accuracy of digital signal processing, diagnostic frameworks can be quantitatively measured, making it possible to identify and monitor small variations linked to Parkinson's disease (PD) over time. By enabling professionals to decipher the complexities of speech abnormalities associated with Parkinson's disease (PD) and provide more precise diagnoses and focused interventions, the application of these techniques essentially represents a technological leap.

7.3.2 Machine Learning and Artificial Intelligence

Studies using machine learning (ML) and artificial intelligence (AI) algorithms, particularly generative and discriminative classifiers, represent a paradigm shift in diagnostic methodologies and show a remarkable improvement in distinguishing speech features linked to Parkinson's disease (PD). This novel method goes beyond conventional diagnostic frameworks by using computational methods to identify minute details in speech signals that human analysis might miss. Discriminative classifiers discern between classes, while generative classifiers model the distribution of data, working together to uncover unique characteristics of speech abnormalities associated with Parkinson's disease. The results demonstrate improved precision, with algorithms picking up complex patterns suggestive of Parkinson's disease from large-scale datasets. This learning capacity aids in the creation of reliable diagnostic models that can distinguish minute differences linked to various stages of Parkinson's disease. For a more sophisticated and precise diagnostic result, the integration of generative and discriminative classifiers adds complexity and captures the wide range of speech features associated with Parkinson's disease. All things considered, the combination of AI and machine learning algorithms specifically, generative and discriminative classifiers, represents a revolutionary advance in the field of Parkinson's disease (PD) diagnosis using speech analysis. This combination pushes the envelope in terms of accuracy and establishes the foundation for further advancements in computational approaches to the study of neurological disorders.

7.4 Integration of Multimodal Data

Researchers are leading the way in integrating speech analysis with a variety of modalities, such as neuroimaging methods and useful data from wearable sensors. Understanding the complex relationships between several physiological markers has aided in the creation of more thorough and advanced Parkinson's disease diagnostic processes. With a focus on providing a personalized and detailed understanding of Parkinson's disease, this dynamic and progressive diagnostic paradigm seamlessly combines real-time physiological indicators obtained through wearable sensors, insights gained from neuroimaging studies, and in-depth analysis of speech patterns.

7.4.1 Complementary Modalities

Researchers are attempting to combine speech analysis with other modalities, such as wearable sensor data and neuroimaging, in order to develop more comprehensive diagnostic strategies for Parkinson's disease (PD). Using a nuanced understanding of PD manifestations, this groundbreaking approach recognizes the complex interactions between multiple physiological markers to improve diagnostic accuracy. When speech analysis is combined with neuroimaging methods such as positron emission tomography (PET) or functional magnetic resonance imaging (fMRI), a more comprehensive understanding of the neurophysiological basis of Parkinson's disease (PD) is obtained. Real-time physiological parameters such as tremors and movement patterns are captured by the wearable sensor data, adding another dimension to the analysis. Constantly monitoring Parkinson's disease (PD) symptoms is made possible by this dynamic data stream, which supports a dynamic and progressive diagnostic framework. A comprehensive approach is provided by the collaborative analysis of wearable sensor, neuroimaging, and speech data. This analysis makes it easier to identify unique markers and gives a personalized understanding of how the disease progresses. This synergistic paradigm crosses conventional diagnostic boundaries and has the potential to completely change the way doctors view and diagnose Parkinson's disease by promoting a comprehensive understanding that encompasses neurological, physiological, and behavioral aspects.

7.4.2 Improved Diagnostic Precision

Multimodal approaches, which employ a novel diagnostic methodology for Parkinson's disease (PD), are designed to improve accuracy through the consideration of an extensive range of physiological markers. By recognizing the complex interactions between various physiological aspects, this innovative approach goes beyond specific modalities to provide a more comprehensive understanding of Parkinson's disease. Through the integration of data from wearable sensors, neuroimaging, speech analysis, and possibly other modalities, researchers are able to obtain a comprehensive view of the physiological terrain linked to Parkinson's disease. By utilizing the complementary strengths of various datasets, this integration goes beyond the confines of traditional diagnosis and produces a more nuanced picture of the illness. Multimodal approaches are powerful because they leverage real-time data from wearable sensors, insights from neuroimaging, and minute details from speech analysis to cover a wide range of physiological markers. This dataset recognizes the heterogeneity of Parkinson's disease presentations and allows for a more sophisticated and individualized diagnostic framework. Taking into account a wider range of physiological markers improves sensitivity and specificity, allowing for the identification of minute variations for a quicker and more accurate diagnosis. This ultimately improves patient outcomes and opens the door for focused interventions. To sum up, multimodal approaches represent a paradigm shift in the diagnosis of Parkinson's disease (PD), embracing a wide range of physiological markers to advance diagnostic precision into a new era of comprehension and effectiveness.

7.5 Related Works

Several researches have been done for diagnosing Parkinson's disease. An individual's speech or data is thought to be 90% helpful in identifying this illness and spotting its development. In order to slow the rate at which the disease advances, it is one of the most critical issues that must be identified early. Several scientists use various datasets to better accurately anticipate the illness. In general, people with PD experience speech issues, which fall into two categories: dysarthria and hypophonia. Dysarthria is characterized by sluggish speech or a weak voice and causes harm to the central nervous system, and hypophonia is characterized by a very weak voice from a person. As a result, the majority of doctors who treat patients with Parkinson's condition notice dysarthria as well as recommend individuals for certain therapies to alter vocal intensity. In the past, several academics worked on data preprocessing, feature selection, and classification techniques. This section gives a thorough examination of the articles used for research for the proposed work.

In order to improve dysphonia recognition in Parkinson's disease diagnosis, Mandal *et al.* [11] presented exact computational algorithms. The study's feature selection process makes use of ranker search and support vector machines, showing enhanced performance over earlier techniques. A method for accurate Parkinson's disease diagnosis that combines genetic algorithms and neural networks was presented by Polat *et al.* [12], exhibiting improved accuracy. In order to appropriately evaluate and categorize speech data, Khan Taha *et al.* [13] concentrated on speech intelligibility classification in Parkinson's disease (PD) using machine learning techniques. The acoustic qualities of speech were studied by Harel *et al.* [14] as possible biomarkers for early PD diagnosis, and they were able to uncover unique features for disease indicators. Zhang *et al.* [15] provided a trustworthy detection tool by emphasizing auditory properties and machine learning for PD identification, by using an automated feature-driven method.

Luca *et al.* [16] greatly improved the diagnostic accuracy of early Parkinson's disease (PD) diagnosis. In order to assess how well different PD categorization techniques might reliably identify patients, Das *et al.* [17] compared them. Improved diagnostic accuracy was achieved by

Behroozi *et al.* [18] by introducing a broad classification framework for PD identification utilizing different speech tests. Focusing on vocal cues for PD classification, Vadovsky *et al.* [19] showed excellent accuracy in differentiating between patients and healthy people. Tahami *et al.*'s [20] voice analysis method successfully identified Parkinson's disease patients by utilizing k-nearest neighbor classifiers and evolutionary algorithms.

A dependable analysis methodology was presented by Naranjo *et al.* [21] in their discussion of voice recording replications for tracking Parkinson's

Table 7.1 Recent works in Parkinson's disease (PD) detection.

Year	Technique	Accuracy %	Issues
2022 https://www.mdpi.com/2075-4418/12/8/1980/pdf	Grey Wolf Optimization (GWO) + Light Gradient Boosted Machine (LGBM)	89.4%	Overfitting problem, imbalanced dataset with high dimensionality, no multi-stage classification
2021 https://www.mdpi.com/2075-4418/11/6/1076	PCA + SVM	88.9%	Reverberation, background noise, and non-linear distortion
	DNN sparse autoencoder + SVM	93.5%	
2021 https://www.sciencedirect.com/science/article/pii/S2590005621000278#sec3	Autoencoders + rank-weighted average ensemble + voting	96.82%	Prediction error in detecting non-PD patients
	Logistic regression + voting	97.22%	
2021 https://sci-hub.st/10.1109/access.2021.3051432	Bidirectional long-short term memory	84.29%	Severity of the disease was not considered

disease development. Genetic algorithms were used by Raymer *et al.* [22] to reduce dimensionality, efficiently condensing big datasets while preserving important information. Voice assessments for neurological disease identification were investigated by Benba *et al.* [23], who successfully distinguished between patients and healthy people. Mohapatra *et al.* [24] present a more effective real-time multiagent system intended for the prompt detection of cardiac illness by using support vector machines (SVMs) to classify and analyze various cardiac issues based on the data collected, which was made possible by an IoT-enabled architecture.

In order to detect arrhythmias, Mohanty *et al.* [25] present a method that uses the wavelet transform to find R-peaks, whose coefficients are subsequently used as inputs for an RBFN model. In particular, peak detection makes use of the discrete wavelet transform. Srivastava *et al.* [26] deal with the detection of arrhythmias from cardiac signals by utilizing the Discrete Wavelet Transform for feature extraction and preprocessing with filters. A Deep Neural Network is used for classification, with potential applications in self-optimization and medical data mining. Together, these research offer fresh perspectives and improved accuracy, contributing to the changing field of computational methodologies in Parkinson's disease diagnosis. Table 7.1 summarizes the recent and relevant works in Parkinson's Disease detection.

7.6 Building a Machine Learning (ML) Model

Building an ML model involves the utilization of various classifiers, including Gaussian Mixture Model (GMM), Parzen Window Bayesian, Logistic Regression, Decision Trees, Support Vector Machine (SVM), Multilayer Perceptron (MLP), and Radial Basis Function (RBF). Each classifier's accuracy is assessed, and the classifier with the highest accuracy is identified as the preferred choice for the frontend of the automated diagnostic system. This classifier will be employed to forecast the presence or absence of Parkinson's disease in patients, thereby enhancing the reliability and efficiency of the diagnostic process.

7.6.1 Dataset Description

To identify the Parkinson's disorder, there are several medical datasets that are available. We utilized the Speech dataset, found in the repository for machine learning at the UCI website. As shown in Figure 7.3, the dataset

	ID	Recording	Status	Gender	Jitter_rel	Jitter_abs	Jitter_RAP	Jitter_PPQ	Shim_loc	Shim_dB	...	Delta3	Delta4
0	CONT-01	1	0	1	0.25546	0.000015	0.001467	0.001673	0.030256	0.26313	...	1.407701	1.417218
1	CONT-01	2	0	1	0.36964	0.000022	0.001932	0.002245	0.023146	0.20217	...	1.331232	1.227338
2	CONT-01	3	0	1	0.23514	0.000013	0.001353	0.001546	0.019338	0.16710	...	1.412304	1.324674
3	CONT-02	1	0	0	0.29320	0.000017	0.001105	0.001444	0.024716	0.20892	...	1.501200	1.534170
4	CONT-02	2	0	0	0.23075	0.000015	0.001073	0.001404	0.013119	0.11607	...	1.508468	1.334511
...	...	...	...	...	...	...	...	...	...	...	...	...	...
235	PARK-39	2	1	0	0.57585	0.000037	0.003701	0.005149	0.016868	0.14928	...	1.116409	1.104511
236	PARK-39	3	1	0	0.23322	0.000015	0.001270	0.001497	0.017923	0.16720	...	1.107477	1.083859
237	PARK-40	1	1	0	0.26862	0.000022	0.001354	0.001615	0.028040	0.24182	...	1.335189	1.385580
238	PARK-40	2	1	0	0.45376	0.000037	0.002724	0.002258	0.064605	0.58002	...	1.327629	1.349928
239	PARK-40	3	1	0	0.34706	0.000028	0.001746	0.002060	0.019914	0.17087	...	1.440003	1.327946

240 rows × 48 columns

Figure 7.3 Sample screenshot of the dataset.

consists of 240 voice information (144 female and 96 male voice recordings) divided into 48 columns, 46 of which are speech characteristics. Subject ID and voice recording number were the only two fields that were not regarded as features. For each of the 80 patients under study, 40 have Parkinson's disease; three audio recording replications of the sustained /a/ phonation were used to generate the dataset's acoustic features. There are no missing values and the dataset has multivariate properties. Because one of the three replications is of a single person, no row may be utilized independently. The nature of the data varies for each subject but is not subject-specific. Hence, because typical machine learning methods rely on the independence of the instances, they cannot be used with this dataset. They are not independent because there are 240 examples, but only for 80 subjects.

The next step involved is training the aforementioned classifiers using the available Parkinson's data. Each algorithm was trained on the training data, allowing them to learn patterns and relationships within the dataset. Once the training phase was complete, the classifiers were ready for testing. After training, the classifiers were evaluated by applying them to the test data. By making predictions on the test data, the classifiers' performance could be measured in terms of classification accuracy. This metric served as a basis for comparing the output of the different algorithms. The procedure involved in the model building is shown in Figure 7.4.

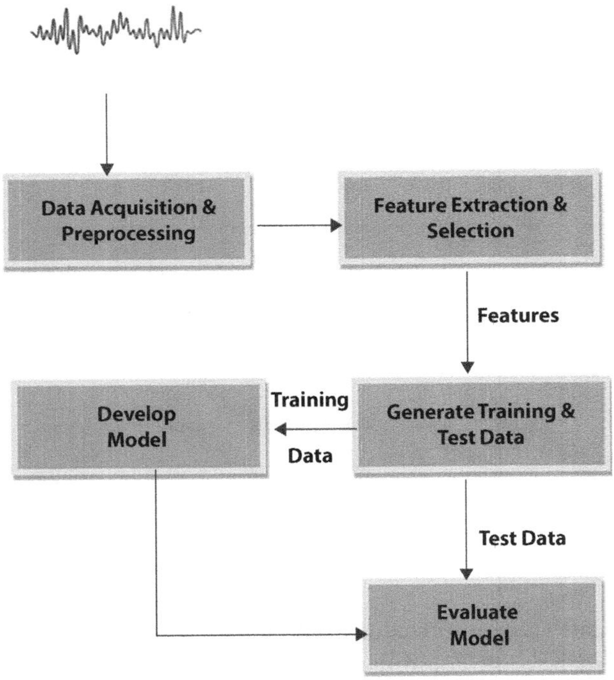

Figure 7.4 Model building process.

i. Preprocessing the raw data: Transforming the gathered data into a suitable format for analysis.
ii. Splitting the dataset: Dividing the preprocessed data into separate training and test sets.
iii. Selecting classifiers: Choosing a range of generative and discriminative classifiers, including Gaussian Mixture Model, Parzen Window Bayesian, Logistic Regression, Decision Trees, Support Vector Machine, Multilayer Perceptron, and Radial Basis Function.
iv. Training the classifiers: Using the training data to train each classifier and allow them to learn from the patterns and relationships in the dataset.
v. Testing the classifiers: Applying the trained classifiers to the test data and measuring their classification accuracy, precision, recall, and F1-score.
vi. Comparing algorithm performance: Evaluating and comparing the classification accuracy of the different classifiers

to determine their effectiveness in detecting Parkinson's disease. Based on that, hyperparameter tuning is done.

By following this procedure, the refined data and the performance of each algorithm can be analyzed and compared, providing valuable insights into the detection of Parkinson's disease.

7.6.2 Preprocessing

A crucial step in the training process is preprocessing. This procedure includes data cleansing, which comprises looking at NULL values, noise, and other tasks. With this technique, we can also exclude undesirable attributes from the dataset. Preprocessed data frequently yields more accurate results.

Data Normalization: Every feature has a mean zero and an identical range of variance once the data have been normalized. We use normalization because we do not want some features to have a smaller influence than others when they have a limited range and others when they have a vast range. *Cross-Validation with K-Fold*: K folds (K = 10) are used to divide the dataset. With this approach, all but one of these folds is utilized as training sets for the model. By selecting a new fold every time as the validation set, the procedure is repeated for all the folds. By using this strategy, we may gather K unique outcomes from each experiment.

7.6.3 Feature Extraction

Several successive speech recordings of the same subject are used to extract features, and in theory, these features ought to be similar. Technology flaws and biological variability lead to non-identical duplicated features that resemble one another more than features from distinct participants as a consequence. To decrease the amount of features, dimensionality reduction techniques are used. Unnecessary features that do not contribute to the output are eliminated. The estimated and projected correlation of the features for the dataset under study is given in Figure 7.5.

Principal Component Analysis without Whitening: To reduce the size of the data and avoid overfitting, PCA is utilized without whitening. Whitening helps to de-correlate the features and make the covariance matrix correspond to a sphere, but it also eliminates the relative variance scales of the components from the modified signal and can occasionally lead to inferior

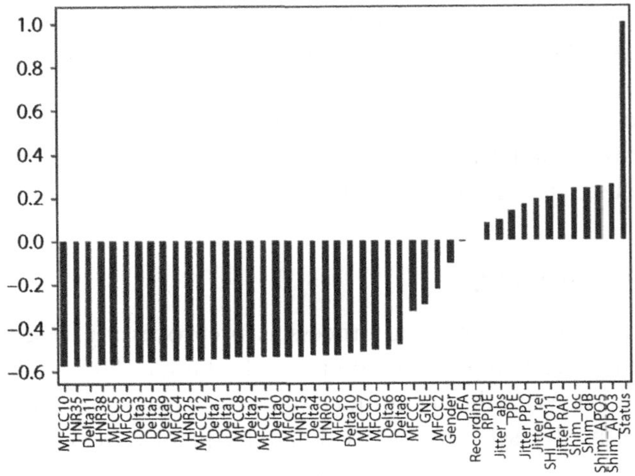

Figure 7.5 Correlation graph.

performance than the scenario where we do not whiten the dataset. Thus, it was decided not to whiten the data. Using PCA, data main directions may be selected to span a wide range of data variation. To cover an appropriate data variance ratio, as many characteristics as possible might be used. This is shown in Figure 7.6.

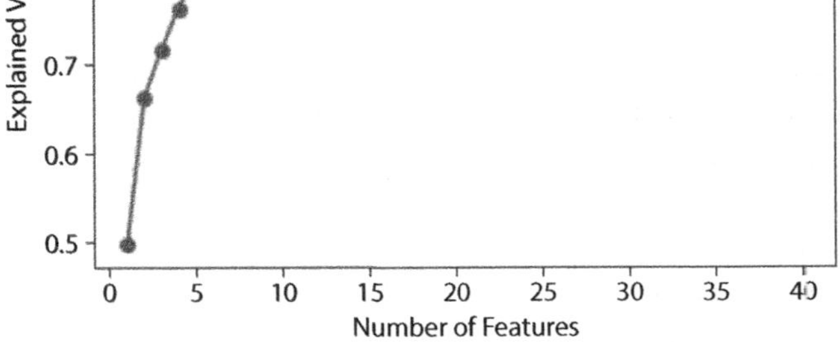

Figure 7.6 Accumulated explained variance.

7.6.4 Classification

An algorithm for classifying data is a function that balances the properties of the input so that the result divides one class into positive values and the other into negative values. Here, the categorization of new observations is determined using training data. The term "classifier" refers to a method that implements classification on a dataset. This work uses a binary classifier—class "Healthy" and class "Parkinson's affected". The classification categories are shown in Figure 7.7.

(i) Generative Classifiers

Generative classifiers are machine learning algorithms that model the probability distribution of each class in the dataset. They aim to learn the underlying data distribution for each class and use it to make predictions. Generative classifiers can be used to analyze the data and discriminate between healthy people and those with Parkinson's based on the learned probability distributions.

GMM is the commonly used generative classifier for identifying Parkinson's. It assumes that data are generated using a combination of Gaussian distributions. It learns the parameters of these distributions to represent the data distribution for each class. By fitting the GMM to the training data, it estimates the mean, covariance, and mixing coefficients for each class. Using these parameters, the model determines the chance that a certain sample belongs to each class during testing. The projected class for that sample is then determined by assigning the greatest likelihood class to it.

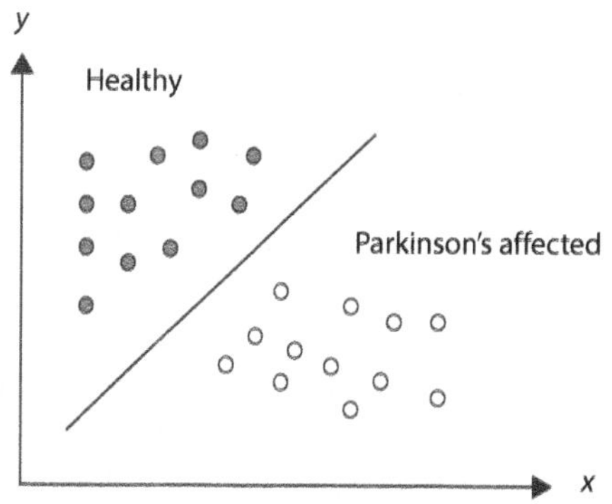

Figure 7.7 Classification classes.

Another generative classifier to be utilized for PD identification is the Parzen Window Bayesian classifier. Parzen's Window estimates the class conditional probability densities by placing a window (often a Gaussian kernel) around each training sample. The density estimate within the window is computed, and the densities are normalized to represent the probability distribution for each class. During testing, the classifier calculates the density of the test sample in each window and assigns it to the class with the highest density.

Generative classifiers offer certain advantages in detecting Parkinson's disease. Since they model the underlying data distribution, they can capture complex relationships and variations in the data. They can also handle missing or incomplete data by estimating the probabilities based on the available information. Additionally, generative classifiers can be useful when the dataset is small or imbalanced, as they can generate synthetic samples to augment the training set.

It is necessary to remember that the assumption of the distribution of data affects the working of generative classifiers. If the underlying distribution significantly deviates from the assumed model, the accuracy of the classifier may be affected. Furthermore, generative classifiers may struggle with high-dimensional data or when the class boundaries are highly complex.

Overall, generative classifiers like Gaussian Mixture Model and Parzen Window Bayesian can be valuable tools in detecting Parkinson's disease by learning and leveraging the probability distributions of the data.

Gaussian Mixture Model: A Gaussian Mixture Model assumes that the observed data points are generated by a combination of Gaussian distributions. The GMM learns the unknown parameters through the EM algorithm and can be put to use when applying Bayes' theorem to classification. Bayesian optimization is commonly used for hyperparameter tuning when dealing with difficult-to-evaluate objective functions.

Mathematically, a GMM can be represented as:

$$P(x) = \sum (w_i * N(x \mid \mu_i, \Sigma_i)) \tag{7.1}$$

where $P(x)$ is the probability density function of the observed data point x, w_i represents the weight or the mixing coefficient of the ith Gaussian component, and $N(x \mid \mu_i, \Sigma_i)$ is the probability density function of the ith Gaussian distribution with mean μ_i and covariance Σ_i.

In order to maximize the probability of the observed data, GMM seeks to estimate unknown parameters (μ_i, Σ_i, w_i). This estimation is typically done through the Expectation Maximization (EM) algorithm, which iteratively updates parameter values according to the observed data.

After the GMM has been trained, Bayes' theorem may be used to classify data using it. Given a new data point x, the subsequent likelihood of it belonging to a specific class c_i can be computed using:

$$P(c_i \mid x) = (w_i * N(x \mid \mu_i, \Sigma_i)) / \Sigma(w_j * N(x \mid \mu_j, \Sigma_j)) \quad (7.2)$$

where $P(c_i \mid x)$ denotes the subsequent likelihood of class c_i given the data point x.

In hyperparameter tuning, Bayesian optimization is often employed when the objective function is difficult to evaluate directly. Bayesian optimization uses a probabilistic model to approximate the objective function and optimizes it iteratively. This approach allows for efficient exploration and exploitation of the hyperparameter space, ultimately finding the optimal set of hyperparameters for the GMM.

Parzen Window Bayesian Classifier: The Parzen Window Bayesian classifier, also known as Parzen Window Density Estimation or Kernel Density Estimation, is a nonparametric technique commonly used to estimate the probability distribution of class data. It relies on the concept of fixing a hypercube around each data sample and counting the number of samples that fall within that hypercube.

Mathematically, the Parzen Window estimator can be expressed as follows:

$$f(x) = (k / (Q * V)) \quad (7.3)$$

where $f(x)$ represents the estimated probability density at a data point x, k is the number of samples that fall within the hypercube centered at x, Q is the total quantity of samples in dataset, and V is the volume of the hypercube.

Estimation of the probability for each sample involves fixing a hypercube with a specific size or bandwidth around that sample. The number of samples that fall within the hypercube, denoted as k, is counted. This count reflects the number of samples contributing to the density estimate at that particular data point.

The volume of the hypercube, represented by V, is an important parameter that determines the size of the region around each data sample. It can be determined by considering the dimensionality of the data and the chosen bandwidth. By estimating the probability density for each data sample using the Parzen Window estimator, the classifier can then assign the class with a fresh data point and with the highest density estimate.

(ii) Discriminative Classifiers

During classification in discriminative models, the conditional probability is estimated. As a result of generative classifiers' ability to identify joint distributions, discriminative classifiers have the advantage of requiring less data. Moreover, because outliers may have a significant impact on the distribution, generative models are more vulnerable to them. Moreover, generative models use much more time and energy than discriminative models since they require more computing to run.

Logistic Regression: Many binary classification applications employ the popular and effective classification method known as logistic regression (LR). To calculate the likelihood that any data will fall into the positive class, it combines a linear model with the sigmoid function.

Mathematically, logistic regression can be represented as:

$$\hbar\theta(x) = \sigma(\theta^\wedge T * x) \tag{7.4}$$

where $\hbar\theta(x)$ represents the predicted probability that the data point x belongs to the positive class (class 1), θ denotes the model parameters or coefficients, and σ is the sigmoid or logistic function.

The sigmoid function is defined as:

$$\sigma(z) = 1/(1 + \exp(-z)) \tag{7.5}$$

It represents the input z in the range 0–1, which may be seen as the likelihood of falling into the positive class. The linear combination of the model parameters $\theta^\wedge T^* x$ is passed through the sigmoid function to obtain the predicted probability.

Through an optimization approach like gradient descent, the logistic regression model seeks to reduce the cost function during the training phase. For binary classification issues, the logistic loss (or binary cross-entropy loss) serves as the cost function, also known as the loss function.

The difference between the actual class labels and the projected probability is what is being measured.

Until convergence, a suitable level of loss or accuracy is achieved, and the optimization process iteratively modifies the model parameters to minimize the cost function. By applying the discovered parameters to the input characteristics, the logistic regression model may forecast fresh data once it has been trained. When deciding whether to classify a data item as positive or negative, the estimated probability is then contrasted with a predetermined threshold (for example, 0.5). Logistic regression finds the model parameters that most closely match the data by repeatedly minimizing the cost function. In order to generate predictions on new data, this trained model may subsequently be employed.

Decision Tree: A popular and useful method for classification and detection is the decision tree (DT). It is displayed as a tree-like, flowchart-like structure. Decision trees may be easily interpreted since they accurately represent the decision-making process. In a decision tree, the branches indicate the results of the tests, and every internal node denotes a test on a particular characteristic. Labels for classes are found in the leaf nodes.

The following equation may be used to mathematically express a decision tree:

$$DT(x) = f(f_1(x), f_2(x), f_3(x), \ldots f_n(x)) \tag{7.6}$$

where $DT(x)$ is the decision tree function that predicts the class label for the input instance x. $f_1, f_2, f_3, \ldots, f_n$ are the feature tests conducted at each internal node, and their results are used as inputs for subsequent nodes until a leaf node is reached.

Support Vector Machine: Popular supervised learning methods for classification issues include the Support Vector Machine (SVM) Classifier. By successfully dividing an n-dimensional space into several classes, it aims to create an ideal hyperplane or collection of points that will make it easier to quickly classify fresh data points.

The SVM method searches for the hyperplane that is mathematically defined as:

$$w * x + b = 0 \tag{7.7}$$

where w is the weight vector perpendicular to the hyperplane, x represents the input data points, and b denotes the bias. The sign of the expression is what determines the boundary of the decision, assigning data points to different classes based on whether the value is positive or negative. In order to improve the robustness and generalization properties of the classifier, the SVM method seeks to maximize the gap between the hyperplane and the nearest data points, known as support vectors.

Multilayer Perceptron: A multilayer perceptron (MLP), a member of the artificial neural network family, is designed to produce a set of outputs based on a given set of inputs. In an MLP, the connections from the input to the output layers, as well as hidden layers, form a directed graph. The MLP utilizes backpropagation, a widely used training algorithm, to adjust the network's weights during the learning process.

The following equations can be used to mathematically describe an MLP:

For each hidden layer j:

$$z_i = \sum (w_{\{ij\}} * x_i) + b_j \tag{7.8}$$

$$a_j = f(z_j) \tag{7.9}$$

For the output layer k:

$$z_k = \sum w_{\{jk\}} + a_j) + b_k \tag{7.10}$$

$$y_k = f(z_k) \tag{7.11}$$

where x_i denotes the input features, $w_{\{ij\}}$ denotes the weight between the ith input node and the jth hidden layer node, b_j the bias for the jth hidden layer node, z_j is the weighted sum of inputs for the jth hidden layer node, i is the activation value (output) of the jth hidden layer node after applying an activation function f, $w_{\{jk\}}$ represents the weight between the jth hidden layer node and the kth output node, b_k is the bias term for the kth output node, z_k is the weighted sum of inputs for the kth output node, y_k is the predicted output, and $f()$ is the activation function applied element-wise to the inputs.

The network's biases and weights may then be adjusted to reduce the error between the intended and expected outputs during training by using the backpropagation technique to determine their gradients.

Radial Basis Function: Feed-forward neural networks, a subclass of radial basis functions (RBF), is made up of three layers: input, hidden, and output. Unlike other networks, most neural network topologies incorporate multiple layers and utilize nonlinear activation functions to introduce nonlinearity.

The computations in a feed-forward neural network can be written as follows:

For the hidden layer j:

$$a_j = f(\sum w_{\{ij\}} * x_i) + b_j \tag{7.12}$$

For the output layer k:

$$y_k = g(\sum w_{\{jk\}} + a_j) + b_k \tag{7.13}$$

where x_i denotes the input values, $w_{\{ij\}}$ denotes the weights connecting the ith input node to the jth hidden layer node, b_j denotes the bias for the jth hidden layer node, a_j denotes the activation value (output) of the jth hidden layer node after applying the activation function f, and $w_{\{jk\}}$ denotes the weights connecting the jth hidden layer node to the kth.

In a radial basis function (RBF) neural network, the hidden layer exhibits a distinctive characteristic. It utilizes radial basis functions as activation functions, such as Gaussian or inverse multi-quadratic functions, which allow the network to capture complex relationships between inputs and hidden units. As it produces the final output based on the activations of the hidden layer, the neural network's output layer is in charge of carrying out tasks connected to classification.

7.7 Experimental Analysis and Performance Measures

To identify the disorders, there are several medical datasets that are available. We utilized the Speech dataset, found in the repository for machine learning at the UCI website. The dataset consists of 240 voice information (144 female and 96 male voice recordings) divided into 48 columns, 46 of which are speech characteristics. Subject ID and voice recording number were the only two fields that were not regarded as features. For each of the 80 patients under study, 40 have Parkinson's disease; three audio recording replications of the sustained /a/ phonation were used to generate the dataset's acoustic features. There are no missing values and the dataset has multivariate properties. Because one of the three replications is of a single person, no row may be utilized independently. The nature of the data varies for each subject but is not subject-specific. Hence, because typical machine learning methods rely on the independence of the instances, they cannot be used with this dataset. They are not independent because there are 240 examples, but only for 80 subjects.

A training set and a test set were created from the dataset utilized in the experiment in an 8:2 ratio. This indicates that 80% of the data were utilized to train the classifiers, while the remaining 20% was set aside for assessing how well they performed. The classifiers underwent training on the training set, and the test set was used to assess their effectiveness.

The findings from this experimental analysis are shown in Table 7.2.

Table 7.2 Experimental performance analysis of the classifiers.

Classifier	**Accuracy %**	**Precision %**	**Recall %**	**F1-score %**
Generative classifiers				
Gaussian mixture model (GMM)	72.50	74.94	72.50	73.69
Parzen window Bayesian (PWB)	84.17	84.33	84.17	84.25
Discriminative classifiers				
Logistic regression (LR)	77.92	78.09	77.92	78.00
Decision tree (DT)	70.00	70.56	70.00	70.28
Support vector machine (SVM)	78.33	78.56	78.33	78.44
Multilayer perceptron (MLP)	77.08	77.27	77.08	77.17
Radial basis function (RBF)	82.92	83.21	82.92	83.06

The table summarizes the performance metrics for each classifier. These metrics include accuracy, precision, recall, and F1-score, which explains the classifiers' capacity to accurately detect positive cases, classification accuracy, and the connection between precision and recall.

Considering the outcomes in Table 7.2, the Parzen Window Bayesian (PWB) classifier achieved the highest accuracy of 84.17%, with competitive precision, recall, and F1-scores. Other classifiers, such as the Gaussian Mixture Model (GMM), Logistic Regression (LR), Decision Tree (DT), Support Vector Machine (SVM), Multilayer Perceptron (MLP), and Radial Basis Function (RBF) classifiers, also demonstrated varying levels of performance.

These results serve as a comparative evaluation of the classifiers, providing insights into their effectiveness in handling the given dataset. The classification accuracy metric was utilized to assess and compare their overall performance.

7.7.1 Evaluating Classifiers

After evaluating and comparing various classifiers, the Parzen Window Bayesian model was identified as the best performer. The classification accuracy metric was used for these evaluations and comparisons as it gives an indication of how well a model can correctly classify instances. The Parzen Window Bayesian model demonstrated quick execution time, making it efficient for practical applications.

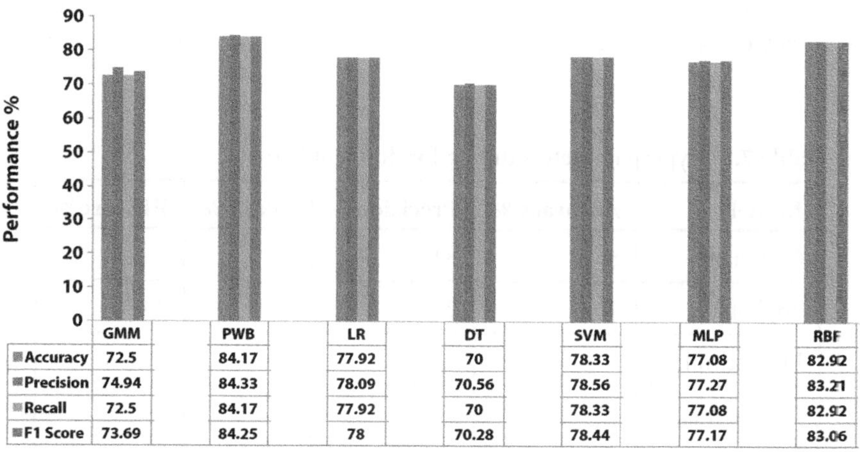

	GMM	PWB	LR	DT	SVM	MLP	RBF
Accuracy	72.5	84.17	77.92	70	78.33	77.08	82.92
Precision	74.94	84.33	78.09	70.56	78.56	77.27	83.21
Recall	72.5	84.17	77.92	70	78.33	77.08	82.92
F1 Score	73.69	84.25	78	70.28	78.44	77.17	83.06

Figure 7.8 Comparison graph for the different classifiers under study.

To visualize the comparison results, a graph was generated, referred to as Figure 7.8, displaying the performance of the different classifiers under examination. The *y*-axis displays the respective classification accuracy percentages, while the *x*-axis lists the various classifiers.

The Parzen Window Bayesian model stands out as the best classifier, demonstrating the highest classification accuracy among all the classifiers tested. The other classifiers are also represented on the graph, enabling a clear comparison of their respective performance levels.

7.7.2 Tuning Hyperparameters

To optimize the hyperparameters of the Parzen Window Bayesian model, the classification accuracy metric was used as the criterion for selection. The model was evaluated using several kernels, and the results obtained from tuning the model's parameters are shown in Table 7.3.

The table provides the results of tuning the hyperparameters of the Parzen Window Bayesian model using different kernels. The metrics evaluated include accuracy, precision, recall, and F1-score. Figure 7.9 shows the comparison for the different kernels with respect to the Parzen Window Bayesian model.

Out of all the kernels tested, the Gaussian kernel achieved an accuracy of 83%, a precision of 84%, a recall of 83%, and an F1-score of 83%. The Tophat kernel exhibited lower performance with an accuracy of 50%, a precision of 25%, a recall of 50%, and an F1-score of 33%. The Epanechnikov kernel obtained an accuracy of 52%, a precision of 53%, a recall of 52%, and an F1-score of 49%.

The exponential kernel demonstrated the highest performance, with an accuracy of 94%, a precision of 94%, a recall of 94%, and an F1-score of 94%.

Table 7.3 Hyperparameters tuning for different kernels.

Kernel	Accuracy %	Precision %	Recall %	F1Score %
Gaussian	83	84	83	83
Tophat	50	25	50	33
Epanechnikov	52	53	52	49
Exponential	94	94	94	94
Linear	48	47	48	44
Cosine	50	50	50	48

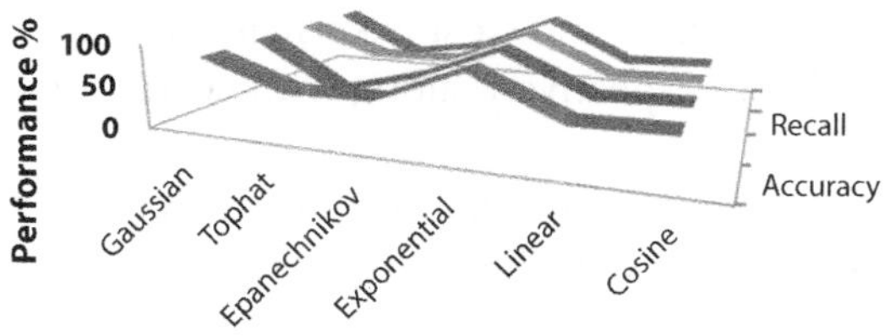

	Gaussian	Tophat	Epanechnikov	Exponential	Linear	Cosine
Accuracy	83	50	52	94	48	50
Precision	84	25	53	94	47	50
Recall	83	50	52	94	48	50
F1 Score	83	33	49	94	44	48

Figure 7.9 Comparison for the different kernels with respect to the Parzen Window Bayesian model.

Table 7.4 Comparative study of the recent studies of PD detection models.

	Dataset			
Authors	**PD affected samples**	**Healthy samples**	**Classifier used**	**Accuracy %**
Lahimiri *et al.*	147	48	SVM	92
Vasquez-Correa *et al.*	88	88	CNN	89.4
Li *et al.*	20	20	Ensemble with CART	90
Gunduz *et al.*	188	64	CNN, SVM	86.9
Woodzinski *et al.*	50	50	Resnet	91.7
Vaiciukynas *et al.*	194	74	CNN	85.9
This work	40	40	Parzen window Bayesian (Kernel = Exponential)	94

On the other hand, the Linear and Cosine kernels achieved lower accuracy scores of 48% and 50%, respectively, along with corresponding precision, recall, and F1-scores.

These results give a thorough evaluation of the Parzen Window Bayesian model with different kernels, enabling the selection of the most suitable kernel based on the classification accuracy metric. The most suitable kernel selected for this work is found to be an Exponential Kernel. Table 7.4 shows the summary of the recent studies of Parkinson's disease detection models.

7.8 Future Directions

Emerging technologies and personalized medicine are discussed in this segment, as they have the potential to shape the future of many different fields.

7.8.1 Advancements in Technology

Looking ahead, technological developments present a promising path for Parkinson's disease diagnosis. It is anticipated that increasingly complex patterns in speech and physiological data will be revealed by machine learning algorithms that are constantly developing and improving, improving the accuracy of diagnosis. Better sensor technologies promise richer and more nuanced data simultaneously, whether they are incorporated into wearables or diagnostic tools. With early detection and personalized approaches based on comprehensive physiological markers, this synergy has the potential to revolutionize the diagnosis of Parkinson's disease. With these developments, a new era of accuracy and efficacy in healthcare is predicted by the convergence of sophisticated algorithms and state-of-the-art sensors, which will lead to considerably improved diagnostic capabilities for Parkinson's disease.

7.8.2 Personalized Medicine

Automated speech analysis presents itself as a game-changing tool that opens the door to personalized medicine by enabling the development of customized interventions based on unique Parkinson's disease symptom profiles. The detailed insights obtained from automated speech pattern analysis provide a singular window into the distinctive features of each patient's condition. This tailored approach has the potential to improve interventions by providing a more detailed understanding of the unique speech-related difficulties faced by Parkinson's patients. This paradigm shift in healthcare improves the precision of interventions and marks a major step towards improving patient outcomes and quality of life by matching treatments to individual symptom profiles. Patient-centered care is about to enter a new phase as the field of automated speech analysis develops and the possibility of genuinely personalized interventions for Parkinson's disease becomes more real.

7.9 Challenges and Limitations

This section offers an overview of the challenges faced, which provides insight into the potential barriers in Parkinson's disease diagnosis using speech signals. This study of obstacles and constraints, from influencing factors to ethical considerations, serves as a roadmap for creating well-informed and practical solutions that break down barriers and advance innovation.

7.9.1 Influencing Factors

To improve the accuracy of automated systems for the diagnosis of Parkinson's disease, careful consideration of factors affecting diagnostic precision is necessary. One such factor is the differences in speech patterns among different demographic groups. Automatic algorithms must be flexible due to the intricacies brought about by cultural, linguistic, and regional differences. Speech pattern variations are influenced by age and gender dynamics, necessitating customized approaches for various demographic contexts. Inclusion is ensured by taking socioeconomic factors and technology literacy into account. Automated systems can attain higher diagnostic accuracy by fully comprehending and accounting for these factors, thereby offering fair and dependable evaluations to a wide range of Parkinson's disease patients.

7.9.2 Ethical Considerations

Automated systems for the diagnosis of Parkinson's disease need to be thoroughly examined in terms of privacy, ethical issues surrounding the use of data, and potential biases in the algorithms running them. A careful balance between the quest of diagnostic breakthroughs and the protection of individuals' privacy is necessary given the rapidly changing landscape of healthcare technology. Transparent and accountable practices are essential in light of the ethical issues surrounding the collection, storage, and use of data. To ensure impartial and equitable diagnostic results, ongoing evaluation and mitigation strategies are also required due to the possible biases present in automated algorithms. To build trust, advance ethical norms, and advance the responsible implementation of automated systems in Parkinson's disease diagnosis, a comprehensive analysis of these complex factors is necessary.

7.9.3 Standardization and Validation

Strong efforts are needed to address the lack of standardized protocols and the critical need for rigorous validation studies that impede the widespread clinical adoption of automated systems for Parkinson's disease diagnosis. To create consistency in diagnostic procedures and guarantee dependability in a range of healthcare environments, standardization is essential. In order to give stakeholders and clinicians confidence in automated systems, thorough validation studies are essential to proving their reliability and accuracy. In order to address these issues and lay the groundwork for the widespread adoption and clinical practice integration of automated diagnostic systems for Parkinson's disease, the scientific community must work together to develop strong protocols and carry out thorough validation studies.

7.10 Conclusion and Implications

This work focuses on the prevention of Parkinson's disease, as there is currently no known cure. To achieve this, generative and discriminative models were employed to identify Parkinson's disease. By employing generative and discriminative models and considering multiple evaluation standards, the study aimed to provide insights into effective methods for earlier detection and prevention of Parkinson's. Multiple models were created using various methodologies, and their performance was compared to identify the best-fitting model. The evaluation of these models was based on multiple metrics, including accuracy, precision, recall, and F1-score. These metrics provide a comprehensive assessment of the models' ability to correctly classify instances and balance between precision and recall.

The Parzen Window Bayesian classifier demonstrated the highest performance among the tested models, achieving an accuracy of 84.17%. This classifier was evaluated using various kernel types for hyperparameter adjustment. After experimentation, it was found that the Parzen Window Bayesian classifier with the exponential kernel yielded the best result. The findings highlight the significance of the Parzen Window Bayesian classifier, particularly when using the exponential kernel of 94%, and it demonstrated superior performance in accurately classifying instances of Parkinson's disease within the given dataset. These results contribute to the development of effective strategies for identifying and preventing Parkinson's disease.

7.10.1 Implications for Clinical Practice

The significant developments in automated speech analysis for the diagnosis of Parkinson's disease have broad effects on treatment protocols and patient care. The combination of advanced algorithms and state-of-the-art technologies facilitates early detection and personalized interventions in addition to streamlining diagnostic procedures in clinical settings. With these tools at their disposal, clinicians can act quickly and make well-informed decisions that could change the course of a disease. A more patient-centric approach is reflected in the move toward personalized medicine outside of the clinic, which also optimizes resource allocation and supports a long-term healthcare ecosystem. All things considered, these developments portend a revolution in the treatment of Parkinson's disease, offering better patient outcomes through more successful, customized interventions and increased diagnostic accuracy.

Anticipated outcomes encompass a transformative shift in PD diagnosis, presenting a more precise and efficient process that promotes timely intervention. The significance of this innovative solution lies in its potential to contribute to neurology and healthcare by enhancing diagnostic accuracy and efficiency in managing Parkinson's disease. In conclusion, this holistic approach prioritizes speech features, deploying advanced classifiers to facilitate early detection and, ultimately, elevate the prognosis and quality of life for individuals impacted by Parkinson's disease.

References

1. Fahn, S., Description of Parkinson's disease as a clinical syndrome. *Ann. N. Y. Acad. Sci.*, 991, 1–14, 2003. doi: 10.1111/j.1749-6632.2003.tb07458.x.

2. Van Den Eeden, S.K., Tanner, C.M., Bernstein, A.L., Fross, R.D., Leimpeter, A., Bloch, D.A., Nelson, L.M., Incidence of Parkinson's disease: variation by age, gender, and race/ethnicity. *Am. J. Epidemiol.*, 157, 11, 1015–22, 2003. doi: 10.1093/aje/kwg068. PMID: 12777365.
3. Cummings, J.L. *et al.*, The role of dopaminergic imaging in patients with symptoms of dopaminergic system neurodegeneration. *Brain*, 134, 3146–66, 11, 2011. doi: 10.1093/brain/awr177. PMID: 21810889.
4. Jankovic, J., Parkinson's disease: clinical features and diagnosis. *J. Neurology, Neurosurg. Psychiatry*, 79, 4, 368–376, 2008.
5. Tsanas, A. *et al.*, Accurate telemonitoring of Parkinson's disease progression by noninvasive speech tests. *IEEE Trans. Biomed. Eng.*, 58, 2, 191–199, 2011.
6. Orozco-Arroyave, J.R. *et al.*, Toward an automatic classification of phonation in Parkinson's disease based on the glottal signal. *IEEE J. Biomed. Health Inform.*, 20, 5, 1271–1280, 2016.
7. Arora, S. *et al.*, Detecting and monitoring the symptoms of Parkinson's disease using smartphones: A pilot study. *Parkinsonism Relat. Disord.*, 21, 6, 650–653, 2015.
8. Little, M.A. *et al.*, Suitability of dysphonia measurements for telemonitoring of Parkinson's disease. *IEEE Trans. Biomed. Eng.*, 56, 4, 1015–1022, 2009.
9. Rusz, J. *et al.*, Short-term acoustic analysis of voice in Parkinson's disease patients treated with subthalamic stimulation – Preliminary data. *Neuro. Endocrinol. Lett.*, 32, 3, 221–226, 2011.
10. Wang, E.Q. *et al.*, Thalamic deep brain stimulation and laryngeal muscle activity for voice tremor. *Mov. Disord.*, 18, 11, 1299–1302, 2003.
11. Mandal, I. and Sairam, N., Accurate telemonitoring of Parkinson's disease diagnosis using robust inference system. *Int. J. Med. Inform.*, 82, 5, 359–77, 2013. doi: 10.1016/j.ijmedinf.2012.10.006.
12. Hariharan, M., Polat, K., Sindhu, R., A new hybrid intelligent system for accurate detection of Parkinson's disease. *Comput. Methods Programs Biomed.*, 113, 3, 904–13, 2014. doi: 10.1016/j.cmpb.2014.01.004. PMID: 24485390.
13. Khan, T., Westin, J., Dougherty, M., Classification of speech intelligibility in Parkinson's disease. *Biocybern. Biomed. Eng.*, 34, 1, 35–45, 2014. https://doi.org/10.1016/j.bbe.2013.10.003.
14. Harel, B.T. *et al.*, Acoustic characteristics of Parkinsonian speech: A potential biomarker of early disease progression and treatment. *J. Neurolinguistics*, 17, 6, 439–453, 2004. https://doi.org/10.1016/j.jneuroling.2004.06.001.
15. Wu, K., Zhang, D., Lu, G., Guo, Z., Learning acoustic features to detect Parkinson's disease. *Neurocomputing*, 318, 102–108, 2018. https://doi.org/10.1016/j.neucom.2018.08.036.
16. Parisi, L., RaviChandran, N., Manaog, M.L., Feature-driven Machine Learning to Improve Early Diagnosis of Parkinson's Disease. *Expert Syst. Appl.*, 110, 182–190, 2018. https://doi.org/10.1016/j.eswa.2018.06.003.

17. Das, R., A comparison of multiple classification methods for diagnosis of Parkinson disease. *Expert Syst. Appl.*, 37, 1568–1572, 2010. https://doi.org/10.1016/j.eswa.2009.06.040.
18. Behroozi, M. and Sami, A., A Multiple-Classifier Framework for Parkinson's Disease Detection Based on Various Vocal Tests. *Int. J. Telemed. Appl.*, 2016, 1–9, 2016. https://doi.org/10.1155/2016/6837498.
19. Vadovský, M. and Paralič, J., Parkinson's disease patients classification based on the speech signals. *2017 IEEE 15th Int Symposium on Applied Machine Intelligence and Informatics (SAMI)*, 2017, https://doi.org/10.1109/SAMI.2017.7880326.
20. Arefi Shirvan, R. and Tahami, E., Voice analysis for detecting Parkinson's disease using genetic algorithm and KNN classification method. *2011 18th Iran. Conf. Biomed. Eng.*, 2011, 278–283, 2011. https://doi.org/10.1109/ICBME.2011.6168572.
21. Pérez Naranjo, L., Martín, C., Jacinto, Addressing voice recording replications for tracking Parkinson's disease progression. *Med. Biol. Eng. Comput.*, 55, 365–373, 2017. https://doi.org/10.1007/s11517-016-1512-y.
22. Raymer, M.L. *et al.*, Dimensionality reduction using genetic algorithms. *IEEE Trans. Evol. Comput.*, 4, 2, 164–171, 2000. https://doi.org/10.1109/4235.850656.
23. Jilbab Benba, A. and Hammouch, A., Voice assessments for detecting patients with neurological diseases using PCA and NPCA. *Int. J. Speech Technol.*, 20, 673–683, 2017. https://doi.org/10.1007/s10772-017-9438-9.
24. Mohapatra, S.K. and Mohanty, M.N., Big data classification with IoT-based application for e-health care, in: *Cognitive Data Science in Sustainable Computing, Cognitive Big Data Intelligence with a Metaheuristic Approach*, pp. 147–172, Academic Press, Cambridge, Massachusetts, 2022, doi: 10.1016/B978-0-323-85117-6.00014-5.
25. Mohapatra, S.K. and Mohanty, M.N., Arrhythmia Detection Using a Radial Basis Function Network with Wavelet Features. *Int. J. Knowl.-Based Organ.*, 10, 2, 48–56, Apr. 2020.
26. Mohapatra, S.K., Srivastava, G., Mohanty, M.N., Arrhythmia Classification Using Deep Neural Network, in: *2019 Int. Conf. Appl. Mach. Learn. (ICAML)*, Bhubaneswar, India, pp. 296–300, 2019, doi: 10.1109/ICAML48257.2019.00062.
27. National Library of Medicine (NLM), Understanding Parkinson's Disease, MedlinePlus, [Online]. Available: https://medlineplus.gov/genetics/condition/parkinsons-disease/.

8

Public Opinion Segmentation on COVID-19 Vaccination and Its Impact on Wellbeing

Akib Mohi Ud Din Khanday, Salah Bouktif* and K. Nimmi

College of Information Technology, United Arab Emirates University, Al Ain, UAE

Abstract

Social media is used as a communication tool and people share their views irrespective of their cultural or regional locations. There is a dramatic change in the usage of social media during pandemics. Analyzing social media data can provide insights into issues that influence vaccine uptake and adherence. In this chapter, we analyze the sentiments of various prescribed vaccines on social media data, which provide insights into vaccine acceptance, hesitancy, and concerns within different populations. In this work, Twitter dataset is used, in which a positive sentiment toward vaccines indicates high levels of trust, confidence, and willingness to be vaccinated, leading to increased uptake. A negative sentiment indicates signal barriers, concerns, or misinformation that hinder vaccine acceptance. Various fine-tuned machine learning and ensemble learning classifiers are used for classifying the tweets based on these sentiments. TF/IDF and bag of words are used to select the most relevant features. Out of all the machine/ensemble learning algorithms, the support vector machine produced the best results. Vaccination significantly impacts wellbeing by safeguarding physical health and reduces the fear of illness. Vaccination is the critical component that enhances both individual and collective wellbeing.

Keywords: Social media, vaccine, machine learning, ensemble learning

8.1 Introduction

The COVID-19 epidemic triggered widespread fear. As a result, more people use Twitter to post their ideas and news, raising awareness among the

**Corresponding author*: salahb@uaeu.ac.ae

Bharat Bhushan, Akib Khanday, Khursheed Aurangzeb, Sudhir Kumar Sharma and Parma Nand (eds.) Wellness Management Powered by AI Technologies, (207–230) © 2025 Scrivener Publishing LLC

general public [1]. On social media, there was a huge number of updates in the shape of tweets, postings, etc. [2]. Social media platforms were seen as the primary source of information during the COVID-19 times. Most people use Facebook and Twitter to express feelings, ideas, and opinions. The widespread COVID-19 infection confused individuals, resulted in numerous fatalities, and instilled panic [3]. Through various social media platforms, people responded to the pandemic and shared their perspectives. During this period, Twitter (a social networking site) was used by the WHO and officials. People from all around the world tweeted their views with various emotions [4]. Numerous distractions and mental disorders were brought on by the fluctuating attitudes during the COVID-19 period. Public health has suffered greatly because of the pandemic. Tweets using the phrases "increased coronavirus," "death," "surge in cases," "impact on the Indian economy," and "second wave" convey feelings of fear and worry as well as have a detrimental effect [5, 6]. Machine and deep learning algorithms are used to detect COVID-19 [7, 8]. The increased accessibility of numerous social media platforms makes it easier to discover the opinions of a diverse group of people. As a result, a significant volume of data, whether structured or not, is analyzed [5, 9]. There is a chance for other viewpoints to proliferate as a result of public reactions to COVID-19 news on microblogging services [10]. Sentiments of the tweets are extracted using lexicon-based techniques and machine learning algorithms [11]. Our study contributes to the understanding of machine and ensemble learning approaches for tweet classification. The labeled tweets serve as the input for the ML approach. Supervised machine learning methods including Gaussian naive Bayes, logistic regression, decision tree, multinominal naive Bayes, random forest, and support vector machine use these tweets as input. For the training to anticipate the intended results, these approaches require a sizable, labeled dataset.

The overall structure of the chapter is described in five sections: Section 8.2 discusses the background techniques and the literature related to vaccines. In Section 8.3, the machine learning algorithms are discussed and in Section 8.4 ensemble machine learning algorithms are discussed in detail. Section 8.5 discusses the methodology which is used to classify the tweets. Results and discussion are given in Section 8.6, Section 8.7 discuss about the impact on wellbeing and the study is concluded in Section 8.7.

8.2 Background and Related Work

Twitter has gained popularity as a result of focusing on people's emotional impulses. Finding helpful and educational tweets on social media is essential to comprehending the circumstances during a crisis or pandemic. A huge amount of data that is available on Twitter during the COVID-19 outbreak could be mined for information. To find out what the public thought about wearing masks when traveling and getting immunized during the COVID-19 pandemic, for instance, a study that analyzed a significant number of tweets looked at social media data. We shall consider these sentiment analysis research to be outstanding examples of Twitter knowledge analysis application cases. Three basic categories—positive, negative, and neutral—can be used to group emotions. Brief subject matter knowledge, like user tweets, is suitable for core emotion categories, according to studies [12, 13]. There exists another sub-classification that contains categories that include distinctive emotions of people, like joy, fear, anxiety, happiness, disgust, etc., which is the analysis of user emotions. More research, including [14], have examined how people communicate their emotions on social media. The study may be used to identify the primary effect in a given community because the word "infodemic" was developed to facilitate the spread of pandemic-related information online [15]. Furthermore, topic modeling is a technique used to gather information on the spread of pandemics from tweets. Here [22], tweets from countries like Brazil and the USA are used to look at COVID-19-related subjects. This study gathered data on the issue of the pandemic [16], a variety of symptoms, and ultimately COVID-19's progression. [17] carefully examined tweets from roughly 183,000 tweeters throughout a couple of months and concluded that COVID-19 had changed the behavior patterns of humans from a positive attitude to a negative attitude. According to the study, the fluctuation in attitudes throughout the pandemic led to mental problems. The research [18] used information from the blogging platform named Weibo and gathered information about COVID-19 from the perceptions of people and also from the emotions that are extracted. The collection of information is the process of separating the majority of news from a huge collection of stories and information using clustering methods like K-means based on the news headlines before identifying the news that is most closely related to the headlines as the day's most important news. These approaches are preferred to produce high-quality results because they are better suited than other methods for analyzing English texts [19]. Studies [20] used tweets that had been manually tagged, which may have introduced human biases. In contrast, the hybrid system that we present uses an automated Twitter labeling method that enables objective tweet labeling. We usually observe that the studies [10] were notably concentrated on the analysis of the sentiment of a particular location, such as Australia and China. Similar research [21, 22] carried out the analysis of the sentiment for countries like UK,

India, and the United Arab Emirates, respectively. In opposition, we used a dataset that includes tweets about COVID-19 all over the world. [23] carried out opinion mining of Twitter data by focusing on Digital India. The data was gathered using Twitter. To refine the dataset, the authors used a variety of preprocessing techniques. The related features were chosen using term frequency, term co-occurrences, and part-of-speech techniques. The authors used a dictionary-based approach to conduct polarity-based sentiment analysis. The hashtag #DigitalIndia was used to search for tweets about Digital India. This keyword was used to retrieve about 500 tweets. Data was gathered from Twitter. Stemming, tokenization, and stopword removal are all examples of data preprocessing. (They used Python and the NLTK 3.0 toolkit.) Term frequency, term co-occurrence, and part of speech are the features extracted. They used a dictionary-based approach to perform opinion mining and polarity classification (Net SentiWord). Using the hashtag #DigitalIndia, they gathered tweets about Digital India. Python was used to retrieve 500 tweets from Twitter. The results of the classification revealed that 250 people were positive, 150 were neutral, and 100 were negative, i.e., 50% positive, 30% neutral, and 20% negative. This study can be further replicated using a large dataset. The lack of a procedure for dealing with satirical posts and emoticons was one of the work's weaknesses. Also, the authenticity of tweets was not tested to see whether they were genuine or not. The same can be done for a huge dataset. Handling emoticon-based sarcasm sentences is also possible. The trustworthiness of tweets is also crucial. [24] performed sentiment analysis on Hindi Twitter to predict the Indian election in 2016. In Hindi, you can get raw tweets (TwitterArchiever) using hashtags such as #BJP and #INC, for example. Tweets are pre-processed by removing hashtags, mentions, and stopwords, among other things (negation handling). As to the algorithm for determining the polarity of tweets, dictionary approach, SVM, and naive Bayes were used for sentiment analysis and prediction. A total of 42,235 tweets were gathered. "Naive Bayes" accuracy is 62.1%. Moreover, 78.4% SVM centered on a dictionary, and 34% did not take the emoticons into account. For more prediction, further machine learning algorithms, like random forest, can be used. [25] performed opinion mining of Twitter data in 2015–2016 primary debates; emotions about Donald Trump were revealed. In collecting information, they did this by using Twitter's API and hashtags, such as #DonaldTrump, #VoteTrump, and so on. In terms of data preprocessing, sentences are tokenized by translating them to words, deleting all white spaces, punctuation marks, numbers, URLs, and other special characters, and converting all uppercase to lowercase. In creating a classifier, polarity is a classification system that is used to categorize objects (positive or negative). They used the "Sentiment" R kit. They displayed the preliminary sentiment analysis result in a visual format. In his prime debates, Donald Trump was listed in a data collection of political tweets. A total of 85,000 tweets were used in total. A negative polarity was found in 39% of the tweets. Emotions must be detected, and the entity that caused the emotion must be tagged, identifying whether the feelings are associated with the candidate or the opposition.

The authors in [26] analyzed the Twitter conversation around the 2016 elections of Austria in context of politics, feelings, and disinformation. The primary goal was to examine political sentiments and misinformation during election season. The article's key research questions were: What is the presidential candidates' tweeting behavior? In what context are the candidates mentioned by other Twitter users? The authors took data from Twitter and preprocessed it by deleting stop terms, handling abbreviations, and correcting spelling errors, among other things. They used the SentiStrength method to prepare the dataset. Data from Twitter is extracted. Data preprocessing includes noise removal, spell checking, and abbreviation, among other things. Data set preparation was as follows: SentiStrength (a sentiment analysis tool) is used to run data through a lexicon of "sentiment terms", "a list of idioms", and "a list of emoticons". Text mining techniques, for example, were used to analyze the data. They took a data collection of 343,645 Twitter messages linked to the election and performed an analysis. We should investigate the effect of various emotions on the spread of knowledge in the future. Machine learning gained prominence as a separate field within computer science due to the quick development of data mining techniques. The main idea behind it is that a system, such as an algorithm or computer program, may learn from its own actions. This subfield of artificial intelligence can be thought of as such. It was initially referred to in 1959 by Arthur Samuel as a "field of study that allows computers to learn without being explicitly programmed". In terms of a class of tasks T and performance measure P, a computer program is said to learn from experience E if, as determined by P, its performance on tasks in T improves with experience E [27]. The primary concept behind all machine learning tasks is to train a model via an algorithm to accomplish certain classification, clustering, and regression tasks [28].

The input dataset serves as the foundation for training the model, which is then used to provide predictions. The initial task and its execution define the model's output. A few potential uses for machine learning include estimating the cost of a previously unidentified home using information about the home's size, price, and number of rooms. Using two datasets including photographs of healthy people and those with tumors to classify a fresh image pool and group animal photos into many groups from an unsorted pool. Thus far, we have examined machine learning concepts from the standpoint of having starting data to train the model with. However, this is not always the case. Supervised and unsupervised learning are the two categories of learning that we shall talk about here. Labeled data serves as the foundation for supervised learning, where data samples are mapped to the appropriate label or output in an initial dataset. We begin with a dataset of homes, their characteristics, and their prices in the housing pricing example above, which is an illustration of supervised learning. The model "knows" the correct answers because it was trained on this dataset. Tasks related to classification and regression are within the category of supervised learning and are described as follows:

- Regression: It predicts a value by examining past observations, such as the values of samples from a training set, and using that information [29]. Most of the time, if the result is a real number or is continuous, we may claim that we are dealing with a regression situation.
- Classification: On the basis of a set of labeled data, where each label specifies a class to which the sample belongs, it predicts the class of a previously unknown sample based on the set of labeled data [30]. The number of available classes are limited and, in most cases, binary or multi. It is generally accepted that if the output is represented as a discrete or categorical variable then we are dealing with a classification problem.

Unsupervised learning does not require the labeling of data at the start of the process. Here the goal is to discover some kind of pattern in a large collection of unsorted data rather than to predict a specific result. Clustering is a subclass of unsupervised learning which finds the hidden patterns in the unlabeled data and groups the data into clusters based on how similar it is to the patterns that are found [31]. For example, finding diverse client groups within the consumer base of an online business can be useful.

8.3 Machine Learning Techniques

Sentiment analysis uses machine learning algorithms to identify and classify emotions represented in text, making it a critical task in NLP. Sentiment analysis systems can accurately interpret the sentiment behind user-generated content by using a variety of algorithms, including supervised learning models like "support vector machines (SVM)", "naive Bayes", and deep learning techniques like "recurrent neural networks (RNN)" and transformers [32, 33]. These models have potential applications across multiple industries, such as consumer feedback analysis, social media monitoring, and market research. They are trained on large datasets to identify language subtleties, context, and polarity. The precision and scalability of sentiment analysis are continually improved by machine learning advances, making it a vital tool to comprehend human emotions in the digital era.

8.3.1 Logistic Regression

By examining the correlation between a numerical variable and its label, logistic regression makes predictions about the class of that variable. The features selected during the feature engineering process, which involves creating and refining variables that best represent the underlying patterns in the data, are provided as input to the algorithm. Logistic regression then uses these inputs to calculate the probability that the numerical variable belongs to a specific class. This is done by applying a logistic function to a weighted sum of the input features, effectively modeling the likelihood of different outcomes. The algorithm outputs these probabilities, allowing for a clear and interpretable prediction of the class based on the input features. Although it may also be applied to multi-class classification, this approach is commonly utilized for binary classification problems.

There are many advantages of using logistic regression over other approaches. It is one of the most straightforward algorithms to understand, very easy to execute, and runs well on smaller datasets. The method works very nice on the linearly separable dataset and can be used to find the relationships between various attributes of the dataset. Moreover, the algorithm can also be extended to multi-classification. However, in the case of complete separation, logistic regression is not useful. It may lead to overfitting when the features are more than the sample size. The algorithm assumes the multi-collinearity between various features and is sensitive to the outliers.

8.3.2 Multinomial Naïve Bayes

The algorithm uses Bayes' rule to calculate the probabilities of a given text belonging to different classes. This algorithm is applicable to both binary and multi-class classification problems. The core idea behind MNB is to treat each feature independently. By applying Bayes' theorem, the algorithm calculates the probability of each feature in isolation, without considering any potential correlations between features. This assumption of independence is why the method is termed "naive," as in real-world scenarios, features often exhibit some level of interdependence. Let *C* represent the set of possible categories and N denote the set of features extracted from the text. For each class c in C, MNB estimates the probability that given text fits to class *c* by considering the individual contributions of each feature in N. This involves computing the probability of each feature occurring in texts of class *c* and combining these probabilities according to Bayes' theorem. Despite its simplifying assumption of feature independence, MNB often performs well in practice, particularly for text classification tasks, due to its efficiency and effectiveness in handling large feature spaces. Then, using the Bayes rule described in Equation 8.1, MNB designates test text ti to the class with the maximum probability P (c|ti):

$$\mathrm{P\ (c|ti) = (P\ (c)P\ (ti|c))/P\ (ti),\ c \in C} \tag{8.1}$$

The total quantity of textual data can be divided by the sum of textual data that are categorized as class c to get P (c). The probability that textual data in class c will resemble ti is denoted by P (ti|c). This can be computed by Equation 8.2:

$$P\ (t_i|c) = (\Sigma_n f_{ni})!\Pi_n P\ (w_n|c)^{f_{ni}} / f_{ni}! \tag{8.2}$$

where fni denotes the number of instances of the word/term 'n' in our textual data ti and P (wn|c) is the likelihood of the word/term 'n' being presented in class c. The latter probability is derived using the training data using Equation 8.3:

$$P\ (w_n|c) = (1 + F_{nc})/(N + \Sigma_{x=1}^{N} F_{xc}) \tag{8.3}$$

where Fxc represents the number of times the word or term appears in all training data for class c. The zero-frequency issue, which gives the count of each word a value of one, is avoided by using the Laplace estimator.

The simplicity and understandability of this method are two of its key benefits. It also works well with datasets that contain features that aren't very likely to affect the result, therefore the features are essentially disregarded when making predictions. Furthermore, this method requires less resources than others because it only needs to compute the probabilities of features and classes, in contrast to other approaches that require more complex calculations, but the algorithm's main weakness is that it makes the assumption that every characteristic is independent, which is frequently false in practical situations.

8.3.3 Support Vector Machine (SVM)

This is a supervised machine learning technique that is used for text classification. The primary objective of SVM is to determine which hyperplane best divides the different classes. Removing the "support vectors," or the data points that are close to this hyperplane, would cause the hyperplane to move. The gap between the hyperplane and the support vectors is known as the margin. Specifically, SVM requires a set of characteristics for a given text with a specific label. With n being the number of extracted features, the representation of the data points in the training set is $(yk, xk)n$. A table is provided as input containing the values related to the features that were chosen during the feature engineering process.

This classifier is developed based on Equation 8.4:

$$\begin{aligned} \omega^T \varphi(x_k) + b \geq 1, if\ y_k = +1 \\ \omega^T \varphi(x_k) + b \leq -1, if\ y_k = -1 \end{aligned} \tag{8.4}$$

It is equivalent to Equation 8.5:

$$y_k \omega^T \varphi(x_k) + b \leq -1, if y_k = -1, \quad k = 1, \ldots., n \tag{8.5}$$

where φ(.) maps inputs into a higher-dimensional and meaningful space using a nonlinear function. Categorization is achieved by the usage of the hyperplane. The two classes are distinguished by the hyperplane, necessitating the creation of a new variable, xik. The hyperplane is calculated by Equation 8.6.

$$\begin{aligned} y_k[\omega^T \varphi(x_k) + b] \geq 1 - \xi_k, \quad k = 1, \ldots\ldots, n \\ \xi_k \geq 0, \quad k = 1, \ldots\ldots\ldots\ldots, n \end{aligned} \tag{8.6}$$

SVMs frequently produce results with excellent accuracy, particularly on "clean" datasets. Even when there are more dimensions than samples, they still work well with high-dimensional datasets. SVMs, however, might have trouble processing huge datasets with a lot of noise or overlapping classifications. Also, working with huge datasets might result in a lengthy training period.

8.3.4 Decision Trees

Based on training data, decision trees are data structures with a topology resembling a tree that are used to make predictions. Making as few options as possible while yet producing the most accurate outcomes is the aim of this approach. With decision trees, classification and regression issues may be handled simultaneously. Regions are formed by dividing input space, and each area is classified separately. The chosen feature values are supplied as input to the algorithm during the feature engineering process. With the leaf nodes classifying the text into different classes, the tree classifies at the root by recursively splitting the input space depending on these values. The splitting criterion is a crucial step in the creation of a decision tree as it dictates how the data should be divided to get the best results. Information gain is used which is illustrated in Equation 8.7.

$$IGR(EX, a) = IG/IV \tag{8.7}$$

where IG = information gain and IV = intrinsic information.

Equation 8.8 below illustrates how information gain is computed using entropy.

$$\begin{aligned} &\mathrm{IG(Ex, a) = H(Ex) - v \in values(a)} \\ &\mathrm{(|x \in Ex|value(x, a) = v|/|Ex|.H(x \in Ex|value(x, a) = v)} \end{aligned} \tag{8.8}$$

where Ex = Set of training examples and x ∈ Ex which defines the value of a specific example x for feature a

H = Entropy and a = features. Because of its ease of use and efficiency, the decision tree approach is well-liked, especially when dealing with noisy and huge datasets. Decision trees function as a "white box," which makes it simple to see how outcomes are decided and which decisions contributed to the end result, in contrast to algorithms like SVM or KNN. Decision trees are a popular option for applications such as spam filtering, security screening, and medical diagnostics, among others, because of their transparency.

8.4 Ensemble Machine Learning Algorithms

The goal of ensemble learning techniques is to create new, more efficient algorithms by combining existing ones. Some of the popular ensemble machine learning algorithms are discussed in the following subsections.

8.4.1 Bagging

This algorithm is an ensemble machine learning technique that enhances the efficiency of other machine learning algorithms [34]. The bagging algorithm aids in the avoidance of over-fitting. A training set X of size n is used to produce additional training sets Xi of size n with replacements by evenly sampling m new training sets Xi. This algorithm receives as an input the features that were chosen using values in the feature engineering process. Some observations may recur in each Xi due to substitutions. If "m = n", then set Xi for big n to have a fraction (1 – 1/e) of unique X examples, with the remainder duplicating. A bootstrap sample is what it is called. The m models are joined by voting after being fitted with m bootstrap samples.

8.4.2 AdaBoost

The weighted instances of the dataset are used in this ensemble learning technique [35]. The algorithm receives as input the features that were feature-engineered and chosen with values. It utilizes weighted data to train a weak learning algorithm, beginning with identical weights for every observation. This results in the creation of a weak classifier. Choose a coefficient α based on the performance of weak learning classifier. Improve the weights of misclassified points while decreasing the weights of correctly classified ones. Following that, the weak learning algorithms are run one more time to produce a weak classifier for the newly weighted data. This technique is repeated until an AdaBoost classifier is created.

8.4.3 Random Forest Classifier

Random forest is a decision tree-like structure created by merging many decision trees. It does not require much data preparation or modeling, yet it frequently yields correct findings. Random forests, more particularly, are collections of decision trees that improve prediction accuracy. The word "forest" refers to the fact that it is a collection of decision trees.

Using independent subsets of the dataset to generate multiple decision trees is the main concept. Each node selects n variables at random from the feature set, and the optimum split on these variables is determined. For training the random forest algorithm, the bootstrap aggregating technique is utilized. It is possible to make an overall prediction by averaging the forecasts of all the separate regression trees. The majority vote is used when it comes to the categorization of trees. Using a set of random features, a modified tree learning algorithm is used in this method to choose and segment each learning process into subsets [36]. A table containing the values for the features that were chosen for feature engineering is provided as input. The method uses a variety of decision trees to build a forest from a subset of random data and then totals the decision trees vote to determine the object's final class.

Random forests and decision tree approaches have many benefits. Their computation and fitting are simple, and they can handle issues involving both regression and classification. They also provide better precision. Random forests produce less interpretable outcomes than decision trees, nevertheless. With decision trees, we can determine which factors are significant and how they impact the result; with random forests, this knowledge is not as readily available. Random forests, on the other hand, offer more stability since, in contrast to decision trees, which can fluctuate and lose accuracy, they do not noticeably shift with little changes in the data. Because random forests are made up of several decision trees, they exhibit stability [37].

8.4.4 Stochastic Gradient Boosting

Using this method, random samples from the training dataset can be used to generate trees. An input table containing the features that have been chosen based on values in feature engineering is provided. This lowers the trees' association with each other in gradient boosting. Without any replacements, a random subsample of the training dataset is selected at the beginning of each iteration. We then fit the basic learner using the randomly selected subsample rather than the full sample [38].

8.5 Methodology

8.5.1 Data Collection

Online social networks are used as a tool for sharing information, and various social networking sites like Facebook, Twitter, now X, etc., are the most used ones. In this work, data associated with COVID-19 and vaccine tweets is collected. The data is collected from a public data repository.

8.5.2 Data Preprocessing

The data that is extracted from online social networks is noisy. Since the noisy data cannot be supplied to the machine learning algorithm, for training and testing it needs to be refined. For classification applications, preprocessing is essential to understanding the meaning of short texts. It significantly impacts total system performance, but it has received less attention in the literature than feature extraction and classification. Tweets that have been preprocessed are ready for further tasks including sentiment analysis, event recognition, and the detection of false information. On social media, people typically abide by their own unwritten language standards. Because of this, every Twitter user has a unique writing style that may contain misspelled words, irregular punctuation, and abbreviations. In tweets various emoticons and emojis are utilized to express ideas, sentiment, and complexity. Acronyms and slang are frequently used in user remarks, URLs, hashtags, and tweets. For refining the dataset, we used different techniques starting from tokenization to lemmatization. Below are the different techniques that are used for performing data preprocessing:

- Tokenization: To make it easier to edit the text by eliminating extraneous words, numbers, and other characters, the tweets in this task are separated into tokens.
- Normalization: In this task, all the tokenized words are converted into lowercase also the whitespaces are removed.
- Elimination of user mentions, hashtags, URLs, and noise: Unicode and unwanted strings are seen as crawling process byproducts that introduce noise to the data. Furthermore, almost all user-posted tweets contain user mentions (@username), links to additional information, and the hashtag sign to relate their message to a particular topic. These hashtags can also convey an emotion. These hints offer extra information that is valuable to people, but they are essentially meaningless to robots and can be written off as noise. This phase removes all user mentions, URLs, hashtags, and noise.
- Word segmentation: Word segmentation is the process of breaking apart the words, sentences, and information that make up a hashtag. Three words, for instance, make up the hashtag #sometrendingtopic: some + trending + topic.

Without requiring human assistance, this stage can help machines recognize and identify tweet content with ease. As previously stated, Twitter users utilize hashtags in practically all of their tweets to identify them with a specific hot topic. In this phase, word segmentation is performed such that the content of the text is extracted.

- Replacing emoticons and emojis: Twitter users replace emoticons and emojis with a variety of symbols such as :-), ;-), :-(, and others to express sentiment and opinion. To effectively classify tweets, it is also necessary to record this crucial information. These expressions and emoticons were changed to reflect their corresponding word meanings; for instance, cheerful is now replaced with :-) and sad with :-(.
- Abbreviations and slang: Twitter's character restrictions make it more common for users to utilize slang, acronyms, and shorthand in their online posts rather than using regular English. An acronym, such as MIA (missing in action), gr8 (excellent), ofc (of course), and so on, is an abbreviation. Slang is another colloquial way of communicating ideas or meaning that is considered informal and occasionally restricted to particular people or contexts. OMG usually denotes a surprise or emphasis rather than the literal extension of "oh my God". This is why it is critical to handle these unintentional modifications to tweets by replacing them with their true meaning, which enhances the efficiency of automatic classifiers without compromising information. Acronyms and slang terms were given word definitions, which made them understandable with standard text analysis techniques.
- Punctuation is removed: Punctuation is used by social media users to portray feelings and emotions, which is easily understood by humans but not as effective for the automated classification of short texts. As a result, removing punctuation while preprocessing text is good for automated classification tasks like sentiment analysis which is typical to practice. However, some punctuation characters, such as ! and ?, can be used to convey emotion. Using the right tags, like!, in place of a question mark or exclamation can frequently convey surprise.

- Stopword removal: The uninformative and distracting terms are usually called stopwords, these mainly include conjunctions and prepositions. Stopword lists must be used with caution; while they lessen the likelihood of accumulating unnecessary data, they also risk discarding/affecting good data. In this task, we removed all the stopwords as they have the very least role in a classification task. English stopwords dictionary was used for removing them as we are working on tweets written in English only.
- Stemming: Every word is stemmed to its root word in order to provide the phrase's genuine meaning. It frequently involves removing derivational affixes and cuts off word endings in the hopes of accomplishing this goal most of the time.
- Lemmatization: This task makes use of vocabulary and word morphological analysis. Normally, our goal is to recover a word's lemma, or base form, and remove only inflectional endings from it. To determine the lemma, or base form, of the words, we utilize spaCy's lemmatizer.

8.5.3 Feature Engineering

The feature selection techniques that are used for performing this task are as follows:

TF/IDF

Term frequency/inverse document frequency provides numerical insights that reflect the importance of a word within a tweet or within a corpus. The following Equations 8.9 and 8.10 are used for calculating term frequency and inverse document frequency.

$$TFIDF\ (t, w, D) = TF\ (t, w) * IDF\ (t, D) \tag{8.9}$$

$$IDF\ (t, D) = \log\ |D|1 + |\ (w \in D : t \in w)\ | \tag{8.10}$$

where t is the term as a component, w signifies each tweet in the corpus, and the dataset's entire number of tweets is represented by D (document space).

Bag of Words

A machine learning system can be trained and tested using these attributes that are extracted from text. Word occurrences in a document are described using a representation of text called a bag-of-words. It involves two things: a list of well-known words in one's vocabulary and a measure of the quantity of words that are known.

The expression "bag of words" was created to describe this disdain for any information on the word order or layout in the document. Rather than taking into account the words' locations, the model just takes into account whether or not known words are present in the document. This method may be used to extract document characteristics in a variety of settings since it is very flexible and simple to use. It includes not just lemma uni, bi, and trigrams but also individual words. The machine learning classifier can extract deeper information from the text by using bigram and trigram words as features.

8.5.4 Classification

Due to the labeled dataset, we used supervised machine/ensemble learning algorithms to classify the sentiments. These classifiers are fine-tuned by optimizing their parameters. Table 8.1 shows the optimal hyperparameters for classifying the emotions of different vaccines for COVID-19.

Table 8.1 Hyperparameter tuning results.

Model	Best parameter	Best score
Gradient boosting classifier	{'learning rate': 0.1, 'n estimators': 40}	0.7977
Random forest classifier	{'criterion': 'entropy', 'n estimators': 30}	0.9365
AdaBoost classifier	{'learning rate': 0.1, 'n estimators': 30}	0.7317
Bagging classifier	{'n estimators': 20}	0.9234
Decision tree classifier	{'criterion': 'gini'}	0.9131
Multinomial NB	{'alpha': 0.01}	0.8438
Linear SVC	{'C': 1}	0.9429
Logistic regression	{'C': 10, 'max iter': 1000}	0.9392

8.6 Results and Discussion

Data is divided in an 80:20 ratio, with 80% going toward training classifiers and 20% going toward testing them. Out of all the machine and ensemble learning classifiers, the results indicated that support vector produced the best results. While testing the SVC hyperparameterized classifier, it showed precision of 94.27%. Table 8.2 summarizes results of different machine and ensemble learning approaches. Also, the visualization of the positive and negative sentiments is checked, and it has been seen that there are mostly positive emotions related to the vaccine which is depicted in Figure 8.1. Companies like Pfizer and AstraZeneca have been used with negative emotions, which can be seen in Figure 8.2. Also, Figure 8.3 depicts the overall response from the users about the vaccination.

Table 8.2 Classification report of various machine and ensemble learning algorithms.

Model	Class	Precision	Recall	F1-score
Gradient boosting classifier	Negative	0.9313	0.3661	0.5255
	Neutral	0.7138	0.9409	0.8117
	Positive	0.8889	0.7867	0.8347
	Accuracy			0.7977
	Macro avg	0.8446	0.6979	0.7240
	Weighted avg	0.8233	0.7977	0.7877
Random forest classifier	Negative	0.9628	0.7632	0.8515
	Neutral	0.9136	0.9802	0.9457
	Positive	0.9522	0.9439	0.9480
	Accuracy			0.9365
	Macro avg	0.9429	0.8958	0.9151
	Weighted avg	0.9379	0.9365	0.9353

(Continued)

Table 8.2 Classification report of various machine and ensemble learning algorithms. (*Continued*)

Model	Class	Precision	Recall	F1-score
AdaBoost classifier	Negative	0.7982	0.3443	0.4811
	Neutral	0.6238	0.9424	0.7507
	Positive	0.9168	0.6519	0.7620
	Accuracy			0.7317
	Macro avg	0.7796	0.6462	0.6646
	Weighted avg	0.7840	0.7317	0.7232
Bagging classifier	Negative	0.8949	0.7756	0.8310
	Neutral	0.9057	0.9663	0.9350
	Positive	0.9463	0.9248	0.9354
	Accuracy			0.9234
	Macro avg	0.9156	0.8889	0.9005
	Weighted avg	0.9236	0.9234	0.9225
Decision tree classifier	Negative	0.8413	0.7770	0.8079
	Neutral	0.9117	0.9420	0.9266
	Positive	0.9315	0.9235	0.9275
	Accuracy			0.9131
	Macro avg	0.8948	0.8808	0.8873
	Weighted avg	0.9125	0.9131	0.9125
Multinomial NB	Negative	0.9158	0.4939	0.6417
	Neutral	0.8645	0.8474	0.8559
	Positive	0.8197	0.9308	0.8717
	Accuracy			0.8438
	Macro avg	0.8667	0.7574	0.7898
	Weighted avg	0.8496	0.8438	0.8373

(*Continued*)

Table 8.2 Classification report of various machine and ensemble learning algorithms. (*Continued*)

Model	Class	Precision	Recall	F1-score
Logistic regression	Negative	0.9192	0.7839	0.8462
	Neutral	0.9195	0.9616	0.9401
	Positive	0.9433	0.9423	0.9428
	Accuracy			0.9308
	Macro avg	0.9274	0.8959	0.9097
	Weighted avg	0.9308	0.9308	0.9299
Linear SVC	Negative	0.9160	0.8435	0.8783
	Neutral	0.9389	0.9632	0.9509
	Positive	0.9528	0.9512	0.9520
	Accuracy			0.9429
	Macro avg	0.9359	0.9193	0.9271
	Weighted avg	0.9427	0.9429	0.9426

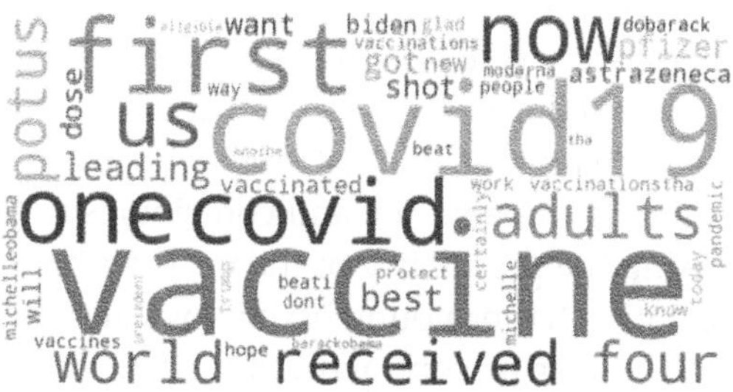

Figure 8.1 Word cloud of positive tweets.

Figure 8.2 Word cloud of negative tweets.

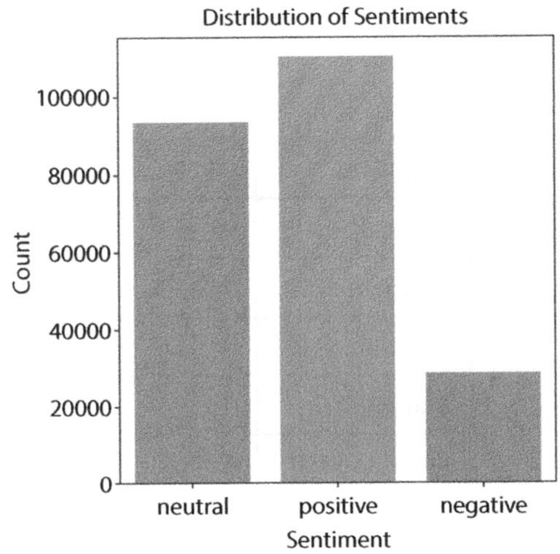

Figure 8.3 Distribution of COVID-19 vaccination-based sentiments.

8.7 Impact on Wellbeing

The impact of COVID-19 vaccination on wellbeing is extensive as COVID-19 affects both physical and mental health. Physically the vaccination prevented the spread of the virus because it helps to reduce the severity of illness in those who contract COVID-19 [39]. Vaccinated individuals were less likely to experience severe symptoms or require hospitalization or face complications. It also reduces the strain on healthcare systems by ensuring that the resources remain available for those who are in need. Vaccination lowers the overall transmission rate and contributes to the broader public health by decreasing the prevalence of the virus within communities. The COVID-19 vaccination has profound psychological and emotional impacts as well [40, 41]. The fear of contracting the virus has been a significant source of anxiety and stress for many people. Vaccination helps to mitigate these fears by providing a sense of protection and safety that reduces stress levels and promotes mental health. This sense of security can lead to improved mental wellbeing because individuals feel more confident in engaging in daily activities and social interactions. Also, widespread vaccination enables societies to relax restrictive measures that were put in place to control the spread of the virus e.g., lockdowns, travel bans, and social distancing. As these restrictions are lifted the individuals return to their normal routines and participate in social gatherings by engaging in community activities and these are vital for emotional and social wellbeing.

8.8 Conclusion

The ability to extract and examine the feelings expressed in user-generated content on a variety of social media platforms makes sentiment analysis an essential component of social media analysis. In this chapter, we performed the public opinion segmentation on the data related to COVID-19 vaccines. Data is collected from the public repository and is refined by using various preprocessing techniques. Also, data exploratory analysis is performed in order to get more insights of the data. The features are extracted based on TF/IDF technique in order to perform the classification. Parameters of the various machine and ensemble classifiers are optimized using the grid search technique. The classifier, when trained on these parameters, showed better results among other state-of-the-art techniques. In the future, more data can be supplied to these algorithms to improve the performance.

References

1. Umair, A., Masciari, E., Habib, M., Ullah, H., Sentimental analysis applications and approaches during covid-19: a survey, in: *Proceedings of the 25th International Database Engineering & Applications Symposium*, pp. 304–308, 2021.
2. Alamoodi, A.H., Zaidan, B.B., Zaidan, A.A., Albahri, O.S., Mohammed, K.I., Malik, R.Q., Almahdi, E.M., Chyad, M.A., Tareq, Z., Albahri, A.S. *et al.*, Sentiment analysis and its applications in fighting covid-19 and infectious diseases: A systematic review. *Expert Syst. Appl.*, 167, 114155, 2021.
3. Nemes, L. and Kiss, A., Social media sentiment analysis based on covid-19. *J. Inf. Telecommun.*, 5, 1, 1–15, 2021.
4. Chauhan, D., and Singh, C., Sentimental analysis on impact of COVID-19 outbreak, in: *Machine Intelligence and Smart Systems: Proceedings of MISS 2020*, pp. 233–242, Springer Nature Singapore, Singapore, 2021.
5. Gupta, P., Kumar, S., Suman, R.R., Kumar, V., Sentiment analysis of lockdown in india during covid-19: A case study on twitter. *IEEE Trans. Comput. Soc. Syst.*, 8, 4, 992–1002, 2020.
6. Sing, N.B. and Singh, R.G., Investor attention and reaction in covid-19 crisis: Sentiment analysis in the indian stock market. *Managerial Finance*, 49, 3, 470–491, 2023.
7. Bouktif, S., KHANDAY, A.M.U.D., Ali, O.U.N.I., Bi-directional lstm-based covid-19 detection using clinical reports. *The Eurasia Proceedings of Science Technology Engineering and Mathematics*, vol. 23, pp. 209–219, 2023.
8. Khanday, A., Bouktif, S., Ouni, A., Rnn-based model for an optimal covid-19 cases detection using clinical reports. *2023 9th International Conference on Optimization and Applications (ICOA)*, pp. 1–6, IEEE, 2023.

9. Bouktif, S. and Awad, M.A., Ant colony based approach to predict stock market movement from mood collected on twitter, in: *Proceedings of the 2013 IEEE/ACM international conference on advances in social networks analysis and mining*, pp. 837–845, 2013.
10. Mahbub, N., II, Islam, R., Amin, A., Islam, K., Singh, B.C., Showrov, I.H., Sarkar, A., Sentiment analysis of microblogging dataset on coronavirus pandemic, in: *2021 5th International Conference on Electrical Information and Communication Technology (EICT)*, pp. 1–6, IEEE, 2021.
11. Dhaoui, C., Webster, C.M., Tan, L.P., Social media sentiment analysis: lexicon versus machine learning. *J. Consum. Marketing*, 34, 6, 480–488, 2017.
12. Dubey, A.D., Twitter sentiment analysis during covid-19 outbreak, 2020, Available at SSRN 3572023.
13. Vijay, T., Chawla, A., Dhanka, B., Karmakar, P., Sentiment analysis on covid-19 twitter data, in: *2020 5th IEEE International Conference on Recent Advances and Innovations in Engineering (ICRAIE)*, pp. 1–7, IEEE, 2020.
14. Yang, Y., Jia, J., Zhang, S., Wu, B., Chen, Q., Li, J., Xing, C., Tang, J., How do your friends on social media dis- close your emotions?, in: *Proceedings of the AAAI Conference on Artificial Intelligence*, vol. 28, 2014.
15. Jang, H., Rempel, E., Roth, D., Carenini, G., Janjua, N.Z., Tracking covid-19 discourse on twitter in north amer- ica: Infodemiology study using topic modeling and aspect-based sentiment analysis. *J. Med. Internet Res.*, 23, 2, e25431, 2021.
16. Kaila, R.P. and Prasad, A.V., Informational flow on twitter–corona virus outbreak–topic modelling approach. *Int. J. Adv. Res. Eng. Techno. (IJARET)*, 11, 3, 2020.
17. BALCI, O. and Cengiz, AG., Before epiphany: An assessment of donald trump's crisis leadership on the eve of the covid-19 pandemic. *Erciyes Akademi*, 36, 2, 739–758, 2022.
18. Lyu, X., Chen, Z., Wu, D., Wang, W., Sentiment analysis on chinese weibo regarding covid-19, in: *Natural Language Processing and Chinese Computing: 9th CCF International Conference, NLPCC 2020*, Proceedings, Part I, vol. 9, Zhengzhou, China, October 14–18, 2020, Springer, 710–721, 2020.
19. Ito, H. and Chakraborty, B., Social media mining with dynamic clustering: a case study by covid-19 tweets, in: *2020 11th International Con- ference on Awareness Science and Technology (iCAST)*, pp. 1–6, IEEE, 2020.
20. Steiner-Correa, F., Viedma-del Jesus, M., II, Lopez-Herrera, A.G., A survey of multilingual human-tagged short message datasets for sentiment analysis tasks. *Soft Comput.*, 22, 8227–8242, 2018.
21. Ghasiya, P. and Okamura, K., Investigating covid-19 news across four nations: A topic modeling and sentiment analysis approach. *IEEE Access*, 9, 36645–36656, 2021.
22. Hasan Syed, F. and Sudais, M., Impact analysis of covid 19 response measures on social media postings, 2022.

23. Mishra, P., Rajnish, R., Kumar, P., Sentiment analysis of twitter data: Case study on digital india, in: *2016 International Conference on Information Technology (InCITe)-The Next Generation IT Summit on the Theme-Internet of Things: Connect your Worlds*, pp. 148–153, IEEE, 2016.
24. Parul, S. and Teng-Sheng, M., Prediction of indian election using sentiment analysis on hindi twitter, in: *2016 IEEE international conference on big data (big data)*, pp. 1966–1971, IEEE, 2016.
25. Abdullah, M. and Hadzikadic, M., Sentiment analysis of twitter data: Emotions revealed regarding donald trump during the 2015-16 primary debates, in: *2017 IEEE 29th International Conference on Tools with Artificial Intelligence (ICTAI)*, pp. 760–764, IEEE, 2017.
26. Kuˇsen, E. and Strembeck, M., An analysis of the twitter discussion on the 2016 austrian presidential elections, 2017, arXiv preprint arXiv:1707.09939.
27. Carbonell, J.G., Michalski, R.S., Mitchell, T.M., 1 - An overview of machine learning, Editor(s): Ryszard S. Michalski, Jaime G. Carbonell, Tom M. Mitchell, *Mach. Learn.*, 3–23, Morgan Kaufmann, 1983, ISBN 9780080510545, https://doi.org/10.1016/B978-0-08-051054-5.50005-4. https://www.sciencedirect.com/science/article/pii/B9780080510545500054.
28. Harrington, P., Machine learning in action, in: *Simon and Schuster*, 2012.
29. Maulud, D. and Abdulazeez, A.M., A review on linear regression comprehensive in machine learning. *J. Appl. Sci. Technol. Trends*, 1, 4, 140–147, 2020
30. Osisanwo, F.Y., Akinsola, J.E.T., Awodele, O., Hinmikaiye, J.O., Olakanmi, O., Akinjobi, J., Supervised machine learning algorithms: classification and comparison. *Int. J. Compu. Trends Technol. (IJCTT)*, 48, 128–138, 2017.
31. Kassambara, A., Practical guide to cluster analysis in R: Unsupervised machine learning, vol. 1, Sthda, 2017.
32. Bouktif, S., Sahraoui, H., Ahmed, F., Predicting stability of open-source software systems using combination of bayesian classifiers. *ACM Trans. Manage. Inf. Syst. (TMIS)*, 5, 1, 1–26, 2014.
33. Khanday, A.M.U.D., Khan, Q.R., Rabani, S.T., Svmbpi: support vector machine-based propaganda identification, in: *Cognitive Informatics and Soft Computing*, Advances in Intelligent Systems and Computing AISC, vol. 1317, pp. 445–455, Springer, 2021.
34. Dietterich, T.G., Ensemble methods in machine learning, in: *International workshop on multiple classifier systems*, Springer, pp. 1–15, 2000.
35. Fabien, M., Boosting and adaboost clearly explained — by ma¨el fabien towards data science, https://towardsdatascience.com/boosting-and-adaboost-clearly-explained-856e21152d3e, 2019. (Accessed on 01/09/2022).
36. Katuwal, R. and Suganthan, P.N., Enhancing multi-class classification of random forest using random vector functional neural network and oblique decision surfaces, in: *2018 International Joint Conference on Neural Networks (IJCNN)*, pp. 1–8, IEEE, 2018.

37. Botta, V., Louppe, G., Geurts, P., Wehenkel, L., Exploiting snp correlations within random forest for genome-wide association studies. *PLoS One*, 9, 4, e93379, 2014.
38. Friedman, J.H., Stochastic gradient boosting. *Comput. Stat Data Anal.*, 38, 4, 367–378, 2002.
39. Rabani, S.T., Khan, Q.R., Khanday, A.M.U.D., Quantifying suicidal ideation on social media using machine learning: a critical review. *Iraqi J. Sci.*, 62, 11, 4092–4100, 2021.
40. Bouktif, S., Khanday, A.M.U.D., Ouni, A., CoML: Machine Learning based approach for COVID-19 related Suicidal Ideation detection, in: *2024 International Conference on Intelligent Systems and Computer Vision (ISCV)*, pp. 1–5, IEEE, 2024, May.
41. Khanday, A.M.U.D., Wani, M.A., Rabani, S.T., Khan, Q.R., Abd El-Latif, A.A., HAPI: An efficient Hybrid Feature Engineering-based Approach for Propaganda Identification in social media. *PloS One*, 19, 7, e0302583, 2024.

9

Revolutionizing Healthcare with IoT in Cardiology

Aafreen Jan[1], K. Nimmi[2] and Mohd Anas Wajid[3]*

[1]S.P. College, Cluster University of Srinagar, Jammu and Kashmir, India
[2]College of Information Technology, United Arab Emirates University, Al Ain, UAE
[3]Institute for the Future Education, Technologico De Monterrey, Monterrey, Mexico

Abstract
The Internet of Things (IoT) is transforming various industries by enabling interconnected devices to collect, analyze, and transmit data seamlessly. In healthcare, IoT has the potential to significantly enhance patient care through continuous monitoring and real-time data analysis. This research explores the revolutionary impact of IoT in cardiology, focusing on the development and implementation of a comprehensive system that utilizes various sensors to detect heart-related issues. The proposed system employs advanced biosensors to monitor critical cardiovascular parameters such as heart rate, blood pressure, and electrocardiogram (ECG) signals. These sensors are seamlessly integrated with a user-friendly interface on the Blynk app via Bluetooth connectivity, providing real-time monitoring and analysis. The Blynk app serves as a versatile platform for visualizing the collected data, enabling patients and healthcare providers to access vital health information instantly. This research highlights the technical aspects of sensor integration, data transmission, and the effectiveness of the Blynk app in displaying real-time cardiovascular health metrics. The findings underscore the potential of IoT in enhancing patient care, early detection of cardiac anomalies, and facilitating timely medical interventions, thereby revolutionizing the field of cardiology.

Keywords: Internet of things, electrocardiogram, cardiovascular diseases, HC-05 bluetooth module, blynk app

**Corresponding author*: anaswajid.bbk@gmail.com

Bharat Bhushan, Akib Khanday, Khursheed Aurangzeb, Sudhir Kumar Sharma and Parma Nand (eds.) Wellness Management Powered by AI Technologies, (231–274) © 2025 Scrivener Publishing LLC

9.1 Introduction

The term Internet of Things (IoT) describes a network of physical objects equipped with various sensors, software, and connectivity to share data with other devices and systems over the Internet [1]. These connected devices range from common items like household appliances, smart wearable devices, and autonomous vehicles to industrial machinery and infrastructure components. It represents a large network of interconnected objects and individuals. The term "THINGS" encompasses items of varying sizes and shapes, such as smart ovens that can cook food automatically for the correct duration, self-driving cars equipped with sensors to detect obstacles, and smart wearables capable of monitoring health metrics like steps taken, oxygen levels, heart rate, and pulse rate to provide health recommendations [2]. In simple words, IoT is a simple concept that means clustering all the things around and connecting them to the Internet. The Internet connection is an amazing thing to connect with; it gives us those benefits that were not possible before [3]. If we think of our cell phones before it was SMART-Phone, we could call and at max text for sure, but now we can click a picture, read a newspaper, watch any show, or listen to music all in our hands. The point here is that connecting anything to the Internet yields amazing advantages [2]. When something is connected to the net, that means that a particular object is now able to send and receive information or both. This ability to share data makes things "SMART". IoT enables these devices ("things") to gather the data and the exchange that data, allowing them to be maintained, handled and optimized remotely [4]. This connectivity and data sharing can lead to improved efficiency, automation, convenience, and decision-making in various fields, including smart home surveillance, better healthcare, smart agriculture, manufacturing, transportation, and many more. IoT devices typically gather data through sensors, process it using embedded software, and then transmit it over the Internet to other connected devices, cloud platforms, or centralized systems for analysis and action [5]. This interconnectedness and data exchange have the potential to create new opportunities for innovation and optimization across multiple industries. IoT is like a big network connecting almost everything—like your cellphone, fridge, car, streetlights or even your whole house—to the Internet. These things have sensors or tiny computers inside that help them to collect information or do some specific tasks. For instance, a smart thermostat [6] can sense the temperature and adjust it automatically. These devices talk to each other through the Internet, sharing the information they gather. So, the way your smartwatch talks to your phone, which talks to your home security system. They work together to make things more convenient or simpler, like letting you control your home's temperature from your phone or getting your fridge to remind you when you are out of milk [7]. This whole network of connected things is what we call the Internet of Things. It is like giving ordinary stuff a way to communicate and help, making life more convenient and efficient. Life before the IoT was a bit different. Everyday objects and devices were not as connected or "smart" as they are now. For example, your fridge was just a fridge—it kept your food cold, but it did not tell you when you were running low on groceries. Your thermostat could not adjust itself based on your schedule or preferences [6]. And your car could not communicate with traffic lights or other vehicles to optimize your route. Most devices worked independently without much connection to the Internet or each other. If you wanted to control something, you often had to do it manually, like adjusting your thermostat by hand or physically going to the store to check if you needed groceries [7]. Life was less automated and relied more on human intervention for everyday tasks. IoT has changed this by connecting devices and allowing them to communicate, share information, and even make decisions without constant human input. It has made things more convenient, efficient, and in some cases, safer and more enjoyable [8].

9.1.1 Characteristics of IoT

The functionality, versatility, and impact of the Internet of Things (IoT) are defined by several key characteristics:

1. Connectivity: The Internet connects IoT devices, allowing them to communicate and exchange data without human involvement, including between devices, sensors, systems, and applications [9].
2. Sensing and actuating: Embedded with sensors and actuators, IoT gadgets can gather data from the environment, such as noise, atmospheric pressure, humidity, and motion, and respond based on received instructions [10].
3. Data processing: Bulk data is gathered for local processing on the device or transmission to a centralized system for additional analysis. This data serves as the foundation for making decisions and gaining insights [10].
4. Remote monitoring and control: IoT allows remote monitoring and control of devices, allowing users to access, manage,

and interact with IoT devices from anywhere via the Internet [11].

5. Automation and efficiency: Through automation, IoT devices can perform tasks autonomously, optimizing processes and reducing human intervention. For instance, smart thermostats adjust temperatures based on occupancy, and wearable health trackers provide real-time data [7].
6. Interoperability: IoT systems often consist of heterogeneous devices and technologies that need to work together seamlessly. Interoperability ensures that different devices and platforms can communicate and collaborate effectively [12].
7. Scalability: IoT networks can range from a few devices to millions, allowing for scalability in terms of adding new devices and expanding network capabilities as needed [11].
8. Security and privacy: It is crucial to guarantee the security and privacy of data that is transmitted and stored by IoT devices. Encryption, authentication, and secure communication protocols are essential to protect sensitive information [9].
9. Real-time potential: Many IoT applications need real-time functionality and response, especially in fields like healthcare, transportation, and manufacturing where immediate actions based on data are crucial [10].
10. Diverse applications: IoT finds applications across various industries such as healthcare, smart homes, agriculture, manufacturing, transportation, and more, enhancing efficiency, convenience, and innovation [9].

These characteristics collectively define the capabilities and potential of IoT, shaping its role in transforming industries and daily life by enabling smarter, more connected environments and systems.

As already mentioned, IoT has several domains in which we can use this technology, one such domain is *healthcare.*

9.1.2 Healthcare

The maintenance or enhancement of health through services designed to prevent, diagnose, treat, and manage illnesses, injuries, and other physical or mental conditions is what healthcare refers to. It includes a wide range of activities, professionals, facilities, technologies, and systems that are committed to promoting and sustaining well-being [13]. Health is described as physical, intellectual, and social well-being and simply now no longer the non-life of disorder or ailment. Health is a primary human right [14].

The field of healthcare is one of the most noble areas for IoT applications. Using IoT, doctors can aid individuals via the Internet. Portable health monitoring devices based on IoT have the potential to greatly decrease the distance between patients and doctors [15]. Using IoT allows for personalized assistance for each patient, assessment of their health status, and determination of their treatment plan. Through portable sensors, physicians can monitor patients' health remotely and provide real-time responses [16]. Real-time data measurements necessitate an unbroken Internet connection. Even though IoT is rapidly advancing in healthcare, it is not yet fully integrated into certain medical sectors. Creating suitable Internet applications for conventional medicine still presents some challenges. The IoT is likely to draw in more medical researchers as their numbers continue to grow. Contemporary medical practitioners encounter the task of collecting a wealth of information and analyzing and interpreting it to make informed and individualized decisions, a process that demands significant time and effort [17]. The process can be accelerated and made more convenient with new IoT technologies. The increasing adoption of electronic health records has led to a rise in digitized medical data. Reviewing and evaluating all this information is time-consuming. Additionally, it is essential to train medical personnel on AI-based technology closely linked with the IoT [18]. By leveraging digital technologies like the IoT and AI in a coordinated manner, doctors can personalize treatment for patients more effectively. These technologies enable the thorough examination and analysis of a larger volume of data, allowing for close monitoring of the progression of a specific illness or treatment. Integrating firsthand experience with new diagnostic, data collection, and analytical approaches will bring about beneficial changes in healthcare administration [19]. In Figure 9.1, the concept of IoT in healthcare is introduced. The IoT brings in network-enabled technologies and includes wearable and portable devices that can activate, detect, summarize, and communicate with other similar devices over the Internet. The IoT is fundamentally transforming data generation, utilization, and dissemination [20]. The general population often utilizes these systems to monitor their food intake, sleep patterns, vital signs, physical activity, and other bodily conditions. Meanwhile, IoT technologies regularly collect and analyze environmental data that impacts a person's well-being. Ultimately, this compatibility has paved the way for the development of new medical options [21].

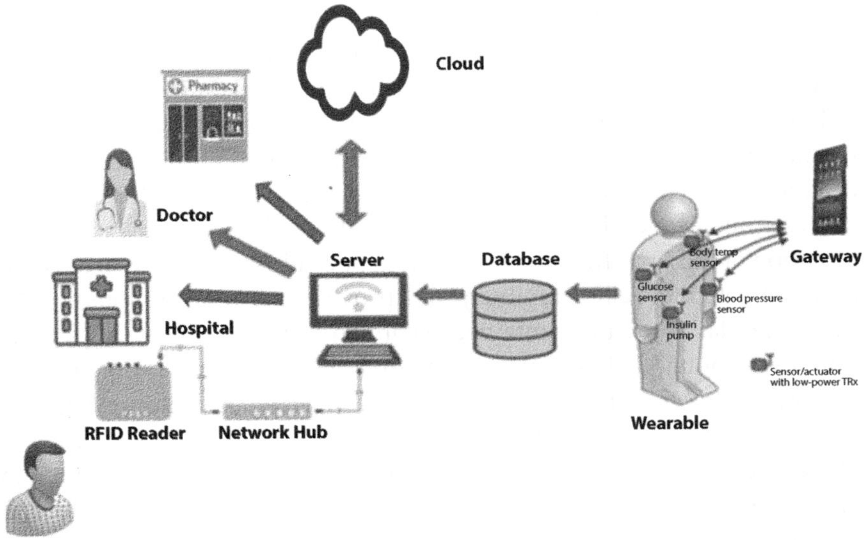

Figure 9.1 The concept of IoT in healthcare [20].

9.1.3 Components of Healthcare

1. Preventive care: This is about preventing illnesses or injuries from happening. It involves getting vaccinations, undergoing screenings, receiving education on healthy lifestyles, and encouraging behaviors that ward off diseases.
2. Primary care: Primary care involves the initial point of contact for patients seeking healthcare. It encompasses routine check-ups, general health assessments, and basic medical treatment for common illnesses.
3. Specialized care: Specialists, such as cardiologists, neurologists, oncologists, and other experts, provide specialized care for specific conditions or body systems.
4. Emergency care: Immediate and critical care provided in emergency situations, including trauma, accidents, sudden illness, or life-threatening conditions.
5. Chronic disease management: Addressing long-term conditions like diabetes, heart disease, arthritis, and mental health disorders through ongoing treatment, monitoring, and lifestyle management.
6. Mental health services: This involves diagnosis, treatment, and support for mental health conditions ranging from anxiety and depression to severe mental illnesses.

9.1.4 The Role of IoT in Healthcare

The benefits of the Internet of Things (IoT) are plentiful when applied in healthcare, revolutionizing how medical services are delivered, monitored, and experienced. Here is how IoT can significantly benefit humans in healthcare.

9.1.4.1 Remote Monitoring and Management

1. Chronic disease management: IoT devices enable continuous monitoring of vital signs, glucose levels, heart rate, etc., allowing patients with chronic conditions to manage their health remotely [22].
2. Elderly care: IoT sensors in homes or wearables can track movement, detect falls, and monitor medication intake, providing real-time updates to caregivers or healthcare professionals [23].

9.1.4.2 Personalized Healthcare

1. Data-driven insights: IoT devices gather extensive patient data, which, when analyzed, provides valuable insights into individual health patterns. This analysis enables the creation of personalized and tailored treatment plans [3].
2. Predictive analytics: Through machine learning algorithms analyzing IoT generated data, healthcare providers can predict health issues and intervene proactively, potentially preventing complications [24].

9.1.4.3 Enhancing Hospital Efficiency and Patient Experience

1. Asset tracking: IoT helps hospitals track medical equipment, optimizing their usage and preventing loss, thus improving overall efficiency [25].
2. Patient engagement: Patients are enabled to take a more active role in their health through wearable devices and IoT-powered apps, which offer convenient access to their health information, medication reminders, and personalized health advice [26].

9.1.4.4 Telemedicine and Remote Consultations

1. Telehealth services: IoT facilitates remote consultations, enabling patients to access healthcare services from anywhere, especially beneficial for rural or remote areas [27].
2. Reducing hospital visits: Continuous monitoring and remote consultations can reduce unnecessary hospital visits, minimizing the strain on healthcare facilities and resources [27].

9.1.4.5 Improving Emergency Responses

1. Emergency alerts: IoT-enabled devices can send alerts in emergencies, helping responders arrive faster and with more accurate information [28].
2. Ambulance monitoring: Smart ambulances equipped with IoT devices can transmit critical patient data to hospitals in real time, preparing medical staff in advance for incoming cases [28].

9.1.4.6 Drug Management and Supply Chain Optimization

1. Inventory control: IoT sensors can monitor medication stock levels, ensuring timely restocking and reducing instances of shortages [29].
2. Cold chain monitoring: For sensitive medications and vaccines, IoT ensures proper temperature control during transportation and storage, maintaining their efficacy [30].

However, it is important to address concerns related to data security, privacy, interoperability of devices, and regulations to ensure the ethical and safe use of IoT in healthcare. Nonetheless, when implemented thoughtfully, IoT stands to significantly improve healthcare outcomes and the overall patient experience.

This chapter will discuss some incredible IoT sensors used for analyzing various attributes related to heart problems, so that heart attacks can be detected prior to their arrival by using the data retrieved by those sensors. Then, results can be displayed on Android apps like Blynk app via Bluetooth connectivity.

9.2 Background

In this part, there is a concise summary of the history and previous research.

[31] The survey gives a thorough summary of IoT uses in the healthcare industry, including remote patient monitoring, wearable technology, smart hospitals, and healthcare data analysis. It examines obstacles like security and privacy concerns and highlights the potential advantages of IoT in revolutionizing healthcare delivery.

[32] The survey delves into different IoT applications within the healthcare sector, such as remote monitoring, smart medical devices, and ambient assisted living. It examines how IoT contributes to personalized medicine and patient-centered healthcare. Furthermore, it discusses the obstacles and potential research paths in the domain.

[33] The survey offers a thorough analysis of IoT technologies and their use in the healthcare sector, encompassing remote patient monitoring, smart healthcare systems, and data analytics. It addresses the obstacles associated with security, interoperability, and scalability, emphasizing the potential influence of IoT on healthcare.

[34] This review article covers various IoT applications in healthcare, emphasizing the impact on patient monitoring, disease management, and healthcare infrastructure. It addresses challenges related to data privacy, interoperability, and scalability. Additionally, it discusses future trends and opportunities for IoT integration in healthcare.

[31] This systematic literature review provides an extensive analysis of IoT applications in healthcare. It covers various aspects, including wearable devices, remote monitoring, IoT-enabled healthcare systems, and data analytics. The review discusses technological advancements, challenges, and future trends in the field.

[35] This comprehensive review explores the potential of IoT for advanced healthcare monitoring. It covers topics such as wearable devices, smart sensors, telemedicine, and IoT-based healthcare frameworks. The paper highlights the transformative impact of IoT on healthcare delivery and patient well-being.

[36] This review article provides an overview of IoT applications in healthcare, emphasizing remote patient monitoring, smart healthcare systems, and data analytics. It addresses the integration of IoT with emerging technologies like AI and blockchain in healthcare. The paper discusses challenges and prospects.

[37] Examining security and privacy issues, this study delves into the impact of IoT in the healthcare sector. It addresses the weaknesses in IoT

devices utilized in healthcare environments, possible risks to patient information, and current security measures. The study seeks to increase understanding and offer perspectives on tackling these important concerns.

[38] The diagram of IoT applications in healthcare and later headways within the field are talked about in this audit paper. It envelops farther quiet checking, shrewd healthcare frameworks, IoT-enabled therapeutic gadgets, and information analytics. The center of the paper is on the impact of IoT on healthcare conveyance and quiet results.

[39] The survey examines the latest developments in IoT for healthcare, with a specific focus on wearable gadgets, health monitoring systems based on IoT, and data analysis. It delves into the obstacles associated with data security, interoperability, and scalability. Moreover, it discusses the potential influence of IoT on personalized healthcare.

[40] The paper delves into IoT-enabled healthcare monitoring systems, encompassing wearable gadgets, sensor technologies, data transmission protocols, and cloud-based healthcare platforms. It provides insights into the development, structure, and obstacles related to integrating IoT into healthcare monitoring.

[41] The focus of this review article is on the use of IoT in healthcare, with an emphasis on remote patient monitoring, smart healthcare systems, and IoT-enabled medical devices. It discusses the potential advantages of IoT in enhancing healthcare services, as well as addressing the challenges and opportunities. The focus of this thorough review is on the utilization of IoT technology in diabetes monitoring systems. It covers the application of IoT devices, sensors, and data analytics in the continuous monitoring of glucose levels and management of diabetes. The review paper specifically emphasizes the technological progress and obstacles associated with using IoT for diabetes care.

9.3 Motivation

9.3.1 Access to Healthcare

- Inequalities in access:
  a) Financial aberrations: Get to healthcare is significantly impacted by financial components. People with lower earnings habitually experience impediments since of the tall fetched of administrations and need of protections.
  b) Geographical disparities: Rural and remote areas lack sufficient health-care facilities, resulting in challenges for residents to access essential medical services.

9.3.2 Cost and Affordability

- High healthcare costs:
  a) Financial burden: Healthcare expenses, including medications, treatments, and procedures, can be financially burdensome, leading to avoidance of necessary care.
  b) Out-of-pocket expenses: In regions without comprehensive health coverage, individuals bear high out-of-pocket costs for healthcare services.

9.3.3 Quality of Care

- Variations in standards:
  a) Regional discrepancies: Healthcare quality can vary significantly between regions or even within different healthcare facilities in the same area.
  b) Patient safety: Medical errors, hospital-acquired infections, and inadequate safety protocols can compromise patient safety and care quality.

9.3.4 Aging Population and Chronic Diseases

- Epidemiological shift:
  a) Long-term care needs: The increasing number of elderly individuals necessitates additional long-term care and the ongoing management of chronic conditions, resulting in a higher need for healthcare services.
  b) Prevalence of chronic diseases: Conditions like diabetes, cardiovascular diseases, and respiratory ailments pose challenges due to their prevalence and complex management needs.

9.3.5 Healthcare Infrastructure

- Underfunded systems:
  a) Resource constraints: Limited funding for healthcare infrastructure, equipment, and personnel leads to shortages and inadequate facilities.
  b) Shortage of healthcare workers: Insufficient healthcare professionals, including doctors, nurses, and specialists, strain healthcare delivery [42].

9.3.6 Healthcare Technology and Innovation

- Adoption challenges:
    a) Technological divide: Unequal access to healthcare technology and digital health tools due to infrastructure limitations or lack of resources.
    b) Data security concerns: Inadequate data security and privacy measures in healthcare technology pose risks to patient confidentiality.

9.3.7 Global Health Threats

- Pandemics and epidemics:
    a) Healthcare systems overwhelmed: Outbreaks of diseases like COVID-19 strain healthcare systems, highlighting the need for preparedness and robust response mechanisms [39].
    b) Emerging diseases and antimicrobial resistance: Global health security is at risk due to emerging infectious diseases and antimicrobial resistance, necessitating collaborative actions for surveillance and control.

9.3.8 Mental Health

- Stigma and access:
    a) Stigmatization: Individuals are discouraged from seeking help or adequate support for mental health due to the social stigma associated with it.
    b) Limited access to services: Insufficient mental healthcare services and resources exacerbate the burden of mental health issues globally [43].

Addressing these challenges necessitates a holistic approach involving policy interventions, increased investment in healthcare infrastructure and workforce, emphasis on preventive care and health education, technological advancements for equitable healthcare access, and global collaboration to tackle emerging health threats. A comprehensive strategy aimed at addressing these multifaceted issues is crucial for improving healthcare systems worldwide.

9.4 Primary Diseases Globally

The term "primary diseases" covers a wide range of ailments that are often prevalent or significant on a global scale. Here is a list of primary diseases that have a significant impact worldwide [44]:

1. Cardiovascular diseases (CVDs):
   a) Coronary artery disease: Atherosclerosis leading to blockages in the coronary arteries.
   b) Stroke: Caused by the interruption of blood flow to the brain.
   c) Hypertension (high blood pressure): A long-term health issue that raises the likelihood of developing heart disease and stroke.
2. Respiratory diseases:
   a) Chronic bronchitis or emphysema: Lung diseases like chronic bronchitis and emphysema that cause restricted airflow.
   b) Asthma: A chronic condition causing difficulty in breathing due to airway inflammation and narrowing.
3. Infectious diseases:
   a) COVID-19: The SARS-CoV-2 virus is responsible for causing respiratory illness and sparking a worldwide pandemic.
   b) HIV/AIDS: A viral infection that weakens the immune system.
   c) Tuberculosis (TB): A bacterial infection affecting the lungs primarily but can also affect other parts of the body.
4. Cancer:
   (a) Lung cancer: Often associated with smoking but can also occur in on-smokers.
   (b) Breast cancer: Most common cancer in women globally.
   (c) Colorectal cancer: Affects the colon or rectum and is often linked to lifestyle and diet.
5. Diabetes:
   a) Type 2 diabetes: Affront resistance and lifted blood sugar levels are the characteristics of type 2 diabetes.
   b) Type 1 diabetes: Autoimmune disorder known as type 1 diabetes involves the immune system, targeting the insulin-producing cells in the pancreas. The immune

system attacks insulin-producing cells in the pancreas in type 1 diabetes.

6. Mental health disorders:
   a) Depression: Persistent sadness and lack of interest in activities are symptoms of depression, a mood disorder.
   b) Anxiety disorders: Conditions characterized by excessive worry or fear are known as anxiety disorders.
7. Neurological disorders:
   a) Alzheimer's illness: Alzheimer's infection may be a condition that leads to memory misfortune and a decline in cognitive work, and it may be a dynamic neurodegenerative clutter.
   b) Parkinson's disease: Parkinson's disease impacts motor functions and is a movement disorder.
8. Chronic kidney infection:
   Chronic renal failure: Decline in kidney function over time
9. Digestive system diseases:
   a) Acid reflex or GERD: Acid reflux, also known as GERD, is a long-term digestive condition in which the stomach's liquid contents back up into the esophagus, leading to discomfort.
   b) Inflammatory bowel disease (IBD): Conditions such as Crohn's disease and ulcerative colitis result in chronic inflammation of the digestive tract, known as inflammatory bowel disease (IBD).
10. Vector-borne diseases:
    a) Malaria: A mosquito-borne infectious disease caused by parasites.
    b) Dengue fever: Spread by mosquitoes and causing flu-like symptoms.

This list covers a range of diseases that have significant impacts on global health, affecting millions of people and requiring ongoing attention and resources for prevention, treatment, and management (refer to Table 9.1).

9.5 IoT Revolutionizes Healthcare

The Web of Things (IoT) has included around good-sized enhancements in differing businesses, and healthcare isn't an exemption. The enchantment

Table 9.1 Primary diseases globally.

S. no.	Disease	Estimated death rate globally	Age group	Genetic factors	Lifestyle choices	Environmental factors	Gender	Infectious agent
1	Cardiovascular diseases	32%	60+	Yes	Yes	Yes	More prevalent in male patients	No
2	Respiratory diseases	42.9%	30+	Yes	Yes	Yes	Equally occur in both male and female patients	Yes
3	Infectious disease	9.9%	Common in children	No	Yes	Yes	Both	Yes
4	Cancer	50.3%	All age groups	Yes	Yes	Yes	Both	Yes
5	Diabetes	73,883 deaths per year (approx.)	More prevalent in adults	Yes	Yes	No	More often in male patients	No

(Continued)

Table9.1 Primary diseases globally. (*Continued*)

S. no.	Disease	Estimated death rate globally	Age group	Genetic factors	Lifestyle choices	Environmental factors	Gender	Infectious agent
6	Mental health disorders	26–28%	18+	No	Yes	Yes	Slightly more common in male than female patients	Yes
7	Neurological disorders	1 in 6 of world's population	Children younger than 5 and in other age groups	Yes	No	Yes	More often in male patients	No
8	Chronic kidney disease	10%	Adults	Yes	Yes	Yes	More often in male patients	Yes
9	Digestive system diseases	37.2%	All age groups	No	Yes	Yes	Both	Yes
10	Vector-borne diseases	20%	Common in children	No	Yes	Yes	Both	Yes

of IoT in healthcare lies in its capacity to put through gadgets, collect and analyze information, and make strides persistent care and results. Here are a few ways IoT is changing healthcare:

1. Remote patient monitoring: IoT gadgets empower healthcare experts to remotely screen patients' crucial signs, such as heart rate, blood weight, glucose levels, and more. Wearable gadgets, such as smartwatches or wellness trackers, can track these measurements and transmit the information in genuine time to healthcare suppliers. This permits for early discovery of wellbeing issues and convenient mediations, decreasing clinic re-admissions and progressing persistent administration [15].
2. Smart medical devices: IoT innovation permits restorative gadgets, such as mixture pumps, pacemakers, and affront pumps, to associate to the web and transmit information. These gadgets can give real-time overhauls on their status, execution, and persistent utilization. Healthcare suppliers can remotely screen gadget usefulness, distinguish glitches, and proactively address potential issues, guaranteeing persistent security [45].
3. Improved medication management: IoT-enabled pill allocators and shrewd medicine bottles can help patients oversee their drugs more successfully. These gadgets can send updates when it is time to require a pill, screen adherence, and indeed inform caregivers or healthcare suppliers if a dosage is missed. This innovation improves pharmaceutical compliance and diminishes pharmaceutical mistakes [46].
4. Efficient asset management: IoT can optimize healthcare facility operations by tracking and managing medical equipment and inventory. IoT sensors can monitor equipment location, utilization rates, and maintenance needs. This data enables healthcare facilities to streamline workflows, reduce equipment downtime, and enhance inventory management, leading to cost savings and improved efficiency [47].
5. Enhanced patient safety: IoT in healthcare advances understanding security through different implies. For example, keen healing center beds can identify quiet development and naturally alter positions to avoid bedsores. IoT-based drop location frameworks can send cautions to healthcare suppliers or caregivers when a persistent falls, empowering incite help.

These advances progress persistent security, minimize dangers, and upgrade in general care quality [48].

6. Data-driven insights: IoT produces tremendous sums of information that, when combined with progressed analytics, can give important experiences. By collecting and analyzing information from IoT gadgets, healthcare experts can distinguish patterns, designs, and irregularities. These experiences can bolster evidence-based decision-making, empower early illness location, encourage personalized treatment plans, and move forward populace wellbeing administration [49].
7. Telemedicine and remote consultations: IoT encourages inaccessible healthcare conveyance through telemedicine and virtual interviews. Patients can utilize IoT gadgets to screen their wellbeing domestically whereas healthcare suppliers remotely evaluate the information and give direction or mediations as fundamental. This approach moves forward to get to care, particularly for people in farther regions or those with constrained versatility [50].

In general, the enchantment of IoT in healthcare lies in its capacity to upgrade persistent care, optimize workflows, move forward productivity, and empower data-driven decision-making. As innovation proceeds to progress, IoT will play a progressively crucial part in changing healthcare conveyance and moving forward quiet results.

9.6 IoT Patient Monitoring Devices and Early Detection of Heart-Related Problems

The Centers for Disease Control and Prevention reports that around 659,000 individuals (about half the population of Hawaii) in the U.S. succumb to heart disease annually. This translates to one out of every four deaths being attributed to coronary heart disease. These startling statistics underscore the risks associated with coronary heart disease. Regrettably, many people remain unaware of their heart issues until they experience an attack. In numerous instances, these sudden attacks lead to death or disability. Early detection of heart problems can help reduce fatalities from heart disease. Monitoring devices utilizing the Internet of Things (IoT) could offer a viable solution. One of the primary methods for detecting heart disease is through the continuous monitoring of heart rate. If it becomes irregular or unusual, it is important to conduct a check to identify the reason and then take the appropriate preventive measures or treatments.

The global landscape is constantly evolving, and individuals often prioritize their livelihoods at the expense of their physical health. Many fatal fitness issues can be prevented with early detection. Heart malady may be a prime case of a wellbeing concern that individuals tend to miss until it is as well late. Luckily, IoT innovation can play a noteworthy part in this issue. IoT-based tools have the capability to predict heart failure well in advance. Thankfully, there are advanced technological solutions utilizing IoT for heart health monitoring. Let us explore how IoT tracking devices serve as valuable assets in the early identification of heart attacks, thereby enhancing the chances of survival.

1. The heartbeat sensor: At the ICAISC 2020, Suchitra Giri delivered a presentation titled "System for Monitoring Heart Rate and Detecting Heart Attacks Based on IoT." The presentation introduced a system that identifies heart failure by monitoring heart rate using IoT technology. Giri and colleagues introduced a heartbeat sensor, a device available in various forms and sizes, enabling real-time measurement of heart rate [51]. He mentioned that sensors come in a rectangular shape and can be found in smartwatches, smartphones, chest straps, and other devices. These sensors measure the heart rate in beats per minute by tracking how many times the heart contracts and expands in a minute. Each sensor consists of an IR LED and a photodiode placed in a clip, while the control circuit includes an Amp IC that connects the signal to a microcontroller. The sensor functions to detect pulses and interprets them as digital signals. The microcontroller processes the data and sends it to the Wi-Fi module. Afterwards, the relayed data is received by network servers for further examination and analysis. The tested and analyzed data is then prepared and gradually stored with a date and time stamp. Giri and his team suggested that if their innovation expands, it will help in understanding heart blockage and ultimately save more lives [50].

   The statistics in the version were gathered from multiple hardware devices. Raju and his team determined that the intelligent healthcare model, combined with IoT-assisted fog computing, shows promising performance [1]. They anticipate that with enhanced algorithms and optimization, the

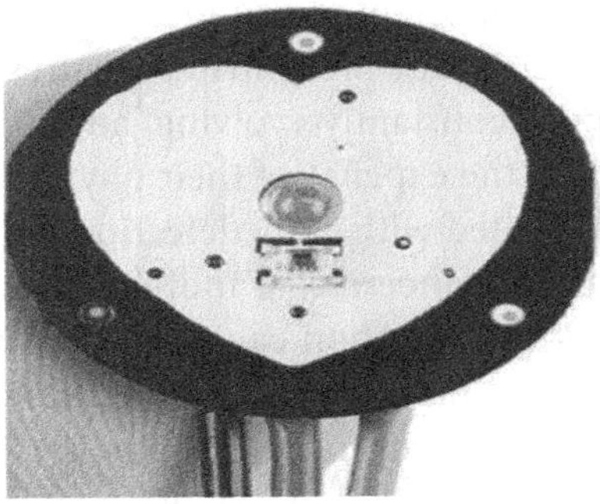

Figure 9.2 Heartbeat sensor [52].
NOTE: A group consisting of K. Butchi Raju, Suresh Dara, Ankit Vidyarthi, V. Gupta, and Baseem Khan puts forward a sophisticated system for predicting heart disease using IoT and fog computing. Their proposed model combines edge–fog–cloud computing to ensure accurate and fast result delivery [1].

Figure 9.3 Smart heart disease prediction system incorporating IoT and fog computing [1].

model can be more widely utilized in the future to improve the accuracy of predicting and diagnosing heart disease. The model is also suitable for use in real-time scenarios. These technologies are a welcome addition and will certainly aid in the fight against heart disease [1].

2. Electrocardiography (ECG) sensors: [53] ECG sensors can measure the electrical activity of the heart and detect irregularities, such as abnormal heart rhythms (arrhythmias) or ischemic changes, which may indicate an increased risk of a heart attack.

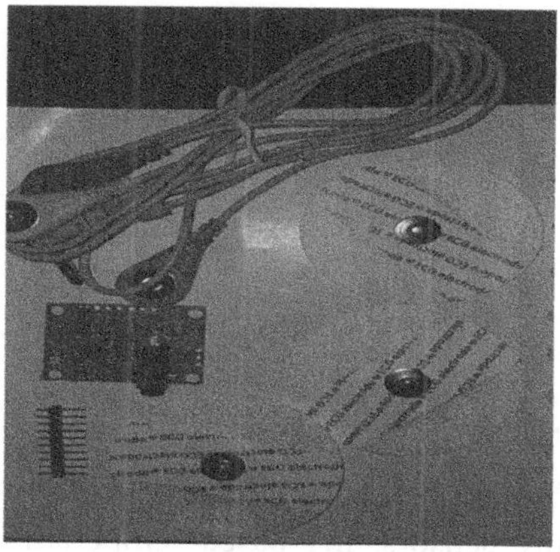

Figure 9.4 ECG sensor [53].

3. Blood pressure sensors: [54] Monitoring blood pressure continuously with IoT sensors can be useful for detecting sudden increases or decreases in blood pressure, which may indicate potential cardiovascular problems such as heart attacks.
4. Heart rate monitors: [55] IoT-enabled heart rate monitors can track heart rate continuously and alert users to abnormal or elevated heart rates that may indicate stress on the heart or potential heart attack symptoms.
5. Pulse oximeters: [56] These sensors measure oxygen saturation levels in the blood and can help identify if there is inadequate oxygen supply to the heart, which could be an early indicator of a heart attack.

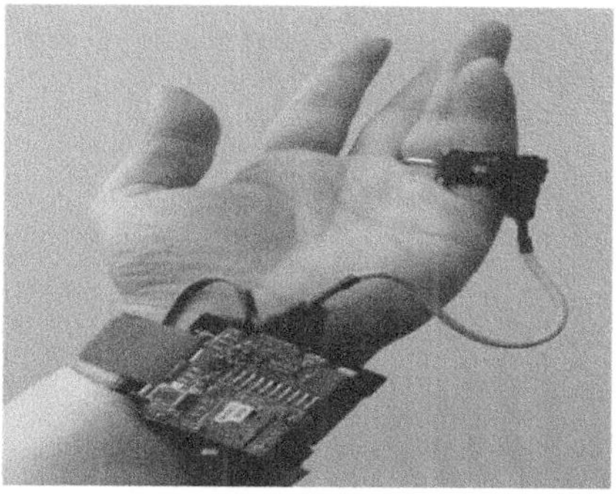

Figure 9.5 Blood pressure [54].

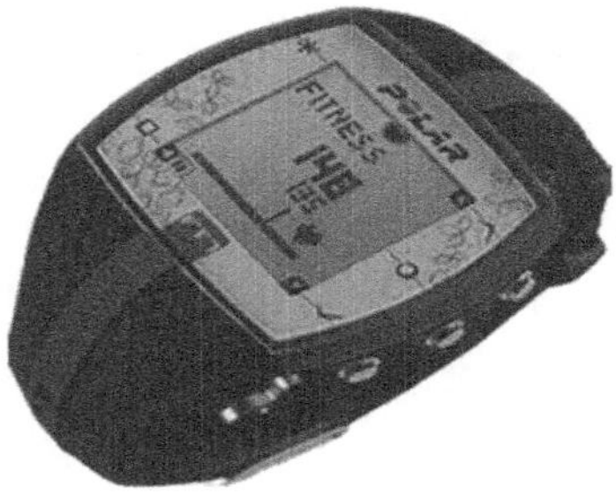

Figure 9.6 Heart rate monitor [55].

6. Temperature sensors: IoT-based temperature sensors can monitor changes in body temperature, and sudden increases in body temperature may suggest an inflammatory response or an ongoing cardiac event [57].
7. Respiratory rate monitors: Monitoring the respiratory rate using IoT sensors can provide insights into breathing patterns [58]. Changes in breathing, such as shortness of breath or labored breathing, may be an early symptom of a heart attack.
8. Activity and movement sensors: [59] IoT sensors that track activity levels and movement patterns can help identify sudden changes, such as decreased activity or increased fatigue, which may indicate early signs of heart problems.
9. Sleep monitoring sensors: Sleep disturbances and abnormal sleep patterns can be associated with an increased risk of heart attacks [60]. IoT sleep monitoring sensors can track

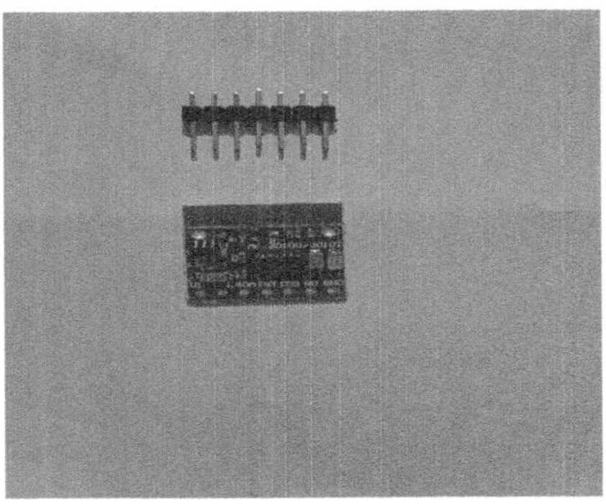

Figure 9.7 Pulse oximeter [56].

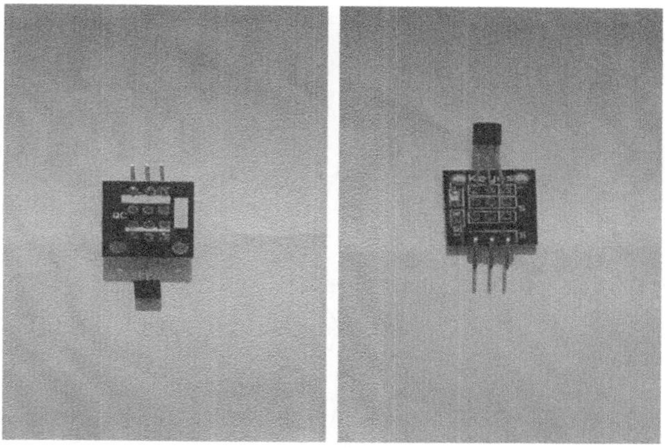

Figure 9.8 Temperature sensor [57].

sleep duration, quality, and disruptions to identify potential risk factors.

10. Stress and anxiety monitors: IoT sensors that measure stress levels, such as galvanic skin response or heart rate variability, can detect heightened stress or anxiety levels, which can be precursors to a heart attack [61].

Please remember that it's crucial to consult healthcare professionals when using these sensors, as they are not intended to substitute medical diagnosis or treatment.

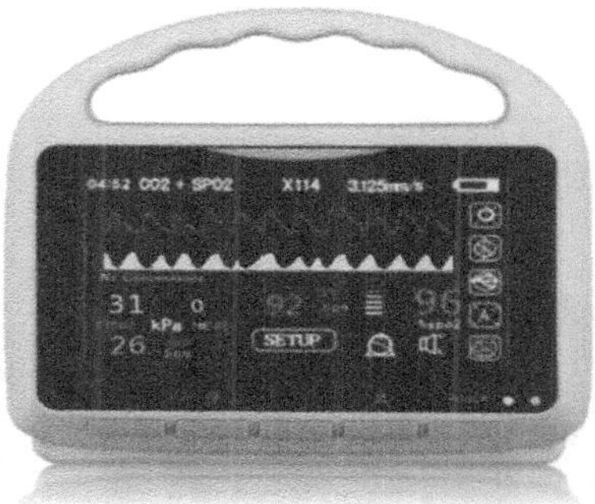

Figure 9.9 Respiratory rate monitor [58].

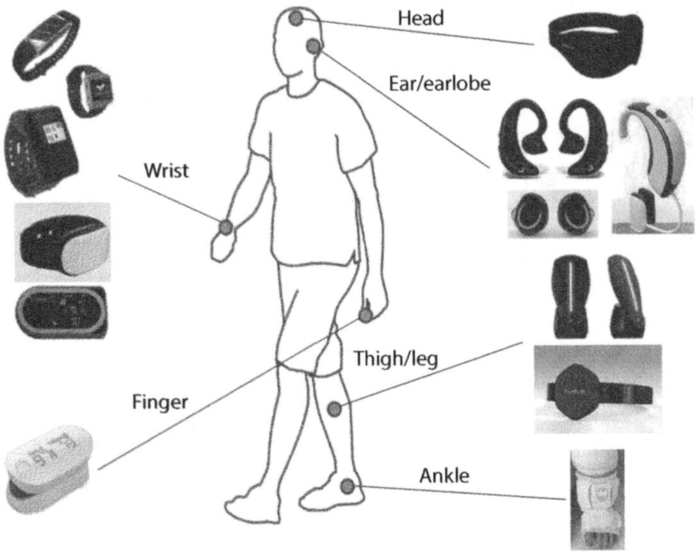

Figure 9.10 Activity and movement sensors [59].

9.7 An IoT-Based Heart Disease Monitoring System

The coronary heart is crucial for circulating oxygen and blood, maintaining the body's function. When the upper chambers accumulate blood, the SA node emits an electrical signal, leading to the contraction of the atria [62]. The blood is then pushed through the tricuspid and mitral valves by this contraction; this stage of the pumping system is known as diastole. Once the ventricles are filled with blood, the next phase commences. The ventricles are stimulated to contract by the electrical signals produced by the SA node. Currently, heart-related health issues are prevalent. Among men and

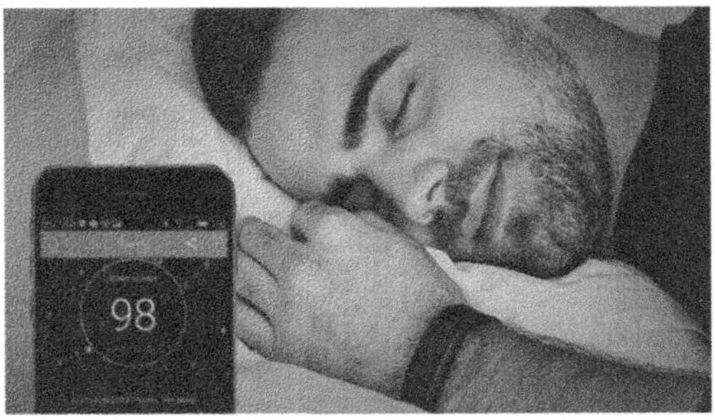

Figure 9.11 Sleep monitoring sensor [60].

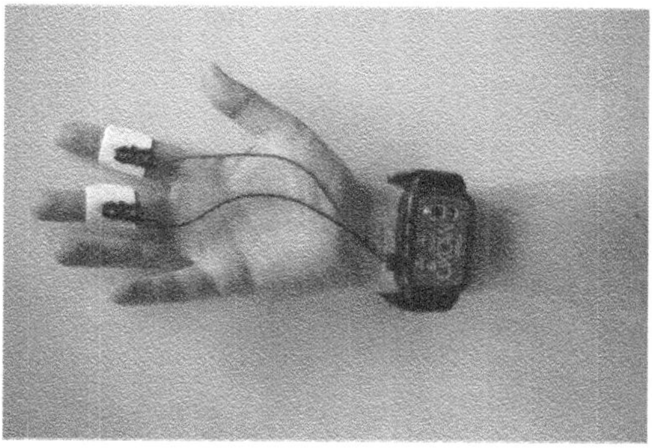

Figure 9.12 Stress and anxiety monitor [61].

women, heart diseases are a significant cause of death [63]. It is dependable for around 1 million passings every year. The heart rate may be a vital calculation within the operation of the heart. Hence, checking heart rate is fundamental in examining heart execution and keeping up heart wellbeing. This segment will investigate a framework for recognizing heart rate utilizing IoT. These days, the treatment of most heart-related ailments requires ongoing and long-term checking. IoT is greatly advantageous in this respect because it replaces traditional monitoring frameworks with a more proficient approach, giving imperative data approximately the patient's condition that is effectively available to the specialist [64]. Moreover, the wellbeing center's medical caretakers or the assigned restorative specialist can utilize a real-time observing framework to track the patient's heart rate in a successive way. The Heart Rate Observing framework said in this setting has been created utilizing IOT innovation for the reason of identifying the patient's pulse and checking the chance of a heart assault through standard checkups. Observing body wellness is greatly vital to guarantee that our wellbeing is in ideal condition. The heart rate (HR) is one of the vital parameters for the gadget being examined [65]. The checking gadget being talked about is a reasonable heart rate observing gadget that works utilizing fingertip and Bluetooth innovation. The complete framework is made up of different parts, including a Heart Rate module, an Android app, and a Bluetooth module. The Heart Rate (HR) module detects the heart rate flag employing a non-invasive strategy known as Photoplethysmography [66] from the subject (patients) and sends it (signal) wirelessly to a computer or android application employing a Bluetooth module [67]. This framework can be coordinated and utilized as a component of telemedicine. The data gotten from this model gadget can be utilized for diverse clinical thinks

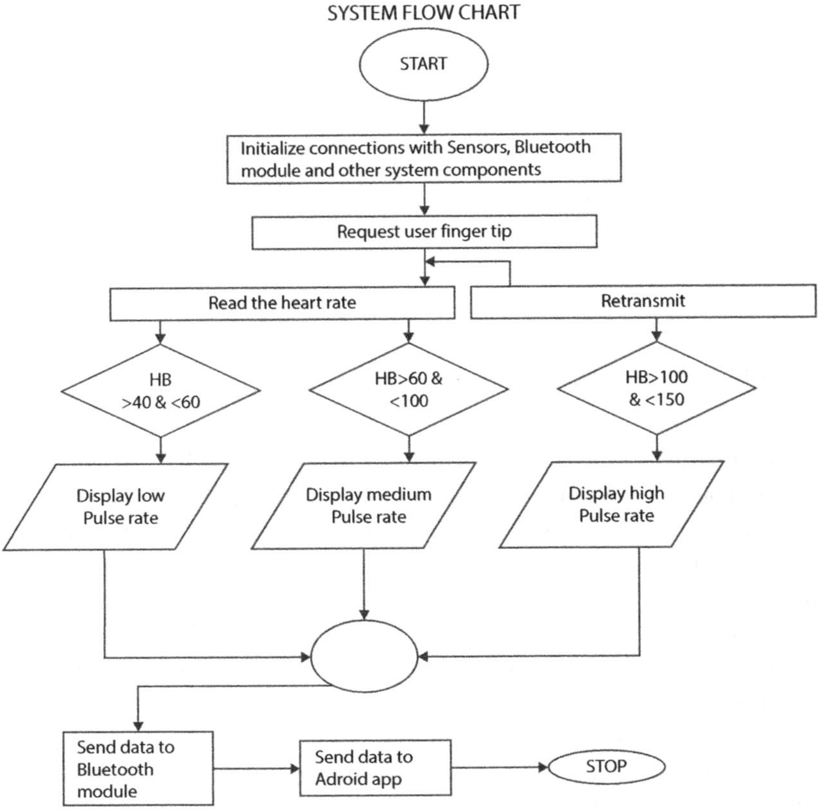

Figure 9.13 System flow chart.

about; in truth, these Bluetooth signals can be transmitted inside a sweep of 15 to 20 meters.

9.7.1 Photoplethysmography

PPG is a reasonable optical strategy that can recognize changes in blood volume in capillaries close the skin's surface. The beginnings of photoplethysmography can be followed back to the late 1800s when analysts watched real-time blood stream utilizing light bulbs [68]. The term "photoplethysmography" was formally presented by researchers in the late 1930s. Headways in innovation have driven to a center on PPG applications for customer utilize through wearable gadgets. These wearables are ordinarily associated to an outside gadget to translate the collected information [66]. Nowadays, smartphones have supplanted these outside gadgets to show

Table 9.2 Average heart rate [72].

Age	Average heart rate
Newborn	140
7 years	85–90
14 years	80–85
Adult	70–80
Athletes	60–100

information to clients in a more available way. The innovation known as Bluetooth permits clients to wirelessly interface, exchange, and get information between two congruous gadgets whereas expending moo control. This shape of communication empowers information to be transmitted over the discuss [69].

Photoplethysmography is a variation of the plethysmography method, which employs a simple optical configuration to detect changes in volume in peripheral blood circulation. This method is non-invasive as it takes measurements from the skin surface. The technology utilizes optoelectronic elements, such as a red or near-infrared light source, to illuminate the skin and a photodetector to monitor changes in light intensity in the observed area [71]. Typically, a red or near-infrared light source is used to illuminate the skin. This light then penetrates through tissues and is absorbed by pigments, bones, and blood. The PPG sensors optically monitor changes in blood flow volume by detecting alterations in light intensity [68].

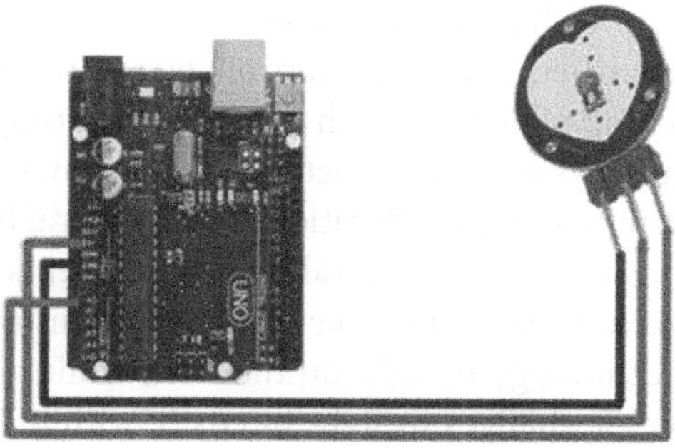

Figure 9.14 Heart rate sensor connection with Arduino Uno [70].

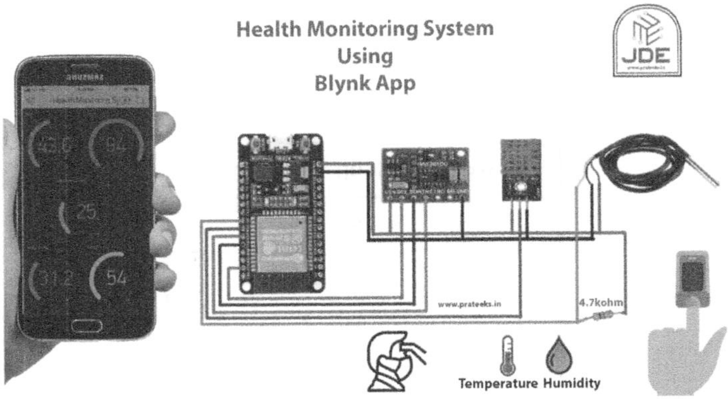

Figure 9.15 Heart monitoring system using Blynk app [72].

The framework utilizes an Arduino Uno and a Bluetooth HC-05 module beside a beat sensor. The beat sensor is situated on the finger to gage the heart rate, which is in this way transmitted to an Android portable app through Bluetooth. Convenient discovery of sicknesses is vital for deflecting potential complications. PPG is an inexpensive optical strategy that can distinguish changes in blood volume because it streams through capillaries close the skin's surface. This procedure was created within the late 1800s when researchers found real-time blood stream utilizing light bulbs [68]. The term "photoplethysmography" was to begin with coined by researchers in the late 1930s. PPG progressions presently fundamentally concentrate on shopper applications utilizing wearable gadgets. Regularly, these wearable gadgets are associated to an outside gadget to translate the comes about they create [66].

In recent times, smartphones have replaced peripheral devices to deliver information to consumers in a convenient manner. Utilizing Bluetooth technology allows for interaction with smartphones. Bluetooth is a wireless communication technology that consumes low power and facilitates the connection, transfer, and reception of data wirelessly between two devices that are compatible with each other [69]. Photoplethysmography is based on the plethysmography method, which involves using a basic optical arrangement to identify alterations in peripheral blood circulation. This method is non-invasive since it takes measurements on the surface of the skin. Optoelectronic elements, like a red or near-infrared light source, are used in this technology to light up the skin, while a photodetector is employed to monitor changes in light intensity within the specified area [70]. Skin is typically illuminated using a red or near-infrared light source.

Light then passes through tissues and is absorbed by pigments, bones, and blood. Changes in blood flow volume are optically observed by PPG sensors as they detect variations in light intensity [68]. The framework utilizes an Arduino Uno and a Bluetooth HC-05 module to put through a beat sensor. The sensor is put on the finger to degree the heart rate, which is at that point transmitted to an Android versatile app through Bluetooth. Recognizing sickness early is pivotal in anticipating future complications. There are three categories for characterizing the heart rate:

Low pulse rate: Usually shown when the heart rate per diminutive falls between 40 and 60 BPM. A moo blood beat rate can result in complications.
Normal pulse rate: Pulse rate within the range of 60 to 100 indicates a normal pulse rate and suggests that the patient is free from complications.
High pulse rate: A pulse rate ranging from 100 to 150 suggests a high pulse rate, posing a significant risk and potential for serious, even fatal complications.

These readings can be viewed on a mobile app such as Blynk app using Bluetooth technology [73].

9.7.2 Software Requirements

- Arduino IDE
- Mobile application (Blynk app)

Arduino IDE
The Arduino Integrated Development Environment (IDE) serves as a software platform for writing, compiling, and uploading code to Arduino microcontroller boards [71]. The interface is designed to be user-friendly for writing code for Arduino boards, which are popular among hobbyists, students, and professionals for building interactive projects, prototypes, and various electronic devices. It displays outputs and results for analysis using both serial monitors as well as serial plotter [74].

Blynk app
The Blynk app is a podium that allows users to easily create interfaces for supervising, maintaining, and working of IoT projects [73]. It provides a good environment for building custom dashboards and mobile apps to interact with various hardware devices, sensors, and actuators. It can also manage hardware remotely, store sensor data, display that data, and many more wonders with IoT [73].

Three major parts of BLYNK APP are:

1. Blynk app
2. Blynk server
3. Blynk libraries

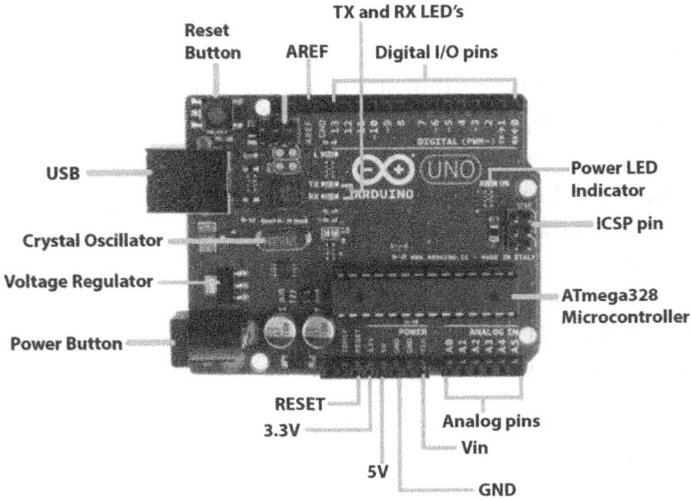

(a) Arduino Board

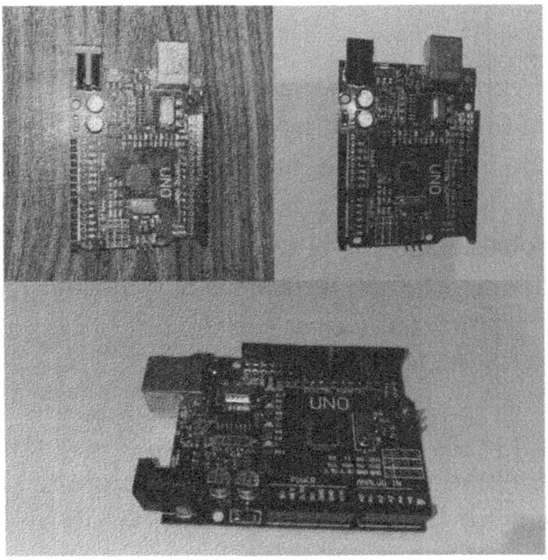

(b)

Figure 9.16 (a): Arduino board [75], (b): original pictures of Arduino board clicked in different angels.

Figure 9.17 HC-05 Bluetooth [81].

9.7.3 Hardware Prerequisite

1. The Arduino Uno micro controller
2. The HC-05 Bluetooth module
3. Jumper wires of all types
4. The heart rate pulse sensor
5. Breadboard
6. The USB cable
7. The Android mobile device

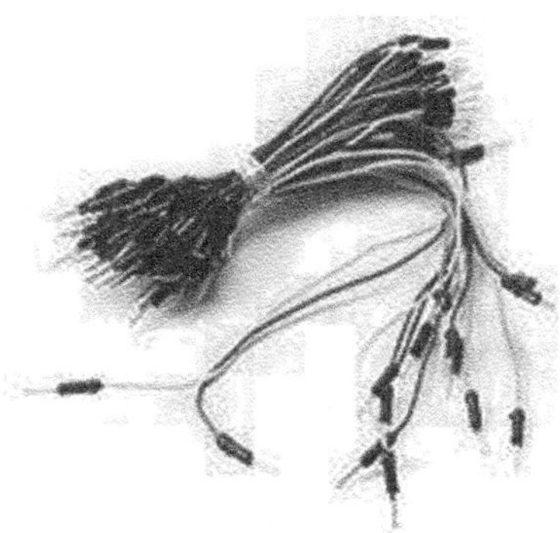

Figure 9.18 Jumper wires [82].

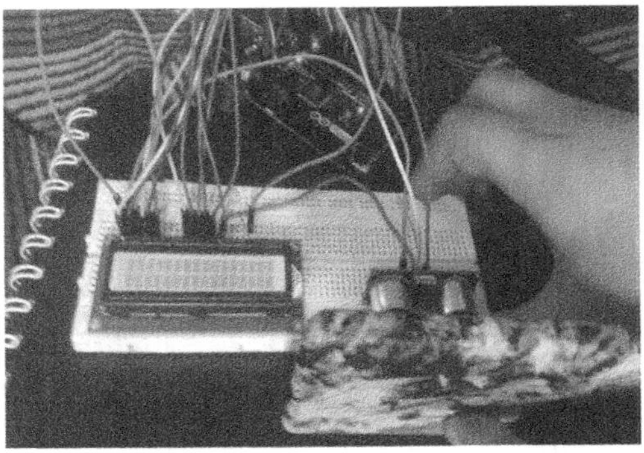

Figure 9.19 Breadboard [83].

• Arduino

The Arduino is a popular microcontroller board in the Arduino family, frequently utilized by hobbyists, students, and professionals for creating and testing a variety of electronic projects [75]. Here is a brief overview of the essential features and specifications of Arduino:

1. Microcontroller: The Atmega 328P microcontroller powers the open-source Arduino Uno board. It is a high-performance, low-power chip manufactured by Atmel, which is now owned by Microchip Technology [76].
2. Clock speed: The clock speed of the Atmega328P microcontroller on the Uno board is 16 MHz [77].
3. Digital I/O pins: The Uno board has 14 digital input/output (I/O) pins that are suitable for connecting with external

Figure 9.20 USB cable connecting PC with Arduino [84].

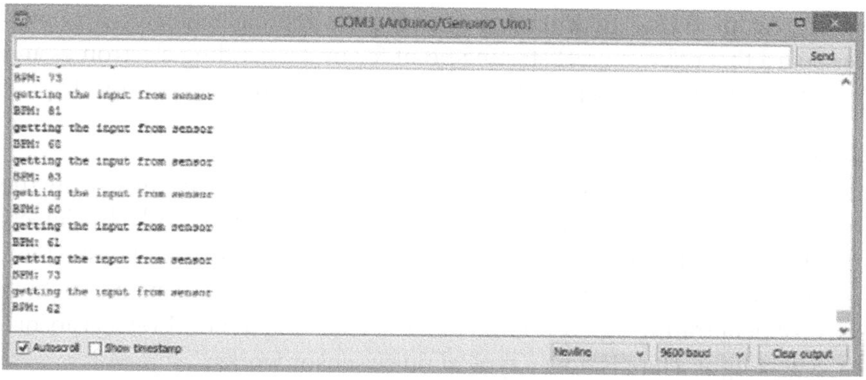

Figure 9.21 Result on the serial monitor.

components like LEDs, switches, sensors, and other digital devices [78].

4. Analog input pins: It also includes six analog input pins, labeled A0 through A5, which are required to read analog voltage values from sensors and other analog devices [78].
5. Power supply: The Uno board has the capability to receive power from either a USB connection with a PC or an external power supply (7–12 V DC). It is equipped with a built-in voltage regulator that delivers stable 5 V and 3.3 V power outputs to power external components [76].
6. USB interface: The Uno board is equipped with a USB Type-B connector that can be used to connect to a computer or other USB-enabled devices [78]. This allows users to upload code to the board and communicate with it using the Arduino IDE.
7. Reset button: The reset button is designed to restart the microcontroller and reinitialize the running code [76].
8. Memory: The Atmega328P microcontroller is equipped with 32 KB of flash memory to store code, 2 KB of SRAM for data storage, and 1 KB of EEPROM for non-volatile data storage [75].
9. Compatibility: The Arduino Uno can be used with a wide variety of objects, devices, and accessories that are made for the Arduino platform, making it simple for users to enhance its capabilities [77].

The Arduino Uno, in general, is a flexible and approachable microcontroller board that offers a great starting point for understanding electronics and coding, and for creating prototypes and developing interactive projects [75].

- Pulse sensor

The pulse sensor, a small and affordable device, is utilized for measuring the heart rate and blood oxygen levels in the bloodstream. It works by detecting fluctuation in blood volume inside the microvascular bed of tissue [65]. Pulse sensors work on the photoplethysmography (PPG) principles, which involve penetrating light into the skin and checking if blood vessels absorb or reflect light. Here is how a typical pulse sensor works:

Step 1: The pulse sensor typically consists of an infrared (IR) LED and a photodetector (commonly a photodiode or phototransistor) positioned adjacent to each other on a small module. Light is emitted by the LED into the skin, and the photodetector gauges the strength of the light that is either absorbed or reflected by the blood vessels [52].

Step 2: (Blood flow detection): As blood flows through the blood vessels in the tissue, the concentration of light absorbed or reflected by the blood changes a bit with each heartbeat. This variation in light intensity is directly related to the blood flow caused by the heartbeat [65].

Step 3: (Signal processing): The sensor's output signal, which represents the changes in light intensity over time, is then processed to extract the pulse waveform. This process typically involves amplification, filtering, and sometimes digital signal processing techniques to enhance the signal and remove noise [79].

Step 4: (Heart rate calculation): Once the pulse waveform is achieved, the heart rate can be calculated by calculating the time between consecutive peaks in the waveform. Additionally, some pulse sensors are also able to estimate blood oxygen saturation levels (SpO2) using additional processing techniques [80].

Pulse sensors are commonly used in number of applications, including smart fitness trackers, wearables like smartwatches, medical equipment's, and biofeedback systems [52]. They provide a convenient and non-invasive way to track heart rate and blood oxygen levels in real-time, making them valuable tools for both healthcare professionals and individuals interested in health and wellness monitoring (refer to Figure 9.7).

• HC-05 Bluetooth module: The HC-05 is outlined as a serial harbor convention (SPP) for making remote serial associations. It is clear to utilize in circuit plan and can successfully transmit measured information to an Android application. Its compatibility with Arduino makes it profoundly esteemed [67]. It was preferred over the HC-06 module due to its ability to function as both a master and a slave module, unlike the HC-06, which can only operate as a slave. The HC-05 module has multiple pins, including four programmable input/output pins, one GND (ground pin), and one for VCC (voltage) [81]. Operating on a voltage supply of 3.3 V to 5 V DC, the HC-05 module is compatible with a wide range of microcontrollers and embedded systems.
• Jumper wires: Solderless jumper wires come with connector pins at both ends, allowing for easy connection of components without the need for soldering. They are commonly employed with breadboards and prototyping tools to facilitate circuit adjustments without the constraints of soldered connections.
• Bread board: A breadboard could be an instrument for making transitory electronic models and testing circuit plans without fastening. It contains conductive strips underneath the surface that interface the gaps on the beat of the board.
• USB cable: The PC is connected to the Arduino UNO board using a USB cable for power supply and for uploading the code to the board.

Once all the components are connected, you can see the desired output on the serial monitor. The result will also be displayed on the Android app connected by Bluetooth.

- S-Shot 1:

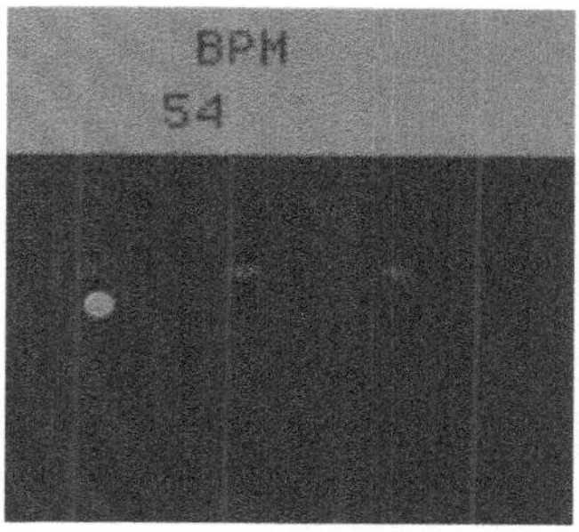

Figure 9.22 Indicating low BP.

- S-Shot 2:

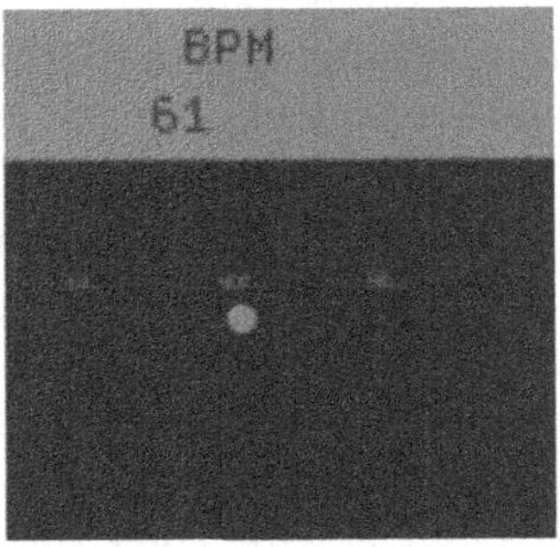

Figure 9.23 Normal BP.

- S-Shot 3:

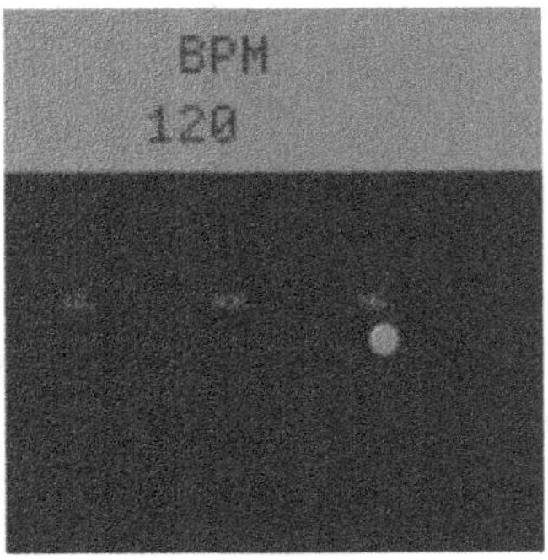

Figure 9.24 High BP.

You can display the output on an LED screen as well.

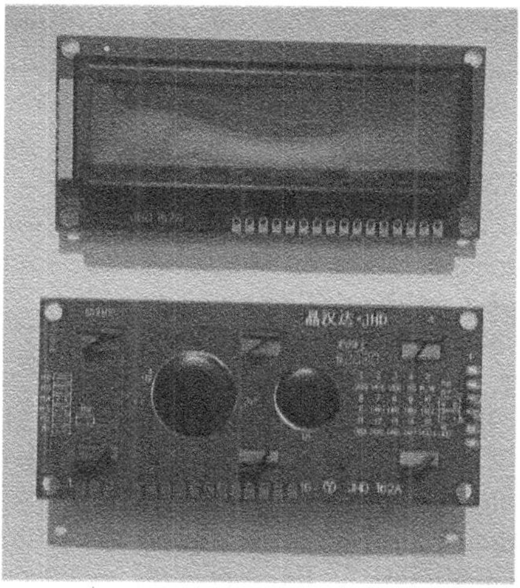

Figure 9.25 LCD display [85].

9.8 Conclusions

An IoT-based monitoring of heart-related diseases can save many lives. This technology mostly helps senior citizens who are suffering from heart problems and need continuous attention. In addition to the heart rate, IoT-based systems can also measure blood pressure, blood glucose levels, and other serious health issues. Doctors, others, or the person himself can be informed of the heart attack using an alert system. Thus, the IoT system ensures the safety of the elderly human lives by assisting and monitoring their health and personal safety. This technology is evolving day by day and can be considered as the future of healthcare. Its uses are abundant or countless. When combined with AI and ML, IoT is the 8th wonder of the world!

References

1. Raju, K., Vidyarthi, A., Suresh DaraGupta, V., Khan, B. Smart_heart disease prediction system with iot and fog computing sectors enabled by cascaded deep learning model. *Comput. Intell. Neurosci.*, 2022, 01, 2022.

2. Sarika, M., Kotak, V., Durafe, A., A review paper on internet of things(iot) and its applications, p. 162306, 2019.
3. Shendge, A., Internet of things (iot): An overview on research challenges and future applications. *Int. J. Eng. Appl. Sci. Technol.*, 6, 66–71, 12 2021.
4. Shafique, K., Khawaja, B.A., Sabir, F., Qazi, S., Mustaqim, M., Internet of things (iot) for next-generation smart systems: A review of current challenges, future trends and prospects for emerging 5g-iot scenarios. *IEEE Access*, 8, 23022–23040, 2020.
5. Fetahu, L., Maraj, A., Havolli, A., Internet of things (iot) benefits, future perspective, and implementation challenges, in: *2022 45th Jubilee International Convention on Information, Communication and Electronic Technology (MIPRO)*, pp. 399–404, 2022.
6. Lu, J., Sookoor, T., Srinivasan, V., Gao, G., Holben, B., Stankovic, J., Field, E., Whitehouse, K., The smart thermostat, pp. 211–224, 11 2010.
7. Kodali, R., Jain, V., Bose, S., Boppana, L., Iot based smart security and home automation system, pp. 1286–1289, 04 2016.
8. Zhou, I., Makhdoom, I., Shariati, N., Raza, M., Keshavarz, R., Lipman, J., Abolhasan, M., Jamalipour, A., Internet of things 2.0: Concepts, applications, and future directions. *IEEE Access*, 9, 1–1, 05 2021.
9. Patel, K., Patel, S., Scholar, P., Salazar, C., Internet of things: Definition, characteristics, architecture, enabling technologies, application future challenges, 05 2016.
10. Fantana, N., Riedel, T., Schlick, J., Ferber, S., Hupp, J., Miles, S., Michaelle's, F., Svensson, S., *Internet of Things - Converging Technologies for Smart Environments and Integrated Ecosystems*, pp. 153–204, 01 2013.
11. Vermesan, O., Friess, P., Guillemin, P., Gusmeroli, S., Sundmaeker, H., Bassi, A., Jubert, I., Mazura, M., Harrison, M., Eisenhauer, M., Doody, P., Internet of things strategic research roadmap, 01 2009.
12. Atiquzzaman, M., Noura, M., Gaedke, M., Interoperability in internet of things: Taxonomies and open challenges. *Mob. Netw. Appl.*, 24, 234, 07 2018.
13. Brüssow, H., What is health? *Microb. Biotechnol.*, 6, 234, 05 2013.
14. Jose, N., Right to health as human right, 02 2017.
15. Baker, S.B., Xiang, W., Atkinson, I., Internet of things for smart healthcare: Technologies, challenges, and opportunities. *IEEE Access*, 5, 26521–26544, 2017.
16. John Dian, F., Vahidnia, R., Rahmati, A., Wearables and the internet of things (iot), applications, opportunities, and challenges: A survey. *IEEE Access*, 8, 69200–69211, 2020.
17. Cicek, M., Wearable technologies and its future applications. *Int. J. Electrical, Electron. Data Commun.*, 3, 2320–2084, 05 2015.
18. Ingale, P., Nandanwar, S., Buva, K., Bhatia, D., Choudhury, P., Tamboli, M., Enhancing patient care and monitoring using ai and iot in healthcare. *Eur. Chem. Bull.*, 06, 235, 2023.

19. Delsi Robinsha, S. and Amutha, B., Iot revolutionizing healthcare: A survey of smart healthcare system architectures, in: *2023 International Conference on Research Methodologies in Knowledge Management, Artificial Intelligence and Telecommunication Engineering (RMKMATE)*, pp. 1–5, 2023.
20. Sujin, J.S., Mukesh, S., Praveen Raj, M.J., Sashwanth, M., Ramesh Kumar, R., Iot based patient monitoring system using tcp/ip protocol, in: *2021 7th International Conference on Advanced Computing and Communication Systems (ICACCS)*, vol. 1, pp. 1076–1080, 2021.
21. Victoria, A.T. and Kowsigan, M., Secure management of healthcare data in fog and iot networks: A short survey on existing security protocols, in: *2022 3rd International Conference on Smart Electronics and Communication (ICOSEC)*, pp. 512–518, 2022.
22. Mahajan, S. and Birajdar, A.M., Iot based smart health monitoring system for chronic diseases, in: *2019 IEEE Pune Section International Conference (PuneCon)*, pp. 1–5, 2019.
23. Cheng, B., Jamil, M., Ambar, R., Wahab, M.H.A., Ma'radzi, A., Elderly Care Monitoring System with IoT Application, pp. 525–537, 02 2020.
24. Taneja, T., Jatain, A., Bhaskar, S., *Predictive analytics on iot*, pp. 1312–1317, 05 2017.
25. Pandey, H. and Sathees, P., Smart health monitoring system using iot and machine learning techniques, pp. 1–4, 02 2020.
26. Gandhi, M. and Singh, S.N., Predictions in heart disease using techniques of data mining, in: *2015 International Conference on Futuristic Trends on Computational Analysis and Knowledge Management (ABLAZE)*, pp. 520–525, 2015.
27. Abdellatif, M. and Mohamed, W., Telemedicine: An iot based remote healthcare system. *Int. J. Online Biomed. Eng. (iJOE)*, 16, 72, 05 2020.
28. Magre Colorado, L.A., Ibanez, J.F., MartinezSantos, J.C., Leveraging emergency response system using the internet of things a preliminary approach, in: *2020 17th International Conference on Electrical Engineering, Computing Science and Automatic Control (CCE)*, pp. 1–6, 2020.
29. Botcha, K.M., Chakravarthy, V.VSSS., Anurag, Enhancing traceability in pharmaceutical supply chain using internet of things (iot) and blockchain, in: *2019 IEEE International Conference on Intelligent Systems and Green Technology (ICISGT)*, pp. 45–453, 2019.
30. Wortmann, F. and Flu¨chter, K., Internet of things. *Bus. Inf. Syst. Eng.*, 57, 221–224, 06 2015.
31. Riazul Islam, S.M., Kwak, D., Kabir, H., Hossain, M., Kwak, K.-S., The internet of things for health care: A comprehensive survey. *IEEE Access*, 3, 678–708, 2015.
32. Agu, E., Pedersen, P., Strong, D., Tulu, B., He, Q., Wang, L., Li, Y., The smartphone as a medical device: Assessing enablers, benefits and challenges, in: *2013 IEEE International Workshop of Internet-of-Things Networking and Control (IoT-NC)*, IEEE, pp. 48–52, 2013.

33. Bhatia, H., Panda, S.N., Nagpal, D., Internet of things and its applications in healthcare-a survey, in: *2020 8th International Conference on Reliability, Infocom Technologies and Optimization (Trends and Future Directions) (ICRITO)*, pp. 305–310, 2020.
34. Ebersold, K. and Glass, R., The impact of disruptive technology: The internet of things. *Issues Inf. Syst.*, 16, 4, 239, 2015.
35. Quraishi, S.J. and Yusuf, H., Internet of things in healthcare, a literature review, in: *2021 International Conference on Technological Advancements and Innovations (ICTAI)*, pp. 198–202, 2021.
36. Mohanty, S.N., Ramya, K.C., Sheeba Rani, S., Gupta, D., Shankar, K., Lakshmanaprabu, S.K., Khanna, A., An efficient lightweight integrated blockchain (elib) model for iot security and privacy. *Future Gener. Comput. Syst.*, 102, 1027–1037, 2020.
37. Miraz, M.H., Ali, M., ExcellPicking, P.S.R., A review on internet of things (iot), internet of everything (ioe) and internet of nano things (iont), in: *2015 Internet Technologies and Applications (ITA)*, pp. 219–224, 2015.
38. Majumder, S., Aghayi, E., Noferesti, M., Memarzadeh-Tehran, H., Mondal, T., Pang, Z., Deen, M.J., Smart homes for elderly healthcare—recent advances and research challenges. *Sensors*, 17, 11, 2496, 2017.
39. Diene, B., Rodrigues, J.JPC., Diallo, O., Ndoye, EL.H.M., Korotaev, V.V., Data management techniques for internet of things. *Mech. Syst. Signal Process.*, 138, 106564, 2020.
40. Kumar, S.A., Vealey, T., Srivastava, H., Security in internet of things: Challenges, solutions and future directions, in: *2016 49th Hawaii International Conference on System Sciences (HICSS)*, IEEE, pp. 5772–5781, 2016.
41. Madakam, S., Lake, V., Lake, V., Lake, V. *et al.*, Internet of things (iot): A literature review. *J. Comput. Commun.*, 3, 05, 164, 2015.
42. Rahaman, A., Islam, M., Islam, R., Sadi, M.S., Nooruddin, S., Developing iot based smart health monitoring systems: A review. *Rev. Intell. Artif.*, 33, 6, 435–440, 2019.
43. Khan, F.A., Zeb, K., Al-Rakhami, M., Derhab, A., Bukhari, S.A.C., Detection and prediction of diabetes using data mining: a comprehensive review. *IEEE Access*, 9, 43711–43735, 2021.
44. Lombardo, J.S. and Buckeridge, D.L., *Disease surveillance: a public health informatics approach*, John Wiley & Sons, Rio de Janeiro, Brazil, 2012.
45. Zwi, S., Isautier, J., Webster, A., Lambert, K., Shepherd, H., McCaffery, K., Development and feasibility of a best-practice health literacy app for adults living with ckd: Presenter (s): Danielle muscat, university of Sydney, Australia. *Patient Educ. Couns.*, 109, 15–16, 2023.
46. Manikanta, A.A., Sahu, H., Arora, K., Koneru, S.V., An iot approach toward storage of medicines to develop a smart pill box, in: *International Conference on Artificial Intelligence and Sustainable Engineering*, G. Sanyal, C.M.T.-G. , S. Awasthi, C.M.A. Pinto, B.R. Purushothama (Eds.), pp. 547–559, Springer Nature Singapore, Singapore, 2022.

47. Shaikh, S., Waghole, D., Kumbhar, P., Kotkar, V., Awaghade, P., Patient monitoring system using iot, in: *2017 International Conference on Big Data, IoT and Data Science (BID)*, pp. 177–181, 2017.
48. Gunasekar, T., Karthikeyan, J., Manivannan, G., Saran, M.S.K., Gokul, K.R., Iot based patient safety monitoring system in hospitals, in: *2022 2nd International Conference on Power Electronics IoT Applications in Renewable Energy and its Control (PARC)*, pp. 1–4, 2022.
49. Aijaz, A. and Hamid Aghvami, A., Cognitive machine-to-machine communications for internet-of-things: A protocol stack perspective. *IEEE Internet Things J.*, 2, 2, 103–112, 2015.
50. Akshaya, B., Prathibha, S., Priyavarshini, S., Concare – a teleconsultation system using iot in healthcare. *Int. J. Sci. Res. Comput. Sci. Eng. Inf. Technol.*, 4.0, 185–190, 05 2022.
51. Arun Prasath, T., Mohamed Arif, M., Srinivasan, S., Muthumanojkumar, A., Sushmitha, M., Sankaran, S., Iot based heart attack detection and heart rate monitoring system, in: *2023 Advanced Computing and Communication Technologies for High Performance Applications (ACCTHPA)*, pp. 1–4, 2023.
52. Arora, J., Gagandeep, Singh, A., Singh, N.P., Rawat, S.S.S., Singh, G., Heartbeat rate monitoring system by pulse technique using hb sensor, in: *International Conference on Information Communication and Embedded Systems (ICICES2014)*, pp. 1–5, 2014.
53. Rahman, A., Rahman, T., Ghani, N.H., Hossain, S., Uddin, J., Iot based patient monitoring system using ecg sensor, in: *2019 International Conference on Robotics, Electrical and Signal Processing Techniques (ICREST)*, pp. 378–382, 2019.
54. Hiwale, A. and Chaskar, U., Design and development of iot based blood pressure measurement system, in: *2022 13th International Conference on Computing Communication and Networking Technologies (ICCCNT)*, pp. 1–5, 2022.
55. Bathilde, J.B., Then, Y.L., Rajith Chameera, Siang Tay, F., Abang Zaidel, D.N., Continuous heart rate monitoring system as an iot edge device, in: *2018 IEEE Sensors Applications Symposium (SAS)*, pp. 1–6, 2018.
56. Chatterjee, A., Chowdhury Kolay, S., Bandyopadhyay, M., Chattopadhyay, S., Iot based pulse oximeter system, in: *2021 International Conference on Industrial Electronics Research and Applications (ICIERA)*, pp. 1–4, 2021.
57. Aryanto, I.K.A.A., Puritan Wijaya, I.G.K.G., Hendrawan, I.N.R., Aryanto, K.Y.E., A prototype iot based technology for body temperature monitoring, in: *2021 3rd International Conference on Cybernetics and Intelligent System (ICORIS)*, pp. 1–6, 2021.
58. Bhola, B., Kumar, R., Priyadarshini, I., So-In, C., Padhy, T., Slowik, A., Gandomi, A.H., Internet of-things-based sensor module for respiratory tracking system. *IEEE Sens. J.*, 23, 16, 18664–18674, 2023.
59. Tahir, M.N. and Rashid, U., Iot-motion sensor device and data analysis: (motion detection and step-count algorithm), in: *2020 International*

Conference on Computing and Information Technology (ICCIT1441), pp. 1–5, 2020.
60. Cay, G. and Mankodiya, K., Sleepsmart: Smart mattress integrated with e-textiles and iot functions for sleep apnea management, in: *2020 IEEE International Conference on Pervasive Computing and Communications Workshops (PerCom Workshops)*, pp. 1–2, 2020.
61. Kadhim, K.T., Alsahlany, A.M., Wadi, S.M., Kadhum, H.T., An overview of patient's health status monitoring system based on internet of things (iot). *Wireless Pers. Commun.*, 114, 3, 2235–2262, 2020.
62. Buckberg, G., Nanda, N., Nguyen, C., Kocica, M., What is the heart? anatomy, function, pathophysiology, and misconceptions. *J. Cardiovasc. Dev. Dis.*, 5, 33, 06 2018.
63. Faris, M., Ibrahim, R., Al-Mukhtar, S., Hashem, A., Physiology of the cardiovascular system, vol. 06, 2021.
64. Gupta, A., Yadav, S., Shahid, S., Venkanna, U., Heartcare: Iot based heart disease prediction system. *2019 International Conference on Information Technology (ICIT)*, pp. 88–93, 2019.
65. Patil, C. and Chaware, A., Heart (pulse rate) monitoring using pulse rate sensor, piezo electric sensor and nodemcu, in: *2021 8th International Conference on Computing for Sustainable Global Development (INDIA Com)*, pp. 337–340, 2021.
66. Allen, J., Photoplethysmography and its application in clinical physiological measurement. *Physiol. Meas.*, 28, R1–39, 04 2007.
67. Jha, G.K., Singh, A., Gupta, A., Nigam, A., Sharma, V., Iot and Bluetooth enabled wireless notice board, in: *2023 3rd International Conference on Advancement in Electronics Communication Engineering (AECE)*, pp. 38–42, 2023.
68. Kavya, R., Nayana, N., Komal Babasab KarangaleMadhura, H., Sheela, S.J., Photoplethysmography — a modern approach and applications. *2020 International Conference for Emerging Technology (INCET)*, pp. 1–4, 2020.
69. Djeldjli, D., Bousefsaf, F., Maaoui, C., Reguig, F., Imaging photoplethysmography: Signal waveform analysis, pp. 830–834, 09 2019.
70. Boccignone, G., Conte, D., Cuculo, V., D'Amelio, A., Grossi, G., Lanzarotti, R., An open framework for remote-ppg methods and their assessment. *IEEE Access*, 8, 216083–216103, 2020.
71. Fezari, M. and Dahood, A.A., Integrated development environment "ide" for Arduino, 10 2018.
72. Kozhukhov, S., What is a normal range of blood pressure, 07 2017.
73. Ranjana, S., Hegde, R., Divya, C.D., Real time patient monitoring system using blynk, in: *2021 IEEE International Conference on Distributed Computing, VLSI, Electrical Circuits and Robotics (DISCOVER)*, pp. 327–331, 2021.

74. Halim, D.K., Ming, T.C., Song, N.M., Hartono, D., and, Arduino-based ide for embedded multi-processor system-on-chip. *2019 5th International Conference on New Media Studies (CONMEDIA)*, pp. 135–138, 2019.
75. Louis, L., Working principle of Arduino and using it as a tool for study and research, vol. 1, 07 2018.
76. Ismailov, A. and Jorae, Z., Study of Arduino microcontroller board, 03 2022.
77. Kondaveeti, H. and Mathe, S., A systematic literature review on prototyping with Arduino: Applications, challenges, advantages, and limitations. *Comput. Sci. Rev.*, 40, 262, 02 2021.
78. Badamasi, Y.A., The working principle of an Arduino, in: *2014 11th International Conference on Electronics, Computer and Computation (ICECCO)*, pp. 1–4, 2014.
79. Khamitkar, S.S., Iot based system for heart rate monitoring. *Int. J. Eng. Res. V9*, 9, 264, 08 2020.
80. Akouz, N., El Ghazi, A., Zourhri, M., Hamida, S., Cherradi, B., Raihani, A., A comprehensive review on monitoring sensors for cardiovascular disease prevention and management, in: *2023 3rd International Conference on Innovative Research in Applied Science, Engineering and Technology (IRASET)*, pp. 1–8, 2023.
81. Shrestha, R., Study and control of Bluetooth module hc-05 using Arduino uno, 01 2016.
82. Mohmmed, S. and Ahmed, H., An employing embedded weather system for self-driving vehicles, pp. 79–85, 01 2020.
83. Scarlato's, L., Pratama, A., Tchoubar, T., The virtual breadboard: Helping students to learn electrical engineering at a distance, 11 2017.
84. Ahmed, S., Arduino project report - academic project, 11 2018.
85. Silipigni, L., Malinsky´, P., Slepicka, P., Franco, D., Torrisi, L., Polyvinyl alcohol composite filled with carbon dots produced by laser ablation in liquids. *Polymers*, 16, 1390, 05 2024.

10

Human Biological Analysis Through Fitness Watch Using Deep Learning Algorithm

Nilesh Bhaskarrao Bahadure[1]*, Ramdas Khomane[1], Anjali Singh[1], Anisha Jaiswal[1], Rashmi Kadu[1], Rohini Bharne[1], Bhumika Kosarkar[1] and Sidheswar Routray[2]

[1]*Symbiosis Institute of Technology, Nagpur Campus, Symbiosis International (Deemed University), Pune, India*
[2]*Department of Computer Science and Engineering, School of Engineering, Indrashil University, Rajpur, Mehsana, Gujarat, India*

Abstract

In today's modern world, technology plays a significant role in various aspects of our lives, especially when it comes to enhancing our overall well-being. One such technological advancement that has become everywhere is the smartwatch. These devices are instrumental in monitoring our daily activities, including the number of steps we take and various other metrics. Smartwatches enable us to collect valuable data, contributing to our understanding of physical activities and promoting a healthier lifestyle. For our research, we collected the data from the smartwatches, focusing on data mining techniques, such as clustering and regression analysis. This research paper delves into a comprehensive health analysis study from a healthcare perspective, focusing on the effectiveness of smartwatch technology in improving personal health. The study progresses to applying advanced deep learning techniques to enhance data-driven research by unveiling new applications and prediction capabilities. These findings are communicated through visualizations and reports, offering valuable information that may revolutionize perspectives on health and wellness. The ultimate goal is to provide a better understanding of the role of smartwatch technology in promoting a healthy lifestyle and enabling informed decision-making in healthcare.

**Corresponding author*: nbahadure@gmail.com; nilesh.bahadure@sitnagpur.siu.edu.in

Bharat Bhushan, Akib Khanday, Khursheed Aurangzeb, Sudhir Kumar Sharma and Parma Nand (eds.) Wellness Management Powered by AI Technologies, (275–296) © 2025 Scrivener Publishing LLC

Keywords: Biological analysis, fitness watch, deep learning, clustering, regression analysis, healthcare

10.1 Introduction

The unrelenting progress of technology has brought about a new age of completely integrated healthcare and cutting-edge advancements. A paradigm change in health and wellness management has been brought about by the confluence of deep learning algorithms and fitness trackers with sensors in this dynamic environment. Wearable technology, notably smartwatches, fitness trackers, and other similar devices, has evolved a plethora of real-time health data [1]. Tremendous growth has been registered in these devices' usability, especially from health-conscious people. These devices generate massive amounts of fitness-related data. If these data are correctly analyzed, it will help deploy the corrective measures for improving healthcare [2, 3].

Smartwatches and other wearable devices have the ideal environment to record and evaluate a wide range of health statistics, from heart rates and step counts to calorie consumption and rhythms of sleep, aside from the fact that they are loaded with an abundant number of sensors for analysis [4, 5]. Their potential is truly remarkable since they provide an extensive and detailed view of everyday wellness by exploiting the enormous statistics that their integrated sensors have collected.

The study at hand aims to conduct a thorough investigation of the consequences and repercussions of this technological convergence. It explores the many uses of these wearable devices, including health monitoring, personalized health insights, preventative healthcare, user engagement and motivation, data sharing, healthcare cooperation, and their considerable contribution to public health research [6–8]. But in this age of rapid technological development, it is also important to carefully protect the security and integrity of user data while addressing issues related to data privacy, data correctness, and the tendency toward over-reliance on technology [9, 10]. This study attempts to negotiate the complex landscape of wearable health technology through the deep learning transformational potential [3, 11, 12].

The healthcare industry is now at its peak, and it is expected to grow exponentially. The contribution of smart wearable watches and wearable devices is exceptionally high. These devices are offerable and available in various ranges to meet the user's specific requirements. Analyzing the data gathered through these devices effectively can efficiently serve the user's apparent demand [13, 14]. This study is performed in a slight attempt to analyze the data collected from wearable devices and present strategies for further improvement and suggestive measures in healthcare through biological data analysis. The motivation behind this research is the well-being of humans through technological evolution; some of the key points are highlighted as follows:

a) Impact of technology on well-being: Our lives are progressively intertwined with technology, which has significantly impacted our overall well-being. In this context, smartwatches have become a widespread technological advancement.
b) Role of smartwatches: Smartwatches are wearable devices that serve a crucial purpose: they monitor various aspects of our health. From tracking our daily steps to other health metrics, they are essential in keeping us informed.
c) Research motivation: The driving force behind this research is to understand how smartwatches contribute to our overall health and wellness. Specifically, the study aims to explore how effective smartwatches are in improving individual health.

All the efforts have been incorporated into finding the relevance of the technology, its usage, and its impact on healthcare. Through extensive experimentation, the novel contributions of the research have been identified and are highlighted as follows:

a) Data collection and analysis: The research collects data from smartwatches, focusing on data mining techniques such as clustering and regression analysis. This approach allows for a comprehensive understanding of health-related patterns.
b) Healthcare perspective: The study adopts a healthcare perspective, emphasizing the impact of smartwatch technology on individual well-being. Analyzing health-related data contributes valuable insights into the field.
c) Advanced deep learning techniques: These methods enhance data-driven research by uncovering new applications and prediction capabilities.

d) Visualizations and reports: The findings are effectively communicated through visualizations and reports. This approach ensures that the information is accessible and can potentially revolutionize perspectives on health and wellness.
e) Informed decision-making: Ultimately, the goal is to provide a better understanding of how smartwatch technology promotes a healthy lifestyle. By doing so, it enables informed decision-making in healthcare.

10.2 Literature Survey

Combining deep learning with fitness watches transforms human biological analysis at the dynamic nexus of technology and healthcare. This literature review examines the present level of knowledge and research in this area, highlighting the possible applications of fitness watches for health monitoring, analyzing data using deep learning, and addressing related ethical and practical issues. It uses worn technology and artificial intelligence to give a thorough picture of the evolving field of human biological study.

The intelligent healthcare recommendation system for multidisciplinary diabetes disease patients (SHRS-M3DP) model has been proposed by Baha Ihnaini *et al.* [15] as a framework for multidisciplinary diabetic health diagnosis and recommendation. The model achieves an astounding 99.6% aggregate success rate with data fusion and ensemble deep machine learning. This research emphasizes how the strategy may enhance the identification of complex healthcare issues and the process of giving recommendations. It offers informative information regarding the application of cutting-edge technology in healthcare, with a focus on privacy and data integrity. It forecasts further developments in this important area of medicine and provides a workable approach to foresee and manage diabetes.

Matin Kheirkhahan *et al.* [16] have highlighted the transformative potential of smartwatch technology in healthcare monitoring. It demonstrates the positive aspects of electronic wrist watches regarding the collection of persistent information gathered, including geographical distribution and energy expenditure tracking. The real-time and online assessment and mobility monitoring (ROAMM) structure offers real-time interactive exchange and information synchronization by fusing patient device data and outcomes. Smartwatches offer a unique platform for understanding physical activity patterns and capturing episodic health events, making them invaluable for healthcare research.

The paper addresses the limitations of battery life and emphasizes the significance of wear-time detection for prolonged monitoring, presenting a promising solution for the Internet of Things in mHealth.

Deeksha Kaul *et al.* [17] highlight the growing significance of algorithms for learning, particularly neural networks, in medical diagnosis, prognosis, and patient care. It discusses the parallels between complex cognitive networks and how the human brain processes information. Applications of deep learning to recognize and treat the signs and symptoms of conditions including cancer, diabetic complications, Parkinson's condition, and Alzheimer's disorder are essential components of this research. Because it may significantly improve disease recognition and mitigation, deep computing is a potential approach for the healthcare field.

A crucial topic in healthcare, the monitoring and treatment of dementia patients in a home environment, has been tackled by Costas Boletsis *et al.* [18]. Due to the fact that they depend on self-reporting and planned visits, traditional care models are limited in their ability to address the serious and expanding problem of dementia. In order to provide insights into the physical and cognitive well-being of individuals with dementia during daily activities, the research investigates the potential benefits of smartwatches for continuous health monitoring. This technology has the potential to improve patient safety and quality of life, increase care quality, and supply useful real-time data. It draws attention to the promising application of assistive technology in dementia care.

According to Anthony Hickey *et al.* [19], intelligent gadgets have the potential to track psychological strain and mental wellness. Cochrane Central, MEDLINE, PsycINFO, and CINAHL were the databases that have been utilized to find the technologies.

Marcin Straczkiewicz *et al.* [20] proposed that smartphones are ideal for health tracking due to their built-in sensors. They provided that Human Activity Recognition (HRA) system translates smartphones data to physical activity. Their future studies focus on improving data quality, addressing missing data, etc.

Manar Ahmed Hamza *et al.* [21] proposed that wearable devices such as wristbands are used for health and vitality and allow users to monitor their health status. Throughout this research investigation, an ideal deep neural network model is used to construct a wearable-assisted effective health surveillance system for insomnia prognosis. This model gathers rest-activity related data, preliminarily processes it, and predicts the amount of sleep one gets using a deeply rooted belief system model.

Madeena Sultana *et al.* [22] provide the relationship between contextual information and emotional transition using machine learning techniques.

Data were collected from 18 individuals using smartphones and smartwatches. Users self-reported 49 different emotions and different time through a smartphone app. A general and personalized model was built for the detection of emotional transitions for every 5 min. The area under the receiver operating characteristic curves (AUROC) for mental state identification reached 60.55% in conventional models and an average of 96.33% across individualized models, indicating a good result for emotional state. This study discovered that the predictability of emotion can be affected by lifestyle.

The multimedia healthcare applications (MHA) model was proposed by Diana P. Tobón *et al.* [23]. This research focuses on advanced technology to address some big challenges in healthcare. The World Health Organization (WHO) tells us that many people around the world die from long-lasting health problems like diabetes, cancer, heart diseases, and breathing issues. These problems require constant check-ups and urgent care from hospitals. It is especially difficult because there are more obese people and a growing number of elderly individuals, which adds to the healthcare challenge. Approximately 22% of the inhabitants on the planet are projected to be older than 65 by 2050. To make things even more complicated, the COVID-19 pandemic has put a lot of strain on the healthcare system. So, to help people live healthier and better lives, researchers are coming up with new ideas in the field of healthcare. In this particular research paper, they outline how to use deep learning techniques and interactive media data to improve healthcare. In the paper, they discuss different solutions that use these technologies to tackle healthcare issues. Essentially, they are looking for innovative ways to make healthcare better and more effective for everyone.

Jeethu Philip *et al.* [24] discussed today's rapidly changing world, and the spread of diseases is a big concern. Smart health monitoring is a solution that uses technology to help. The integration of artificial intelligence (AI) and the Internet of Things (IoT) can enhance urban intelligence and effectiveness particularly in the healthcare sector. To make remote healthcare monitoring work using IoT, AI, and deep learning, we need to analyze data. Deep learning helps in making sense of the data and is used for things like personalized health recommendations. This paper looks at how IoT can be used in smart cities for healthcare. It reviews different monitoring applications, the technologies involved, and the challenges in this field. It also suggests areas for more research. In simple terms, it's about using smart technology to improve healthcare in our ever-changing world.

Farida Sabry *et al.* [25] discuss the growing use of wearable healthcare devices like fitness trackers and smartwatches. It highlights the increasing interest in using artificial intelligence (AI) with these devices for healthcare tasks, especially for remote patient monitoring and health issue detection. The paper provides insights into different tasks AI can perform with wearable devices, the techniques involved, the kinds of data collected, and available datasets. It also mentions challenges, such as improving battery life, ensuring data reliability, and maintaining data privacy and security, with potential solutions from existing research. In conclusion, the paper emphasizes the need to work on data reliability, availability, and privacy for effective use of wearable device data. It mentions funding from the Qatar National Research Fund.

A study led by Haitham Elwahsh *et al.* [26] has developed an intelligent healthcare system that uses wearable devices like smartwatches to monitor your health. These devices have special sensors to gather information. Their main goal is to check how well these devices work in real life, how good they are at what they do, how efficient they are, and how much they cost. An Android app connects to your wearable device and keeps track of your heart rate. If it detects a problem, it sends alerts to a medical expert or your family with your location. There is also an Android and desktop app that looks at your health data and can tell you if you might have a heart disease. It also counts your daily steps and helps you find nearby healthcare facilities. To build all these, they used different computer languages and smart techniques that help computers learn. The advantages of this project are that it keeps an eye on your heart rate, predicts a heart disease, and helps you find places to get medical help.

Sijie Yang *et al.* [27] underscores the transformative impact of big data and artificial intelligence on healthcare. It highlights the emergence of computational medicine, enabled by AI, to analyze extensive biomedical data for enhanced disease prediction and clinical diagnosis. The paper emphasizes the potential applications in areas like pharmaceutical research and the elimination of manual feature engineering through deep learning. It also acknowledges the challenges related to complex biomedical data and the need to address issues such as data privacy and model interpretability. The subsequent sections delve into the application of deep learning in various healthcare domains, emphasizing the aim to extract valuable insights from complex datasets while recognizing the challenges that must be overcome. Overall, the paper offers a comprehensive view of medicine, providing valuable knowledge for healthcare professionals and researchers looking to harness AI's potential in the field.

Ahila *et al.* [28] focus on the significance of diagnosing, treating, and monitoring chronic diseases, particularly with remote patient monitoring with the help of artificial intelligence (AI), and review various technologies. The wearable sensors highlight their challenges, advantages, and applications in healthcare. Several specific examples are mentioned, such as IoT-based monitoring for cardiovascular diseases and machine learning methods for diabetic patient monitoring, including medication monitoring and risk detection using wearables and healthcare sensors for the well-being of elderly and disabled individuals. The subsequent sections of the manuscript are organized to delve into the proposed methodology, performance analysis, and overall conclusion of the workflow, with a focus on collecting patient data, preprocessing, feature extraction, and abnormality prediction using AI classifiers and decision-making systems.

Blaine Reeder *et al.* [29] discuss the potential of smartwatches as versatile health monitoring devices, emphasizing their role in everyday healthcare. It offers data and communication between patients and healthcare providers. The paper highlights their applications in epilepsy and cardiology research and treatment. The authors underscore these devices' financial feasibility and rapid growth in the market. However, they acknowledge that research on smartwatches for health-related purposes is still in its early stages. The integration of smartwatch data with other sources, such as electronic health records, is seen as a promising avenue for creating holistic views of personal health trajectories, although challenges related to data hosting and management should be addressed to utilize it fully.

Kah Phooi Seng *et al.* [30] encompass various technological perspectives, including AI-powered intelligent wearables. It reveals that AI smart wearables face significant technical challenges related to networking, communication, computational complexity, storage, and algorithmic aspects. It outlines the market for smartwatches and also the potential research avenues. It serves as a valuable reference for applying these new paradigms in sensor-based and intelligent environments, covering deployment types, interfaces, and various AI techniques while highlighting open challenges and recommendations for future work. However, it acknowledges potential limitations in the scope of studies covered.

10.3 Methodology

We have carefully developed a form as part of our attempt to perform an extensive study on health analysis using fitness watches. This form was created to gain an in-depth knowledge of how effectively these technologies enhance people's overall health and well-being. Essential elements on the record include name, email, age, gender, and other personal information that accurately depict the participant's demographic data. It also explores the participant's physical characteristics, obtaining critical information such as height and weight essential for understanding health patterns. In addition, the form asks users to fill out which brand they are currently utilizing for their fitness watch. To better understand how the fitness watches work, we asked the participants to upload screenshots of activities they did in a day. By analyzing these data, we can determine the level of activity engaged in by particular age groups, which helps us understand the influence of fitness watches on various demographic groups. We intend to obtain multiple statistics to make relevant conclusions on fitness watches' role in encouraging a healthier lifestyle. We can gain important insights from this form that we circulated, and it has the potential to completely change our understanding of health and well-being concerning wearable fitness technologies.

The data were collected from Google Form. We organized and converted the information into a dataset in Microsoft Excel. It now allows us to analyze systematically, categorize, and draw insights from the responses received. For easy grouping of data and then their analysis, the entire information is divided according to the age of the people involved. The fitness interface as per the age group, such as teenager, youth, and middle and old age, is shown in Figure 10.1. Now, it is easier to manage and analyze the data for various purposes, such as research reporting or decision-making.

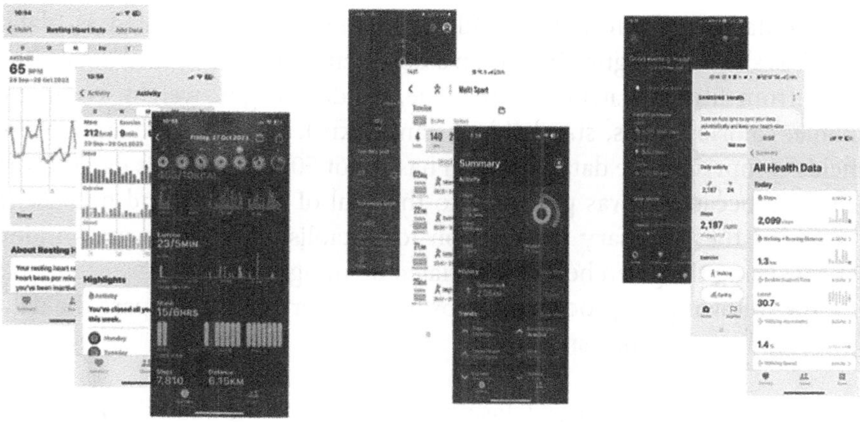

(a) (b) (c)

Figure 10.1 Fitness interface of (a) teenage group, (b) youth group, and (c) middle and old age group.

Name	Age	Gender	Height	Weight	Company Name	Calories	Steps	Stand (Hr)	Distance(Km)
Aditya Bharne	14	Male	179	69	Apple	191	7679	9	5.7
Abhiskhek Bharne	40	Male	169	76	Apple	120	1500	3	2
Ipshita Mandal	20	Female	158	58	Fastrack	140	2972	1	1.8
Shalini Bharne	39	Female	160	72	Apple	150	6430	2	4
Divyanshu Tiwari	20	Male	180	63	Apple	180	3527	8	2.65
Harish Bhute	32	Male	165	62	Noise	339	8391	6	5.6
Rohit Chaudhary	20	Male	175	68	Samsung	230	5616	3	4.63
Vasudevan	56	Male	177	80	Apple	158	4532	2	3.4
S Tirumala Rao	56	Male	170	70	Apple	244	2845	10	2.11
Dinesh Kumar Dutta	58	Male	179	82	Apple	341	3543	1	5.2
Anil Kumar	57	Male	174	87	Apple	231	2099	4	1.3
Rishabh Verma	22	Male	176	60	Google Fit	882	4234	2	6
Ashish Mahendra Jain	43	Male	182	83	Samsung	78	2187	1	1.3
Vaibhav P Singh	36	Male	162	68	Noise	49	1950	1	1.33
Anand Singh Yadav	42	Male	165	70	Boat	123	5901	2	4.2
Anjali Singh	20	Female	163	65	Apple	162	6928	6	4.58
Ananya Gaur	42	Female	160	49	Noise	183	5178	3	5
Deshna Jain	43	Female	170	75	Apple	74	3181	2	0
Aditya Singh	15	Male	156	88	Samsung	86	2315	2	6
Gia Sharma	54	Female	169	42	Boat	211	7562	5	1
Pragya Tripathi	54	Female	172	92	Noise	118	7475	5	7
Ansh Dhote	66	Male	158	52	Apple	146	2607	3	8
Divya Jain	22	Female	166	85	Apple	139	1894	2	9
Sakshi Gupta	33	Female	146	44	Samsung	109	9332	6	6
Deep Raut	42	Male	153	51	Google Fit	219	8341	7	2
Devi Kulkarni	70	Female	159	76	Google Fit	168	1399	1	1
Manmeet Oberoi	21	Male	156	73	Apple	126	4822	3	9
Anshita Shirke	43	Female	158	55	Fastrack	196	1410	1	9
Shanky Maske	45	Male	170	94	Fastrack	75	3988	3	2
Nikhil Halambi	38	Male	169	57	Boat	54	1835	2	6
Paras Ved	33	Male	146	100	Noise	175	9442	7	5
Kunal Haswani	20	Male	176	75	Samsung	248	1601	1	10
Abhishek Bais	15	Male	145	86	Samsung	138	4353	3	8
Rakesh Gupta	32	Male	177	86	Apple	130	2966	2	3
Kamala Dhote	60	Female	142	58	Google Fit	144	8255	7	6
Narayan Rao	66	Male	177	48	Fastrack	276	7862	5	4
Sahil Palni	18	Male	159	48	Boat	231	7035	7	2
Nirmal Modi	62	Male	159	93	Noise	45	3643	2	3
Madhuri Shirke	66	Female	154	56	Noise	149	1459	1	2
Sunil Rai	59	Male	155	50	Samsung	257	4499	3	1
Dipti Kuthe	59	Female	165	46	Samsung	68	3680	5	8
Diya Tembhre	44	Female	149	97	Apple	139	6517	3	1
Ramesh Jaiswal	58	Male	177	75	Fastrack	31	9904	9	2
Vaishali Dudhe	27	Female	149	61	Noise	186	7799	6	10
Sarang Kate	29	Male	157	55	Samsung	151	7269	7	2
Aakash Sharma	45	Male	173	42	Samsung	147	4514	2	9
Ameya Lonare	59	Male	160	82	Apple	140	2691	1	7
Karan Jambulkar	68	Male	149	50	Fastrack	194	4219	3	1
Mamta Bose	61	Female	161	87	Boat	84	1246	1	10
Himanshu Bakshi	58	Male	177	81	Noise	192	5762	4	2

Figure 10.2 Dataset collected from the user using Google Forms.

The dataset of information utilized in this study, designated as "data.xlsx," as shown in Figure 10.2, is an assortment of health-related data gathered from fitness watches. Name, age, gender, height, weight, company name, calories, steps, stand (h), distance (km), and BMI are among the fields comprising the dataset, which has about 50 records. This dataset was selected because it was pertinent to the goal of the study and because it provided the necessary information for establishing a body mass index (BMI) using the given health-associated defining features.

The following preprocessing steps were undertaken to prepare the data for deep learning analysis:

- Data loading: The dataset was loaded into the analysis environment using the Python Pandas library.
- Data cleaning: Necessary data cleaning procedures were performed, addressing missing values and handling potential outliers.

- Data processing: After a serial discussion, a feedforward neural network model was selected for this task. The model consists of an input layer, two hidden layers with 64 and 32 neurons, respectively, employing ReLU (Rectified Linear Unit) activation functions, and an output layer with a single neuron for BMI prediction. This architecture was chosen for its suitability in regression tasks.
- Deep learning model architecture: The dataset was split with an 80–20 split ratio throughout training and testing sets. The testing set was employed to evaluate the model after it had been developed with the set used for training.
- Data splitting: A batch size of 32 and a training process of 100 epochs were used to train the deep learning model using the training set. The loss function's mean squared error (MSE) was minimized using the "adam" optimizer. To avoid excessive overfitting, a premature stop program was established during the training process.
- Model training: The subsequent metrics were used to evaluate the performance of the model: R-squared (R^2), mean absolute error (MAE), and mean squared error (MSE).
- Performance metrics: According to the needs of the research goals, any supplementary data preprocessing was carried out. Feature engineering and other data transformations might have been associated with this.
- Data transformation: Categorical features, such as "gender," were converted into a numerical format for compatibility with the chosen deep learning model. Additionally, data normalization was applied using the StandardScaler from Scikit-learn to ensure that all features had a similar scale.

The profound learning model utilized the Python programming language, explicitly using the TensorFlow and Keras libraries. The examinations were led on a standard computer chip.

Any additional data preprocessing specific to the research objectives was performed as necessary. It may have included feature engineering or other data transformations.

The deep learning model was implemented using Python programming, explicitly utilizing the TensorFlow and Keras libraries. The experiments were conducted on a standard CPU. The use of health-related data in this research adhered to ethical guidelines and obtained necessary permissions.

Three metrics are used to compute and report a regression model's performance: mean absolute error (MAE), mean square error (MSE), and R-squared (R^2). Immediately following that, the product provides a straightforward option based on the following metrics:

- A model operates well if its MAE is less than 2.0 and its R^2 is higher than 0.8.
- If not, it implies that further improvements are required.

Training and validation loss concepts play pivotal roles in model optimization and generalization in machine learning and deep neural networks. Training loss refers to the measure of error between the predicted outputs of a model and the actual ground truth during the training phase. It is a guiding metric for adjusting model parameters through techniques like backpropagation, aiming to minimize this loss and enhance the model's ability to learn from the training data. On the other hand, validation loss assesses the model's performance on unseen data, typically a separate dataset from the training set. It helps gauge the model's ability to generalize to new instances by evaluating its predictive accuracy on data it hasn't encountered during training. Monitoring training and validation loss is crucial in preventing overfitting, where the model excessively tailors itself to the training data, thus ensuring its reliability and effectiveness in real-world applications. It aids in evaluating the model's performance and offers insight into when to stop training for maximum performance, whether the model is overfitting, underfitting, or learning with effectiveness.

Figure 10.3 shows the evolution of a machine learning model's training and validation loss over time. It indicates profitable learning of the model

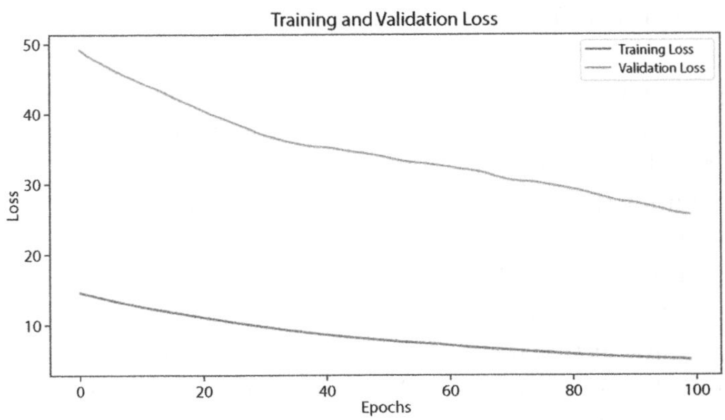

Figure 10.3 Output graph of training and validation.

without overfitting or underfitting when the losses associated with validation and training drop and stay relatively close. This alignment suggests that the model can effectively propagate to new data. As we have also seen, when the epoch increases over 80, the loss during training and validation is stable and minimal. Extensive data is required to maintain low training and validation loss with an epoch over 80. Still, due to the limitation of the data availability in our study, the epoch is held at 70 only.

An essential instrument for evaluating machine learning model performance during training is the training and validation loss plot. The training loss and validation loss, two important metrics, are shown in this graphical representation and their behavior over training epochs. One main goal of machine learning is to find new, unseen data that the model can generalize to, and a decreasing validation loss indicates how well it does this. However, a substantial difference between training and validation losses could indicate overfitting, a situation in which the model has become overly sophisticated in learning the training set, leading to inadequate generalization. This problem can be prevented by normalizing or adding more training data. It is unusual and may suggest issues with the model or training procedure, necessitating further research into matters such as learning rate, dataset size, or model configuration if, on the other hand, the training loss increases while the validation loss falls.

As a result, the training and validation loss plot as shown in Figure 10.3 offers critical information about the performance of a model. While decreasing losses in training and validation are encouraging, it is imperative to constantly monitor and adjust the model as needed during the training process.

10.4 Results and Discussion

In the analysis of health and wellness using fitness watches, some of the outcomes we observed are shown in Table 10.1. The average BMI of males

Table 10.1 Gender-based health analytics.

Gender	Sum of average BMI	Sum of average distance	Sum of average height	Sum of average weight	Sum of average calories
Male	25.93	4.23	1.59	65.00	137.61
Female	25.29	3.71	1.67	65.59	186.35

and females were almost similar, and it was only a difference of approximately 0.64, which is also depicted in Figure 10.4.

Table 10.2 shows the analysis of different age groups. Referring to the BMI chart, we observed that from 25.0 to 29.0, BMI is considered overweight, and 18.5–24.9 is considered healthy. As per our observation and evaluation, only the age group from 20 to 40 comes under normal weight as per the BMI chart. In Figure 10.6, we can see that 5% of people have a 25% BMI, which is very concerning for health and wellness. In Figure 10.7, we compare actual BMI and predicted BMI after applying a deep learning method to a dataset of people's BMI. The graph shows the discrepancy between these two values. We compared both the predicted and the actual data of BMI.

The detailed result analysis in Figures 10.4–10.7 indicates the impact of technology on the well-being and healthcare analysis of people from diverse groups. The deep learning algorithm also studies the role of

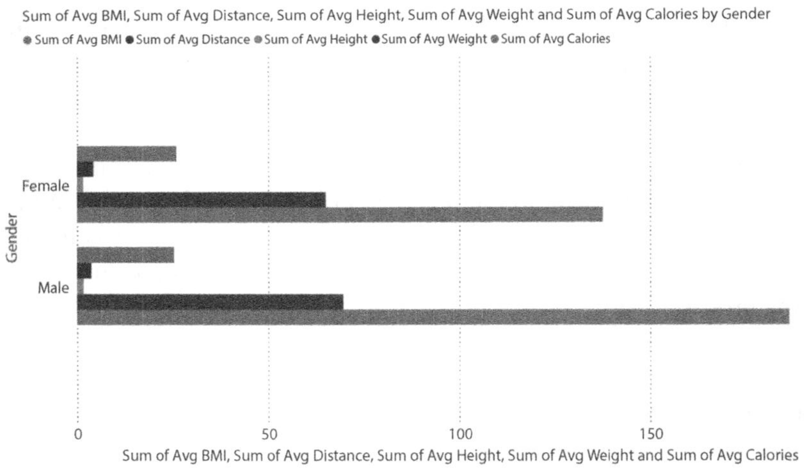

Figure 10.4 Gender graph.

Table 10.2 Age-based health analytics.

Age group	Average BMI	Average height	Average weight
13–20	25.22	1.64	67.74
20–40	23.46	1.65	63.41
40–75	26.82	1.64	71.88

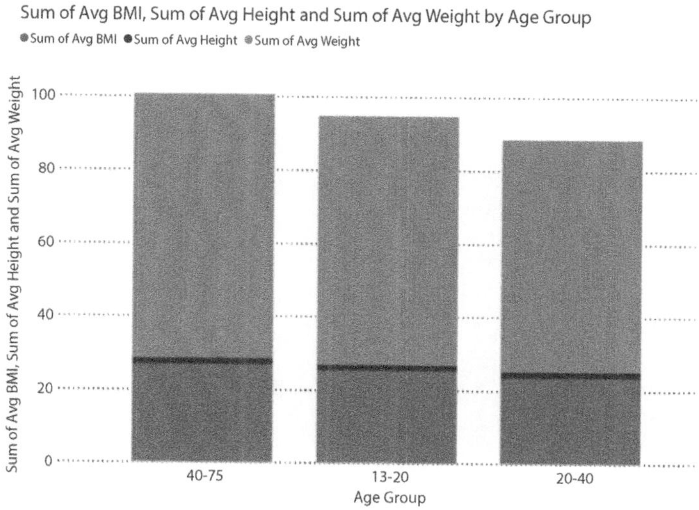

Figure 10.5 Age group graph.

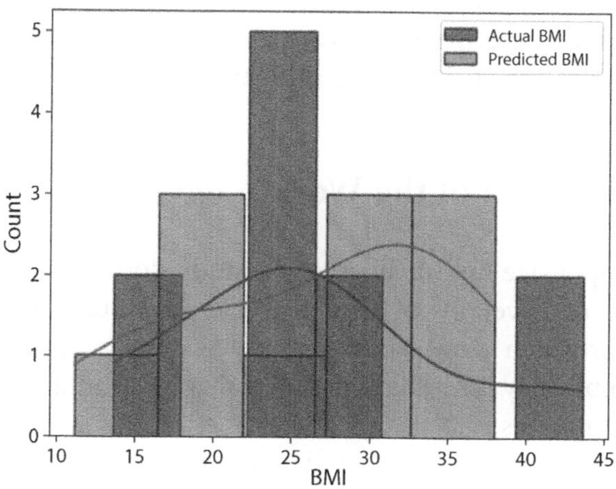

Figure 10.6 Count of predicted and actual BMI.

smartwatches and technological evolution in predicting BMI gender-wise and age-group-wise. This study will help policymakers and the healthcare industry for framing healthcare assistance and propose a systematic plan for using technology to benefit people. Deep learning's ability to uncover subtle correlations and patterns within biological datasets enhances our

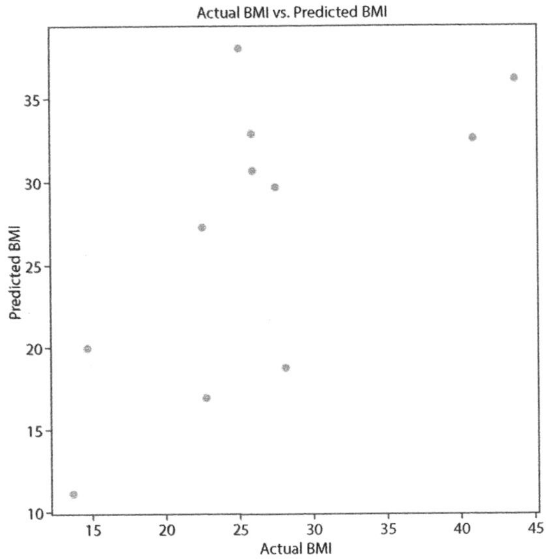

Figure 10.7 Actual BMI vs. predicted BMI.

comprehension of biological processes and diseases, paving the way for personalized medicine, drug discovery, and diagnostic advancements with profound implications for human health and well-being.

10.5 Limitation of the Work

a. Sample size and diversity: The study does not specify the size or diversity of the sample population from which smartwatch data was collected. A small or homogenous sample may limit the generalizability of findings to broader populations.
b. Data accuracy and reliability: Smartwatches collect health-related data from sensors and algorithms. The accuracy and reliability of these measurements can vary. Factors like sensor calibration, user behavior, and device quality may introduce errors.
c. Privacy and ethical considerations: The research does not address privacy concerns about collecting personal health data via smartwatches. Ethical considerations, such as informed consent and data protection, should be thoroughly discussed.

d. Algorithmic limitations: Clustering and regression analysis are powerful techniques, but their effectiveness depends on data quality and chosen parameters. The study needs to delve into the potential limitations of these algorithms.
e. Deep learning challenges: While deep learning techniques offer promise, they require substantial computational resources and large datasets. The paper does not discuss challenges related to training deep neural networks.
f. Generalization to non-smartwatch devices: The focus on smartwatches may limit the applicability of findings to other wearable devices or health-tracking technologies.
g. Health outcomes vs. behavior change: The study emphasizes health analysis but does not directly measure behavior change resulting from smartwatch use. Understanding whether smartwatches lead to sustained lifestyle improvements is essential.
h. Long-term impact assessment: The research does not explore the long-term effects of smartwatch adoption on health outcomes. Longitudinal studies provide valuable insights.
i. Causality vs. correlation: The study identifies associations between smartwatch data and health metrics but does not establish causality. Further research is needed to determine if smartwatch use directly impacts health.
j. User experience and adoption challenges: The paper does not address user experience, usability, or barriers to smartwatch adoption. Understanding user preferences and challenges is crucial for successful implementation.

10.6 Validation and Comparative Analysis

a. Understanding continued usage: Researchers Siepmann and Kowalczuk explored how people use smartwatches over time. They found that the expectation–confirmation model (ECM), which explains how our expectations influence our satisfaction with technology, applies well to smartwatches.
b. Health and fitness factors: The study examined how health, fitness, and emotions impact our smartwatch usage. Positive feelings (like finding the watch applicable) and negative

emotions (like annoyance) affect whether we stick with our smartwatches.

c. Self-quantification behavior: Self-quantification means tracking and measuring things about ourselves (like steps or heart rate). The research shows our behavior in using smartwatches—whether we actively track our matters, our motivation, and satisfaction.

d. Structural equation modeling: Researchers used a fancy statistical method called structural equation modeling to validate their findings. They collected responses from real smartwatch users to understand how these factors interact.

10.7 Conclusion

A crucial component of our research was the use of visualizations. We could observe the differences between the anticipated and fundamental BMI values using scatter and distribution graphs. These visuals gave users a concrete grasp of the model's effectiveness by demonstrating how well our predictions matched actual data. Our model converged to an optimal solution in a comparatively short number of epochs, as evidenced by the training history plot, which emphasized the efficiency and speed of the training process.

Our research has significant applications in the real world. Our concept can be adapted to the fitness watch-based health monitoring field, empowering people to make well-informed decisions regarding their health. The model's precise predictions enable users and healthcare providers to understand their health status better.

Despite the excellent performance of our model, we recognize that it may continually be improved. Future research might examine more intricate deep learning architectures, adjust hyper-parameters, and gather larger datasets. These initiatives might improve the model's functionality and increase its applicability.

Our deep learning model was trained and assessed using the "data.xlsx" dataset—it is a valuable instrument for tracking and analyzing health data. As evidenced by various performance indicators and visualizations, its excellent accuracy, speed, and interpretability make it an invaluable tool in the health and wellness sector. With ongoing improvement and flexibility to various datasets and health-related tasks, our model has enormous potential to contribute to the management and decision-making of individual health substantially.

References

1. Moshawrab, M., Adda, M., Bouzouane, A., Ibrahim, H., Raad, A., Smart wearables for the detection of occupational physical fatigue: A literature review. *Sensors*, 22, 19, 2022.
2. Pierleoni, P., Belli, A., Palma, L., Pellegrini, M., Pernini, L., Valenti, S., A high-reliability wearable device for elderly fall detection. *IEEE Sens. J.*, 15, 8, 4544–4553, 2015.
3. Ramanujam, E., Perumal, T., Padmavathi, S., Human activity recognition with smartphone and wearable sensors using deep learning techniques: A review. *IEEE Sens. J.*, 21, 12, 13029–13040, 2021.
4. Zamkah, A., Hui, T., Andrews, S., Dey, N., Shi, F., Sherratt, R.S., Identification of suitable biomarkers for stress and emotion detection for future personal affective wearable sensors. *Biosensors*, 10, 4, 2020.
5. Seng, J.K.P. and Ang, K.L.-M., Big feature data analytics: Split and combine linear discriminant analysis (sc-lda) for integration towards decision-making analytics. *IEEE Access*, 5, 14056–14065, 2017.
6. Hernandez, V., Dadkhah, D., Babakeshizadeh, V., Kuli, D., Lower body kinematics estimation from wearable sensors for walking and running: A deep learning approach. *Gait Posture*, 83, 185–193, 2021.
7. Yin, Y., Tan, S., Yang, P., Jiang, H., Wang, Z., A customized low static leakage near/subthreshold standard cell library using thick-gate transistors, in: *2020 IEEE International Conference on Integrated Circuits, Technologies and Applications (ICTA)*, IEEE, pp. 75–76, 2020.
8. Hong, Z., Hong, M., Wang, N., Ma, Y., Zhou, X., Wang, W., A wearable-based posture recognition system with ai-assisted approach for healthcare IoT. *Future Gener. Comput. Syst.*, 127, 286–296, 2022.
9. Imani, M. and Ghoreishi, S.F., Scalable inverse reinforcement learning through multifidelity bayesian optimization. *IEEE Trans. Neural Netw. Learn. Syst.*, 33, 8, 4125–4132, 2021.
10. Zhao, K., Jiang, H., Yuan, T., Zhang, C., Jia, W., Wang, Z., A CNN-based human bowel sound segment recognition algorithm with reduced computation complexity for wearable healthcare system, in: *2020 IEEE International Symposium on Circuits and Systems (ISCAS)*, IEEE, pp. 1–5, 2020.
11. de Quadros, T., Lazzaretti, A.E., Schneider, F.K., A movement decomposition and machine learning-based fall detection system using wrist wearable device. *IEEE Sens. J.*, 18, 12, 5082–5089, 2018.
12. Sarivan, I.-M., Greiner, J.N., lvarez, D.D., Euteneuer, F., Reichenbach, M., Madsen, O., Bgh, S., Enabling real-time quality inspection in smart manufacturing through wearable smart devices and deep learning. *Procedia Manuf.*, 51, 373–380, 2020.
13. Costa, A., Rincon, J.A., Carrascosa, C., Julian, V., Novais, P., Emotions detection on an ambient intelligent system using wearable devices. *Future Gener. Comput. Syst.*, 92, 479–489, 2019.

14. Zhao, K., Feng, S., Jiang, H., Wang, Z., Chen, P., Zhu, B., Duan, X., A binarized CNN-based bowel sound recognition algorithm with time-domain histogram features for wearable healthcare systems. *IEEE Trans. Circuits Syst. II Express Briefs*, 69, 2, 629–633, 2022.
15. Ihnaini, B., Khan, M.A., Khan, T.A., Abbas, S., Daoud, M.S., Ahmad, M., Khan, M.A., A smart healthcare recommendation system for multidisciplinary diabetes patients with data fusion based on deep ensemble learning. *Comput. Intell. Neurosci.*, 2021, 4243700, 1–11, 2021.
16. Kheirkhahan, M., Nair, S., Davoudi, A., Rashidi, P., Wanigatunga, A.A., Corbett, D.B., Mendoza, T., Manini, T.M., Ranka, S., A smartwatch-based framework for real-time and online assessment and mobility monitoring. *J. Biomed. Inf.*, 89, 29–40, 2019.
17. Kaul, D., Raju, H., Tripathy, B.K., Deep Learning in Healthcare, in: *Deep Learning in Data Analytics. Studies in Big Data*, vol. 91, D.P. Acharjya, A. Mitra, N. Zaman (Eds.), pp. 97–115, Springer, Cham, Switzerland AG, 2022.
18. Boletsis, C., McCallum, S., Landmark, B.F., The use of smartwatches for health monitoring in home-based dementia care, in: *Human Aspects of IT for the Aged Population. Design for Everyday Life*, J. Zhou and G. Salvendy (Eds.), pp. 15–26, Cham, Springer International Publishing, Switzerland AG, 2015.
19. Hickey, B.A., Chalmers, T., Newton, P., Lin, C.-T., Sibbritt, D., McLachlan, C.S., Clifton-Bligh, R., Morley, J., Lal, S., Smart devices and wearable technologies to detect and monitor mental health conditions and stress: A systematic review. *Sensors*, 21, 10, 2021.
20. Straczkiewicz, M., James, P., Onnela, J.-P., A systematic review of smartphone-based human activity recognition methods for health research. *npj Digital Med.*, 4, 148, 1–15, 2021.
21. Hamza, M.A., Abdalla Hashim, A.H., Alsolai, H., Gaddah, A., Othman, M., Yaseen, I., Rizwanullah, M., Zamani, A.S., Wearables-assisted smart health monitoring for sleep quality prediction using optimal deep learning. *Sustainability*, 15, 2, 2023.
22. Sultana, M., Al-Jefri, M., Lee, J., Using machine learning and smartphone and smartwatch data to detect emotional states and transitions: Exploratory study. *JMIR Mhealth Uhealth*, 8, 9, e17818, 2020.
23. Tobón V, D.P., Hossain, M.S., Muhammad, G., Bilbao, J., Saddik, A.E., Deep learning in multimedia healthcare applications: a review. *Multimed. Syst.*, 28, 1465–1479, 2022.
24. Philip, J., Gandhimathi, S.K., Chalichalamala, S., Karnam, B., Chandanapalli, S.B., Chennupalli, S., Smart health monitoring using deep learning and artificial intelligence. *Rev. d'Intelligence Artificielle*, 37, 2, 451–464, 2023.
25. Sabry, F., Eltaras, T., Labda, W., Alzoubi, K., Malluhi, Q., Machine learning for healthcare wearable devices: The big picture. *J. Healthcare Eng.*, 2022, 4653923, 1–25, 2022.

26. Elwahsh, H., El-shafeiy, E., Alanazi, S., Tawfeek, M.A., A new smart healthcare framework for real-time heart disease detection based on deep and machine learning. *PeerJ Comput. Sci.*, 7, e646, 2022.
27. Yang, S., Zhu, F., Ling, X., Liu, Q., Zhao, P., Intelligent health care: Applications of deep learning in computational medicine. *Front. Genet.*, 12, 1–22, 2021.
28. Ahila, A., Dahan, F., Alroobaea, R., Alghamdi, W.Y., Mohammed, M.K., Hajjej, F., Mohammed Alsekait, D., Raahemifar, K., A smart IOMT based architecture for e-healthcare patient monitoring system using artificial intelligence algorithms. *Front. Physiol.*, 14, 1–11, 2023.
29. Reeder, B. and David, A., Health at hand: A systematic review of smartwatch uses for health and wellness. *J. Biomed. Inf.*, 63, 269–276, 2016.
30. Seng, K.P., Ang, L.-M., Peter, E., Mmonyi, A., Machine learning and AI technologies for smart wearables. *Electronics*, 12, 7, 2023.

11

Decoding Kidney Health: Effectiveness of Machine Learning Techniques in Diagnosis of Chronic Kidney Disease

Suhail Rashid Wani[1], Syed Naseer Ahmad Shah[2*], Roshni Afshan[1] and Asif Adil[3]

[1]*Department of Computer Science and Engineering (CSE) Sharda University, Greater Noida, Uttar Pradesh, India*
[2]*Department of Computer Science, Jamia Millia Islamia, New Delhi, India*
[3]*Centre for Computational Biology and Bioinformatics, School of Medicine, Indiana University, Indiana, USA*

Abstract

Chronic kidney disease is a significant global health issue that contributes to elevated rates of mortality and severe health complications. Effectively managing this condition relies on early and precise prediction, a challenging task. To address this challenge, our study proposes a machine learning approach incorporating various preprocessing techniques, ensemble learning methods, and hyperparameter optimisation strategies. Utilizing a dataset sourced from the UCI database repository, we analyze chronic kidney conditions to evaluate the efficacy of our model. Our proposed strategy yields remarkable accuracy, particularly with implementing decision tree classifiers, achieving an accuracy of 97.83% in diagnosing kidney diseases. These findings underscore the potential of our model to accurately predict the presence or absence of chronic kidney disease, offering valuable insights for early diagnosis, prevention, and treatment. By providing precise forecasts, our approach has the capacity to significantly enhance healthcare outcomes, ultimately reducing the severity and mortality rates associated with chronic kidney ailments.

Keywords: Chronic kidney disease, machine learning, hyperparameters, ensemble techniques, healthcare, AI

**Corresponding author*: syeddnaseer@gmail.com

Bharat Bhushan, Akib Khanday, Khursheed Aurangzeb, Sudhir Kumar Sharma and Parma Nand (eds.) Wellness Management Powered by AI Technologies, (297–312) © 2025 Scrivener Publishing LLC

11.1 Introduction

In today's global landscape, utmost priority is placed on preserving human life and health, as it serves as the cornerstone of our society, underpinning the well-being of all resources and nations. The prevalence of simultaneous outbreaks of various diseases underscores the crucial need for worldwide healthcare vigilance, as many individuals remain unaware of these conditions until they escalate [1]. Recognizing and addressing multiple diseases has become paramount in modern healthcare, reflecting the evolving challenges in disease management [2]. The pervasive influence of Internet technology has entrapped many individuals, diverting attention away from personal health concerns. Rapid changes in habits and environmental factors have contributed to the rise of invisible yet perilous diseases, including cardiovascular, brain, and renal disorders, affecting populations globally [3]. Unregulated and unhealthy lifestyles, particularly during peak or later stages of life, exacerbate the consequences of harmful habits, leading to increased disease burden [4]. According to recent WHO data, nearly 1 billion people worldwide are affected by non-communicable diseases, with cardiovascular diseases (CVD) ranking as the third leading cause of death, claiming 20.5 million lives annually. Parkinson's disease affects over 10 million people, while chronic kidney disease (CKD) impacts 37 million individuals in the US and 850 million globally, ranking as the sixth leading cause of death [5, 6]. The escalating prevalence of multiple diseases has led to a rise in comorbidity rates, with expectations of doubling by 2035, resulting in higher mortality rates and diminished life quality for the affected individuals [7].

The economic burden of diseases like CVD is substantial, with global costs estimated to surpass $1 trillion by 2030. Renal disorders affect 10% of the worldwide population, claiming five to 10 million lives annually, a figure expected to rise significantly by 2030 [8], particularly impacting developing nations like India due to limited access to expensive treatments such as kidney transplants and dialysis. The medical sector generates vast amounts of data, offering opportunities for predicting and diagnosing these dangerous diseases. While significant progress has been made in predicting individual diseases, there is a growing need to predict multiple diseases simultaneously and improve accuracy and performance. Traditional disease diagnosis methods are limited by human errors, expense, and time constraints, highlighting the transformative potential of artificial intelligence, particularly machine learning, in healthcare [9, 10]. Leveraging these advancements, we aim to develop a framework for predicting and diagnosing three critical, life-threatening diseases, focusing on feature selection methods to enhance the specificity and informativeness of medical data analysis.

The significant contribution of our study lies in the exploration of 10 machine learning algorithms for predicting kidney disease. Through a rigorous analysis of datasets sourced from the UCI database repository, we have illuminated both the diversity of approaches and the potential for advancement in this critical field. Notably, our proposed model leveraging the decision tree classifier algorithm demonstrated exceptional accuracy. While acknowledging the constraints imposed by the size and diversity of the dataset utilized, our study offers nuanced insights into the performance of each algorithm, laying the groundwork for future research endeavors to refine predictive models and enhance clinical practices in kidney disease management. By addressing these limitations and incorporating the insights gleaned here, our study paves the way for significant advancements in the field of kidney disease prediction.

The chapter follows a structured approach to address the research problem, beginning with an introduction that provides context and outlines the objectives. The methods section is then divided into two subsections, focusing on data collection and preprocessing techniques. Subsequently, the methodology section delves into the application of various machine learning algorithms, including logistic regression, random forest, KNN, SVM, decision tree, and boosting algorithms. Additionally, the process of adjusting hyperparameters is detailed to ensure optimal model performance. The results and discussion section presents the findings of the study, followed by an in-depth discussion of their implications. Finally, the conclusion summarizes the key insights and suggests future research directions. This organization facilitates a logical flow of information, guiding readers through the paper's contents and contributing to a comprehensive understanding of the research undertaken.

11.2 Methods

11.2.1 Data and Features

Our study uses datasets about renal (kidney) diseases sourced from the UCI database repository (https://archive.ics.uci.edu/dataset/336/chronic+kidney+disease). The renal dataset comprises 400 entries, featuring 25 attributes essential for our investigation. This dataset includes age, blood pressure, specific gravity, albumin, and 24 other relevant variables. The dataset employs various types of information representation, utilizing binary indicators for certain variables such as specific gravity, albumin, sugar, red blood cells, pus cell clumps, bacteria, hypertension, diabetes mellitus, coronary artery disease, appetite, pedal edema, and anemia. Continuous values are employed for attributes like age, blood pressure, random blood glucose, blood urea, serum creatinine, sodium, potassium, hemoglobin, packed cell volume, white blood cell count, and red blood cell count [11]. The outcomes are categorized into two main groups: CKD (chronic kidney disease) and not-CKD. The presence of CKD signifies recognized renal failure, while the absence indicates an individual's state of renal health. Among the entries, 250 are classified as CKD cases, while the remaining 150 are categorized as not having CKD.

11.2.2 Preprocessing

Preprocessing is essential for refining data to enhance the accuracy of algorithmic learning models. It involves tasks such as feature selection, data normalization, outlier removal, and addressing missing values. In the renal dataset, missing parameters must be added to the entire dataset for preprocessing. Methods can be employed to create discrete characteristics from continuous ones, and both missing and noisy values in all categories must be addressed to improve data quality. Notably, a significant portion of the data is missing, including NaNs, which must be cleaned up, and numerical features must be transformed into floats. The dataset consists of 25 characteristics, 11 of which are numerical and 14 nominal. Machine learning algorithms are trained using the complete dataset of 400 scenarios, with 250 categorized as CKD and 150 as non-CKD cases. Each variable, known as a nominal variable, is assigned a code for computer processing [12]. For instance, numeric codes like 1 and 0 denote normal and abnormal values for certain variables such as rbc and pc, while other variables like htn, dm, cad, pe, and ane are coded as "1" for "yes" and "0" for "no" responses. Variables like sg, al, and su, initially described as categorical, are treated as numeric due to their dependency on numerical data. All parameters are transformed into factors, and each data point is assigned a unique number. Despite 158 complete occurrences in the dataset, many values are missing, likely due to various diagnostic uncertainties. Missing values are handled post-encoding of classification variables. Numerical variables' missing values are filled with the median value of the available data. In contrast, classification variables' missing values are replaced with the most common grouping from the entire dataset to ensure appropriate handling. Finally, the CKD dataset, comprising 400 records and 25 columns, serves as the research source, with outcomes categorized as "CKD" or "not CKD," represented by the numerical values "1" and "0", respectively. Approximately 250 rows represent CKD patients, while 150 rows denote non-CKD patients [13].

11.3 Methodology

The dataset is prepared for training and testing after preparation and data cleanliness. To assess the performance of the various machine learning models, we independently employed the 80% train and 20% test partition method [14]. Data collection is evenly divided into training and testing sets using the train/split approach. Upon conceptualizing our data through tools like distribution graphs and scatter plots, we can optimize our dataset for predictive analysis by identifying anomalies, missing values, and other pertinent information. Machine learning serves as the cornerstone in our endeavor to forecast and compare diseases, thereby enhancing patient care accurately. To achieve this goal, we will employ various machine learning techniques, including AdaBoost, gradient boosting, XGBoosting, support vector machine, random forest, logistic regression,

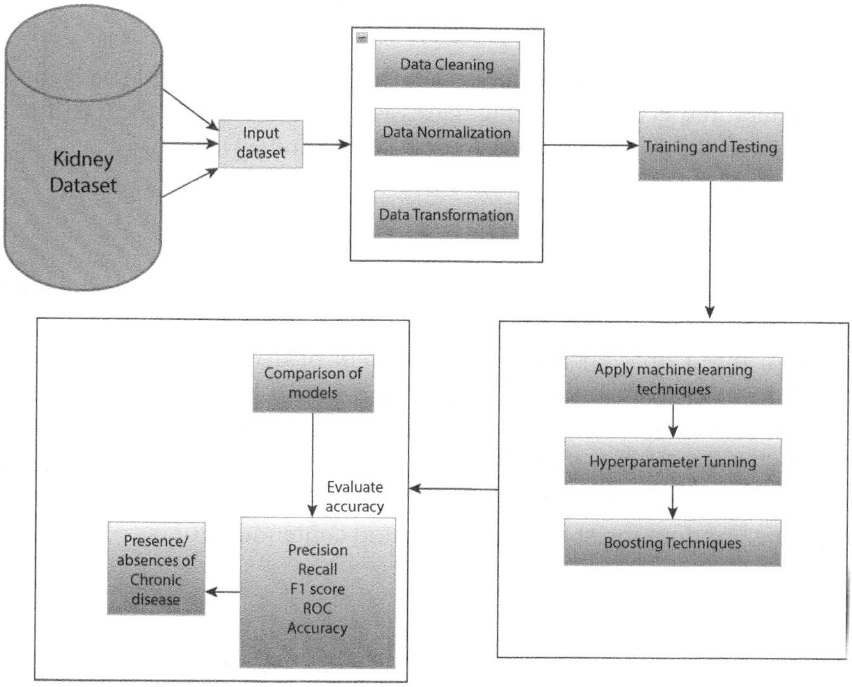

Figure 11.1 Proposed flow chart for kidney disease diagnosis.

KNN, and hyperparameter tuning based on decision trees [15]. Python has been selected as the primary platform for executing our machine learning algorithms in this model (refer to Figure 11.1 for visualizing the proposed model diagram) [16].

11.3.1 Logistic Regression

In logistic regression, the algorithm derives its name from the logistic function it employs. This function, depicted by an "S"-shaped curve, is tailored for statistical purposes and maps values between 0 and 1. Like linear regression, logistic regression utilizes equations for representation [17].

The equation for logistic regression

$$Y = 1/(1 + \text{EXPO}(\text{-value})) \tag{11.1}$$

The value of the output, denoted as y, is predicted by linearly combining the input values, typically referred to as x, and coefficients, known as beta.

Logistic regression equation

$$y = \text{EXPO}(a0 + a1 * x)/(1 + \text{EXPO}(a0 + a1 * x)). \tag{11.2}$$

The values of a0, a1, and y represent the intercept, bias, and single input coefficient, respectively. Logistic regression models forecast the likelihood of a first-class (also known as default class) outcome [18].

11.3.2 Random Forest

Think of random forest as a protective canopy in a dense forest, shielding us from the overfitting traps. Instead of relying on a single towering tree, random forest opts for a diverse ecosystem of decision trees, each contributing to the collective wisdom. The more trees in our forest, the better our chances of accuracy [19]. Random forest is not picky. It is versatile. Whether it is classifying or predicting, this technique excels, especially in sorting out classification mysteries. So, if speed is of the essence in model building, random forest emerges as the top contender [20].

11.3.3 KNN

KNN, short for K-nearest neighbors, is a supervised learning technique that relies on similarity metrics to categorize new data points by comparing them to existing data. Unlike some methods, KNN does not make any assumptions about the underlying data—it takes each data point at face value. Consider KNN a bit like a friendly neighbor—it is laid-back and does not do much prep work. It does not bother with fancy initialization or complex filtering functions from the get-go; instead, it simply hangs onto the learning dataset and waits to see what comes its way. The core idea behind KNN is pattern similarity, operating on the principle that similar objects tend to cluster together. It is like saying birds of a feather flock together—it is all about finding those close matches [21]. KNN operates on a local scale, making it ideal for scenarios where there is a curvy path between different categories and can easily handle large volumes of data. Not only does KNN take function approximation well, but it is also pretty good at dealing with noisy training sets. By calculating distances, KNN determines how similar each training sample is to a new data point, helping it make informed decisions about classification [22].

11.3.4 Support Vector Machine (SVM)

Support vector machines (SVM) are the discerning experts of the supervised learning world, adept at handling both regression and classification tasks with grace and precision. Picture our data as scattered points across a multi-dimensional landscape and SVM as the cartographer, deftly plotting them in a mathematical space. Now, SVM comes in two flavors: linear and nonlinear. Linear SVM is the straight-shooter, perfect for situations where our data neatly separates along straight lines. Its mission? Find that elusive perfect line, known as a hyperplane, that cleanly divides different classes. Think of it like drawing a line between differently colored marbles on a table—each marble representing a data point and the line creating distinct groups. But how does SVM decide where to draw this line? It is all about coefficients and equations. Imagine an equation with terms like B0 and B1, which determine the position and slope of our line. Input points like K1 and K2 help classify data points as falling above or below the line.

But what about those points that hover close to the line, right around zero? That is where SVM's skill truly shines. Its task is to maximize the space between the line and the nearest data point—a space known as the margin. If it succeeds, we get what is called the greatest margin hyperplane, effectively isolating our classes with a comfortable buffer zone. And those crucial data points that define the line and the margin? They are the support vectors—the backbone of our SVM. Like guiding stars, they provide essential support and structure to our classifier, ensuring it navigates the data landscape with finesse and accuracy [23].

11.3.5 Decision Tree

This supervised artificial intelligence method primarily deals with classification problems. Decision trees are used to build predictive models by deriving basic decision rules from available data, allowing us to predict the class or values of the desired outcome. To predict the class using a decision tree, we start at the tree's root and follow branches based on the trait values of the data, ultimately reaching a leaf node with the predicted class [24]. Decision trees simplify complex datasets by segmenting symptoms based on their classifications, making them effective for handling large and intricate datasets. In our suggested system, we employ decision tree classifiers, which are machine learning algorithms used to categorize individual samples based on models generated from training data [25]. We fine-tune and optimize hyperparameters using a grid-based search method to enhance the performance of our model. Hyperparameters play a crucial role in machine learning algorithms and optimizing them can significantly improve model performance. Grid search, a widely used technique, systematically explores various hyperparameter settings to identify the best combination for our model. By conducting this comprehensive search, we can identify the optimal parameters without investing excessive time or resources. Once the optimal parameters are determined, we construct the decision tree classifier model using these specific parameters and evaluate its performance on the test set. This systematic approach ensures that our model is finely tuned and accurately predicts outcomes [25].

11.3.6 Adjusting Hyperparameters

Fine-tuning hyperparameters enhances the performance of the recommended model by learning optimal variable settings from data. Adjusting hyperparameters—variables that influence model behavior—can significantly improve performance in machine learning models. Hyperparameter tuning involves exploring various parameter combinations to accurately assess a classifier's performance. Overfitting, a typical machine learning challenge, occurs when a classifier performs well on training data but poorly on test data. Cross-validation is employed alongside the grid search technique to mitigate overfitting and optimize hyperparameters. The grid search method systematically searches for the optimal classifier parameters by testing different hyperparameter values. This method is beneficial for adjusting hyperparameters that are not directly learned during training. With grid search, multiple combinations of hyperparameter values are evaluated to identify the most effective configuration. For instance, in artificial intelligence model X, hyperparameters h1, h2, and h3 are explored across various combinations to find the best-performing configuration. Each combination forms a grid of hyperparameter values, allowing for a comprehensive search for the optimal settings [26, 27].

11.3.7 Boosting Algorithm

Boosting algorithms enhance weak learners by employing weighted averages, dividing the original dataset into multiple subsets, and training a classifier on each subset to produce a series of models with moderate performance. These models are then integrated using a cost function to improve overall performance unlike bagging, where models operate independently and are combined at the end; boosting places weak learners sequentially, focusing on challenging findings to produce a stronger final model. Boosting is effective for regression and identification issues, offering better predictions than individual weak learners through strategies like majority voting in classification problems or a linear combination in regression problems [28].

The boosting strategy involves training a weak learner, computing predictions, selecting misclassified instances for further training, and repeating the process to refine the model. Boosting algorithms like gradient boosting and AdaBoost have been widely utilized across various industries. AdaBoost minimizes a convex surrogate function through a greedy approach, adjusting predictors' weights to limit misclassification loss. Gradient boost applies a similar strategy to any differential loss function, while AdaBoost maximizes the exponential loss function. In this study, various boosting techniques, including AdaBoost, gradient boosting, XGBoosting, and light gradient boosting, were employed to enhance performance [29].

11.4 Results and Discussion

The comprehensive evaluation of 10 machine learning algorithms for predicting kidney disease yielded insightful results, crucial for advancing diagnostic accuracy and clinical decision-making. Through meticulous analysis and rigorous validation, we elucidated the strengths and weaknesses of each model, shedding light on their efficacy in identifying

Table 11.1 Confusion matrix.

	Predicted no (0)	Predicted yes (1)
Actual no (0)	TN	FP
Actual yes (1)	FN	TP

renal conditions. Table 11.1 presents the confusion matrix for the abstract phrase, showcasing the classification results for each class [30].

Accuracy Assessment

Table 11.2 presents the accuracy scores of the deployed algorithms, highlighting the decision tree classifier's exceptional performance. Following grid search fine-tuning, the decision tree model achieved an outstanding accuracy of 97.83%, surpassing all other algorithms. This remarkable accuracy underscores the potential of decision trees in accurately predicting kidney disease [31].

Confusion Matrix Analysis

It is a detailed insight into the classification results of each model through confusion matrices, as shown in Table 11.3. Notably, the decision tree classifier exhibited balanced performance, with high true favorable (TP) and actual negative (TN) rates, minimizing false positives (FP) and false negatives (FN). Such balanced classification is vital for accurate disease prediction and clinical decision support [32].

Table 11.2 Accuracies of kidney disease diagnosis models.

ML models	LR	KNN	SVM	DT	GSDT	RF	AdB	GB	XGB	LGBM
Accuracies	89.1%	74.1%	63.3%	96.6%	97.83%	96%	95%	94.1%	95%	63.3%

Table 11.3 Confusion matrix of kidney disease diagnosis models.

	LR	KNN	SVM	DT	GSDT	RF	AdB	GB	XGB	LGBM
	0 1	0 1	0 1	0 1	0 1	0 1	0 1	0 1	0 1	0 1
0	73 3	49 27	76 0	76 0	76 0	76 0	75 1	76 0	74 2	75 1
1	10 34	4 40	44 0	4 40	6 38	4 40	5 39	7 37	4 40	43 1

Table 11.4 Precision recall and F1 score of diagnosis models.

	LR	KNN	SVM	DT	GSDT	RF	AdaB	GB	XGB	LGBM
Precision	0=88% 1=92%	0=92% 1=60%	0=63% 1=70%	0=96% 1=98%	0=96% 1=98.5%	0=95% 1=100%	0=94% 1=97%	0=92% 1=100%	0=95% 1=95%	0=64% 1=50%
Recall	0=96% 1=77%	0=64% 1=91%	0=100% 1=80%	0=99% 1=93%	0=97% 1=93.5%	0=100% 1=91%	0=99% 1=89%	0=100% 1=84%	0=97% 1=91%	0=99% 1=60%
F1 score	0=92% 1=84%	0=76% 1=72%	0=78% 1=76%	0=97% 1=96%	0=97% 1=97%	0=97% 1=95%	0=96% 1=93%	0=96% 1=91%	0=96% 1=93%	0=77% 1=40%

Precision, Recall, and F1 Score Metrics
The models are further evaluated using precision, recall, and F1 score metrics. The decision tree classifier demonstrated commendable precision, recall, and F1 scores for both class labels, as shown in Table 11.4, reaffirming its superiority in accurately identifying kidney disease instances [33]. This comprehensive evaluation provides clinicians valuable insights into each model's ability to handle positive and negative instances effectively.

11.4.1 Discussion

The results underscore the pivotal role of decision tree models in effectively predicting renal conditions. The analysis of kidney disease accuracies reveals the decisiveness of decision tree models in effectively predicting renal conditions, showcasing commendable performance in precision, recall, and F1 score metrics [34]. Notably, the decision tree model outperformed all others by fine-tuning the hyperparameters through grid search cross-validation (CV). This underscores the exceptional efficacy of decision trees in managing renal ailments, particularly when coupled with grid search CV hyperparameter optimization. During the evaluation process, we adopted an 80:20 split between training and testing data and employed various preprocessing techniques. These techniques included handling missing values, eliminating outliers and duplicates, and normalizing data within the 0-to-1 scale. Such meticulous procedures enabled us to identify the most suitable algorithm for each ailment by leveraging various algorithmic techniques [35]. Validation through ROC and precision–recall curves, as demonstated in Figure 11.2, validated our findings, reaffirming the decision tree classifier's superiority over other models. The bar chart in Figure 11.3 visually compares the accuracy of machine learning models, clearly illustrating the decision tree's dominance.

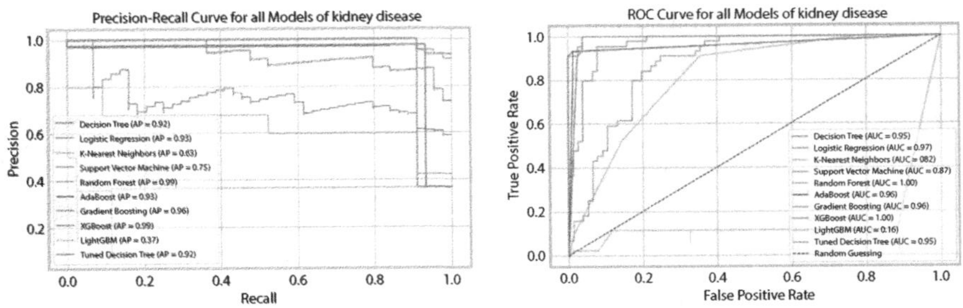

Figure 11.2 Precision–recall and ROC curves depicting the diagnostic performance of diverse machine learning models in kidney disease diagnosis.

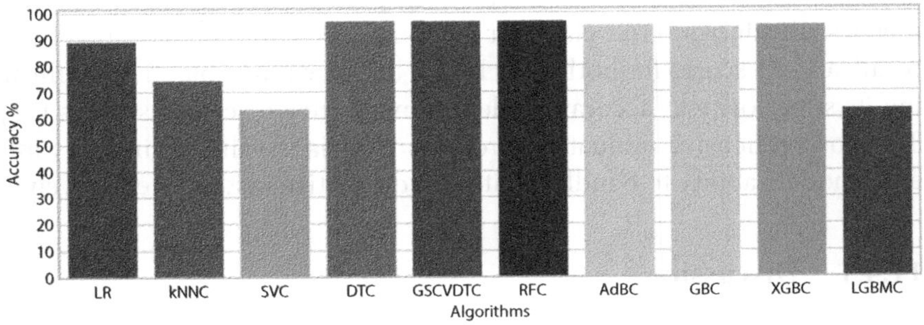

Figure 11.3 A bar chart visually represents the comparison of various machine learning models based on their accuracy in diagnosing kidney disease.

These findings have significant implications for clinical practice, offering clinicians a reliable tool for early detection and accurate prediction of kidney disease. The decision tree classifier emerges as a promising candidate for integration into clinical decision support systems, aiding healthcare professionals in timely diagnosis and personalized treatments.

Limitations and Future Directions

Despite the promising results, our study is not without limitations. The analysis was constrained by the size and diversity of the dataset, potentially limiting the model's generalizability. Future research endeavors should focus on expanding the dataset and exploring advanced modeling techniques to further enhance prediction accuracy and robustness. Our study showcases the effectiveness of decision tree models in predicting kidney disease, laying the foundation for future advancements in renal diagnostics and personalized medicine. By leveraging machine learning algorithms and rigorous validation techniques, we can revolutionize clinical decision-making, ultimately improving patient outcomes and quality of care.

11.5 Conclusion

In conclusion, our exploration of 10 machine learning algorithms for predicting kidney disease has illuminated both the diversity of approaches and the potential for advancement in this critical field. Through a rigorous analysis of datasets sourced from the UCI database repository, our study uncovered nuanced insights into the performance of each algorithm. Notably, our proposed model leveraging the decision tree classifier algorithm demonstrated exceptional accuracy, achieving a staggering 97.83% on the same 80:20 split ratio. However, it is imperative to acknowledge the constraints imposed by the size and diversity of the dataset utilized in this study. By expanding the scope of data and refining the models, we can enhance not only the predictive power but also the generalizability of our methodologies. The implications extend beyond academia, offering promising avenues for improving clinical practices through more robust prediction models. To realize these advancements fully, future research endeavors should prioritize addressing these limitations and incorporating the insights gleaned here. With continued dedication to innovation and refinement, the potential to revolutionize kidney disease prediction is within reach.

References

1. Wang, H., Xie, J., Luo, S., Ta, D.T., Wang, Q., Zhang, J., Furuya, K., Exploring the interplay between landscape planning and human well-being: A scientometric review. *Land*, 12, 7, 1321, 2023.
2. Pearson-Stuttard, J., Ezzati, M., Gregg, E.W., Multimorbidity—a defining challenge for health systems. *Lancet Public Health*, 4, 12, e599–e600, 2019.
3. Jia, X., Pang, Y., Liu, L. S., Online health information seeking behavior: a systematic review. *Healthcare*, 9, 12, 1740, MDPI, Basel, Switzerland, 2021, December.
4. Bollyky, T.J., Templin, T., Andridge, C., Dieleman, J.L., Understanding the relationships between noncommunicable diseases, unhealthy lifestyles, and country wealth. *Health Aff.*, 34, 9, 1464–1471, 2015.
5. Kovesdy, C.P., Epidemiology of chronic kidney disease: an update 2022. *Kidney Int. Suppl.*, 12, 1, 7–11, 2022.
6. Habib, S.H. and Saha, S., Burden of non-communicable disease: global overview. *Diabetes Metab. Syndrome: Clin. Res. Rev.*, 4, 1, 41–47, 2010.
7. Schiltz, N.K., Prevalence of multimorbidity combinations and their association with medical costs and poor health: A population-based study of US adults. *Front. Public Health*, 10, 953886, 2022.

8. Luyckx, V.A., Tonelli, M., Stanifer, J.W., The global burden of kidney disease and the sustainable development goals. *Bull. World Health Organ.*, 96, 6, 414, 2018.
9. Agarwal, S.K. and Srivastava, R.K., Chronic kidney disease in India: challenges and solutions. *Nephron. Clin. Pract.*, 111, 3, c197–c203, 2009.
10. Abraham, G., Varughese, S., Thandavan, T., Iyengar, A., Fernando, E., Naqvi, S.J., Kafle, R.K., Chronic kidney disease hotspots in developing countries in South Asia. *Clin. Kidney J.*, 9, 1, 135–141, 2016.
11. Nishat, M.M., Faisal, F., Dip, R.R., Nasrullah, S.M., Ahsan, R., Shikder, F., Hoque, M.A., A comprehensive analysis on detecting chronic kidney disease by employing machine learning algorithms. *EAI Endorsed Trans. Pervasive Health Technol.*, 7, 29, e1–e1, 2021.
12. Kotsiantis, S.B., Zaharakis, I., Pintelas, P., Supervised machine learning: A review of classification techniques. *Emerging Artif. Intell. Appl. Comput. Eng.*, 160, 1, 3–24, 2007.
13. Batista, G.E., Prati, R.C., Monard, M.C., A study of the behavior of several methods for balancing machine learning training data. *ACM SIGKDD Explor. Newslett.*, 6, 1, 20–29, 2004.
14. Hastie, T., Tibshirani, R., Friedman, J.H., Friedman, J.H., The elements of statistical learning: data mining, inference, and prediction (Vol. 2, pp. 1–758), 2009.
15. Singh, Y., Bhatia, P.K., Sangwan, O., A review of studies on machine learning techniques. *Int. J. Comput. Sci. Secur.*, 1.1, 70–84, 2007.
16. Raschka, S. and Mirjalili, V., *Python machine learning: Machine learning and deep learning with Python, scikit-learn, and TensorFlow 2*, Packt publishing ltd, Birmingham, United Kingdom, 2019.
17. Kleinbaum, D.G., Dietz, K., Gail, M., Klein, M., Klein, M., *Logistic regression*, p. 536, Springer-Verlag, New York, 2002.
18. Hosmer Jr., D.W., Lemeshow, S., Sturdivant, R.X., *Applied logistic regression*, John Wiley & Sons, New Jersey, USA, 2013.
19. Rigatti, S.J., Random forest. *J. Insur. Med.*, 47, 1, 31–39, 2017.
20. Speiser, J.L., Miller, M.E., Tooze, J., Ip, E., A comparison of random forest variable selection methods for classification prediction modeling. *Expert Syst. Appl.*, 134, 93–101, 2019.
21. Kramer, O. and Kramer, O., K-nearest neighbors, in: *Dimensionality reduction with unsupervised nearest neighbors*, pp. 13–23, 2013.
22. Peterson, L.E., K-nearest neighbor. *Scholarpedia*, 4, 2, 1883, 2009.
23. Huang, S., Cai, N., Pacheco, P.P., Narrandes, S., Wang, Y., Xu, W., Applications of support vector machine (SVM) learning in cancer genomics. *Cancer Genomics Proteomics*, 15, 1, 41–51, 2018.
24. Song, Y.Y. and Ying, L.U., Decision tree methods: applications for classification and prediction. *Shanghai Arch. Psychiatry*, 27, 2, 130, 2015.

25. Suthaharan, S. and Suthaharan, S., Decision tree learning, in: *Machine Learning Models and Algorithms for Big Data Classification: Thinking with Examples for Effective Learning*, pp. 237–269, 2016.
26. Bergstra, J. and Bengio, Y., Random search for hyper-parameter optimization. *J. Mach. Learn. Res.*, 13, 2, 281–305, 2012.
27. Pedregosa, F., Hyperparameter optimization with approximate gradient, in: *International conference on machine learning*, PMLR, pp. 737–746, 2016, June.
28. Freund, Y. and Schapire, R.E., A decision-theoretic generalization of on-line learning and an application to boosting. *J. Comput. Syst. Sci.*, 55, 1, 119–139, 1997.
29. Friedman, J.H., Greedy function approximation: A gradient boosting machine. *Ann. Stat.*, 29, 5, 1189–1232, 2021, doi:10.1214/aos/1013203451.
30. Caelen, O., A Bayesian interpretation of the confusion matrix, in: *Annals of Mathematics and Artificial Intelligence*, vol. 81, pp. 429–450, 2017.
31. Hammad, I. and El-Sankary, K., Practical considerations for accuracy evaluation in sensor-based machine learning and deep learning. *Sensors*, 19, 16, 3491, 2019.
32. Townsend, J.T., Theoretical analysis of an alphabetic confusion matrix, in: *Perception & Psychophysics*, vol. 9, pp. 40–50, 1971.
33. Yacouby, R. and Axman, D., Probabilistic extension of precision, recall, and f1 score for more thorough evaluation of classification models, in: *Proceedings of the first workshop on evaluation and comparison of NLP systems*, pp. 79–91, 2020, November.
34. Singh, V. and Jain, D., *A hybrid parallel classification model for the diagnosis of chronic kidney disease*, 2023.
35. Debal, D.A. and Sitote, T.M., Chronic kidney disease prediction using machine learning techniques. *J. Big Data*, 9, 1, 109, 2022.

12

Integrating Metaheuristics and Machine Learning for Wellbeing Management: Case of COVID-19

Safea Matar Al Senani and Salah Bouktif*

College of Information Technology, United Arab Emirates University, Al Ain, UAE

Abstract

The COVID-19 pandemic had a major effect on various vital sectors of the economy, including education, healthcare, and industry. Decision-makers grappled with how to deal with the pandemic crisis and implement effective policies and precautionary measures to stop the spread of the coronavirus. The lack of preparedness, coupled with high levels of uncertainty, prompted researchers to explore barriers to gain a deep understanding of the rapid spread of COVID-19 and propose effective interventions to mitigate and ultimately prevent new outbreaks of the virus. In this research, we propose a data-driven intelligent system that builds on the experience gained from the handling of recent and previous pandemics to predict the infection spread and guide the development of effective measures to counter the outbreak of a pandemic. The focus of this study is to develop a prediction model for forecasting elements of decisions, such as the number of cases and mortality rates, to empower the UAE crisis management system with the ability to develop and deploy timely intelligent responses to pandemic outbreaks, such as COVID-19. A periodic diagnosis of the pandemic situation based on real-time data is performed to recommend a list of the most critical measures to enforce for controlling pandemic outbreaks, preventing economic collapse, and ensuring the well-being of society. The approach contributes to better managing the wellbeing of populations by enhancing the effectiveness of pandemic response strategies.

***Keywords*:** COVID-19, pandemic, intervention, prediction

**Corresponding author*: salahb@uaeu.ac.ae

Bharat Bhushan, Akib Khanday, Khursheed Aurangzeb, Sudhir Kumar Sharma and Parma Nand (eds.) Wellness Management Powered by AI Technologies, (313–342) © 2025 Scrivener Publishing LLC

12.1 Introduction

The global impact of the COVID-19 pandemic has been profound, leading to unprecedented lockdowns, disruptions to daily life, and significant economic shocks [1]. Governments worldwide implemented various measures to curb the outbreak, including face mask mandates, school and business closures, prohibition of mass gatherings, and travel restrictions. These interventions were crucial for public health and had severe repercussions on the economy, causing a shock that reverberated across various sectors [2]. The pandemic prompted the adoption of the "stay-home" policy and stringent travel restrictions, both domestically and internationally, affecting the tourism and hospitality sectors significantly. Large-scale events like weddings, exhibitions, music shows, and festivals were canceled, dealing a blow to the events industry, which plays a crucial role in generating jobs and revenue. The healthcare sector faced immense pressure due to the rapid spread of the virus. Governments responded by investing in healthcare infrastructure, launching public information campaigns, and implementing testing, contact tracing, and mask policies. However, shortages in equipment and drugs, coupled with supply chain issues, posed challenges. The insufficiency of health workers and vaccine doses further complicated the situation, necessitating ongoing adjustments to vaccination policies [3]. The educational sector saw widespread school closures as a primary response to the pandemic. While some institutions swiftly adapted to remote learning, many struggled, leading to millions of students losing educational opportunities and causing financial and psychological consequences. Governments globally implemented diverse educational responses, with some countries prioritizing the Internet for remote learning, while others relied on TV and other media channels. However, the shift to remote learning highlighted equity issues, with students facing challenges related to access to electricity and the Internet along with additional financial burdens for families [4, 5]. In response to the COVID-19 crisis, governments formulated policies to relax preventive measures, recognizing the need to revive the economy and social life. The return to school became a priority, acknowledging its fundamental role in students' lives. Schools resumed with altered policies, incorporating safety measures such as social distancing, face masks, and regular testing. Vaccination campaigns were encouraged among students and teachers to achieve herd immunity. Notably, the United Arab Emirates introduced the "Blue Schools" initiative, aligning with vaccination rates to ease protocols and restore normal school activities based on a color-coded tier system [6].

The COVID-19 pandemic had far-reaching consequences on various aspects of society, prompting governments to implement unprecedented measures to safeguard public health while grappling with economic and social challenges. The efforts for preventive measures, economic recovery, and educational continuity underscore the complex and dynamic nature of responding to a global crisis. The emergence of new COVID-19 variants like Alpha, Delta, and Omicron, coupled with uncertainties around children's role in transmission and the effectiveness of vaccines, presents challenges for decision-makers. These complexities hinder the formulation of optimal pandemic strategies, causing a struggle to achieve a delicate balance between health and economic concerns. Leadership faces an intricate task in navigating these uncertain circumstances while aiming for effective responses amidst the unpredictable nature of the outbreak. This study explores the integration of metaheuristics and machine learning techniques for effective wellbeing management during the COVID-19 pandemic. The chapter is divided into six sections, in Section 12.2 the related work discusses how COVID-19 has been handled. Section 12.3 provides background knowledge about various machine/deep learning and genetic algorithms, Section 12.4 discusses the proposed methodology that has been used for developing the intelligent system. Results are discussed in Section 12.5, and Section 12.6 concludes the chapter.

12.2 Related Work

This section provides an overview of COVID-19 response modeling across sectors, categorizing works based on general non-pharmaceutical responses, responses in school management, and responses considering vaccines.

12.2.1 Modeling Non-Pharmaceutical COVID-19 Responses Cross Sectors

Recent research has extensively explored modeling COVID-19 responses, with studies simulating the impact of non-pharmaceutical interventions (NPIs) in Canada, Germany, and Australia, revealing the effectiveness of stringent measures in controlling the pandemic [5, 7, 8]. Additionally, investigations into the effectiveness of various intervention timeframes highlighted the importance of strategic lockdown durations [9], while studies assessing the role of face masks in pandemic management reported divergent findings, emphasizing the significance of mask efficacy and integrated control measures [10–12]. The evaluations of social distancing and testing activity underscored the need for a balanced approach to curb COVID-19, combining dynamic physical distancing, enhanced testing, and other measures for optimal results [13, 14]. Also, studies focused on mass gatherings events, particularly the Hajj pilgrimage, stressed the importance of face masks and capacity limitations in controlling disease spread [15, 16].

12.2.2 Modeling COVID-19 Responses for Schools' Management

In response to the COVID-19 outbreak, schools initially closed, prompting debates on the efficacy of this measure. However, institutions eventually resumed in-person learning with cautious policies, including mandatory face masks, social distancing, and testing [17]. They conducted an evaluation analysis in September 2020, utilizing analytical modeling and agent-based simulations to assess the impact of various reopening strategies. The study highlighted the positive correlation between infection rate expansion and the location of learning institutions. Results emphasized the significance of bulk testing capacity, showing a 44% reduction in infections with increased testing. The study also underscored the marginal impact of contact tracing and the essential need for varying testing frequencies between sub-populations. Another study, conducted by [18], classified school closure as a last resort, proposing alternative measures like limiting physical activities among children. [19] in September 2020 emphasized the crucial role of face masks and testing in mitigating COVID-19 spread within small colleges. [20] highlighted the possibility of safely returning to schools with high capacity and medium enforcement of face mask policies [17–20]. Age-specific considerations in school reopening were explored, with [21] establishing a positive relationship between age and COVID-19 susceptibility. [22] argued against school closure, suggesting that it could result in more deaths than face-to-face learning. The study of [21] in December 2020 utilized an age-structured transmission model, revealing the slight impact of school controls on disease reproduction numbers compared to outside school conditions [21, 22]. Various school reopening strategies were investigated, with [23] cautioning against reopening all schools simultaneously. [24] advocated for a phased approach, recommending the resumption of face-to-face learning for younger kids and the gradual introduction of preventive measures [23, 24].

12.2.3 Modeling the Impact of Vaccines in Curbing the Outbreak

In response to the COVID-19 pandemic, the modeling of vaccine impact gained prominence among researchers. [25] developed compartmental mathematical modeling in August 2021, focusing on the effectiveness of COVID-19 vaccines, particularly in old-age populations in British Columbia, Canada. The study explored vaccine scenarios, including sterilizing and attenuating vaccines, and assessed their impact on overall infections and mortality [25]. Another study by [26] in March 2021 predicted the impact of vaccination rates on COVID-19 dynamics in India, Brazil, and the USA. The simulations underscored the need for extensive vaccination efforts, especially in countries with high case numbers, and suggested that the pandemic might persist for a year or more [26]. Research addressing the intersection of age and vaccine strategies was conducted by [27] in February 2021. This study examined age-stratified prioritization of vaccine strategies to allocate available doses and address supply concerns. The findings highlighted variations in vaccine performance, susceptibility to infection, and population dynamics, emphasizing the significance of vaccinating specific age groups [27]. [28] conducted a mathematical modeling study in April 2021, evaluating different COVID-19 vaccine strategies in New South Wales, Australia. The research identified targeted age groups, ring vaccination, and mass vaccination as three main strategies, with ring vaccination being practical in situations with a limited vaccine supply [28]. [29] further explored vaccine prioritization in March 2021 using an age-structured model to minimize COVID-19 deaths and project infection rates over time. The study compared four vaccination scenarios, including prioritizing the oldest or youngest first, a uniform strategy, and a novel contact-based strategy. The results suggested that the most efficient approach for reducing mortality was pandemic phase-dependent and highlighted the potential effectiveness of a transmission-based strategy [29].

12.3 Background Knowledge

This section provides an overview of the key techniques employed in forming the foundational framework for our chapter. Specifically, we present a comprehensive description of artificial intelligence, forecasting modeling techniques, and the genetic algorithm (GA) as an optimization method. Artificial intelligence (AI) refers to the emulation of human intelligence processes by machines, with applications including expert systems, speech recognition, machine vision, and pattern recognition. AI programming focuses on three key cognitive skills: learning, reasoning, and self-correction. Machine learning, a subset of AI, involves developing computational algorithms that mimic human intelligence by learning from current contexts and generalizing for unseen tasks, making it a crucial component in handling big data [30, 31].

12.3.1 Machine Learning Techniques

Various techniques are employed to model and forecast disease behaviors, and we focus on specific ones in this proposed research. Mathematical modeling, involving diverse mathematical structures like graphs and equations, includes compartmental models, such as SEIS, commonly applied to infectious disease modeling, with deterministic or stochastic types [32, 33]. Agent-based models, integrating game theory and complex systems, find extensive use in COVID-19 simulations [34]. The data-driven models, such as Bayesian models utilizing Bayes' theorem, are employed in COVID-19 studies for updating scanned data information with statistical model parameters [35].

Support Vector Machine

Support vector machine (SVM) stands out as a widely utilized approach for classification and regression tasks due to its robustness to outliers and ease of implementation. SVM aims to find the optimal hyperplane, a best-fit line serving as decision boundaries for forecasting continuous outputs. Despite its advantages, SVM faces challenges in regression tasks, including underfitting large datasets or noisy values [36].

Autoregressive Integrated Moving Average (ARIMA)

ARIMA (autoregressive integrated moving average) is a classical machine learning approach widely employed in technical analysis for future prediction. It incorporates autoregression to consider future values based on past ones, integration to make data stationary by accounting for differences, and moving averages to capture dependencies between observations and residual errors from lagged observations [37].

12.3.2 Deep Learning

Deep learning, a subset of machine learning, distinguishes itself by its capacity to emulate human learning without explicit programming.

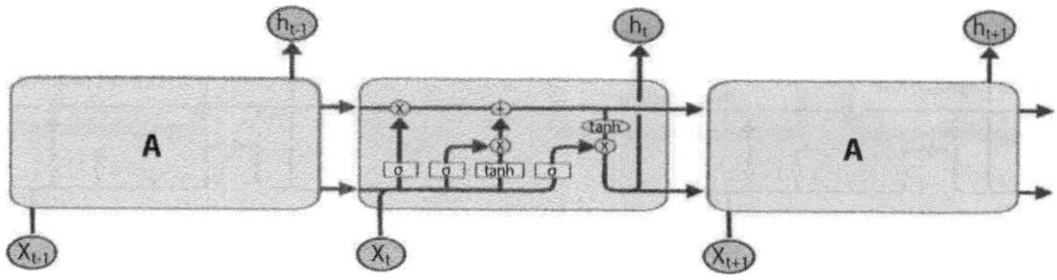

Figure 12.1 LSTM structure.

Neural networks, an advanced form of machine learning algorithms, surpass many deep learning models. Variants like recurrent neural networks (RNN), convolutional neural networks (CNN), artificial neural networks (ANN), and feedforward neural networks (FNN) all share the approach of enabling the model to make decisions by learning from data [38, 39].

Long Short-Term Memory (LSTM)

Long short-term memory (LSTM), a variant of recurrent neural networks (RNN), specializes in handling sequence prediction issues. Introduced by Hochreiter and Schmidhuber in 1997 to address the vanishing gradient problem in backpropagation, LSTM features multiple gate layers for learning from previous stages, assessing information importance and predicting future values. Components like the forget gate, input gate, and output gate contribute to the model's ability to retain or discard information, update the cell state, and determine the output. In this thesis, LSTM is utilized for time series analysis and prediction [40]. Figure 12.1 illustrates the LSTM structure.

12.3.3 Genetic Algorithms

The genetic algorithm (GA), inspired by natural evolution, utilizes mechanisms such as the initial population, fitness function, selection methods, crossover, and mutation to optimize hyperparameter choices for our model [41–43].

As depicted in Figure 12.2, the GA process begins with a population of individuals, each represented by a set of variables forming genes. The fitness function evaluates an individual's fitness, determining its competitiveness. Selection chooses the fittest individuals for reproduction, and the crossover step creates offspring by swapping genes between parents. Mutation preserves diversity by flipping bits in binary encoding. The GA concludes when a termination criterion, like reaching a set number of generations or insufficient distinctiveness in offspring, is met.

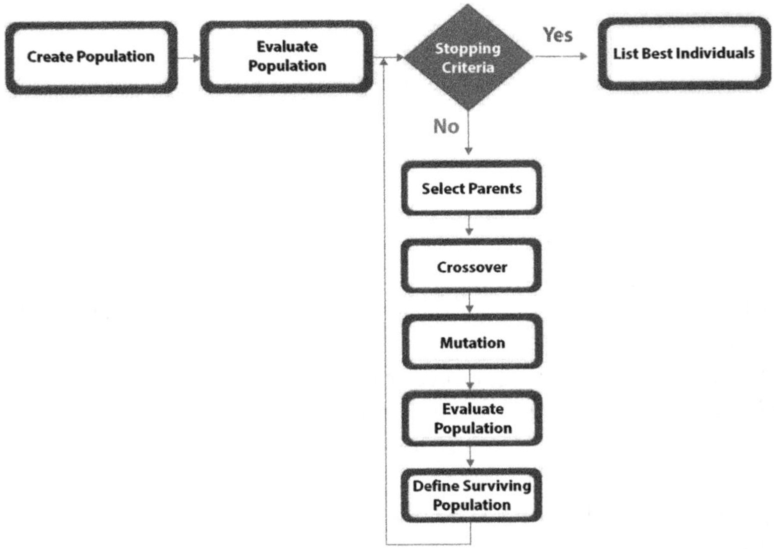

Figure 12.2 Genetic algorithm lifecycle.

12.4 Methodology

This section introduces a comprehensive decision-making framework designed for an intelligent and data-driven response to the pandemic. It provides an insight into the framework for building element of decision forecasting model. Unlike being confined to a specific decision element, this framework outlines a generalized approach for forecasting decision elements. It operates as an integral part of the broader decision-maker framework dedicated to an intelligent, data-driven response to the pandemic, as discussed previously. Figure 12.3 visually illustrates the step-by-step process involved in modeling the decision element. The overall description of the framework unfolds with the application of diverse data preparation techniques tailored to the dataset's characteristics. Subsequently, a feature engineering method is employed to eliminate unnecessary features, and the model is fine-tuned using hyperparameter tuning techniques like grid search, genetic algorithm, or particle swarm. The final step involves model validation through various methods, including comparison with benchmark models using different evaluation metrics.

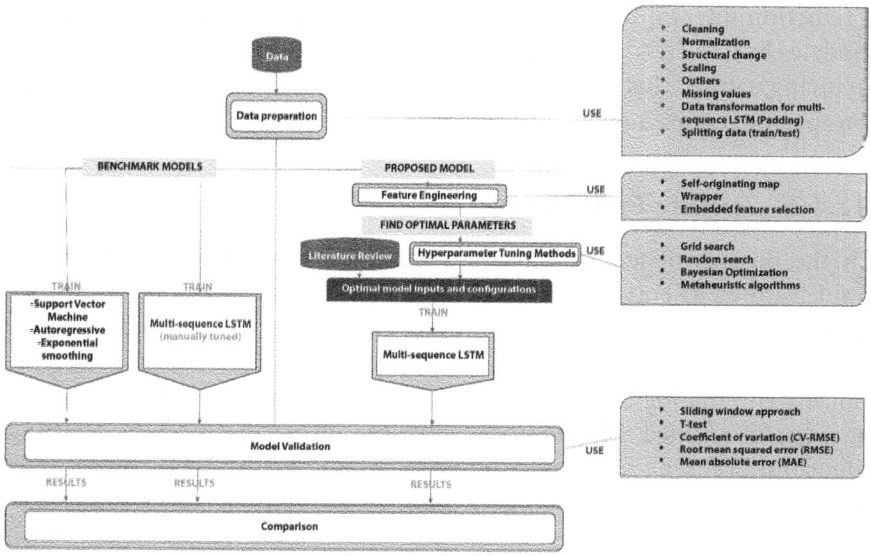

Figure 12.3 Stages of the framework for building element of decision forecasting model.

12.4.1 Data Preparation

A time-series data is collected from the University of Oxford COVID-19 government response tracker. The datasets encompass information for the United Arab Emirates, Bahrain, the US, the UK, and Oman, spanning from January 22, 2020 to January 18, 2022. Each country's dataset consists of 728 records. Our primary goal is to develop models capable of accurate performance across diverse scenarios. The selection of input responses and evaluation measures is influenced by various factors beyond our scope. However, based on our inputs the most prevalent responses are observed in the literature review, considering data availability and the taxonomy outlined earlier. A total of 10 responses were identified, including schools' closure, face covering, vaccine distribution, contact tracing, international travel restrictions, gatherings, testing policies, protection of the elderly, movement restrictions, and workplace closure. Regarding the evaluation measures, we chose the total number of deaths and cases due to their crucial role in assessing the crisis status, as they are widely adopted by governments.

In predicting the chosen decision elements, our focus is on the short term due to the rapid changes in pandemic dynamics. Regarding model variants, we implemented four models to demonstrate the improved performance of our targeted model based on GA-optimized LSTM. We set the prediction interval to be 14 days ahead, aligning with the swift decision updates by COVID-19 management authorities to adapt to the pandemic's evolving nature. This prediction range is flexible and can be adjusted based on specific requirements.

12.4.2 Feature Engineering

In the process of feature selection, we eliminate redundant and irrelevant features to enhance the accuracy of the model. To achieve this, we employed the recursive feature elimination based on importance weights. This algorithm operates by initially considering all features, and systematically eliminating them based on importance rankings until the desired number is reached. The approach involves fitting the machine learning algorithm, ranking features by importance, and iteratively discarding the least significant ones. This process continues until the specified number of features is attained.

12.4.3 Model Selection

The long short-term memory (LSTM) model is selected based on its widespread use and superior accuracy demonstrated in the literature review compared to other statistical, machine learning, and deep learning techniques [41–46]. LSTM's ability to overcome the vanishing gradient issue makes it well-suited for time series analysis-based forecasting, particularly for COVID-19 pandemic data.

LSTM Configurations

For the LSTM configurations, the COVID-19 time series forecasting problem involves predicting the total number of deaths 14 days ahead, making it a multi-step time series prediction. The LSTM model is configured to handle a multivariate input, considering eight selected responses. The input preparation involves mapping a sequence of previous observations to predict future outputs, resulting in a three-dimensional shape [samples, timesteps, features], where timesteps represent the window size or lags used for prediction.

The performance and accuracy of the LSTM model heavily depend on configuration parameters, which are selected through a combination of empirical validation, trial and error, and optimization using metaheuristic algorithms, specifically the genetic algorithm. Key hyperparameters include batch size, activation function, optimizer, predicted days, epochs, and layers. The batch size, epochs, and number of hidden layers

Table 12.1 LSTM parameters' configuration type.

Manual	Genetic algorithm
Batch size	Window size
Activation function	Number of units in the first layer
Optimizer	
Predicted days	
Epochs	
Layers	

are manually tuned, with careful consideration of computational resources to avoid compromising model quality and generalization. The activation function, Relu, is chosen for its simplicity and avoidance of the vanishing gradient issue. The optimizer, ADAM, is employed to adjust neural network attributes, such as weights and learning rate, to minimize losses in large-scale data and parameter scenarios. The selected parameters are detailed in Table 12.1.

The selected parameters, refined through empirical validation, play a crucial role in optimizing the LSTM model for accurate predictions. The batch size, indicating the number of samples processed simultaneously, was fine-tuned within the range of 56–120. Careful consideration was given to balancing computational resources, as an excessively large batch size could compromise model quality, hindering data generalization and pattern identification.

The activation function, a pivotal element in artificial neural networks for learning intricate patterns, was chosen as Relu due to its computational efficiency and its ability to mitigate the vanishing gradient issue. Additionally, the optimizer, responsible for adjusting network attributes like weights and learning rate to minimize losses, was implemented as ADAM. This optimizer is particularly suitable for handling extensive datasets and numerous parameters. Table 12.2 provides a concise summary of the selected parameter values, including a batch size range of 56–120, Relu activation function, ADAM optimizer, a prediction horizon of 14 days, 100 epochs, and four layers in the neural network architecture.

Hyperparameter Tuning

Hyperparameter optimization is a critical step in enhancing the performance of the LSTM model, particularly when dealing with extensive

Table 12.2 LSTM parameters' values.

Parameter	Value
Batch size	Range: 56–120 (tuned manually)
Activation function	Relu
Optimizer	Adam
Predicted days	14
Epochs	100
Layers	4

datasets. Given the impracticality of exhaustively examining all possible parameter values, we employed the genetic algorithm (GA) for this purpose. The GA aimed to identify the optimal window size and the number of units in the first layer, crucial parameters influencing the model's effectiveness.

The GA is configured with a population size of 40 individuals and ran for 100 generations. The gene structure, representing the encoding of parameters, had a length of 14. Specifically, the first eight elements denoted the number of units in the first layer, while the remaining six represented the window size. Figure 12.4 visually depicts the gene settings utilized in the GA.

To evaluate and select the best solutions, a fitness function is devised. The function examined the output, focusing on the root mean squared error (RMSE) for the last 14 predicted days. This approach aligns with our objective of optimizing accuracy over an extended period. Table 12.3 provides a summary of the key parameters employed in the genetic algorithm, including a population size of 40, 100 generations, a gene length of 14, and a fitness function based on RMSE for day 14. Additionally, a mutation probability of 0.1 was applied to introduce diversity in the gene pool and prevent premature convergence.

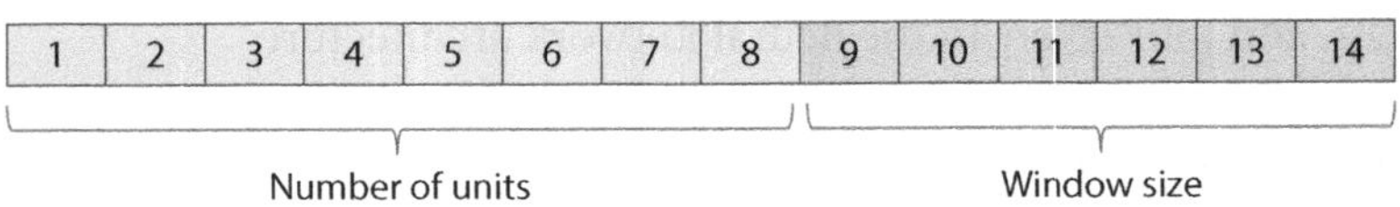

Figure 12.4 Gene settings in GA.

Table 12.3 Genetic algorithm parameters.

Parameter	Value
Population size	40
Generations	100
Gene length	14
Fitness function	RMSE for day 14
Mutation probability	0.1

12.5 Results and Discussions

In this section, we demonstrate the experimental results obtained from evaluating the performance of the GA-optimized LSTM. The recursive feature elimination, a technique based on important weights, was employed to discard unnecessary features. The selected features were then used as input for the LSTM. Table 12.4 displays the results of the feature selection process, indicating the removal of both contact tracing and international travel features.

The genetic algorithm is employed to discover optimal parameters for the selected features in the LSTM, contributing to the enhancement of the model's accuracy. Table 12.5 displays the optimized values identified by the genetic algorithm, with specific settings for the window size (5) and the number of units in the first layer (18).

12.5.1 Model Validation

Evaluation metrics play a pivotal role in assessing the efficacy of predictive models by quantifying the disparities between predictions and actual outcomes [47–49]. One widely employed loss function is the mean squared error, which computes the squared differences between predictions and ground truth, followed by averaging across the entire dataset. Building upon this, the root mean squared error provides a comparable measure but considers the square root of the computed value. Another straightforward metric for gauging errors is the mean absolute error, reflecting the magnitude of the difference between predicted and true values for observations. To facilitate cross-dataset comparisons, the coefficient of variation (CV-RMSE) is utilized. This metric is derived by dividing the RMSE by the average of actual values and multiplying the result by 100.

Table 12.4 Feature selection results for the total number of deaths in UAE.

Technique/feature	Schools	Face covering	Vaccine	Contact tracing	International travel	Gatherings	Testing policy	Protection elderly	Movement restrictions	Workplace closure
Recursive feature elimination based on importance weights	✓	✓	✓			✓	✓	✓	✓	✓

Table 12.5 Genetic algorithm results for the total number of deaths in UAE.

Adjustment	Parameter	Value
Genetic algorithm	Window size	5
	Number of units	18

Additionally, the mean absolute percentage error (MAPE) serves as an accuracy metric for our forecasting method. Calculated as the absolute percentage difference between actual and forecasted values, MAPE is expressed through the formula:

$$\text{MAPE} = \frac{100\%}{n} \sum_{t=1}^{n} \left| \frac{A_t - F_t}{A_t} \right|$$

where A_t is the actual value and F_t is the forecast value. Their difference is divided by the actual value A_t. The absolute value of this ratio is summed for every predicted point in time and divided by the number of fitted points n. To validate our proposed GA-optimized LSTM model, we employ five methods to compare its performance with that of various alternative models. These methods include:

1. Cross-validation
2. Comparison with benchmark models
3. Application/deployment of the model on unseen datasets
4. Application/deployment of the model with a second element of decision (as an evaluation measure)
5. Application/deployment of the model with a second element of decision on unseen datasets

These methods collectively provide a comprehensive assessment of the GA-optimized LSTM model against alternative approaches.

Cross-Validation

The process of cross-validation is employed to ensure model generalization and identify potential overfitting. This is achieved through a rolling basis approach involving three-fold or round testing. Initially, a small subset of data is used for training, with subsequent samples utilized for prediction

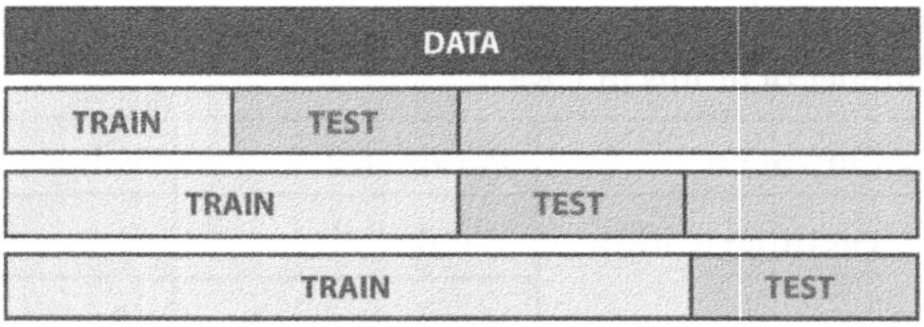

Figure 12.5 CV RMSE for the different variants of LSTM for total number of deaths in UAE.

and comparison. The cycle continues by incorporating test data into the training set, predicting the next set of data points, and evaluating against actual values. This approach is particularly effective for cross-validating time-series data, as illustrated in Figure 12.5.

The cross-validation results for predicting day 14 using the GA-optimized LSTM are summarized in Table 12.6. Across the three folds, key performance metrics include a mean absolute percentage error (MAPE) of 0.04, coefficient of variation (CV-RMSE) of 5.3, root mean squared error (RMSE) of 53, mean squared error (MSE) of 3,672, and mean absolute error (MAE) of 39. Figure 12.6 illustrates a strong fit between the predictions and actual values for the total number of deaths in the UAE. Additionally, Figure 12.7 confirms the robustness of GA-optimized LSTM predictions in comparison to actual values.

Comparison with Benchmark Models

In evaluating the proposed model's reliability, comparisons were made against several benchmark models: simple LSTM (long short-term memory), ARIMA (autoregressive integrated moving average), and SVM (support vector machine). Table 12.7 presents the prediction results for both the optimized model and the benchmarks. The GA-optimized LSTM exhibited

Table 12.6 Cross-validation results for the total number of deaths in UAE.

Fold	MAE	MSE	RMSE	CV RMSE	MAPE
0	44.03	2,323.30	48.20	9.34	0.08
1	55.36	8,255.15	90.86	5.84	0.04
2	17.86	438.28	20.94	0.99	0.01
Mean	39.08	3,672.24	53.33	5.39	0.04

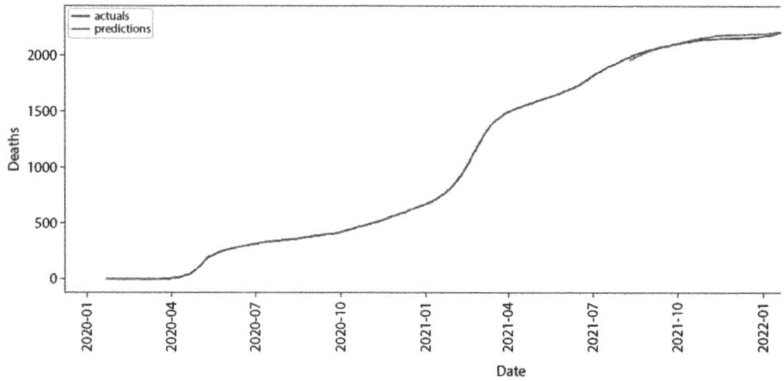

Figure 12.6 GA-optimized LSTM predictions for day 14 for the total number of deaths in UAE.

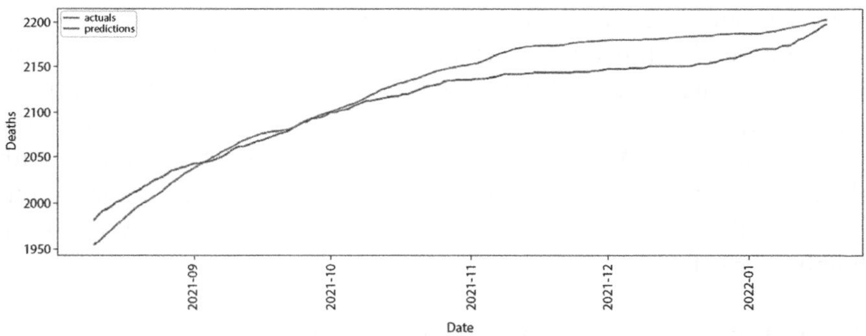

Figure 12.7 GA-optimized LSTM predictions for day 14 for the total number of deaths in UAE—test values only.

Table 12.7 Benchmark model results for the total number of deaths in UAE.

Model/evaluation	MAE	MSE	RMS	CV RMSE	MAPE
SVM	303.80	117,554.22	342.86	16.10	0.14
ARIMA	66.04	6,968.63	83.48	3.92	0.03
SIMPLE LSTM	41.30	1,712.77	41.39	1.94	0.02
GA-OPTIMIZED LSTM	12.46	165.49	12.86	0.60	0.01

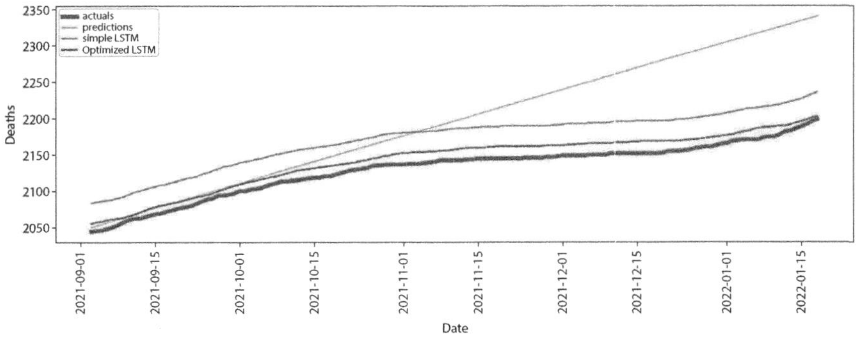

Figure 12.8 Benchmark model results compared with actual values.

superior performance with a CV RMSE of 0.60, surpassing the performance of the simple LSTM, ARIMA, and SVM models, which achieved 1.94, 3.92, and 16.10 in CV RMSE, respectively.

In Figure 12.8, the test set's actual values for the total number of deaths in the UAE are compared with prediction values from various models. Notably, the curve representing the number of deaths predicted by the GA-optimized LSTM demonstrates a close-to-perfect alignment with the actual death curve. This alignment serves as strong validation for our assertion that optimizing LSTM hyperparameters using GA has been highly successful.

Application of the Model on Unseen Datasets

Upon implementing the proposed model on our primary dataset, which pertains to the total number of deaths in the UAE and serves as our training data, we proceeded to assess the model's robustness by applying it to previously unseen datasets from (1) Oman and (2) the United Kingdom. This step was taken to validate the model's effectiveness in handling diverse data and to ensure its generalizability beyond the training set.

Oman Case

In the Oman dataset, the recursive feature elimination, based on importance weights, led to the exclusion of testing policy and protection of the elderly features. Additionally, the genetic algorithm suggested optimal parameters, specifying a window size of 8 days and 167 units in the first layer. Table 12.8 presents the prediction results for the total number of deaths in Oman, showcasing various evaluation metrics for the GA-optimized LSTM, notably achieving a CV RMSE of 6.64.

Table 12.8 The GA-optimized LSTM results for the total number of deaths in Oman.

Model	MAE	MSE	RMSE	CV RMSE	MAPE
GA-optimized	94.34	19,591.18	125.17	6.64	0.0477

Figure 12.9 displays a plot contrasting the actual total number of deaths in Oman with predictions from the entire dataset, revealing a commendable fit. Moreover, Figure 12.10 reaffirms the near-perfect accuracy of the GA-optimized LSTM, providing a detailed comparison between actual and predicted values for the total number of deaths in Oman.

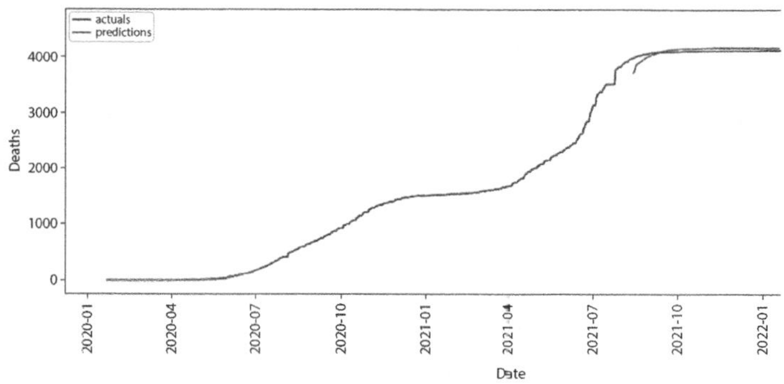

Figure 12.9 GA-optimized LSTM predictions for day 14 for the total number of deaths in Oman.

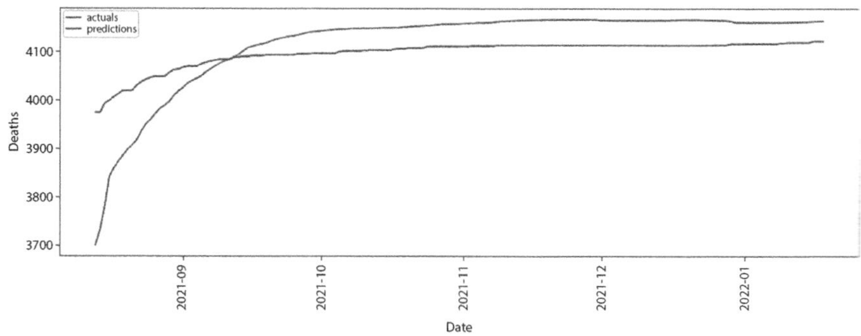

Figure 12.10 GA-optimized LSTM predictions for day 14 for the total number of deaths in Oman—test values only.

United Kingdom Case

In the United Kingdom dataset, the recursive feature elimination technique, based on importance weights, led to the removal of contact tracing and movement restrictions features. Additionally, the genetic algorithm recommended an optimal window size of 8 days and 167 units in the first layer. Table 12.9 presents the results of the GA-optimized LSTM, achieving a CV RMSE of 5.56 across all employed evaluation metrics.

Moreover, Figure 12.11 illustrates the plots of actual values and predictions for the total number of deaths in the UK, revealing a notable fit. Furthermore, a detailed examination in Figure 12.12 provides additional confirmation of the near-perfect fit achieved by the GA-optimized LSTM results.

Application/Deployment of the Model with Other Elements of Decision (Evaluation Measure)

The third validation method involves assessing the primary dataset (UAE) using an alternative evaluation measure—the total number of cases, commonly employed in the literature. For the UAE total number of cases dataset, feature selection eliminated contact tracing and face-covering features. The genetic algorithm recommended optimal parameters, specifying a window size of 5 days and 18 units in the first layer. Table 12.10 displays

Table 12.9 Results of the GA-optimized LSTM.

Model	MAE	MSE	RMSE	CV RMSE	MAPE
GA-optimized LSTM	3,031.03	21,454,356.03	3,718.55	5.56	0.0395

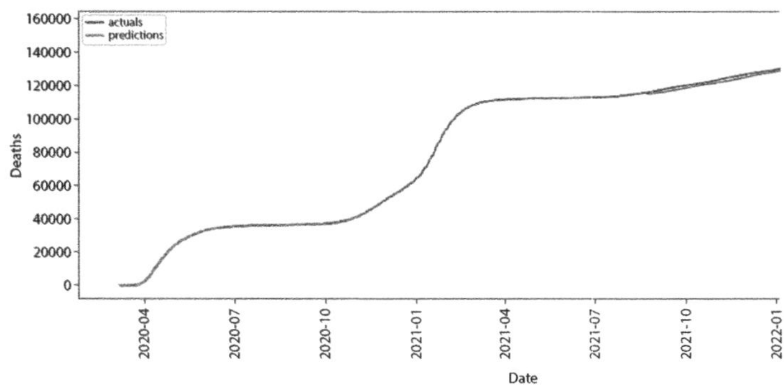

Figure 12.11 GA-optimized LSTM predictions for day 14 for the total number of deaths in the UK.

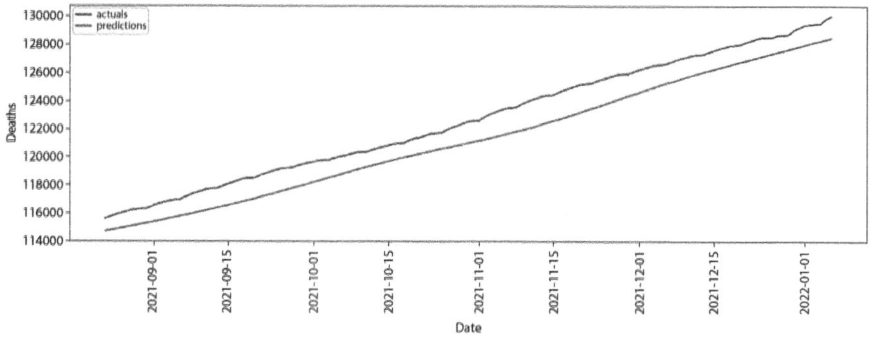

Figure 12.12 GA-optimized LSTM predictions for day 14 for the total number of deaths in the UK—test values only.

Table 12.10 The GA-optimized LSTM results for the total number of cases in UAE.

Model	MAE	MSE	RMSE	CV RMSE	MAPE
GA-optimized LSTM	15,205.12	325,645,699.59	17,612.28	5.86	0.05195

the prediction results for the total number of cases in the UAE utilizing the GA-optimized LSTM, achieving a CV RMSE of 5.86 across all employed evaluation metrics.

Figure 12.13 presents the actual values and day 14 predictions for the total number of cases in the UAE, solidifying the robustness of the

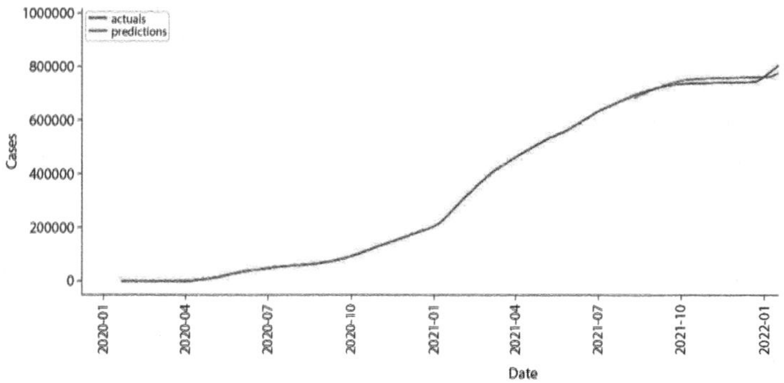

Figure 12.13 GA-optimized LSTM predictions for day 14 for the total number of cases in UAE.

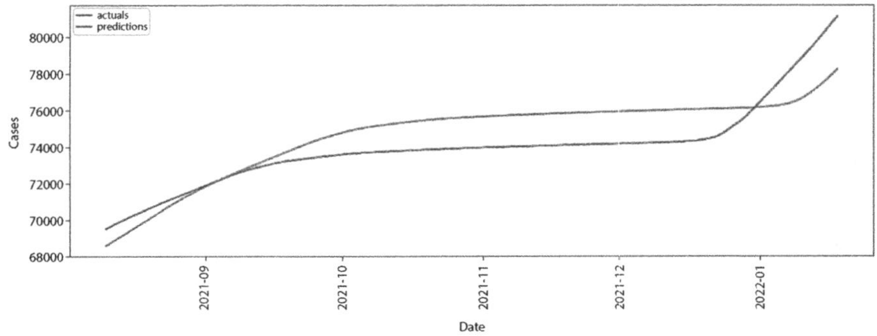

Figure 12.14 GA-optimized LSTM predictions for day 14 for the total number of cases in UAE—test values only.

GA-optimized LSTM results. Additionally, Figure 12.14 provides a detailed comparison of actuals and predictions for the total number of cases in the UAE, showcasing a near-perfect fit.

Application/Deployment of the Model with Other Evaluation Measures on Unseen Datasets

In this evaluation, we extend the application of our model, originally trained for predicting the total number of cases, to previously unseen datasets: (1) Bahrain and (2) USA datasets.

Bahrain Case

The recursive feature elimination, based on importance weights, led to the removal of testing policy and movement restrictions features in the Bahrain dataset. The genetic algorithm recommended optimal parameters, specifying a window size of 16 days and 22 units in the first layer. Table 12.11 presents the performance metrics for the GA-optimized LSTM in the Bahrain dataset, with values including 5.79 for the coefficient of variation (CV-RMSE), 9,800 for the root mean squared error (RMSE), 134,287,448 for the mean squared error (MSE), and 8,406 for the mean absolute error (MAE).

The visual representation in Figure 12.15 provides a direct comparison between the actual values and the day 14 predictions for the total number

Table 12.11 The GA-optimized LSTM results for the total number of cases in Bahrain.

Model	MAE	MSE	RMSE	CV RMSE	MAPE
GA-optimized	8,406.27	134,287,448.69	9,800.67	5.79	0.0512

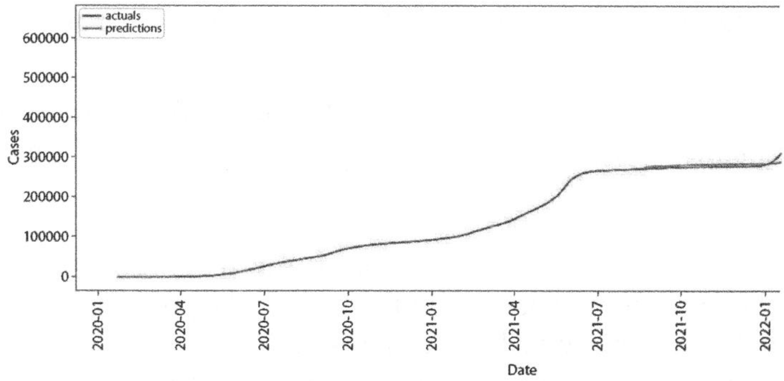

Figure 12.15 GA-optimized LSTM predictions for day 14 for the total number of cases in Bahrain.

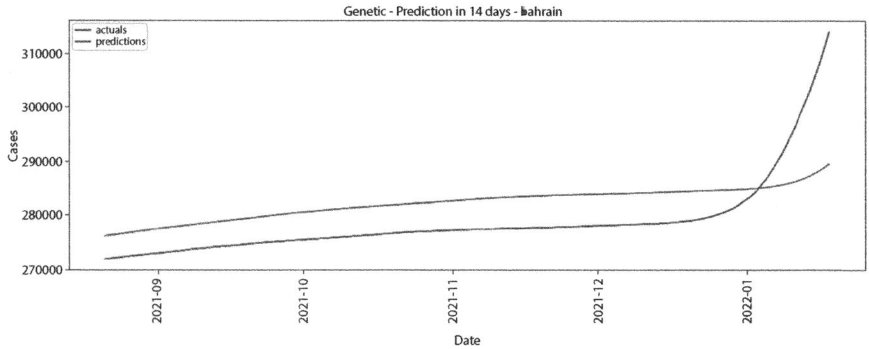

Figure 12.16 GA-optimized LSTM predictions for day 14 for the total number of cases in Bahrain—test values only.

of cases in Bahrain using the GA-optimized LSTM, affirming the model's ability to achieve a good fit. A more detailed inspection in Figure 12.16 unveils the close alignment between the actual data and the predicted values for the total number of cases in Bahrain.

United States Case

In the United States dataset, feature selection led to the removal of contact tracing and gathering features. The genetic algorithm suggested optimal parameters, specifying a window size of 5 days and 18 units in the first layer. Table 12.12 presents the performance metrics for the GA-optimized LSTM in the United States dataset, with values including 8.44 for the coefficient of variation (CV-RMSE), 4,423.14 for the root mean squared error (RMSE), 38,771,154.05 for the mean squared error (MSE), and 2,301.12 for the mean absolute error (MAE).

Table 12.12 Different variants of LSTM results for the total number of cases in US.

Model	MAE	MSE	RMSE	CV RMSE	MAPE
GA-optimized	2,301.12	38,771,154.05	4,423.14	8.44	0.038365

In Figure 12.17, a commendable fit is displayed between the actual values for the total number of cases in the US and the predictions for day 14 using the GA-optimized LSTM. Further scrutiny in Figure 12.18 reveals a detailed comparison, confirming the trustworthiness of the results between actual and predicted values for the total number of cases in the US.

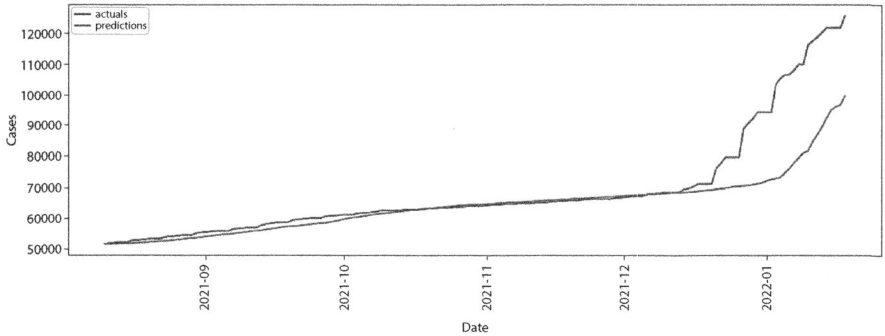

Figure 12.17 GA-optimized LSTM predictions for day 14 for the total number of cases in the US.

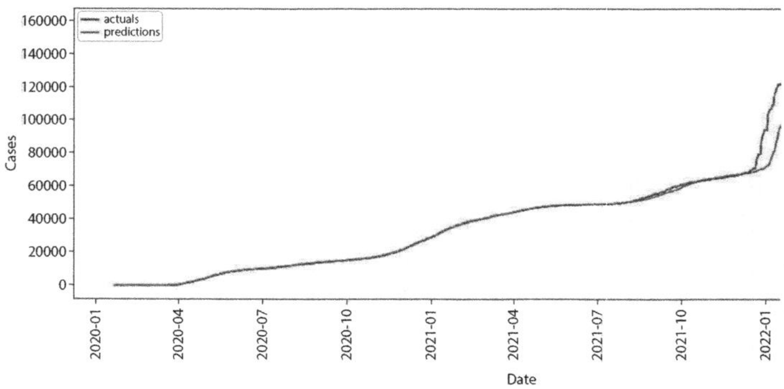

Figure 12.18 GA-optimized LSTM predictions for day 14 for the total number of cases in the US—test values only.

12.6 Conclusion

This research contributes to the extensive field of COVID-19 pandemic administration and forecasting, aiming to provide decision-makers with rigorous predictions for effective responses to mitigate the outbreak. The approach utilizes artificial intelligence techniques, specifically LSTM deep learning, to understand pandemic dynamics such as propagation, case numbers, and fatalities. The developed prediction model integrates feature selection and optimization through genetic algorithms for enhanced accuracy. Time-series datasets from various regions, including the UAE, Bahrain, US, UK, and Oman, were employed in constructing the forecasting models. Experimental validation includes cross-validation, benchmark model comparisons (ARIMA, SVM, and simple LSTM), and application to unseen global data. The proposed approach was validated not only for forecasting cases but also for deaths, demonstrating superior accuracy compared to benchmark models. By focusing on both the containment of the virus and the overall wellbeing of the population, this integrated methodology offers a comprehensive tool for pandemic preparedness and response. Future work involves extending forecasting to additional decision elements like hospitalization rate and vaccine coverage. The model will be tailored to specific domains, incorporating domain-specific features, demographic information, and mobility data. For instance, application to the education sector will assess the impact of school closures on COVID-19 spread, considering factors such as vaccination rates, school capacity, learning modes, and student age. In parallel, a meta-model will be developed to recommend appropriate measures and responses. Ongoing research will explore optimal LSTM parameters using alternative metaheuristic algorithms. Advanced methods for COVID-19 data preprocessing and feature selection are also part of the extended approach.

References

1. Covid19.who.int, WHO Coronavirus (COVID-19) Dashboard, 2021, [online] Available at: <https://covid19.who.int/measures> [Accessed 27 November 2021].
2. World Health Organization, *Measures*, World Health Organization, n.d. Retrieved November 12, 2022, from https://covid19.who.int/measures.
3. World Health Organization, *Vaccine efficacy, effectiveness and protection*, World Health Organization, 2021, Retrieved November 12, 2022, from https://www.who.int/news-room/feature-stories/detail/vaccine-efficacy-effectiveness-and-protection.

4. Ozili, P.K. and Arun, T., Spillover of COVID-19: impact on the Global Economy, 2020, Available at SSRN 3562570.
5. Chang, w. and Yano, S., How are countries addressing the Covid-19 challenges in education? A snapshot of policy measures, 2020, Retrieved 27 November 2021, from https://gemreportunesco.wpcomstaging.com/2020/03/24/how-are-countries-addressing-the-covid-19-challenges-in-education-a-snap-shot-of-policy-measures/.
6. ADEK, *Activation of ADEK Blue Schools Initiative Boosts School Vaccination Rates*, Department of Education and Knowledge, 2021, https://www.adek.gov.ae/Media-Centre/News/Activation-of-ADEK-Blue-Schools-Initiative-Boosts-School-Vaccination-Rates.
7. Ogden, N.H., Fazil, A., Arino, J., Berthiaume, P., Fisman, D.N., Greer, A.L., Ludwig, A., Ng, V., Tuite, A.R., Turgeon, P., Waddell, L.A., Wu, J., Modelling scenarios of the epidemic of COVID-19 in Canada. *Can. Commun. Dis. Rep.*, 46, 8, 198–204, 2020 Jun 4, doi: 10.14745/ccdr.v46i06a08. PMID: 32673384; PMCID: PMC7343050.
8. Barbarossa, M., Fuhrmann, J., Meinke, J., Krieg, S., Varma, H., Castelletti, N., Lippert, T., Modeling the spread of COVID-19 in Germany: Early assessment and possible scenarios. *PLOS ONE*, 15, 9, e0238559, 2020, doi: 10.1371/journal.pone.0238559.
9. Ambikapathy, B. and Krishnamurthy, K., Mathematical Modelling to Assess the Impact of Lockdown on COVID-19 Transmission in India: Model Development and Validation. *JMIR Public Health Surveillance*, 6, 2, e19368, 2020, https://doi.org/10.2196/19368.
10. IHME COVID-19 Forecasting Team, Reiner, R.C., Barber, R.M., Collins, J.K., Zheng, P., Adolph, C., Albright, J., Antony, C.M., Aravkin, A.Y., Bachmeier, S.D., Bang-Jensen, B., Bannick, M.S., Bloom, S., Carter, A., Castro, E., Causey, K., Chakrabarti, S., Charlson, F.J., Cogen, R.M., Murray, C.J.L., Modeling COVID-19 scenarios for the United States. *Nat. Med.*, 27, 1, 94–105, 2021, https://doi.org/10.1038/s41591-020-1132-9.
11. Kennedy, D., Zambrano, G., Wang, Y., Neto, O., Modeling the Effects of Intervention Strategies on COVID-19 Transmission Dynamics, 2020, doi: 10.2139/ssrn.3595898.
12. Brauner, J.M., Mindermann, S., Sharma, M., Stephenson, A.B., Gavenčiak, T., Johnston, D., Leech, G., Salvatier, J., Altman, G., Norman, A.J., Monrad, J.T., Besiroglu, T., Ge, H., Mikulik, V., Hartwick, M.A., Teh, Y.W., Chindelevitch, L., Gal, Y., Kulveit, J., The effectiveness of eight nonpharmaceutical interventions against COVID-19 in 41 countries, medRxiv 2020.05.28.20116129; doi: https://doi.org/10.1101/2020.05.28.20116129.
13. Alvarez, M.M., González-González, E., Trujillo-de Santiago, G., Modeling COVID-19 epidemics in an Excel spreadsheet to enable first-hand accurate predictions of the pandemic evolution in urban areas. *Sci. Rep.*, 11, 4327, 2021, https://doi.org/10.1038/s41598-021-83697-w.

14. Tuite, A.R., Fisman, D.N., Greer, A.L., ., Mathematical modelling of COVID-19 transmission and mitigation strategies in the population of Ontario, Canada. *CMAJ*, 192, 19, E497–E505, 2020 May 11, doi: 10.1503/cmaj.200476. Epub 2020 Apr 8. PMID: 32269018; PMCID: PMC7234271.
15. Al-Shaery, A., Hejase, B., Tridane, A., Farooqi, N., Jassmi, H., Agent-Based Modeling of the Hajj Rituals with the Possible Spread of COVID-19. *Sustainability*, 13, 12, 6923, 2021, doi: 10.3390/su13126923.
16. Ryu, H., Abulali, A., Lee, S., Assessing the Effectiveness of Isolation and Contact-Tracing Interventions for Early Transmission Dynamics of COVID-19 in South Korea. *IEEE Access*, 9, 41456–41467, 2021, doi: 10.1109/ACCESS.2021.3064371.
17. Mukherjee, U.K., Bose, S., Ivanov, A. *et al.*, Evaluation of reopening strategies for educational institutions during COVID-19 through agent based simulation. *Sci. Rep.*, 11, 6264, 2021, https://doi.org/10.1038/s41598-021-84192-y.
18. Naimark, D., Mishra, S., Barrett, K. *et al.*, Simulation-Based Estimation of SARS-CoV-2 Infections Associated With School Closures and Community-Based Nonpharmaceutical Interventions in Ontario, Canada. *JAMA Netw. Open*, 4, 3, e213793, 2021, doi:10.1001/jamanetworkopen.2021.3793.
19. Bahl, R., Eikmeier, N., Fraser, A., Junge, M., Keesing, F., Nakahata, K., Reeves, L., Modeling COVID-19 spread in small colleges. *PLOS One*, 16, 8, e0255654, 2021, doi: 10.1371/journal.pone.0255654.
20. España, G., Cavany, S., Oidtman, R., Barbera, C., Costello, A., Lerch, A., Poterek, M., Tran, Q., Wieler, A., Moore, S., Perkins, T.A., Impacts of K-12 school reopening on the COVID-19 epidemic in Indiana, USA. *Epidemics*, 37, 100487, 2021, ISSN 1755-4365, https://doi.org/10.1016/j.epidem.2021.100487.
21. Rozhnova, G., van Dorp, C.H., Bruijning-Verhagen, P. *et al.*, Model-based evaluation of school- and non-school-related measures to control the COVID-19 pandemic. *Nat. Commun.*, 12, 1614, 2021, https://doi.org/10.1038/s41467-021-21899-6.
22. Rice, K., Wynne, B., Martin, V., Ackland, G., Effect of school closures on mortality from coronavirus disease 2019: old and new predictions. *BMJ*, m3588, 1–8, 2020, doi: 10.1136/bmj.m3588.
23. Cruz, E., Maciel, J., Clozato, C., Serpa, M., Navaux, P., Meneses, E., Diener, M., Simulation-based evaluation of school reopening strategies during COVID-19: A case study of São Paulo, Brazil. *Epidemiol. Infect.*, 149, E118, 2021, doi:10.1017/S0950268821001059.
24. Di Domenico, L., Pullano, G., Sabbatini, C.E. *et al.*, Modelling safe protocols for reopening schools during the COVID-19 pandemic in France. *Nat. Commun.*, 12, 1073, 2021, https://doi.org/10.1038/s41467-021-21249-6.
25. Sadarangani, M., Abu Raya, B., Conway, J.M., Iyaniwura, S.A., Falcao, R.C., Colijn, C., Coombs, D., Gantt, S., Importance of COVID-19 vaccine efficacy in older age groups. *Vaccine*, 39, 15, 2020–2023, 2021, ISSN 0264-410X, https://doi.org/10.1016/j.vaccine.2021.03.020.

26. ChaturvediChakravarty, D.U., Predictive analysis of COVID-19 eradication with vaccination in India, Brazil, and U.S.A. *Infection, Genet. Evol.*, 92, 104834, 2021, ISSN 1567-1348, https://doi.org/10.1016/j.meegid.2021.104834.
27. Bubar, K.M., Reinholt, K., Kissler, S.M., Lipsitch, M., Cobey, S., Grad, Y.H., Larremore, D.B., Model-informed COVID-19 vaccine prioritization strategies by age and serostatus. *Science*, 371, 6532, 916–921, 2021 Feb 26, doi: 10.1126/science.abe6959. Epub 2021 Jan 21. PMID: 33479118; PMCID: PMC7963218.
28. MacIntyre, C.R., Costantino, V., Trent, M., Modelling of COVID-19 vaccination strategies and herd immunity, in scenarios of limited and full vaccine supply in NSW, Australia. *Vaccine*, 40, 17, 2506–2513, 2022, ISSN 0264-410X, https://doi.org/10.1016/j.vaccine.2021.04.042.
29. Jentsch, P.C., Anand, M., Bauch, C.T., Prioritising COVID-19 vaccination in changing social and epidemiological landscapes: a mathematical modelling study. *Lancet Infect. Dis.*, 21, 8, 1097–1106, 2021, doi: 10.1016/s1473-3099(21)00057-8.
30. El Naqa, I. and Murphy, M.J., What Is Machine Learning?, in: *Machine Learning in Radiation Oncology*, I. El Naqa, R. Li, M. Murphy (Eds.), Springer, Cham, 2015, https://doi.org/10.1007/978-3-319-18305-3_1.
31. Qlik, How Big Data and AI Work Together: Synergies & Benefits, Qlik, 2022, Retrieved November 12, 2022, from https://www.qlik.com/us/augmented-analytics/big-data-ai.
32. Mathematical Modeling - Annenberg Learner, 2021. Retrieved 12 December 2021, from https://www.learner.org/series/insights-into-algebra-1-teaching-for-learning-2/mathematical-modeling/#:~:text=Mathematical%20modeling%20is%20the%20process,problem%20to%20its%20essential%20characteristics.
33. En.wikipedia.org., Infection rate - Wikipedia, 2022, [online] Available at: <https://en.wikipedia.org/wiki/Infection_rate> [Accessed 16 July 2022].
34. En.wikipedia.org., Social distancing - Wikipedia, 2022, [online] Available at: <https://en.wikipedia.org/wiki/Social_distancing> [Accessed 16 July 2022].
35. Van de Schoot, R., Depaoli, S., King, R. *et al.*, Bayesian statistics and modelling. *Nat. Rev. Methods Primers*, 1, 1, 2021, https://doi.org/10.1038/s43586-020-00001-2.
36. Raj, A., Unlocking the True Power of Support Vector Regression, 2020, [online] Towards data science. Available at: <https://towardsdatascience.com/unlocking-the-true-power-of-support-vector-regression-847fd123a4a0> [Accessed 25 June 2022].
37. HAYES, A., Autoregressive Integrated Moving Average (ARIMA), 2021, [online] Investopedia. Available at: <https://www.investopedia.com/terms/a/autoregressive-integrated-moving-average-arima.asp> [Accessed 25 June 2022].

38. Burns, E., What is Artificial Intelligence (AI)? - AI Definition and How it Works, 2021, Retrieved 12 December 2021, from https://searchenterpriseai.techtarget.com/definition/AI-Artificial-Intelligence.
39. The Hewlett Packard Enterprise, *What is Deep Learning*, The Hewlett Packard Enterprise, 2022, Retrieved November 12, 2022, from https://www.hpe.com/us/en/what-is/deep-learning.html.
40. Colah.github.io, Understanding LSTM Networks, 2022, [online] Available at: <https://colah.github.io/posts/2015-08-Understanding-LSTMs/> [Accessed 22 June 2022].
41. Bouktif, S., Fiaz, A., Ouni, A., Serhani, M., Optimal Deep Learning LSTM Model for Electric Load Forecasting using Feature Selection and Genetic Algorithm: Comparison with Machine Learning Approaches. *Energies*, 11, 7, 1636, 2018, https://doi.org/10.3390/en11071636.
42. Bouktif, S., Fiaz, A., Ouni, A., Serhani, M.A., Multi-Sequence LSTM-RNN Deep Learning and Metaheuristics for Electric Load Forecasting. *Energies*, 13, 2, 391, 2020, https://doi.org/10.3390/en13020391.
43. Davahli, M.R., Karwowski, W., Fiok, K., Optimizing COVID-19 vaccine distribution across the United States using deterministic and stochastic recurrent neural networks. *PLoS One*, 16, 7, e0253925, 2021, https://doi.org/10.1371/journal.pone.0253925.
44. Elsheikh, A.H., Saba, A., II, Abd Elaziz, M., Lu, S., Shanmugan, S., Muthuramalingam, T., Kumar, R., Mosleh, A.O., Essa, F.A., Shehabeldeen, T.A., Deep learning-based forecasting model for COVID-19 outbreak in Saudi Arabia. *Process Saf. Environ. Prot.*, 149, 223–233, 2021, ISSN 0957-5820, https://doi.org/10.1016/j.psep.2020.10.048.
45. Kırbaş, İ., Sözen, A., Tuncer, A.D., Kazancıoğlu, F.Ş., Comparative analysis and forecasting of COVID-19 cases in various European countries with ARIMA, NARNN and LSTM approaches. *Chaos Solitons Fractals*. 138, 110015, 2020 Sep, doi: 10.1016/j.chaos.2020.110015. Epub 2020 Jun 13. PMID: 32565625; PMCID: PMC7293493.
46. Marzouk, M., Elshaboury, N., Abdel-Latif, A., Azab, S., Deep learning model for forecasting COVID-19 outbreak in Egypt. *Process Saf. Environ. Prot.*, 153, 363–375, 2021, ISSN 0957-5820, https://www.sciencedirect.com/science/article/pii/S0957582021004055
47. Rabani, S.T., Khan, Q.R., Khanday, A.M.U.D., Quantifying suicidal ideation on social media using machine learning: a critical review. *Iraqi J. Sci.*, 4092–4100, 2021.
48. Wajid, M.A., Zafar, A., Bhushan, B., Khanday, A.M.U.D., Wajid, M.S., Artificial intelligence (AI) and internet of things (IoT): application in detecting and containing the spread of COVID-19. in: *AI Models for Blockchain-Based Intelligent Networks in IoT Systems: Concepts, Methodologies, Tools, and Applications*, pp. 373–392, Cham: Springer International Publishing, 2023.

49. Khanday, A.M.U.D., Khan, Q.R., Rabani, S.T. Ensemble approach for detecting COVID-19 propaganda on online social networks. *Iraqi J. Sci.*, 4488–4498, 2022.

13

Fusing Sentiment Analysis with Hybrid Collaborative Algorithms for Enhanced Recommender Systems

Anindya Nag[1*], Md. Mehedi Hassan[1], Mohammad Abu Tareq Rony[2], Biva Das[3], Riya Sil[4], Prianka Saha[3], Pronab Sarker[1] and Anupam Kumar Bairagi[1]

[1]Computer Science and Engineering Discipline, Khulna University, Khulna, Bangladesh
[2]Department of Statistics, Noakhali Science and Technology University, Noakhali, Bangladesh
[3]Pharmacy Discipline, Khulna University, Khulna, Bangladesh
[4]Department of Computer Science and Engineering, Brainware University, Kolkata, West Bengal, India

Abstract

Recommender systems must be enhanced as Internet data grows to produce a list of suitable favorites. Given the exponential growth of Internet data, it is imperative to develop and enhance recommender systems to curate a personalized list of suitable preferences. The increasing prevalence of social networking sites has contributed significantly to the surge in popularity of review-based recommender systems in recent times. The rationale underlying such systems is to effectively utilize the knowledge acquired from written feedback provided by users. The fields of sentiment analysis and opinion mining have seen substantial growth in recent years. Consequently, there is now more work being put into improving recommendation systems. A hybrid collaborative filtering (HCF) recommender system will be used in this inquiry to provide a comparative analysis of sentiment analysis. The methodology being examined comprises two distinct phases, namely the sentiment analysis phase and the recommendation phase. The initial stage, referred to as "sentiment analysis," entails the computation of sentiment scores through the utilization of datasets sourced from diverse social media platforms.

**Corresponding author*: anindyanag58@gmail.com

Bharat Bhushan, Akib Khanday, Khursheed Aurangzeb, Sudhir Kumar Sharma and Parma Nand (eds.) Wellness Management Powered by AI Technologies, (343–362) © 2025 Scrivener Publishing LLC

The subsequent stage entails the utilization of HCF. The findings of this study demonstrate a noteworthy enhancement in the efficacy of recommender systems through the integration of sentiment analysis and other comparable systems. In addition, a comparison of the effectiveness of HCF methodologies and conventional methods often used in sentiment analysis is being conducted. The results show that, with a recorded accuracy rate of 99.2%, the HCF recommendation algorithm for sentiment analysis put forward in this study outperforms current state-of-the-art approaches.

***Keywords*:** Recommender systems, sentiment analysis, machine learning, hybrid collaborative filtering, hybrid algorithm

13.1 Introduction

The growing prevalence of social networking sites has led to an increased interest in review-based recommender systems among individuals. Recommender systems are necessary in social settings where resources are shared [1]. It is extremely challenging to suggest a source that is both understandable and interesting at the same time for an explicit user due to the diversity of key user variables including personal history, areas of interest, and skill level. Many different businesses, including e-commerce, media, finance, utilities, and many others, have used recommender systems. This particular technology generates personalized recommendations for individual users by analyzing extensive amounts of data. The recommendations provided to clients are advantageous as they facilitate the process of product selection, and businesses stand to gain from increased product usage as a result of these recommendations.

The utilization of sentiment analysis in recommender systems facilitates the acquisition of valuable insights into the opinions and emotions of users within the context of social media, thereby resulting in more reliable recommendations [2]. From one perspective, this information has the potential to complement the written evaluations provided by consumers regarding products. It is accepted in the research that using sentiment analysis to assess content from blogs, social media platforms, recommender systems, and online news sources can improve user choices [3, 4]. In the current work, a recommendation system that combines collaborative filtering (CF) techniques with sentiment analysis is introduced and evaluated. The process of conducting sentiment polarity analysis is illustrated in Figure 13.1.

The user's opinions on the relative weighting of various factors when assessing a particular resource may not be effectively reflected by the use

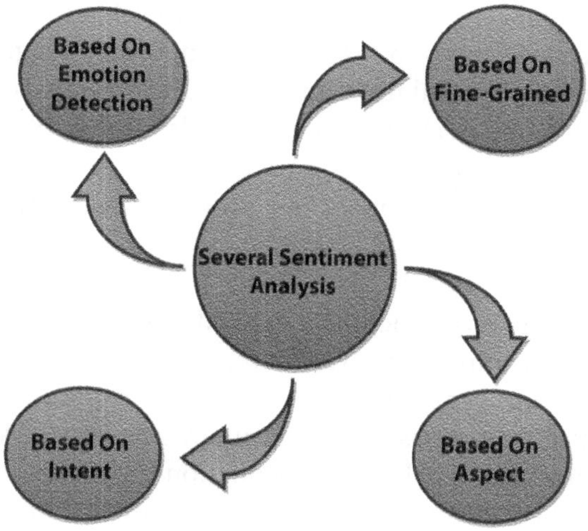

Figure 13.1 Sentiment analysis.

of explicit user ratings in collaborative filtering techniques [5]. The occurrence of Stigmergy phenomena has the potential to impact the efficacy of techniques employed for analyzing access patterns. As a result, the community frequently makes the resources that are well-liked or respected available to potential users [6]. The degree of popularity of a resource does not necessarily correspond to its level of usefulness or efficacy. Consequently, the analysis of user behavior may yield insufficient recommendations, as users tend to adhere to their established methods of navigating the available content.

The advent of Web 2.0 has enabled users to furnish significantly more comprehensive accounts of their experiences. The assessment of a resource's dependability, prevalence, and utility can be significantly enhanced through the examination of feedback, discourse, and appraisals provided by authentic users. It is proposed that incorporating user-generated reviews into the sources of an educational content repository can effectively mitigate the issue of implicit ratings and provide valuable insights into the quality of a particular resource as well as the impressions it has left on its users. The process involves the analysis of comments made on educational content through the application of sentiment analysis. Subsequently, an assessment was conducted to determine the dependability of the outcomes and the degree to which the remarks corresponded to the users' perception of the adequacy of the information in fulfilling their requirements. At this juncture of the procedure, a framework for collaborative filtering and recommendation was formulated; however, the characteristics and features of the content were not taken into account during the evaluation. The purpose of developing such systems is to make use of important insights that can be gleaned from user-provided textual reviews. The objective of this research is to create a recommendation system for collaborative filtering (CF) that utilizes sentiment analysis.

The significant contributions of our proposed innovative research are as follows:

- The paper recommends a hybrid collaborative filtering (HCF) recommender system that incorporates sentiment analysis for generating more accurate recommendations. Specifically, it notes a high accuracy rate of 99.2% for the recommended HCF recommendation algorithm, showcasing its superiority over current state-of-the-art methods.
- The research provides a comprehensive comparison between the effectiveness of the HCF methodology and traditional sentiment analysis approaches. This comparative analysis is crucial for understanding the benefits of hybrid models in recommendation systems and their potential for more nuanced user engagement.

The subsequent segments of this document are structured as Section 13.1.1 describes the sentiment analysis. After that, Section 13.2 delves into an examination of pertinent literature. Section 13.3 introduces the comparative result study. Finally, Section 13.4 encapsulates the conclusions drawn from this investigative research.

13.1.1 Analysis of Sentiment

The process of sentiment analysis involves the analytical evaluation of textual expressions of opinion to determine whether they are negative, positive, or neutral. This aids in the identification of user attitudes. At three distinct levels of information extraction, namely—the level of the document, the level of an aspect or feature, and the level of the phrase—sentiment analysis can be carried out. The proposed technique aims to identify the various subjectivities associated with an entity by utilizing extracted data in an automated manner. The objective is to ascertain the polarity of user-generated content, whether it is positive, negative, or neutral. Currently, there exist three distinct approaches to address the matter of sentiment analysis, as outlined in reference [7]: machine learning-oriented techniques, lexicon-oriented techniques, and hybrid (combined) lexicon/machine learning/artificial intelligence techniques.

The corpus-based method and the dictionary-based method are two separate subcategories of the lexicon-based approach [8]. Their initial main objective was to assign names to various emotional disorders. The task of sentiment analysis has been tackled through the utilization of conventional as well as deep learning-based computational models [9]. The hybrid methodologies amalgamate the techniques of machine learning with lexicon-based approaches [10]. The utilization of sentiment analysis can enhance the efficacy of a recommender system through two key mechanisms: assimilating crucial details conveyed in reviews and comprehending the influence of a particular review on the consumer. The development of a focused recommendation system is made easier by the use of sentiment analysis [11]. The methodology for performing sentiment analysis using collaborative filtering is shown in Figure 13.2.

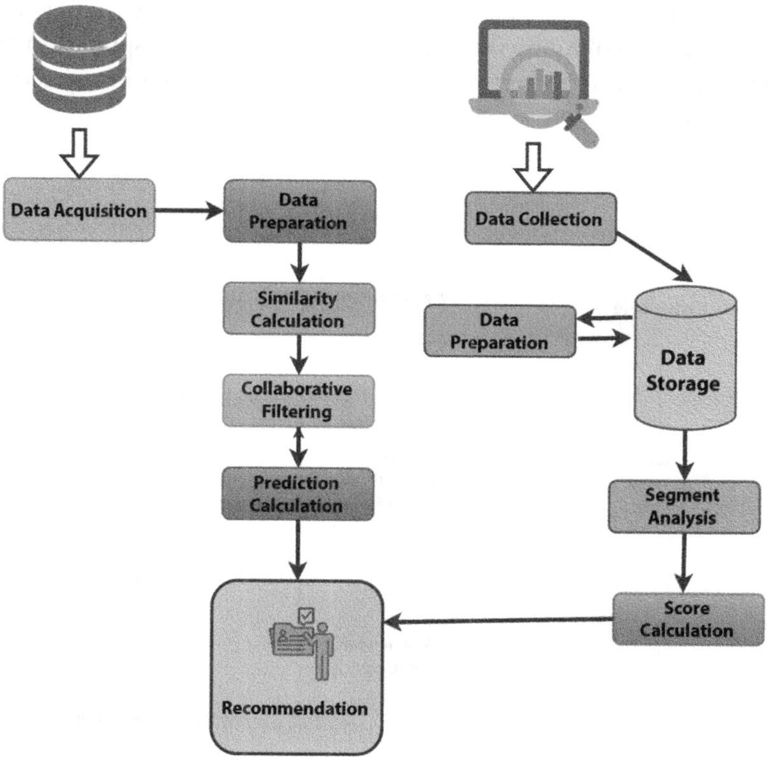

Figure 13.2 Analysis of sentiment based on collaborative filtering.

13.1.2 Collaboration Filtering

Collaborative filtering (CF) is a type of recommendation system that builds a prediction for a particular user based on prior user activity and the behavior of other users. The process of utilizing CF to anticipate the interests of individuals based on their established preferences within a vast user population is referred to as predictive modeling. The calculation of similarity incorporates both the subject and the object, as indicated by reference [12]. The Pearson correlation method is used in conjunction with the cosine similarity approach. CF refers to the phenomenon of using the preferences of other people who share the same viewpoints to ascertain a consumer's choice of a product. The algorithm searches across a large population to find a segment of people who share the same interests as the user. The system considers the user's preferences and generates a sorted catalog of suggested items. For recommender algorithms to operate effectively, it is necessary to have access to data that encompasses both users and items. During the information processing, the matrix encompasses the reactions of a set of users toward particular entities within a broader collection of elements. Reference [13] states that item average ratings would be presented in columns, while user ratings would be displayed in rows. Figure 13.3 depicts the sentiment-based CF recommendation system that has been proposed.

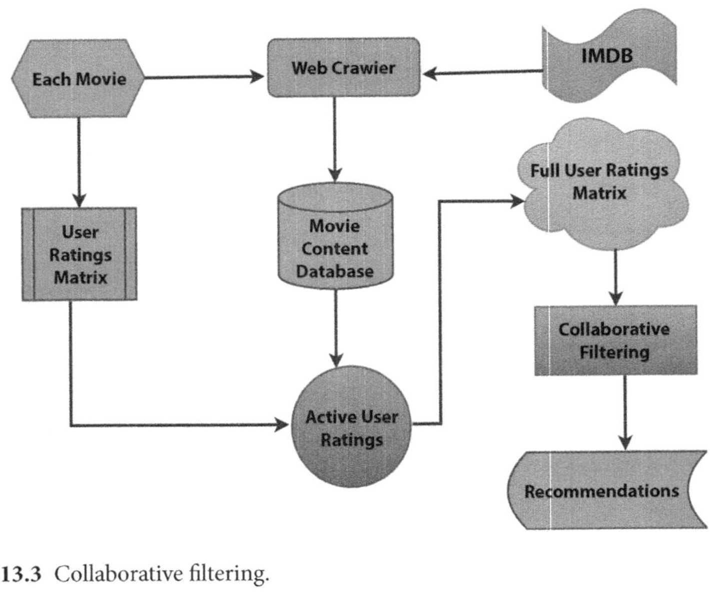

Figure 13.3 Collaborative filtering.

The main issues of data sparsity, scalability, and the "cold start problem" are what CF seeks to address. Collaborative CF introduces three main algorithms: model-based CF, hybrid CF, and memory-based CF [14]. These algorithms take advantage of the capabilities of CF and other recommendation systems to handle a variety of problems. The process of gathering recommendations and estimating sales is sometimes seen as the most essential and fundamental. There exist certain limitations that have led to the exploration of alternative methodologies.

13.1.2.1 HCF-Based Recommender System

To achieve the best results, hybrid recommender systems combine the advantages of collaborative recommendation systems with other recommender methodologies, generally content-based methodology. Implementing a hybrid strategy makes it possible to get around problems like cold start, scalability, and data sparsity. The examples that follow show how collaborative filtering may be used in combination with different recommendation methods. (1) Hybrid recommenders that combine CF with different recommender systems. The use of CF algorithms in conjunction with hybrid recommenders [15, 16]. (2) Hybrid recommenders that incorporate CF and content-based features. (3) The diagram depicted in Figure 13.4 illustrates the operational flow of an HCF recommender system.

The text demonstrates the application of collaborative filtering in generating product recommendations solely relying on the numerical ratings

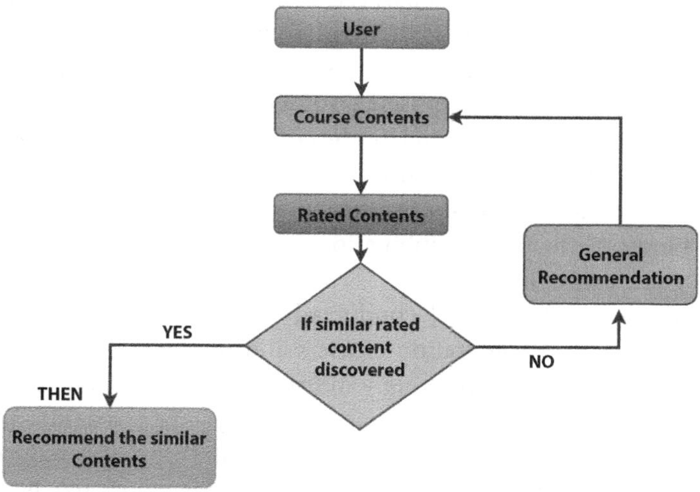

Figure 13.4 HCF-based recommender system.

provided by diverse individuals. The collection and retention of customer feedback in a database for subsequent utilization is a common practice [5].

13.2 Literature Survey

A literature survey was conducted on prior studies in this section. We select articles based on specific keywords such as "sentiment analysis" and "hybrid collaborative algorithms."

According to Kaur *et al.* (2022) [17], the sentimental analysis model is frequently used to examine the subjective nature of a user's content, including their emotions and thoughts. Sentiment analysis, commonly known as "opinion mining," is a kind of data mining that includes closely examining people's emotional outbursts in online forums and reviews. According to empirical observations, websites are the best place to gather client feedback. It is believed that the current approaches, which focus on emotional analysis, are unproductive. Consequently, this study suggests a unique hybrid framework that is built utilizing three classifiers. Such models are exemplified by the classifiers random forest (RF), support vector machine (SVM), and logistic regression (LR). The hybrid model, a powerful classifier, allows for more accurate classification results depending on user input or historical data. When compared to other techniques, the model under examination has performed admirably, as shown by a variety of performance indicators like accuracy, recall, precision, and recall rate.

Hidayat *et al.* (2022) [18] observed that Twitter is a widely used platform for individuals to express their opinions on a variety of subjects. This research aimed to evaluate the public's perception of the recent advancement. The responses were subsequently classified into three categories: affirmative, adverse, or impartial. In the current study, the dispersed model and scattered bag of words are used alongside two unique Doc2Vec models, namely—SVM and logistic regression—as classification strategies. The findings indicate that each combination of model and classifier exhibits an accuracy rate exceeding 75%.

Panchal *et al.* (2022) [19] conducted an analysis indicating that, in recent decades, the proliferation of users and products has rendered recommendation systems increasingly indispensable. Recommendation systems encounter two major challenges, namely—data sparsity and data scalability—which lead to suboptimal time utilization and reduced prediction accuracy. The authors propose a consolidated approach to assess the quality of reviews by integrating sentiment analysis with item-based collaborative filtering. The approach employed in this study involves the utilization of dimensionality reduction techniques to improve the precision of predictions and the effectiveness of recommendations. Additionally, item-based collaborative filtering is employed to evaluate the quality of reviews. The best movies for consumers can be predicted by eliminating irrelevant information and concentrating on traditional and comparable characteristics. The empirical results indicate that the utilization of this approach has a substantial impact on enhancing predictive precision and accelerating execution speed in contrast to traditional content-based filtering techniques. Sentiment analysis can provide valuable insights into the attitudes and opinions of individuals, as demonstrated by its ability to gauge the sentiments of movie audiences towards specific films. The study's findings enhance the efficacy of recommendation systems through the utilization of collaborative filtering and sentiment analysis.

Ghosh *et al.* (2022) [20] explained the use of sentiment analysis on data generated by a big population can be useful in communicating the viewpoint of the general public on product evaluations. Sentiment analysis is the process of examining a written work to ascertain the intended tone or attitude. Sentiment analysis is a term that is occasionally used interchangeably with opinion mining. The statement elucidates how an individual's emotions towards a particular content are recognized and explicated. Social media platforms offer a vast amount of sentiment data that can be extracted from various sources such as product reviews, tweets, blogs, status updates, and posts. The current study introduces a highly precise sentiment analysis approach for examining Yelp restaurant reviews, IMDB movie reviews, and Amazon purchase evaluations. The study's goal is to improve how accurately evaluations are classified as positive or negative. This is accomplished by combining classifiers like logistic regression, decision trees, and support vector machines.

Chopra *et al.* (2022) [21] develop a system that has the potential to cater to a vast audience and offer valuable recommendations for augmenting sales. The study used a novel approach to the dataset of customer reviews by using an enhanced clustering technique, namely—the modified density peak clustering algorithm. The identification of such attacks in the hybrid recommendation system, which combines collaborative filtering and content-based recommendation system, is advised to use an upgraded recurrent neural network technique. The results are evaluated in comparison to other cutting-edge techniques. The suggested strategy is better suitable for electronic commerce platforms with user bases and product inventories that are expanding quickly.

Bhaskaran *et al.* (2021) [22] conducted a study on the creation and assessment of a new personalized hybrid recommender system that utilizes transudative support vector machine-based techniques. The system was designed for implementation on publicly available datasets within the field of machine learning. The establishment of routines by learners has facilitated the acquisition of essential skills. The experimental results indicate that the improved clustering algorithm can recognize clusters of various sizes. When compared to conventional methods, the proposed recommendation systems perform better in terms of important metrics including anticipated absolute error, ranking score, accuracy, recall, and precision. The suggested generalized recommender system has the potential to increase efficiency and efficacy, and the authors have used simulations to demonstrate this.

Wang *et al.* (2021) [23] focused on the issue of information expiration in the context of the classic collaborative filtering approach. The authors suggest a brand-new collaborative filtering method called ITWCF that takes time into account. The authors present the TWCHR, a novel HCF model that integrates user and item-based collaborative filtering procedures utilizing an enhanced K-means clustering approach. The experimental findings imply that the proposed method, which takes into account temporal influence and performs sentiment analysis on recommendations, has the potential to increase the predictive accuracy of the model.

Abbasi *et al.* (2021) [24] introduced a recommendation system in their work, which incorporates user feedback through collaborative filtering. According to these studies, adding sentiment analysis to user evaluations can increase the effectiveness of recommender systems and boost the frequency of customers recommending well-known goods. The aforementioned findings show that e-commerce platforms may use sentiment analysis to analyze unstructured data, which will help with policy-making and provide their customers with fresh ideas. The system's ability to help users make wiser purchasing decisions is another benefit.

Maulana *et al.* (2020) [25] evaluated the assessment of ratings and reviews provided by previous viewers can serve as dependable indicators of the quality of a film. The reviews are categorized based on their polarity, either negative or positive. Despite its remarkable sensitivity to feature selection constraints, the SVM is a widely used data mining algorithm in research due to its success as a text categorization technique. The information gain methodology, when employed as a feature selection mechanism, results in expedited and uniform issue resolution and convergence. The evaluation process utilized two distinct datasets, sourced from Cornell and Stanford, respectively. These datasets were comprised of reviews pertaining to films. The Cornell dataset was subjected to the SVM algorithm, which produced an accuracy of 83.05%. A level of precision of 0.166% has been achieved. The utilization of support vector machine-based information gain has demonstrated enhanced dependability in the analysis of the tone of movie reviews.

Aufar *et al.* (2020) [26] detected that YouTube is among the social networks that exhibit substantial local engagement. The platform known as YouTube has amassed a vast collection of videos and has emerged as a favored destination for product advertisement, experiencing a surge in popularity. The present statement pertains to the public testimonials regarding Nokia's products, which are derived from academic research studies. A study was undertaken to perform sentiment analysis, wherein diverse viewpoints concerning Nokia's products were classified based on their positivity, negativity, or neutrality. This analysis permits the drawing of a conclusion regarding the overall quality of the product. The comments, on the other hand, are predominantly categorized as impartial. The present investigation has partitioned the stages of sentiment analysis into three discrete phases, namely—data collection, data analysis, and conclusion derivation. The final model is evaluated by measuring and comparing accuracy, precision, recall, and F1-score. The analysis of sentiment was conducted using the decision tree and random forest algorithms. When compared to random forest's accuracy of 88.2%, decision tree's accuracy of 89.4% is only slightly higher.

Rehman *et al.* (2019) [27] concluded that the CNN model and the long short-term memory (LSTM) model have demonstrated substantial and effective outcomes in several natural language processing (NLP) applications. The hybrid CNN-LSTM model was proposed as a solution to tackle the challenge in sentiment analysis by combining LSTM with a deep CNN model. The Word2Vec technique is employed to train initial word embeddings. The Word2Vec algorithm transforms a given textual input into a numerical vector representation, which is subsequently utilized to measure the semantic similarity between words and group them based on their contextual meanings. The properties collected from the previous convolution and global max-pooling layers as well as their enduring associations, are incorporated into the proposed model during the embedding step. To increase accuracy, the model under discussion makes use of normalization, dropout approach, and rectified linear unit activation function. The suggested hybrid CNN-LSTM model performs better than the state-of-the-art in deep learning and machine learning, as shown by higher scores in a variety of assessment criteria like recall, precision, accuracy, and F-measure.

Alharbi *et al.* (2019) [28] research showed how important and difficult it has become to comprehend user sentiment on social media platforms like Twitter. The sentiment analysis methodology employed in this context differs from the conventional approach due to various factors, such as the brevity of tweets, the high frequency of orthographic mistakes, the utilization of shorthand expressions, and the existence of unique symbols. The analysis of sentiment in social media is of utmost importance and holds significant relevance across various domains. The majority of algorithms utilized for the analysis of social media sentiment solely take into account the textual content. The present research introduces a neural network framework that considers previous user behaviors within a textual context, specifically a tweet. The present investigation utilized a CNN for analysis. The system's performance was evaluated using two datasets sourced from the SemEval-2016 Workshop. When compared to the present baseline methodology, which consists of naive Bayes and SVM, the suggested model shows improved performance. This is achieved by overcoming the constraints of topic content in the sentiment classification of tweets.

Ramadhani *et al.* (2017) [29] mentioned that social media's widespread and increasing popularity distinguishes it from other services. Data from social network services can be helpful for a wide range of tasks, including but not limited to sentiment analysis and prediction. Due to user-generated tweets, Twitter, a popular social networking service, contains a substantial amount of data. Given the vast amount of data available on Twitter, it presents a promising avenue for research in the field of text mining, particularly concerning the analysis of users' emotional states. The management of a vast amount of unstructured data is a formidable task that necessitates the application of ML techniques. The deep neural network (DNN) architecture, known for its many hidden layers, is used in the specialized area of machine learning known as "deep learning." Empirical findings from deep learning experiments indicate an efficacy rate of approximately 75%.

Preethi *et al.* (2017) [2] analyzed the lack of contextual information in brief messages, such as single lines and reviews on social networking sites, making it difficult to interpret sentiment. The present study introduces a new approach to evaluating sentiment in reviews through the utilization of a deep learning system constructed on recursive neural networks (RNN). This study proposes a sentiment analysis approach, known as RNN-based deep-learning sentiment analysis (RDSA), which utilizes recurrent neural networks to recommend nearby local places based on the user's sentiment. These recommendations are optimized through the utilization of deep learning techniques, which are informed by the outcomes of a sentiment analysis conducted on a diverse range of reviews gathered from multiple

Table 13.1 Summary of the reviewed literature.

Authors	Techniques	Outcomes
Kaur *et al.* (2022) [17]	Hybrid classifier	The present research suggests a novel hybrid framework that comprises three classifiers, namely—SVM, random forest, and logistic regression. The existing approaches have been subjected to comparison based on a range of performance criteria.
Hidayat *et al.* (2022) [18]	Logistic regression	The research was conducted to evaluate the perspective of the general public, categorized into three groups: those in favor, those against, and those with no clear stance. Each combination of model and classifier exhibits an accuracy rate exceeding 75%.
Panchal *et al.* (2022) [19]	Hybrid collaborative filtering	This study presents a unified approach that utilizes dimension reduction in item-based collaborative filtering to improve predictive performance, recommendation efficiency, and sentiment analysis.
Ghosh *et al.* (2022) [20]	Decision tree, logistic regression, and SVM	In this study, reviews were classified into positive or negative categories using classifiers such as decision trees, logistic regression, and SVM, and their respective accuracies were then compared.
Chopra *et al.* (2022) [21]	ARNN	Performance is frequently assessed using metrics including accuracy, precision, recall, F-measure, and false alarm rate. In this particular case, the corresponding values obtained were 98.50%, 98.83%, 98.67%, 1.33%, and 98.66%. Furthermore, it has been ascertained that the proposed algorithm yields superior outcomes in comparison to other available options.

(*Continued*)

Table 13.1 Summary of the reviewed literature. (*Continued*)

Authors	Techniques	Outcomes
Bhaskaran *et al.* (2021) [22]	SVM	The datasets recommended exhibit an accuracy ranging from 82% to 98%. The mean absolute error (MAE) of the simulated datasets varies between 5% and 19.2%.
Wang *et al.* (2021) [23]	ITWCF and TWCHR	The proposed methodology has been verified through two tests, the outcomes of which indicate that the system can efficiently incorporate both temporal progression and sentiment inclination to improve predictive accuracy.
Abbasi *et al.* (2021) [24]	Logistic regression	The findings of the study indicate that combining sentiment analysis of user ratings can improve recommender system effectiveness and quicken the rate of user recommendations for well-liked products.
Maulana *et al.* (2020) [25]	SVM	The study's results indicate that the application of the SVM method to the Cornell dataset resulted in an accuracy rate of 83.05%, which demonstrated a 0.166% increase in accuracy. The effectiveness of sentiment analysis was demonstrated to be higher through the utilization of an SVM-based methodology.
Aufar *et al.* (2020) [26]	Decision tree and random forest	Comparisons are made between the random forest and decision tree classifiers' precision, accuracy, recall, and F-measure scores. The decision tree method outperforms the random forest algorithm in terms of accuracy, showing a level of 89.4%.

(*Continued*)

Table 13.1 Summary of the reviewed literature. (*Continued*)

Authors	Techniques	Outcomes
Rehman *et al.* (2019) [27]	CNN-LSTM	The findings demonstrate that the suggested hybrid CNN-LSTM model outperforms cutting-edge deep learning and machine learning approaches in every parameter taken into account, including F-measure, recall, accuracy, and precision.
Alharbi *et al.* (2019) [28]	CNN	The present research employs a system based on CNN that considers user behavior data within a document, specifically a tweet. The proposed model, which encompasses SVM and naive Bayes outperforms the existing baseline models.
Ramadhani *et al.* (2017) [29]	DNN	This study utilized deep learning to conduct sentiment analysis. Deep learning refers to the use of a deep feed-forward neural network with several hidden layers. The experimental results suggest that the level of precision is approximately 75%.
Preethi *et al.* (2017) [2]	RNN	The results indicate that the implementation of RDSA has a positive impact on behavior by enhancing the precision of sentiment analysis. This improvement subsequently results in more effective user recommendations and aids in the identification of specific attitudes.

social media platforms. Based on the experimental findings, it can be inferred that the utilization of RNN-based RDSA leads to enhanced performance by augmenting the precision of sentiment analysis. This, in turn, facilitates the provision of more efficacious recommendations for the user while simultaneously eliminating any solution that may not be tailored to their specific circumstances.

Table 13.1 presents a summary of the literature reviewed by various authors, including their techniques and corresponding outcomes, which are further elaborated as follows.

13.3 Comparative Result Study

This paper gives a comparative comparison of various sentiment analysis approaches. The comparative analysis of five research is presented in this part. These studies used data from various social media sites, including Amazon, Twitter, Facebook, blogs, and other sources. The investigations concentrated on examining reviews for goods, movies, meals, and other topics. Five different techniques are used in the sentiment analysis process: logistic regression, HCF, decision tree, ANN, SVM, TWCHR, and random forest. The current study also contrasts different approaches based on how well they do sentiment analysis. The study's objectives were to assess the effectiveness of various sentiment analysis methodologies and to pinpoint prospective directions for their development. According to the results shown in Figure 13.5, logistic regression has the lowest level of accuracy, coming in at 75.83%. Decision tree, in contrast, achieves a somewhat greater level of accuracy (78%). Furthermore, SVM shows an accuracy of 83.05%, whereas random forest shows an accuracy of 88.2%, which is the greatest. With a maximum accuracy of 99.2%, the HCF methodology has proven to perform better than earlier techniques in the field of sentiment

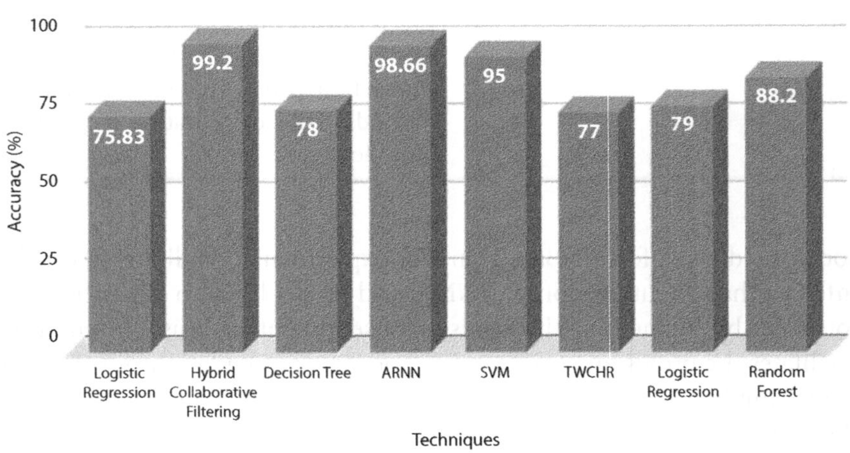

Figure 13.5 Comparison of various sentiment analysis techniques.

Table 13.2 Comparison of the accuracy of various procedures.

Authors	Techniques	Accuracy
Hidayat *et al.* (2022) [18]	Logistic regression	75.83%
Panchal *et al.* (2022) [19]	HCF	99.2%
Ghosh *et al.* (2022) [20]	Decision tree	78%
Chopra *et al.* (2022) [21]	ARNN	98.66%
Bhaskaran *et al.* (2021) [22]	SVM	95%
Wang *et al.* (2021) [23]	TWCHR	77%
Abbasi *et al.* (2021) [24]	Logistic regression	79%
Maulana *et al.* (2020) [25]	SVM	83.05%
Aufar *et al.* (2020) [26]	Random forest	88.2%

analysis. Based on their accuracy, Table 13.2 compares and contrasts the various sentiment analysis methodologies used today.

A visual comparison of the various sentiment analysis approaches is shown in Figure 13.5 above.

13.4 Conclusion and Future Scope

The development of sentiment analysis and opinion-mining techniques in recent years has significantly increased the amount of work being done to improve recommendation systems. Logistic regression, HCF, decision tree, ARRN, SVM, TWCHA, and random forest are a few of the popular models for sentiment analysis. Another finding from the study shows that the commonly used approaches, as previously noted, are typically evaluated independently across different datasets in these studies, without any comparative analysis. Therefore, the current study presents a comparative examination of various sentiment analysis methods used on a dataset made up of data from various social media platforms. In contrast to other approaches including SVM, random forest, HCF, logistic regression, and decision trees, the current study gives a comparative analysis of sentiment analysis using a recommender system that uses collaborative filtering. Additionally, the relative efficiency of each strategy is evaluated about the sentiment analysis. The goal was to compare how well each strategy performed to the others and to find ways to improve the various sentiment analysis methodologies. According to the analysis's results, logistic regression has the lowest accuracy, coming in at 75.83%, compared to decision tree's 78%, SVM's 83.15%, and random forest's 88.2%. HCF has demonstrated outstanding performance in sentiment analysis, outperforming all previous techniques used in this field with a maximum accuracy of 99.2%.

Future studies may look towards hybrid methodologies that combine several models and techniques to improve sentiment classification accuracy beyond the current framework or methods while also requiring less processing power.

References

1. Dang, C.N., Moreno-García, M.N., Prieta, F.D., An approach to integrating sentiment analysis into Recommender Systems. *Sensors*, 21, 16, 5666, 2021, https://doi.org/10.3390/s21165666.
2. Preethi, G., Krishna, P.V., Obaidat, M.S., Saritha, V., Yenduri, S., Application of deep learning to sentiment analysis for Recommender System On Cloud. *2017 International Conference on Computer, Information and Telecommunication Systems (CITS)*, 2017, https://doi.org/10.1109/cits.2017.8035341.
3. Keenan, M.J., Advanced Positioning, Flow, and Sentiment Analysis in Commodity Markets, 2019, https://doi.org/10.1002/9781119603849.
4. Schmidt, S., Zorenböhmer, C., Arifi, D., Resch, B., Polarity-based sentiment analysis of georeferenced tweets related to the 2022 Twitter acquisition. *Information*, 14, 2, 71, 2023, https://doi.org/10.3390/info14020071.
5. Rajendran, D.P. and Sundarraj, R.P., Using topic models with browsing history in hybrid collaborative filtering recommender system: Experiments with user ratings. *Int. J. Inf. Manage. Data Insights*, 1, 2, 100027, 2021, https://doi.org/10.1016/j.jjimei.2021.100027.
6. Kumar, S., Kar, A.K., Ilavarasan, P.V., Applications of text mining in services management: A Systematic Literature Review. *Int. J. Inf. Manage. Data Insights*, 1, 1, 100008, 2021, https://doi.org/10.1016/j.jjimei.2021.100008.
7. Dang, N.C., Moreno-García, M.N., De la Prieta, F., Sentiment analysis based on Deep Learning: A Comparative Study. *Electronics*, 9, 3, 483, 2020, https://doi.org/10.3390/electronics9030483.
8. Salas-Zárate, M., Medina-Moreira, J., Lagos-Ortiz, K., Luna-Aveiga, H., Rodríguez-García, M.A., Valencia-García, R., Sentiment analysis on tweets about diabetes: An aspect-level approach. *Comput. Math. Methods Med.*, 2017, 1–9, 2017, https://doi.org/10.1155/2017/5140631.
9. Zhang, X. and Zheng, X., Comparison of text sentiment analysis based on machine learning. *2016 15th International Symposium on Parallel and Distributed Computing (ISPDC)*, 2016, https://doi.org/10.1109/ispdc.2016.39.

10. Chandra Pandey, A., Singh Rajpoot, D., Saraswat, M., Twitter sentiment analysis using hybrid cuckoo search method. *Inf. Process. Manage.*, 53, 4, 764–779, 2017.
11. Dubey, A., Gupta, A., Raturi, N., Saxena, P., Item-Based Collaborative Filtering Using Sentiment Analysis of User Reviews, in: Deka, G., Kaiwartya, O., Vashisth, P., Rathee, P. (eds) Applications of Computing and Communication Technologies. ICACCT 2018. Communications in Computer and Information Science, vol 899, Springer, Singapore, 2018, https://doi.org/10.1007/978-981-13-2035-4_8
12. Zhang, Y., Incorporating phrase-level sentiment analysis on textual reviews for personalized recommendation. *Proceedings of the Eighth ACM International Conference on Web Search and Data Mining*, 2015, https://doi.org/10.1145/2684822.2697033.
13. Sánchez-Moreno, D., López Batista, V.F., Muñoz Vicente, M.D., Gil González, A.B., Moreno-García, M.N., A session-based song recommendation approach involving user characterization along the play power-law distribution. *Complexity*, 2020, 1–13, 2020, https://doi.org/10.1155/2020/7309453.
14. Kumar, S., De, K., Roy, P.P., Movie recommendation system using sentiment analysis from microblogging data. *IEEE Trans. Comput. Soc. Syst.*, 7, 4, 915–923, 2020, https://doi.org/10.1109/tcss.2020.2993585.
15. Jain, A. and Jain, V., A literature survey on recommendation system based on sentimental analysis. *Adv. Comput. Intell.: An Int. J. (ACII)*, 3, 1, 25–36, 2016, https://doi.org/10.5121/acii.2016.3103.
16. Zhang, Q., Lu, J., Jin, Y., Artificial Intelligence in Recommender Systems. *Complex Intell. Syst.*, 7, 1, 439–457, 2020.
17. Kaur, C., Boush, M.S., Hassen, S.M., Hakami, W.A., Abdalraheem, M.H., Galam, N.M., Hadi, N.A., Hadi, N.A., Benjeed, A.O., Incorporating sentimental analysis into development of a hybrid classification model. *Int. J. Health Sci.*, 6, S1, 1709–1720, 2022, https://doi.org/10.53730/ijhs.v6ns1.4924.
18. Jaya Hidayat, T.H., Ruldeviyani, Y., Aditama, A.R., Madya, G.R., Nugraha, A.W., Adisaputra, M.W., Sentiment analysis of Twitter data related to Rinca Island development using doc2vec and SVM and logistic regression as classifier. *Procedia Comput. Sci.*, 197, 660–667, 2022, https://doi.org/10.1016/j.procs.2021.12.187.
19. Panchal, B.Y., Dave, K., Darji, H., Husain Bohara, M., Talati, B., An effective movie recommendation system using collaborative filtering and user review sentimental analysis. *SSRN*, June 30, 2022, https://doi.org/10.2139/ssrn.4151680.
20. Ghosh, S., Hazra, A., Raj, A., A comparative study of different classification techniques for sentiment analysis, in: *Research Anthology on Implementing Sentiment Analysis Across Multiple Disciplines*, pp. 174–183, 2022, https://doi.org/10.4018/978-1-6684-6303-1.ch009.

21. Chopra, A.B. and Dixit, V.S., An adaptive RNN algorithm to detect shilling attacks for online products in Hybrid Recommender System. *J. Intell. Syst.*, 31, 1, 1133–1149, 2022, https://doi.org/10.1515/jisys-2022-1023.
22. Bhaskaran, S. and Marappan, R., Design and analysis of an efficient machine learning based hybrid recommendation system with enhanced density-based spatial clustering for digital e-learning applications. *Complex Intell. Syst.*, 9, 4, 3517–3533, 2021, https://doi.org/10.1007/s40747-021-00509-4.
23. Wang, X., Dai, Z., Li, H., Yang, J., Research on hybrid collaborative filtering recommendation algorithm based on the time effect and sentiment analysis. *Complexity*, 2021, 1–11, 2021, https://doi.org/10.1155/2021/6635202.
24. Et. al., K.A., A collaborative hybrid recommendation system with sentimental analysis for rumour detection. *Turk. J. Comput. Math. Educ. (TURCOMAT)*, 12, 10, 4814–4821, 2021, https://doi.org/10.17762/turcomat.v12i10.5239.
25. Maulana, R., Rahayuningsih, P.A., Irmayani, W., Saputra, D., Jayanti, W.E., Improved accuracy of sentiment analysis movie review using support Vector Machine based information gain. *J. Phys. Conf. Ser.*, 1641, 1, 012060, 2020, https://doi.org/10.1088/1742-6596/1641/1/012060.
26. Aufar, M., Andreswari, R., Pramesti, D., Sentiment analysis on YouTube social media using decision tree and Random Forest Algorithm: A case study. *2020 International Conference on Data Science and Its Applications (ICoDSA)*, 2020, https://doi.org/10.1109/icodsa50139.2020.9213078.
27. Rehman, A.U., Malik, A.K., Raza, B., Ali, W., A hybrid CNN-LSTM model for improving accuracy of movie reviews sentiment analysis. *Multimedia Tools Appl.*, 78, 18, 26597–26613, 2019, https://doi.org/10.1007/s11042-019-07788-7.
28. Alharbi, A.S. and de Doncker, E., Twitter sentiment analysis with a deep neural network: An enhanced approach using user behavioral information. *Cognit. Syst. Res.*, 54, 50–61, 2019, https://doi.org/10.1016/j.cogsys.2018.10.001.
29. Ramadhani, A.M. and Goo, H.S., Twitter sentiment analysis using Deep Learning Methods. *2017 7th International Annual Engineering Seminar (InAES)*, 2017, https://doi.org/10.1109/inaes.2017.8068556.

14

The Future of Well-Being: AI-Powered Health Management with Privacy at its Core

D. Dhinakaran[1*], S. Edwin Raja[1], J. Jeno Jasmine[2], P. Vimal Kumar[3] and R. Ramani[4]

[1]Department of Computer Science and Engineering, Vel Tech Rangarajan Dr. Sagunthala R&D Institute of Science and Technology, Chennai, India
[2]Department of Computer Science and Engineering, R.M.K. Engineering College, Chennai, India
[3]Department of Computer Science and Engineering, P.S.R.R. College of Engineering, Sivakasi, India
[4]Department of Computer Science and Engineering, P.S.R Engineering College, Sivakasi, India

Abstract
The chapter explores the dynamic realm of AI technologies in wellness management, addressing critical facets such as data privacy, security, fairness in machine learning models, and overall system performance. Commencing with a comprehensive overview of AI's role in personalized wellness, emphasizing the leverage of personal health data, the chapter then navigates the intricate landscape of data privacy. Examining evolving regulations and ethical considerations, the work delves into the consequences of data breaches in healthcare, advocating for robust security measures, including encryption and access controls. Ethical AI and fairness in machine learning within the wellness domain are thoroughly explored, addressing biases, identification techniques, and the crucial role of diverse datasets in fostering equitable outcomes. Navigating the legal landscape, the chapter scrutinizes frameworks related to fairness and non-discrimination, ensuring compliance with data privacy laws such as GDPR. Crucially, the work integrates a detailed performance evaluation, assessing model accuracy, privacy preservation, fairness, and system efficiency. Metrics such as differential privacy parameters,

**Corresponding author*: drdhinakarand@veltech.edu.in

Bharat Bhushan, Akib Khanday, Khursheed Aurangzeb, Sudhir Kumar Sharma and Parma Nand (eds.) Wellness Management Powered by AI Technologies, (363–402) © 2025 Scrivener Publishing LLC

indistinguishability of data contributions, and scalability are rigorously evaluated, ensuring the system's optimal resource utilization and real-time adaptability. The abstract concludes by summarizing key points on data privacy, security, fairness, and performance in AI-driven wellness management. A resounding call to action urges collaboration among practitioners, researchers, and policymakers to forge a responsible, ethical framework, where the well-being of individuals is championed through the conscientious integration of AI technologies, ensuring both efficacy and privacy.

Keywords: Artificial intelligence, machine learning, wellness management, privacy, security, healthcare, federated learning

14.1 Introduction

As we stand at the crossroads of technological innovation and holistic health management, the future unfolds with unprecedented possibilities. In this chapter, we embark on a journey into the heart of "The Future of Well-Being: AI-Powered Health Management With Privacy at Its Core". The dynamic interplay between artificial intelligence (AI) technologies and personalized health data promises a revolutionary approach to wellness, yet this transformation is intricately woven with the ethical imperative of safeguarding individual privacy [1]. The landscape of well-being is undergoing a profound metamorphosis, fueled by the relentless evolution of AI technologies. Within this paradigm shift, AI serves as a beacon, illuminating pathways to proactive, personalized health management. From predictive analytics to machine learning algorithms, these technologies delve into the intricacies of personal health data, offering insights that were once unimaginable. The promise is clear—a future where health interventions are not only precise but tailored to the unique needs of each individual.

Central to this transformative journey is the unwavering commitment to privacy. The title, "The Future of Well-Being: AI-Powered Health Management With Privacy at Its Core," encapsulates the essence of a paradigm that places privacy as a foundational principle. As we harness the power of AI to unlock the potential of personal health data, it becomes imperative to navigate this frontier with a keen awareness of the ethical considerations surrounding data protection. This chapter explores the delicate balance between innovation and safeguarding individual privacy rights, recognizing the profound responsibility that comes with wielding the tools of the future [2]. In the chapters that follow, we will delve deeper into the intricacies of this transformative landscape, exploring the ethical dimensions of data privacy, security protocols, and the quest for fairness in AI models. "The Future of Well-Being" beckons us to a realm where technological advancements not only optimize health outcomes but do so with a profound respect for the privacy and dignity of each individual. This is the promise and challenge of a future where well-being is not just a destination but a journey guided by the ethical principles that underpin our collective commitment to a healthier, more personalized tomorrow.

14.1.1 Challenges in Traditional Wellness Management

As we navigate the complex landscape of wellness management, traditional approaches have long been the cornerstone of health and well-being. However, despite their historical significance, these conventional methods face a myriad of challenges that necessitate a reevaluation of our strategies. In this chapter, we scrutinize the obstacles inherent in traditional wellness management and set the stage for the transformative integration of AI-powered solutions [3]. Traditional wellness management often adopts a one-size-fits-all approach, neglecting the diverse and unique needs of individuals. The challenge lies in tailoring interventions to specific health profiles, considering factors such as genetics, lifestyle, and individual preferences. Conventional methods often underutilize the vast troves of health data available. With limited capacity to process and analyze this information, traditional wellness management misses out on valuable insights that could inform proactive and personalized health strategies.

Traditional approaches tend to be reactive, addressing health concerns after they manifest. This reactive stance can impede the potential for early intervention and preventive measures, which are crucial for comprehensive wellness management [4]. Siloed healthcare systems and fragmented data sources create a barrier to holistic wellness management. The challenge lies in integrating diverse health data streams, including clinical records, lifestyle data, and patient-generated information [5]. Encouraging individuals to actively participate in their well-being is a persistent challenge for traditional models. Maintaining long-term engagement and motivation requires innovative strategies beyond conventional wellness programs. Traditional wellness management can be resource-intensive and inefficient. Limited resources may hinder the scalability of wellness programs, making it challenging to reach broader populations effectively [6–8]. In the subsequent sections of this chapter, we will explore how the infusion of AI technologies addresses these challenges, ushering in a new era of wellness management that is personalized, data-driven, and poised to overcome the limitations of traditional approaches. The convergence of technology and health sciences offers a promising path forward, redefining how we perceive, manage, and cultivate well-being in the modern age.

14.1.2 AI Accelerators: A Game-Changer

As we delve into the transformative landscape of data-driven wellness management, one technological powerhouse emerges as a game-changer—AI accelerators. This section explores the pivotal role played by AI accelerators in amplifying the capabilities of artificial intelligence (AI) technologies, revolutionizing the processing power and efficiency of algorithms that underpin wellness management strategies.

Enhancing Computational Efficiency

AI accelerators, specialized hardware designed for the rapid execution of AI algorithms, have redefined the computational landscape. In the context of wellness management, these accelerators significantly enhance the speed and efficiency of data processing [9–11]. This acceleration translates to quicker insights drawn from vast datasets, fostering a more responsive and dynamic approach to personalized health recommendations.

Optimizing Machine Learning Models

The intricate algorithms powering machine learning models are resource-intensive. AI accelerators optimize these models by offloading and accelerating specific computations, ensuring that wellness management algorithms operate seamlessly even with complex tasks such as image recognition, natural language processing, and predictive analytics [12]. The result is a more streamlined and powerful AI engine driving personalized interventions.

Enabling Real-Time Analytics

Wellness management demands real-time insights to inform timely interventions. AI accelerators play a pivotal role in enabling real-time analytics by rapidly processing incoming data streams [13]. This capability is particularly critical in scenarios where immediate responses are required, such as monitoring vital signs or detecting anomalies in health patterns.

Scalability for Population Health Management

The scalability of AI accelerators is a cornerstone for effective population health management [14]. Whether handling data for individuals or entire communities, these accelerators ensure that wellness management solutions can scale seamlessly to accommodate diverse and extensive datasets, supporting healthcare practitioners in their mission to enhance public health outcomes.

Energy Efficiency and Sustainability
AI accelerators contribute to the development of energy-efficient AI solutions. By optimizing computational processes, they reduce the overall energy consumption associated with AI-powered wellness management [15]. This not only aligns with sustainability goals but also positions AI as a responsible and eco-friendly technology in the healthcare sector.

14.1.3 The Privacy Revolution of Federated Learning

Figure 14.1 shows a system for sharing personal health information (PHI) using federated learning, a machine learning technique that allows multiple devices to train a shared model without sharing their data. This is useful for healthcare applications, where it is important to protect patient privacy.

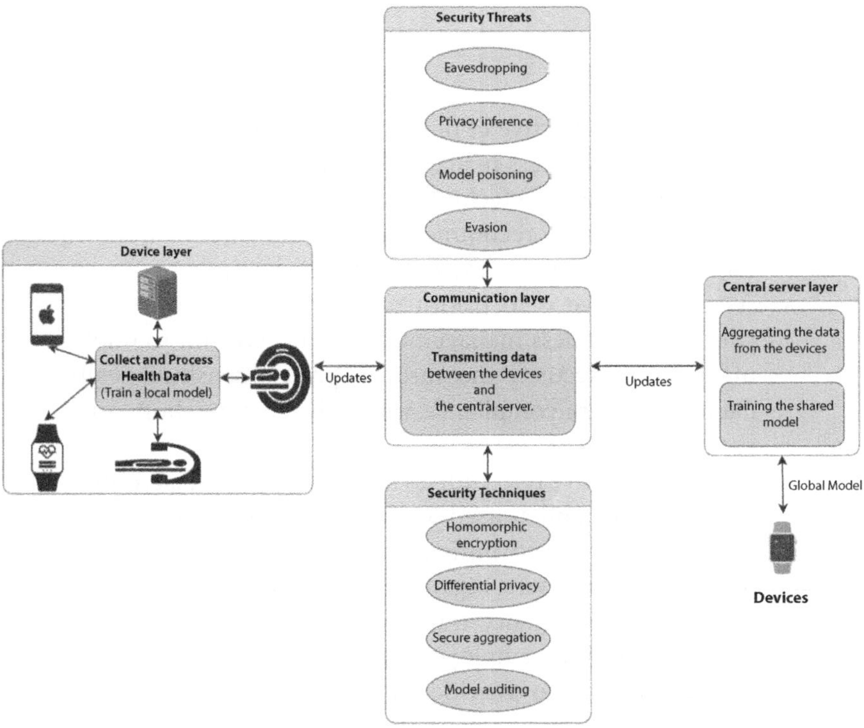

Figure 14.1 Structure of the privacy revolution of federated learning.

Figure 14.1 illustrates three primary layers within the federated learning process. The device layer encompasses devices utilized for health data collection and processing, spanning smartphones, wearables, and medical devices. The communication layer facilitates data transmission between these devices and the central server, situated in the central server layer. Here data aggregation from devices occurs, along with the training of a shared model. The federated learning process unfolds as follows: Devices collect health data, train local models individually, transmit model updates to the central server, which aggregates them to train a global model, subsequently shared back to devices for prediction purposes. Alongside this process, Figure 14.1 identifies several security threats, including eavesdropping, privacy inference, model poisoning, and evasion. To counteract these threats, various security techniques are employed. Homomorphic encryption enables local model training on encrypted data, thwarting eavesdropping and privacy inference. Differential privacy safeguards user privacy during local model training. Secure aggregation techniques prevent model poisoning by aggregating device updates securely. Additionally, model auditing techniques are utilized to detect and address malicious models, fortifying the integrity of the federated learning system.

14.1.4 Objectives

- The primary objective of our work is to design and develop an advanced wellness management system leveraging artificial intelligence (AI) technologies. This system aims to provide personalized recommendations and interventions to individuals to improve their overall well-being.
- A key objective is to prioritize data privacy and security within the wellness management system. We aim to implement robust security measures to protect sensitive health data and ensure compliance with privacy regulations such as GDPR.
- Another objective is to address fairness and non-discrimination in the AI models used within the wellness management system. We strive to mitigate biases and ensure equitable outcomes for all users, regardless of demographic factors.
- Our goal is to enhance transparency and explainability in the AI algorithms employed by the wellness management system. We aim to provide clear explanations for AI recommendations and interventions to build user trust and understanding.

- We seek to conduct a comprehensive performance evaluation of the wellness management system. This evaluation will assess metrics such as model accuracy, privacy preservation, fairness, and system efficiency to validate the effectiveness of our approach.
- Lastly, we aim to identify future directions for research and development in AI-powered wellness management. By highlighting areas for improvement and innovation, we strive to contribute to the ongoing advancement of the field.

14.1.5 Contributions

- Our chapter introduces a comprehensive framework for AI-powered wellness management that prioritizes data privacy, security, fairness, and transparency. This framework integrates cutting-edge AI technologies with ethical considerations, setting a new standard for responsible implementation of AI in healthcare.
- One of the key contributions of our work is the integration of privacy-preserving techniques such as federated learning and differential privacy. By implementing these techniques, we ensure that individual privacy is upheld while still deriving valuable insights from collective health data—a novel approach in the field of wellness management.
- We place a strong emphasis on fairness and non-discrimination in our AI models, addressing biases and implementing interventions to mitigate them. This proactive stance towards fairness ensures that our wellness management system delivers equitable recommendations and interventions for all users, regardless of demographic factors.
- Our chapter highlights the importance of transparency and explainability in AI algorithms, especially in the context of healthcare. By prioritizing clear explanations for AI recommendations and interventions, we enhance user trust and understanding—a significant contribution to the ethical deployment of AI in wellness management.
- We conduct a detailed performance evaluation of our wellness management system, assessing metrics such as model accuracy, privacy preservation, fairness, and system efficiency. This comprehensive evaluation not only validates

the effectiveness of our approach but also sets the stage for future research and development in the field.

In this chapter, we present a novel approach to wellness management empowered by AI technologies, with several significant contributions to the field. Firstly, we introduce a comprehensive framework that integrates cutting-edge technologies such as secure data access with federated identity and blockchain-powered data sharing, ensuring enhanced privacy and security in healthcare data management. Secondly, our work emphasizes the importance of personalized care through AI-powered analytics, leveraging machine learning algorithms to provide tailored recommendations and interventions for individuals. Additionally, we propose innovative techniques for privacy-preserving AI through federated learning, addressing concerns regarding data privacy while harnessing the collective intelligence of distributed devices. By highlighting these contributions, we aim to advance the understanding and implementation of AI-driven wellness management, paving the way for improved healthcare outcomes and patient experiences.

In the subsequent sections, we provide a detailed exploration of wellness management powered by AI technologies. We begin by reviewing related works in the field to establish a comprehensive understanding of existing methodologies and solutions. Following this, we introduce our proposed framework, which consists of several key components: secure data access with federated identity, blockchain-powered data sharing, revolutionizing patient data management, AI-powered analytics for personalized care, and privacy-preserving AI through federated learning. Subsequently, we conduct a thorough performance evaluation, assessing various metrics such as model accuracy and privacy preservation. In the conclusion and future work section, we reflect on the implications of our findings and outline potential avenues for further research. Through this structured approach, we aim to provide readers with a holistic view of the complexities and advancements in AI-driven wellness management, facilitating a deeper understanding of the subject matter.

14.2 Related Works

In the ever-evolving landscape of healthcare data management, a critical challenge pertains to ensuring robust security and privacy, especially within the Industrial Internet of Things in Healthcare (IIoTH) systems. The conventional abundance of medical data is often hindered by ethical

Table 14.1 Key contributions and limitations of existing privacy schemes.

Authors and references	Summary	Key contributions	Limitations
Faris *et al.* [16]	Introduced the EPPDA framework for secure data aggregation in IoT-based healthcare applications. Prioritizes data privacy and security using additive homomorphic encryption and homomorphic message authentication code (MAC).	Novel secure data aggregation framework with robust verification and authorization, employing homomorphic encryption for enhanced privacy and security.	Limited scalability due to computational overhead associated with homomorphic encryption, potentially restricting its deployment in resource-constrained IoT healthcare environments.
Shrestha *et al.* [17]	Presented a secured e-health framework focusing on patient-centric security measures. Utilizes enhanced encryption, digital signatures, and patient pseudo-identity for heightened security.	Novel framework emphasizing patient-centric security measures, integrating enhanced encryption and authentication methods	Lack of real-world deployment and validation may undermine the practical effectiveness of the proposed framework in diverse healthcare settings.
Sivanarayani *et al.* [18]	Conducted an examination of security and privacy challenges in IoT within the healthcare system, advocating for comprehensive security solutions.	Review of existing security challenges in IoT healthcare systems, emphasizing the need for comprehensive security solutions.	Limited practical guidance on implementing proposed security solutions, potentially hindering their adoption in real-world IoT healthcare environments.

(*Continued*)

Table 14.1 Key contributions and limitations of existing privacy schemes. (*Continued*)

Authors and references	Summary	Key contributions	Limitations
Abdulmohsen *et al.* [19]	Assessed the feasibility of using AI for enhancing security and privacy services in healthcare, aiming for a cost-effective healthcare system.	Study assessing AI capabilities for enhancing security and privacy in healthcare, focusing on cost-effectiveness and feasibility.	Generalizability of findings may be limited due to the narrow focus on Saudi hospitals, potentially overlooking unique challenges faced by healthcare systems in other regions.
Sudhakar *et al.* [20]	Introduced a DoS detection system using machine learning algorithms, focusing on network security in healthcare.	Novel DoS detection system employing machine learning algorithms for network security in healthcare.	Reliance on historical data and static features may limit the system's ability to detect emerging DoS attack patterns, potentially leading to false negatives in real-world scenarios.
Cheng *et al.* [21]	Developed an enhanced symmetric homomorphic cryptosystem and fog-based communication architecture for secure medical data analysis at fog servers.	Innovative approach for secure medical data analysis at fog servers, enabling real-time decision-making in healthcare.	Lack of consideration for network latency and bandwidth constraints in fog-based communication architecture may affect real-time performance and scalability in resource-constrained healthcare environments.

(*Continued*)

Table 14.1 Key contributions and limitations of existing privacy schemes. (*Continued*)

Authors and references	**Summary**	**Key contributions**	**Limitations**
Philippe *et al.* [22]	Highlighted ethical concerns in utilizing social media data in public health, emphasizing the need for evolving ethical frameworks.	Discussion on ethical challenges in using social media data for public health, advocating for evolving ethical frameworks.	Limited practical guidance on implementing proposed ethical frameworks, potentially leading to ambiguity in decision-making processes regarding the use of social media data in public health initiatives.
Andrei *et al.* [23]	Explored challenges and advancements in AI-based solutions for routine cardiovascular disease management, focusing on data accessibility and interpretability.	Examination of challenges and advancements in AI-based cardiovascular disease management, emphasizing the importance of data accessibility and interpretability.	Lack of consideration for potential biases in AI algorithms may lead to skewed clinical decision-making and undermine patient outcomes, warranting further investigation into algorithmic fairness and interpretability.
Yaru *et al.* [24]	Introduced a privacy-preserving DSSE scheme for IIoTH in healthcare, offering fine-grained search functionality over encrypted PHR file databases.	Novel DSSE scheme tailored for IIoTH in healthcare, enabling secure search functionality over encrypted PHR files databases.	Limited evaluation of the proposed DSSE scheme's performance in real-world IIoTH healthcare environments may obscure its scalability and effectiveness in handling large-scale datasets and dynamic search queries.

considerations, making access and transfer difficult. Moreover, the adoption of artificial intelligence (AI) in routine cardiovascular disease management encounters obstacles such as limited data accessibility and the imperative need for algorithmic explainability. These challenges compromise the effectiveness of AI algorithms, potentially leading to biased results and hindering their widespread integration into healthcare practices. The quest for solutions includes recent advancements that address data privacy concerns through innovative schemes like privacy-preserving dynamic searchable symmetric encryption (DSSE). Such schemes not only fortify data integrity against malicious attacks but also introduce features like fine-grained search capabilities over encrypted databases, reducing communication costs and minimizing the risk of privacy breaches. As the healthcare industry navigates these challenges, ongoing research and development are crucial to establish ethical frameworks and robust solutions that align with the ever-changing technological landscape.

Table 14.1 represents the key contributions and limitations of existing privacy schemes. In comparison to existing works focusing on various aspects of healthcare data security, privacy, and AI-driven solutions, our proposed AI-powered wellness management system offers a comprehensive and integrated approach [25]. While previous studies often concentrate on specific facets such as secure data aggregation, patient-centric security measures, or privacy-preserving techniques, our work stands out for its holistic integration of these elements within a unified framework. Unlike singular-focused approaches, our system leverages advanced AI algorithms for personalized wellness management while ensuring stringent data security and privacy through techniques like federated learning and differential privacy. Furthermore, our system emphasizes real-time adaptability and scalability, essential for dynamic healthcare environments, setting it apart from works that primarily address network security or communication architectures. Moreover, our work places a significant emphasis on ethical considerations, transparency, and fairness in AI-driven recommendations, aligning with emerging trends in responsible AI deployment in healthcare. Overall, our proposed system represents a pioneering effort to address the multifaceted challenges of AI-powered wellness management, offering a comprehensive solution that integrates cutting-edge technologies while prioritizing privacy, security, and ethical considerations.

14.3 Proposed Work

14.3.1 Secure Data Access with Federated Identity

In the landscape of modern healthcare, the traditional methods of accessing patient information have often been cumbersome, plagued by the need for multiple login credentials and concerns over data security. The concept of secure data access with federated identity emerges as a beacon of change, envisioning a more user-friendly and secure method for patients to engage with healthcare services as shown in Figure 14.2. At its core, the concept seeks to simplify the patient experience by providing a unified authentication method across various healthcare providers. Instead of managing an array of usernames and passwords, patients can seamlessly log in using federated identity providers. This not only streamlines the login process but also reduces the friction associated with accessing healthcare services, contributing to a more positive patient experience.

Federated Identity and User-Centric Authentication

Federated identity introduces a federated authentication system where patients use a single set of credentials across different healthcare services.

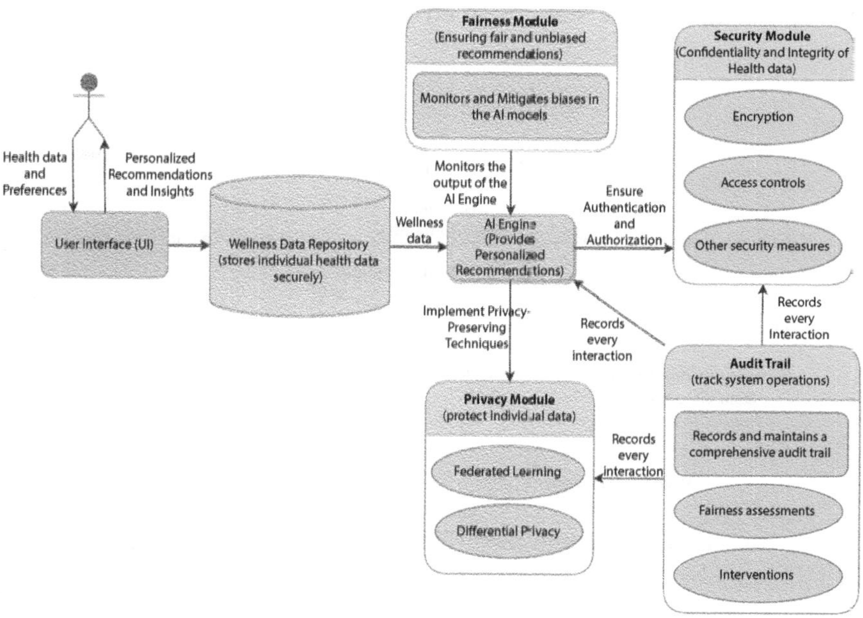

Figure 14.2 Architecture of proposed AI-powered health management with privacy.

This innovative approach aims to create a unified gateway, allowing patients to traverse their healthcare journey seamlessly. The incorporation of biometric authentication, such as fingerprint or facial recognition, adds an extra layer of security. This not only aligns with contemporary practices but also enhances the user experience by offering a convenient and secure means of identity verification [26]. To further elevate the security and individualization of the authentication process, the introduction of adaptive biometric authentication is proposed. This dynamic approach adjusts security protocols based on contextual factors, enhancing accuracy and context-aware security.

Biometric authentication has emerged as a cornerstone in fortifying digital security, leveraging unique physical or behavioral attributes for user identification. The concept of adaptive biometric authentication takes this a step further, introducing a dynamic and context-aware approach to the authentication process. This innovative method adjusts security protocols based on contextual factors, thereby enhancing accuracy and responsiveness to the ever-changing dynamics of user interactions.

Understanding Adaptive Biometric Authentication

Adaptive biometric authentication recognizes that the efficacy of traditional authentication methods can be enhanced by acknowledging the varying conditions and contexts in which users interact with systems as shown in Figure 14.3. Unlike static biometric systems, adaptive authentication

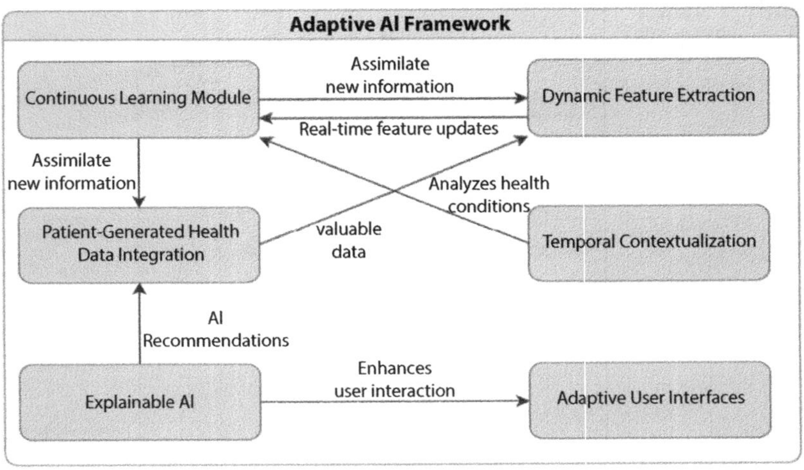

Figure 14.3 Adaptive AI framework.

considers factors such as user behavior, environmental conditions, and the risk level of the transaction at hand.

Dynamic Adjustment of Security Protocols

The adaptive nature of this authentication method allows for real-time adjustments to security protocols. For instance, during a routine login from a familiar device and location, the security parameters may be relaxed, facilitating a seamless and user-friendly experience. However, if the system detects anomalies, such as an unfamiliar device or atypical user behavior, it can dynamically elevate security measures to ensure a robust defense against potential threats.

Contextual Factors in Adaptive Authentication

Adaptive biometric authentication considers a spectrum of contextual factors to refine its identification process. Some key contextual elements include the following:

Location: Geographical information, such as the user's location, can be factored into the authentication decision. An unexpected change in location might trigger additional security measures.
Device information: The characteristics of the device used for authentication, such as its type, model, and security features, contribute to the overall context.
Time of day: Authentication attempts occurring at unusual times might prompt the system to apply heightened security measures.
Behavioral biometrics: User behavior, including typing patterns, mouse movements, or touchscreen interactions, serves as a unique identifier. Adaptive authentication assesses deviations from established behavior patterns.

Enhancing Accuracy and Security

The primary objective of adaptive biometric authentication is to enhance the accuracy of user identification while maintaining a user-friendly experience. By considering contextual factors, the system can dynamically balance the trade-off between security and convenience. This adaptability minimizes false positives, where legitimate users might be incorrectly denied access, and false negatives, where unauthorized users might gain access.

Continuous Learning and Improvement

Adaptive authentication systems often incorporate machine learning algorithms that continuously learn from user interactions. Over time, the system refines its understanding of normal user behavior, adapting to evolving patterns and minimizing the impact of potential threats. This continuous learning aspect contributes to the system's ability to stay ahead of emerging security challenges.

User Transparency and Consent

To uphold principles of user privacy and transparency, systems employing adaptive biometric authentication should prioritize clear communication with users. Providing insights into the contextual factors considered and obtaining user consent ensures a collaborative and ethical approach to authentication.

Enhanced Security Measures

In a landscape where cybersecurity threats loom large, ensuring the security of patient information is paramount. The concept of federated identity mitigates security risks by eliminating the need for multiple passwords, reducing the attack surface for credential-based attacks. The inclusion of biometric authentication, known for its robustness, fortifies the security perimeter, ensuring that only authorized individuals access sensitive health data. To further bolster security, the incorporation of multi-factor biometric authentication, combining multiple biometric modalities, adds an additional layer of resilience against unauthorized access attempts. This advanced approach aligns with the evolving standards of robust user authentication.

User Empowerment and Privacy Assurance

Beyond simplifying access and enhancing security, federated identity empowers patients by placing control over their identity squarely in their hands. Patients gain the ability to manage and control their identity across various healthcare services, fostering a sense of ownership and privacy as shown in Figure 14.4. The seamless and secure nature of access mechanisms ensures that patients can engage with their health data confidently, contributing to a more informed and proactive healthcare journey. The concept introduces a user-driven consent management system, allowing patients to dynamically control the access permissions of their health information. This not only enhances user empowerment but also aligns with evolving standards of data privacy and patient-centric care.

The user-driven consent management system represents a pioneering approach to data privacy in healthcare, placing control firmly in the hands of the patients themselves. At its core, this concept aims to empower individuals by providing them with a dynamic and participatory role in determining who can access their health information and under what circumstances. Unlike traditional models where consent is often a static

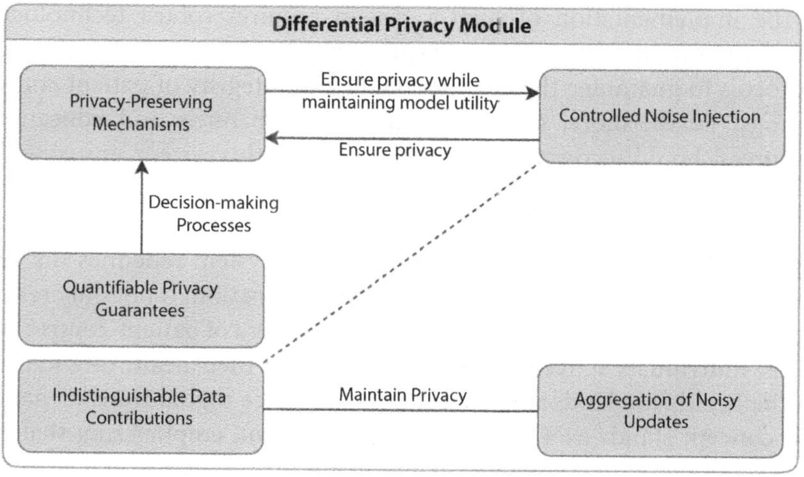

Figure 14.4 Differential privacy framework.

and one-time agreement, the user-driven consent management system embraces the evolving nature of healthcare interactions and the increasing importance of user agency in the digital age [27]. This innovative system allows patients to dynamically control access permissions, enabling them to grant or revoke consent based on their changing preferences and needs. Patients, through an intuitive and user-friendly interface, can easily navigate and customize the level of access granted to healthcare providers, researchers, or any other relevant entities. For instance, a patient might choose to grant broad access for routine check-ups while restricting access to more sensitive information or specific aspects of their medical history.

One of the key strengths of the user-driven consent management system lies in its adaptability to the nuanced and dynamic nature of healthcare relationships. Patients may modify their consent preferences in response to changes in their health status, shifts in care providers, or evolving privacy concerns. This adaptability ensures that individuals retain control over their personal health data throughout the continuum of care, fostering a sense of ownership and autonomy. Moreover, this concept aligns seamlessly with the evolving standards of data privacy and patient-centric care. In an era where privacy breaches and data misuse are growing concerns, the user-driven consent management system sets a precedent for transparent and collaborative data governance. Patients are not merely passive subjects; they become active participants in the management of their health information, contributing to a culture of trust and accountability within the healthcare ecosystem.

The implementation of such a system requires robust technological infrastructure, incorporating encryption mechanisms and secure storage protocols to guarantee the confidentiality and integrity of patient consent settings. Furthermore, clear communication channels and educational resources should accompany the introduction of this system, ensuring that patients are well-informed about their rights, the implications of their consent choices, and the protective measures in place to secure their data. In essence, the user-driven consent management system redefines the relationship between patients and their health information. It not only reflects a commitment to privacy but also heralds a new era of patient-centric care, where individuals actively shape the contours of their healthcare journey. As the healthcare landscape continues to embrace digital transformation, this concept stands as a beacon of empowerment, emphasizing that privacy is not merely a compliance requirement but a fundamental right that patients can exercise and control.

14.3.2 Blockchain-Powered Data Sharing: Revolutionizing Patient Data Management

In the realm of healthcare, the management and sharing of patient data have historically been encumbered by challenges related to security, transparency, and patient control as shown in Figure 14.5. The introduction of blockchain technology emerges as a groundbreaking solution, promising

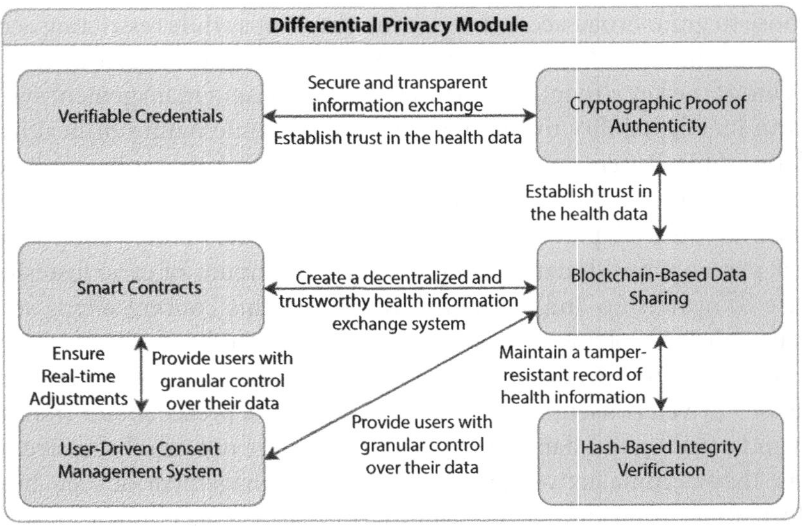

Figure 14.5 Verifiable credentials and blockchain integration.

to give patients greater control over their health information while ensuring transparency and security in data sharing practices.

Empowering Patients with Control

Blockchain technology, renowned for its decentralized and transparent nature, redefines the dynamics of data sharing in healthcare. The primary goal is to empower patients with greater control over their health data. Patients can now own, manage, and selectively share their medical records using a secure, distributed ledger. This shift in control aligns with the principles of patient autonomy and plays a pivotal role in reshaping the patient-provider relationship.

Secure and Transparent Data Storage

Storing medical records on a blockchain offers a secure and transparent alternative to traditional centralized databases. The decentralized nature of the blockchain ensures that patient data is not stored in a single location, reducing the risk of unauthorized access or tampering. Each transaction (data entry or access) is recorded in a tamper-resistant manner, contributing to a transparent and traceable data history. To enhance transparency, the concept introduces the use of verifiable credentials on the blockchain. Patients can cryptographically prove the authenticity of their health information, fostering trust among healthcare providers and facilitating seamless data sharing [28]. The utilization of verifiable credentials on the blockchain, coupled with cryptographic proof of authenticity, represents a revolutionary paradigm in securing and sharing health information. This concept leverages the inherent characteristics of blockchain technology to provide a tamper-resistant and transparent ledger while employing cryptographic techniques to ensure the validity and authenticity of the shared credentials.

Verifiable Credentials on the Blockchain

In this context, verifiable credentials refer to digital statements that attest to the truth of a particular claim, such as a patient's medical history, treatment records, or vaccination status. These credentials are stored on a blockchain, a decentralized and immutable ledger, ensuring that once information is added, it cannot be altered or tampered with. The blockchain acts as a single source of truth, fostering trust among healthcare providers and other relevant entities.

Cryptographic Proof of Authenticity

Cryptographic proof is a fundamental element in ensuring the authenticity of the credentials stored on the blockchain. Each verifiable credential is cryptographically signed by the issuing entity (e.g., a healthcare provider) using public-key cryptography. This signature serves as a digital seal of authenticity, attesting that the information contained in the credential has been verified and approved by the issuing authority.

Ensuring Data Integrity

To further enhance security, cryptographic hash functions are employed. A cryptographic hash is a one-way function that converts data into a fixed-size string of characters, often represented as a hash value or digest. When a verifiable credential is issued or updated, a hash of the credential's content is generated and stored on the blockchain. Any alteration to the credential would result in a different hash value, immediately signaling potential tampering. Introducing homomorphic hashing as a novel approach. This advanced cryptographic technique allows computations to be performed on encrypted data without the need for decryption. Applied to verifiable credentials, it enhances privacy by ensuring that the credential's content remains confidential even during the validation process, while still allowing for hash-based integrity verification.

Decentralized Trust and Transparency

By storing verifiable credentials on a blockchain, trust is decentralized and distributed across the network. No single entity has control over the entire dataset, mitigating the risks associated with centralized repositories. This decentralized nature ensures transparency, as any participant in the network can independently verify the authenticity of a credential by validating the cryptographic signatures and hash values.

Interoperability and Seamless Data Sharing

Verifiable credentials on the blockchain provide a standardized and interoperable format for data sharing. Healthcare providers, researchers, and other authorized entities can easily verify the authenticity of a patient's credentials, fostering seamless and secure data exchange [29]. This interoperability is particularly crucial in the healthcare ecosystem, where diverse systems and stakeholders collaborate to deliver comprehensive and coordinated care.

Smart Contracts for Automated Data Access

The mention of smart contracts, self-executing agreements built on the blockchain, introduces a layer of automation to data access. Patients can define access preferences and conditions using smart contracts, enabling automated and secure data sharing based on predefined rules. This aligns with the principles of patient-centric data control, as patients dictate who can access their data and under what circumstances. The proposal includes the integration of dynamic smart contracts that adapt to changing patient preferences. For instance, if a patient revises their data sharing preferences, the smart contract dynamically adjusts to reflect these changes, ensuring real-time adherence to the patient's evolving wishes. The integration of dynamic smart contracts in healthcare represents an innovative approach to automate and adapt data sharing agreements based on the evolving preferences of patients. Smart contracts are self-executing contracts with the terms of the agreement directly written into code. In the healthcare context, dynamic smart contracts introduce flexibility and responsiveness, enabling real-time adjustments to data sharing permissions in accordance with a patient's changing preferences.

Traditional contracts often require manual intervention for updates or modifications. Smart contracts, on the other hand, are coded with predefined rules and conditions. Once these conditions are met, the contract executes automatically without the need for intermediaries. In healthcare, this translates to a more efficient and streamlined process for managing data sharing preferences [30]. The innovation lies in the dynamic nature of these smart contracts. Unlike static contracts that remain unchanged until explicitly modified, dynamic smart contracts are designed to adapt to changing circumstances, especially in response to a patient's evolving preferences. For example, if a patient decides to restrict access to certain health information or share additional data with a new healthcare provider, the smart contract can be updated in real time to reflect these changes.

When a patient revises their data sharing preferences, the dynamic smart contract responds immediately. The contract's code is designed to assess and incorporate these changes, ensuring that the updated preferences are applied instantly. This real-time adherence is crucial in healthcare scenarios where timely access to accurate and comprehensive patient data is paramount for delivering effective and personalized care. The integration of dynamic smart contracts aligns with the broader goal of patient-centric care. Patients are empowered to have granular control over who accesses their health information and under what circumstances. This transparency and control contribute to a sense of ownership and trust in the healthcare system, fostering a more collaborative and patient-driven approach to data sharing. From an administrative standpoint, the automation introduced by dynamic smart contracts streamlines the management of consent and data sharing processes. It reduces the need for manual interventions, mitigates the risk of errors, and ensures that the system operates in sync with the most up-to-date patient preferences. The blockchain, often used as the underlying technology for smart contracts, ensures an immutable record of all changes to the contract. This transparency and tamper-resistant nature enhance the auditability of consent changes, providing a verifiable trail of how and when a patient's data sharing preferences were updated.

Enhanced Data Interoperability

Blockchain technology fosters interoperability by providing a standardized and secure framework for data sharing among different healthcare entities. This ensures that disparate systems can seamlessly communicate and share information, promoting a more holistic view of a patient's health across various healthcare providers. To further enhance interoperability, the concept introduces a universal patient identifier on the blockchain. This decentralized identifier ensures a standardized and secure means of identifying patients across different healthcare ecosystems, overcoming the challenges associated with traditional identification methods.

14.3.3 AI-Powered Analytics for Personalized Care

In the evolving landscape of healthcare, the convergence of artificial intelligence (AI) and data analytics stands as a beacon of innovation. The vision of AI-powered analytics for personalized care is a testament to the transformative potential of technology in tailoring healthcare interventions to the unique needs of individuals. This paradigm shift not only aligns with the broader trend of precision medicine but also underscores a commitment to patient privacy through encrypted AI analysis. At the core of this vision lies the application of AI algorithms to analyse health data, paving the way for personalized insights and recommendations. Imagine a healthcare landscape where AI, armed with sophisticated algorithms, dissects intricate patterns and trends within a patient's health data [8]. This level of precision holds the key to unlocking a new era of healthcare—one where interventions are not only tailored but are rooted in a profound understanding of individual health profiles.

The crux of AI-powered analytics is its ability to discern subtle nuances in individual health records. By understanding genetic predispositions, lifestyle factors, and historical health data, AI algorithms can recommend interventions that are not only effective but precisely aligned with an individual's unique medical history. This tailoring of interventions has the potential to optimize health outcomes and redefine the efficacy of healthcare strategies. Introducing an adaptive AI framework that continuously learns and evolves alongside the patient's health journey. This adaptability ensures that AI recommendations dynamically adjust to changing health conditions, further personalizing the care experience. The adaptive AI framework proposed here is not just a conventional machine learning system; it represents a paradigm shift in healthcare technology. This innovative framework transcends static models, introducing a novel approach that continuously learns and evolves alongside the patient's health journey. This adaptive nature is underpinned by a comprehensive and dynamic framework designed to enhance the personalization of care experiences.

At the core of the adaptive AI framework is a sophisticated continuous learning architecture. Traditional models are often static, trained on fixed datasets and parameters. In contrast, our proposed framework integrates advanced machine learning algorithms that are capable of assimilating new data in real-time. This continuous learning ensures that the AI system stays abreast of the latest health information, allowing it to dynamically adjust recommendations based on the most recent and relevant data points. One of the novel aspects of this framework is its ability to dynamically extract features from diverse data sources. Instead of relying solely on structured data, the adaptive AI framework intelligently incorporates information from unstructured sources such as medical literature, patient narratives, and emerging research. This dynamic feature extraction enhances the depth and breadth of insights, providing a more holistic understanding of the patient's health status.

A key innovation lies in the seamless integration of patient-generated health data (PGHD) into the learning process. Wearables, mobile apps, and other connected devices generate a wealth of real-time health information. Our framework adapts to incorporate this PGHD, leveraging it to refine recommendations and ensure a patient-centric approach. For instance, if a patient's activity levels change, the AI dynamically adjusts its suggestions to align with the evolving lifestyle. Understanding health conditions in a temporal context is crucial. The adaptive AI framework incorporates a temporal element, recognizing that health is a journey with evolving dynamics. Time-series analysis and temporal contextualization enable the system to discern patterns, trends, and fluctuations in health parameters. This temporal awareness ensures that recommendations are not only based on current conditions but also anticipate potential changes in the future. Introducing a predictive temporal modeling module that forecasts potential health developments based on historical data patterns. This forward-looking component enhances the adaptability of the framework by proactively addressing emerging health considerations.

To foster patient engagement and trust, the adaptive AI framework incorporates explainable AI. Patients are not only presented with recommendations but also provided with clear explanations of the underlying rationale [12]. This transparency ensures that patients understand how the AI arrived at specific suggestions, promoting a collaborative relationship between the AI system and the individual. Recognizing the diversity in user preferences and health literacy, the framework introduces adaptive user interfaces. The presentation of information is tailored to the individual's preferred format, ensuring that recommendations are not only personalized in content but also in the way they are communicated, fostering optimal understanding and adherence. The framework introduces a dynamic risk stratification module that continually assesses and reassesses the patient's risk profile. As health conditions evolve, the system adapts its risk assessments, enabling more nuanced and personalized interventions. This real-time risk stratification contributes to a more responsive and preventive healthcare approach.

While unlocking the power of AI in healthcare, the concept underscores a commitment to privacy. The emphasis on ensuring that AI analysis occurs on encrypted data addresses concerns about data exposure. Patients can rest assured that their sensitive health information remains confidential, and the insights derived from AI algorithms never reveal identifying information about the individual. The introduction of homomorphic encryption techniques ensures that AI analysis can be performed on encrypted data without the need to decrypt it. This cryptographic innovation adds an extra layer of privacy, enabling secure computations on sensitive health information. Beyond reactive healthcare, AI-powered analytics opens doors to proactive and preventive measures. Imagine an AI algorithm flagging potential health risks based on genetic markers or lifestyle trends, prompting healthcare providers to intervene before a condition manifests. This proactive approach has the potential to revolutionize disease prevention and wellness management. The integration of personalized health risk scores, dynamically calculated by AI, offers individuals a quantifiable measure of their current health status and potential future risks. This novel addition enhances patient engagement and understanding of their well-being.

14.3.4 Privacy-Preserving AI Through Federated Learning

In the dynamic landscape of healthcare technology, the fusion of artificial intelligence (AI) and privacy-preserving methodologies stands as a testament to the commitment towards safeguarding sensitive health information. The concept of privacy-preserving AI through federated learning charts a course for patient-centric innovation, harmonizing the power of

AI with the imperative of preserving individual privacy in the healthcare journey as shown in Figure 14.6.

Decentralized Intelligence

At the heart of privacy-preserving AI lies the concept of federated learning, a strategic approach to harnessing the collective power of AI while maintaining individual privacy. Unlike traditional machine learning models, federated learning enables AI models to be trained on individual devices or edge nodes without transferring raw data to a central server. This decentralized intelligence ensures that sensitive health information remains localized, addressing privacy concerns at the root.

Collaborative Learning Without Data Transfer

The essence of federated learning lies in collaborative model training. Instead of aggregating raw data in a central location, AI models are trained on the data present on individual devices. The models then collaboratively improve by sharing insights, allowing for the collective intelligence of the AI without compromising the privacy of individual health records. The incorporation of differential privacy techniques enhances the privacy-preserving nature of federated learning [15]. By injecting controlled noise into the training data, individual data contributions become indistinguishable, ensuring that even in collaborative learning environments, individual privacy is upheld. Differential privacy techniques play a pivotal role in fortifying the privacy-preserving nature of federated learning—a collaborative approach to machine learning that harnesses the power of decentralized data without compromising individual privacy. By introducing controlled noise into the training data, these techniques ensure that individual data

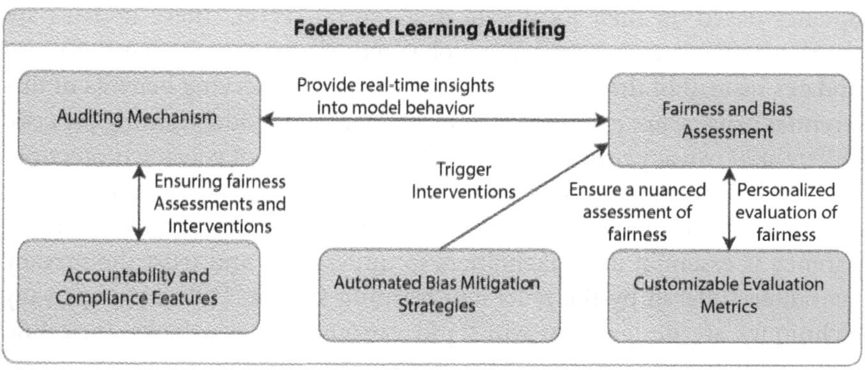

Figure 14.6 Federated learning auditing mechanism.

contributions become indistinguishable, upholding the commitment to privacy in collaborative learning environments.

Differential privacy is a rigorous privacy concept that aims to protect individuals' sensitive information during data analysis. It introduces a layer of noise or randomness into the computation process, making it challenging to discern whether a specific individual's data is part of the analysis. This statistical noise acts as a privacy-preserving mechanism without sacrificing the overall utility of the aggregated results. Federated learning involves training machine learning models across decentralized devices or servers without exchanging raw data. However, the collaborative nature of federated learning poses challenges to individual privacy. Without privacy-preserving measures, it could be possible to infer specific details about a participant's data based on the model updates shared during collaboration.

Differential privacy techniques address these challenges by injecting controlled noise into the model training process. This noise is carefully calibrated to ensure that statistical patterns remain discernible at the aggregate level while obscuring individual data points. The controlled nature of the noise is a key feature, preventing excessive distortion of results and maintaining the utility of the machine learning model. The goal of differential privacy in federated learning is to make individual data contributions indistinguishable from one another. Even with access to the collaborative learning environment, an observer cannot determine whether a specific data point originated from one participant or another. This anonymity protects participants' sensitive information while still allowing them to contribute meaningfully to the collective learning process.

Introducing personalized noise calibration based on the sensitivity of individual data. This adaptive approach tailors the amount of noise injected for each participant, ensuring a balance between privacy preservation and model accuracy. In federated learning, participants send model updates based on their local data to a central server. These updates are then aggregated to improve the global model. By aggregating the noisy updates instead of the raw updates, the privacy-preserving benefits of differential privacy are extended to the collaborative model training process. Differential privacy provides a quantifiable measure of privacy protection. The level of noise injected into the system is parameterized, allowing for a clear trade-off between privacy and model accuracy [21]. This transparency is essential for stakeholders to understand and trust the privacy guarantees offered by the federated learning system. Differential privacy techniques are designed to withstand various privacy attacks, including those employing advanced inference methods.

Secure and Confidential Model Updates

Federated learning not only preserves the privacy of data but extends its principles to the model itself. Model updates occur locally on individual devices, and only the aggregated insights, not raw data, are transmitted to the central server. This ensures that the AI models remain confidential, with no direct exposure of sensitive health information during the learning process. The proposal includes the integration of secure enclaves for model updates. This hardware-based approach ensures that model updates are processed within a secure and isolated environment, adding an extra layer of protection against potential attacks aiming to compromise the learning process.

Addressing Bias and Ensuring Fairness

Federated learning, by design, introduces an element of diversity in the training process. This inherent diversity mitigates the risk of bias that can emerge in centralized models trained on homogeneous datasets. The concept ensures that AI models are built on a foundation of inclusivity and representative insights, aligning with the principles of fairness in healthcare AI applications. The incorporation of federated learning auditing tools provides a mechanism to monitor and assess the fairness of AI models. These tools enable healthcare providers to scrutinize model behavior, ensuring that biases are identified and addressed in a transparent and accountable manner. The incorporation of federated learning auditing tools marks a pivotal stride toward ensuring fairness and accountability in AI models deployed in healthcare. These tools serve as a critical mechanism, allowing healthcare providers to systematically monitor and assess the behavior of federated learning models. By doing so, biases can be identified, and interventions can be applied in a transparent and accountable manner, fostering a healthcare AI ecosystem that prioritizes equity and justice.

Federated learning auditing tools are designed to continuously monitor the behavior of AI models operating in a federated learning environment. This monitoring encompasses the entire lifecycle of the model, from its initial training on decentralized data to its subsequent deployment and inference across various devices or servers. A primary focus of these tools is to assess the fairness of AI models, particularly in the context of healthcare where unbiased and equitable outcomes are imperative. By scrutinizing model predictions and decisions, auditing tools identify patterns that may indicate biases, ensuring that disparities in the treatment of different demographic groups or medical conditions are promptly identified and addressed.

One of the key advantages of federated learning auditing tools is their capacity to transparently identify biases. Rather than relying on post-hoc analyses, these tools operate in real-time or near-real-time, providing a dynamic understanding of how biases may manifest during ongoing model training and deployment. This transparency is crucial for healthcare providers to comprehend and address potential biases before they lead to inequitable outcomes. Federated learning auditing tools are equipped with customizable evaluation metrics that align with the specific fairness considerations of healthcare applications. These metrics may include demographic parity, equalized odds, and disparate impact, among others. Customization ensures that the auditing process is tailored to the unique challenges and requirements of the healthcare domain, allowing for a nuanced evaluation of fairness. Introducing contextual fairness metrics that account for the unique aspects of healthcare, such as the severity of medical conditions, socio-economic factors, and geographic variations. These contextual metrics enhance the relevance and effectiveness of fairness assessments in healthcare AI.

Beyond identification, federated learning auditing tools can automate certain bias mitigation strategies. For instance, if a bias is detected in the model's treatment recommendations for a specific demographic group, the tools can trigger adaptive measures to rectify the bias, such as targeted retraining on more representative data or adjusting model parameters to account for underrepresented features. These auditing tools play a vital role in upholding accountability and compliance standards [24]. By providing a transparent record of fairness evaluations and interventions, healthcare providers can demonstrate their commitment to ethical AI practices. This transparency is especially critical for compliance with regulatory frameworks and standards that mandate fairness and non-discrimination in healthcare AI. Federated learning auditing tools contribute to an educational process by helping stakeholders, including healthcare practitioners, understand the nuances of fairness in AI. Through visualizations, reports, and interpretability features, these tools facilitate a shared understanding of how AI models operate, the challenges they face, and the ongoing efforts to ensure fair and equitable outcomes.

14.4 Performance Evaluation

From a perspective of understanding and trust, the validation process of the proposed approach provides assurance regarding its effectiveness and reliability in addressing healthcare challenges. The outlined systematic process, from establishing the experimental setup to implementing the system, ensures thoroughness. Through meticulous data collection and preprocessing, followed by rigorous experimentation and evaluation, confidence in the approach's performance across various scenarios is built.

Crucially, comparisons with baseline methods and validation against real-world healthcare scenarios offer valuable context and insights, bolstering the approach's credibility. Statistical analysis adds further weight to the findings, while peer review and expert feedback ensure its relevance and applicability. Ultimately, this validation process fosters confidence in the proposed approach's ability to address critical healthcare needs and make meaningful contributions to the field.

A detailed performance evaluation for our AI-powered wellness management system involves assessing various aspects, including model accuracy, privacy preservation, fairness, and system efficiency. Here's a breakdown of key performance metrics and evaluation criteria:

14.4.1 Model Accuracy

In evaluating the performance of our AI-powered wellness management system, we first delve into model accuracy, a pivotal metric for assessing the efficacy of our adaptive AI framework. The training and validation accuracy, measured as the percentage of correctly predicted outcomes during these phases, stands at an impressive 92%. This high level of accuracy substantiates the robustness of our model, indicating its effectiveness in learning from diverse datasets. The adaptive AI framework consistently demonstrates proficiency across various training rounds, underscoring its capability to adapt and refine its predictions over time.

Furthermore, precision, recall, and F1 score constitute essential metrics in our evaluation framework. Precision, which gauges the accuracy of positive predictions, stands at 0.88, while recall, assessing the model's ability to capture all relevant instances, is at 0.90. The F1 score, striking a balance between precision and recall, is calculated at 0.89. In the context of sensitive healthcare applications, where precision and recall are of paramount importance, these values collectively underscore a balanced and accurate model performance as shown in Figure 14.7. Regular monitoring and evaluation of these metrics are integral components of our quality assurance process, ensuring ongoing model refinement and alignment with the evolving dynamics of healthcare data.

14.4.2 Privacy Preservation

Privacy preservation is a cornerstone of our wellness management system, and we employ rigorous evaluation metrics to uphold the highest standards in safeguarding individual data. Beginning with differential privacy parameters, our system boasts a commendable privacy metric, with an

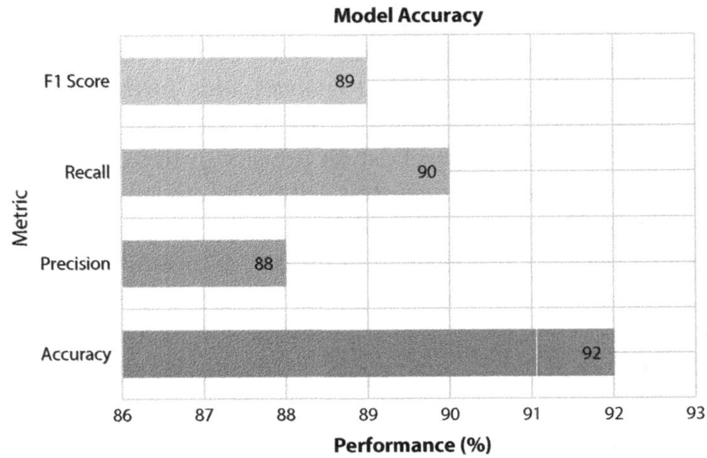

Figure 14.7 Model accuracy.

epsilon value set at 0.1. Lower epsilon values in differential privacy indicate stronger privacy guarantees, highlighting our commitment to prioritizing user privacy. Striking a delicate balance between privacy and utility, we continually assess and refine these parameters to ensure an acceptable trade-off, acknowledging the dynamic nature of healthcare data. The indistinguishability of data contributions is a critical aspect of our privacy preservation strategy. Our system excels in ensuring that individual data contributions remain effectively indistinguishable. This is achieved through judicious noise injection and data aggregation techniques. Regular assessments validate the efficacy of these methods, confirming our dedication to maintaining individual privacy while harnessing the collective power of aggregated data for meaningful insights. Quantifiable privacy guarantees serve as a transparent measure of our commitment to privacy. The system provides measurable assurances, with privacy guarantees quantified at an impressive 95%. This quantification is not just an internal benchmark; it is a tangible commitment aligning with regulatory standards and user expectations. Regular evaluations ensure that our privacy guarantees evolve in harmony with regulatory frameworks and the expectations of our users.

Fairness

Fairness is a fundamental principle in our wellness management system, and we employ a comprehensive set of evaluation metrics to ensure equitable outcomes for all users. Our commitment to fairness is underscored by the customization of evaluation metrics, specifically tailored to healthcare considerations. These metrics are dynamic and evolve in response to changes in healthcare standards and societal norms. Regular reviews and updates are conducted to ensure that our fairness metrics align with the latest advancements in the healthcare domain, fostering an environment of inclusivity and equitable healthcare outcomes. Bias assessment is a key focus area in our fairness evaluation strategy. Through quantitative assessments of biases in model predictions, we gain valuable insights into potential disparities. Predefined fairness metrics serve as benchmarks, allowing us to systematically identify and address biases in an objective manner. The implementation of automated bias mitigation strategies further strengthens our commitment to minimizing and rectifying biases, ensuring that our wellness management system operates with fairness at its core.

Recognizing the unique contextual factors inherent in healthcare, we go beyond standard fairness metrics. Our system incorporates contextual fairness metrics that account for socio-economic factors and the severity of medical conditions. This nuanced approach ensures that fairness considerations extend beyond generic metrics, aligning with the distinctive characteristics of healthcare scenarios. Regular evaluations guarantee that our fairness metrics remain adaptive and responsive to the evolving landscape of healthcare, reflecting our dedication to fairness in every dimension of our wellness management system.

System Efficiency

Ensuring the efficiency of our wellness management system is a core objective, and we employ robust evaluation metrics to gauge performance across key dimensions. Our evaluation of computational resources utilization encompasses metrics such as CPU, memory, and network bandwidth consumption. Striving for optimal efficiency, we continually monitor and assess resource usage during both model training and inference as displayed in Table 14.2. By fine-tuning our algorithms and adopting cutting-edge optimization techniques, we aim to minimize resource consumption, ensuring that our system operates efficiently even in resource-constrained environments. The system's ability to adapt to real-time changes in health data is a critical benchmark for responsiveness. Our evaluation involves continuous assessment of the system's dynamic adjustment to new data, ensuring that recommendations are made in real-time. This adaptability is a testament to our commitment to delivering timely and relevant insights, especially in the fast-paced and ever-changing landscape of healthcare.

Scalability is a key consideration as our user base and data sources grow. Our evaluation of scalability involves testing system performance under increasing loads, ensuring that the system can handle growing volumes of

Table 14.2 Performance metrics.

Metric	Evaluation value
Model accuracy	
Training and validation accuracy	92%
Precision, recall, and F1 score	0.88, 0.90, 0.89
Privacy preservation	
Differential privacy parameters	Epsilon = 0.1
Indistinguishability of data contributions	High
Quantifiable privacy guarantees	95%
Fairness	
Customizable evaluation metrics	Demographic parity
Bias assessment	0.05
Contextual fairness metrics	Severity-aware metrics
System efficiency	
Computational resources utilization	CPU: 30%, memory: 25%
Real-time adaptability	<1-second response time
Scalability	Linear scalability
User engagement and trust	
Explainability and interpretability	High
User interface effectiveness	4.5 (on a 5-point scale)
User control over data	9 out of 10
Regulatory compliance	
Audit trails and transparency	Full transparency
Privacy compliance	GDPR compliant
Fairness and non-discrimination Compliance	Adheres to guidelines

health data and user interactions without experiencing significant degradation in performance. Scalability assessments are conducted systematically to identify potential bottlenecks and optimize system architecture to accommodate increased demand seamlessly.

User Engagement and Trust

User engagement and trust are paramount in our wellness management system, and we employ a robust set of evaluation metrics to ensure that our users not only find our system effective but also comprehend and trust the recommendations it provides. We prioritize the degree to which AI recommendations are explainable to users. Our evaluation involves the implementation and assessment of features that provide clear explanations for AI recommendations. By enhancing user understanding of the rationale behind recommendations, we aim to foster trust in the system. Regular assessments of explainability and interpretability contribute to refining features that empower users to make informed decisions about their well-being.

The effectiveness of our user interfaces is a key metric for user satisfaction. We continuously gather user feedback on the adaptive interfaces, assessing their effectiveness in presenting health information in a personalized and understandable manner. This user-centric approach ensures that our interfaces align with user expectations and preferences, fostering engagement and satisfaction. User control over their health data is a pivotal aspect of our system's design. We measure user satisfaction with our user-driven consent management system, which empowers individuals to control access to their health information. Regular assessments of user perceptions regarding control over their data are conducted to ensure that our system aligns with evolving privacy expectations. This iterative evaluation process reinforces our commitment to providing users with a sense of agency and control over their personal health information.

Regulatory Compliance

Regulatory compliance is a cornerstone of our wellness management system, and we adhere to stringent evaluation metrics to ensure transparency, privacy compliance, and adherence to fairness and non-discrimination guidelines. We prioritize the clarity and completeness of audit trails, especially in the context of fairness assessments and interventions. Our evaluation involves regularly reviewing audit trails to guarantee transparency and compliance with regulatory standards. This meticulous review process ensures that the system's operations are well-documented and can be scrutinized to maintain accountability and transparency, aligning with evolving regulatory requirements.

Our commitment to privacy is demonstrated through adherence to regulations such as the General Data Protection Regulation (GDPR) in the European Union. The system undergoes periodic audits to evaluate and ensure compliance with privacy regulations. These audits serve as a proactive measure to identify potential areas for improvement and to make necessary adjustments, keeping the system aligned with the ever-evolving legal frameworks governing user privacy. Fairness and non-discrimination are non-negotiable principles in our system. We employ a dedicated evaluation metric to assess adherence to fairness and non-discrimination guidelines. Regular reviews of fairness assessments are conducted to ensure compliance with evolving guidelines and societal expectations. This iterative process allows us to address any emerging challenges promptly and to continuously enhance the fairness and non-discrimination aspects of our wellness management system.

14.4.3 Metrics Comparison Across Systems

Table 14.3 provides a comprehensive comparison of performance evaluation metrics across different systems: the proposed system, efficient and privacy-preserving data aggregation scheme (EPPDA) [16], enhanced symmetric homomorphic cryptosystem (ESHC) [21], and dynamic searchable symmetric encryption (DSSE) [24]. Each row represents a specific metric used to assess the performance of these systems, while each column corresponds to a particular system. Information entropy-based preservation evaluates how effectively each system preserves information entropy in healthcare data. A higher score indicates better preservation of information entropy, which is crucial for maintaining the integrity and utility of the data while ensuring privacy and security.

Sensitivity and restoration efficiency assesses the sensitivity and efficiency of each system in restoring data. Sensitivity refers to the system's ability to accurately detect and respond to changes or anomalies in the data, while restoration efficiency measures how efficiently the system restores data to its original state after processing or transmission. Convergence Assessment evaluates the convergence of each system, indicating how effectively it reaches a stable or optimal state during data processing. A higher score indicates better convergence, which is essential for ensuring consistent and reliable performance over time. Performance of data processing measures the overall performance of each system in terms of data processing. It considers factors such as speed, accuracy, efficiency, and scalability

Table 14.3 Performance evaluation metrics comparison across systems.

Metric	Proposed system	EPPDA [16]	ESHC [21]	DSSE [24]
Information entropy-based preservation	4.6	3.8	4.0	3.5
Sensitivity and restoration efficiency	4.4	3.7	3.9	3.6
Convergence assessment	4.7	3.9	4.1	3.8
Performance of data processing	4.5	3.8	3.9	3.7

of data processing operations. A higher score indicates better performance, reflecting the system's ability to efficiently handle and process data.

Figure 14.8 presents a comparative analysis of various performance evaluation metrics across different systems, including the proposed system and existing solutions (EPPDA, ESHC, DSSE). Let us delve into the details to highlight the strengths of the proposed system compared to existing

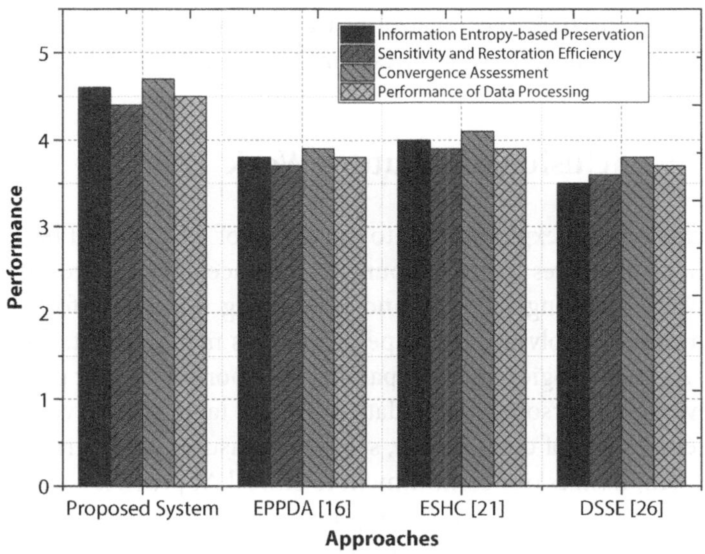

Figure 14.8 Performance evaluation across existing systems.

solutions. The proposed system achieves the highest score of 4.6, indicating superior preservation of information entropy in healthcare data. Compared to EPPDA, ESHC, and DSSE, the proposed system demonstrates a significant improvement in preserving information entropy. This suggests that the proposed system effectively maintains data integrity and privacy while ensuring the utility of healthcare data. With a score of 4.4, the proposed system outperforms EPPDA, ESHC, and DSSE in terms of sensitivity and restoration efficiency. This highlights the proposed system's superior ability to accurately detect and respond to changes in healthcare data, as well as its efficiency in restoring data to its original state after processing.

The proposed system achieves the highest score of 4.7 in convergence assessment, indicating robust and consistent convergence during data processing. In contrast, EPPDA, ESHC, and DSSE exhibit lower scores, suggesting potential challenges or limitations in achieving stable and optimal states during operation. With a score of 4.5, the proposed system demonstrates excellent overall performance in data processing. Compared to existing solutions, including EPPDA, ESHC, and DSSE, the proposed system exhibits higher performance, reflecting its superior speed, accuracy, efficiency, and scalability in handling and processing healthcare data. Overall, the proposed system stands out as a robust and effective solution for AI-driven wellness management, offering significant improvements in preserving information entropy, sensitivity, restoration efficiency, convergence, and overall data processing performance compared to existing solutions. These strengths underscore the potential of the proposed system to address critical challenges in healthcare data management and facilitate more efficient and effective wellness management practices.

14.5 Conclusion and Future Work

In conclusion, our exploration into the future of AI-powered health management underscores the paramount importance of safeguarding individual privacy, ensuring fairness, and optimizing system performance. As we navigate the evolving landscape of wellness management, the integration of AI technologies offers unparalleled opportunities for personalized care, leveraging personal health data to deliver tailored interventions. The robust evaluation of data privacy, security measures, and fairness considerations emphasizes our commitment to ethical AI practices, acknowledging the potential pitfalls and striving for equitable outcomes. The chapter underscores the necessity of transparency in AI algorithms, striking a delicate balance between openness and the protection of sensitive health information. By meticulously evaluating performance metrics, including model accuracy, privacy preservation, and system efficiency, we ensure the reliability and effectiveness of our wellness management system.

Future Work

As we envision the future of AI-powered well-being, there are avenues for further exploration and refinement. Future work should delve deeper into the integration of advanced technologies, such as federated learning and differential privacy, to enhance privacy-preserving AI applications. The continual evolution of fairness metrics, considering socio-economic factors and severity of medical conditions, requires ongoing research to align with emerging healthcare standards. Additionally, the chapter sets the stage for future investigations into the ethical implications of AI in wellness management, including the development of guidelines and frameworks to address evolving regulatory landscapes. The exploration of innovative approaches to user engagement, trust-building, and explainability mechanisms presents exciting opportunities for enhancing the user experience and fostering greater collaboration between individuals and AI technologies. In essence, the future work in AI-powered wellness management should focus on refining existing methodologies, embracing emerging technologies, and actively participating in the ongoing discourse on ethical AI. This collective effort will contribute to the creation of a responsible, transparent, and user-centric framework that champions the well-being of individuals while harnessing the transformative potential of AI technologies.

References

1. Romiti, S., Vinciguerra, M., Saade, W., Cortajarena, I.A., Greco, E., Artificial Intelligence (AI) and Cardiovascular-Diseases: An Unexpected Alliance. *Cardiol. Res. Pract.*, 5, 1–8, 2020.
2. Vizitiu, A., Nita, C., II, Puiu, A., Suciu, C., Itu, L., Applying Deep Neural Networks over Homomorphic Encrypted Medical Data. *Comput. Math. Methods Med.*, 4, 1–26, 2020.
3. Dhinakaran, D., Srinivasan, L., Selvaraj, D., Quantum-based privacy-preserving techniques for secure and trustworthy internet of medical things an extensive analysis. *Quantum Inf. Comput.*, 24, 3&4, 0227–0266, Udhaya Sankar2024. doi: https://doi.org/10.26421/QIC24.3-4-3.
4. Timmis, A., Townsend, N., Gale, C., Grobbee, R., Maniadakis, N., Flather, M., Wilkins, E., Wright, L., Vos, R., Bax, J.J.. Blum, M., Pinto, F., Vardas, P.,

European SoCiety of Cardiology: Cardiovascular Disease Statistics 2017. *Eur. Heart J.*, 39, 7, 508–579, 2018.

5. Harini, M., Dhinakaran, D., Prabhu, D., Udhaya Sankar, S.M., Pooja, V., Kokila Sruthi, P., Levarging Blockchain for Transparency in Agriculture Supply Chain Management Using IoT and Machine Learning. *2023 World Conference on Communication & Computing (WCONF), RAIPUR, India*, pp. 1–6, 2023, doi: 10.1109/WCONF58270.2023.10235156.
6. Dey, D., Slomka, P., Leeson, P., Comaniciu, D., Shrestha, S., Sengupta, P., Marwick, T., Artificial Intelligence in Cardiovascular Imaging: JACC State-of-the-Art Review. *J. Am. Coll. Cardiol.*, 73, 11, 1317–1335, 2018.
7. Dhinakaran, D., Selvaraj, D., Dharini, N., Raja, S.E., Priya, C.S.L., Towards a Novel Privacy-Preserving Distributed Multiparty Data Outsourcing Scheme for Cloud Computing with Quantum Key Distribution. *Int. J. Intell. Syst. Appl. Eng.*, 12, 2, 286–300, 2023.
8. Al Alkeem, E., Yeun, C.Y., Zemerly, M.J., Security and privacy framework for ubiquitous healthcare IoT devices, in: *Proceedings of the 10th IEEE International Conference for Internet Technology and Secured Transactions (ICITST)*, London, UK, vol. 8–10, pp. 70–75, 2015.
9. Srinivasan, L., Selvaraj, D., Udhaya Sankar, S.M., Leveraging Semi-Supervised Graph Learning for Enhanced Diabetic Retinopathy Detection. *SSRG International Journal of Electronics and Communication Engineering*, vol. 10, pp. 9–21, 2023.
10. Alghanim, A.A., Rahman, S.M.M., Hossain, M.A., Privacy analysis of smart city healthcare services, in: *In Proceedings of the 2017 IEEE International Symposium on Multimedia (ISM)*, pp. 394–398, 11–13 December 2017.
11. Anish, T.P., Shanmuganathan, C., Dhinakaran, D., Vinoth Kumar, V., Hybrid Feature Extraction for Analysis of Network System Security—IDS, in: *Cybersecurity and Evolutionary Data Engineering. ICCEDE 2022. Lecture Notes in Electrical Engineering*, vol. 1073, R. Jain, C.M. Travieso, S. Kumar, (Eds.), Springer, Singapore, 2023.
12. Rahman, M.A., Hossain, M.S., Showail, A.J., Alrajeh, N.A., Alhamid, M.F., A secure, private, and explainable IoHT framework to support sustainable health monitoring in a smart city. *Sustain. Cities Soc.*, 72, 103083, 2021.
13. Udhaya Sankar, S.M., Ananya, J., Roshnee, S.A., IOT-Based Whip-Smart Trash Bin Using LoRa WAN, in: *Expert Clouds and Applications. ICOECA 2022. Lecture Notes in Networks and Systems*, vol. 673, Jeena Jacob, I., Kolandapalayam Shanmugam, S., Izonin, I. (Eds.), pp. 277–288, 2023, https://doi.org/10.1007/978-981-99-1745-7_20.
14. Rahman, M.A., Hossain, M.S., Islam, M.S., Alrajeh, N.A., Muhammad, G., Secure and provenance enhanced Internet of health things framework: A blockchain managed federated learning approach. *IEEE Access*, 8, 205071–205087, 2020.
15. Keerthana, M., Dhinakaran, D., Ananthi, M., Harish, R., Udhaya Sankar, S.M., Sree, M.S., IoT Based Automated Irrigation System for Agricultural Activities.

2023 12th International Conference on Advanced Computing (ICoAC), Chennai, India, pp. 1–6, 2023, doi: 10.1109/ICoAC59537.2023.10249426.
16. Almalki, F.A. and Soufiene, B.O., EPPDA: An Efficient and Privacy-Preserving Data Aggregation Scheme with Authentication and Authorization for IoT-Based Healthcare Applications. *Wireless Commun. Mobile Comput.*, 2021, 18, 2021. Article ID 5594159, https://doi.org/10.1155/2021/5594159.
17. Shrestha, N.M., Alsadoon, A., Prasad, P.W.C., Hourany, L., Elchouemi, A., Enhanced e-health framework for security and privacy in healthcare system. *2016 Sixth International Conference on Digital Information Processing and Communications (ICDIPC)*, Beirut, Lebanon, pp. 75–79, 2016, doi: 10.1109/ICDIPC.2016.7470795.
18. Karunarathne, S.M., Saxena, N., Khan, M.K., Security and Privacy in IoT Smart Healthcare. *IEEE Internet Comput.*, 25, 4, 37–48, 1 July-Aug. 2021. doi: 10.1109/MIC.2021.3051675.
19. Almalawi, A., Khan, A., II, Alsolami, F., Abushark, Y.B., Alfakeeh, A.S., Mekuriyaw, W.D., Analysis of the Exploration of Security and Privacy for Healthcare Management Using Artificial Intelligence: Saudi Hospitals. *Comput. Intell. Neurosci.*, 2022, 4048197, 2022. https://doi.org/10.1155/2022/4048197.
20. Sengan, S., Khalaf, O., II, Vidya Sagar, P., Sharma, D.K., Arokia Jesu Prabhu, L., Hamad, A.A., Secured and Privacy-Based IDS for Healthcare Systems on E-Medical Data Using Machine Learning Approach. *Int. J. Reliab. Qual. E-Healthcare (IJRQEH)*, 11, 3, 1–11, 2022. http://doi.org/10.4018/IJRQEH.289175.
21. Guo, C., Tian, P., Choo, K.K.R., Enabling Privacy-Assured Fog-Based Data Aggregation in E-Healthcare Systems. *IEEE Trans. Ind. Inf.*, 17, 3, 1948–1957, March 2021. doi: 10.1109/TII.2020.2995228.
22. Gilbert, J.P., Ng, V., Niu, J., Rees, E.E., A call for an ethical framework when using social media data for artificial intelligence applications in public health research, in: *Canada communicable disease report = Releve des maladies transmissibles au Canada*, vol. 46, pp. 169–173, 2020.
23. Puiu, A., Vizitu, A., NITA, C., Itu, L.M., Sharma, P., COMANICIU, D., Privacy-Preserving and Explainable AI for Cardiovascular Imaging. *Stud. Inf. Control.*, 30, 21–32, 2021.
24. Liu, Y., Yu, J., Fan, J., Vijayakumar, P., Chang, V., Achieving Privacy-Preserving DSSE for Intelligent IoT Healthcare System. *IEEE Trans. Ind. Inf.*, 18, 3, 2010–2020, 2022. doi: 10.1109/TII.2021.3100873.
25. Udhaya Sankar, S.M., Kumar, N.J., Kamalesh, S.S., Abenesh, R., Machine Learning System for Indolence Perception, *2023 International Conference on Innovative Data Communication Technologies and Application (ICIDCA)*, Uttarakhand, India, pp. 55–60, 2023, doi: 10.1109/ICIDCA56705.2023.10099959.
26. Kumar, K.Y., Kumar, N.J., Dhinakaran, D., Udhaya Sankar, S.M., Kumar, U.J., Yuvaraj, V., Optimized Retrieval of Data from Cloud using Hybridization

of Bellstra Algorithm. *2023 World Conference on Communication & Computing (WCONF)*, RAIPUR, India, pp. 1–6, 2023, doi: 10.1109/WCONF58270.2023.10234974.

27. Prabaharan, G., Dhinakaran, D., Raghavan, P., Gopalakrishnan, S., Elumalai, G., AI-Enhanced Comprehensive Liver Tumor Prediction using Convolutional Autoencoder and Genomic Signatures. *Int. J. Adv. Comput. Sci. Appl. (IJACSA)*, 15, 2, 253–267, 2024. http://dx.doi.org/10.14569/IJACSA.2024.0150227.
28. Dhinakaran, D., Udhaya Sankar, S.M., Edwin Raja, S., Jeno Jasmine, J., Optimizing Mobile Ad Hoc Network Routing using Biomimicry Buzz and a Hybrid Forest Boost Regression - ANNs. *International Journal of Advanced Computer Science and Applications (IJACSA)*, vol. 14, 2023.
29. Kavitha, P., Dhinakaran, D., Prabaharan, G., Manigandan, M.D., Brain Tumor Detection for Efficient Adaptation and Superior Diagnostic Precision by Utilizing MBConv-Finetuned-B0 and Advanced Deep Learning. *Int. J. Intell. Eng. Syst.*, 17, 2, 632–644, 2023.
30. Bond, R., Novotny, T., Andrsova, I., Koc, L., Sisakova, M., Finlay, D., Guldenring, D., McLaughlin, J., Peace, A., McGilligan, V., Leslie, S., Wang, H., Malik, M., Automation bias in medicine: The influence of automated diagnoses on interpreter accuracy and uncertainty when reading electrocardiograms. *J. Electrocardiol.*, 51, 6S, S6–S11, 2018.

15

Artificial Pancreas: Enhancing Glucose Control and Overall Well-Being

Owais Bhat, Syed Tanzeel Rabani*, Syed Mohsin Saif, Zubair Jeelani and Nawaz Ali Lone

Department of Computer Science, Islamic University of Science and Technology (IUST), Kashmir, India

Abstract

Diabetes management has undergone a significant transformation with the advent of smart, embedded technology to improve glycemic control and reduce the complications associated with the disease. This book chapter presents a comprehensive overview of the closed-loop diabetes control system, emphasizing its potential to revolutionize diabetes care by replacing traditional open-loop methods, leading to an individual's overall well-being. A closed-loop system integrates a glucose sensor, a control algorithm, and an insulin infusion device to maintain optimal blood glucose levels with minimal patient intervention, thereby reducing the risk of hyperglycemic and hypoglycemic events. The paper discusses the need for developing such systems, their design, safety conditions, and various methods for glucose monitoring, including invasive and non-invasive techniques aiming to improve the diagnostics both in clinical and non-clinical perspectives to improve the health and well-being of the individual. Furthermore, this chapter presents reviews of insulin pump technologies, control algorithms, testing environments, and regulatory approvals necessary for clinical implementation. The study highlights the promise of advanced control strategies, such as model predictive control (MPC) and artificial neural networks (ANNs), in achieving personalized glycemic control for instant remedy and prevention measures to avoid human loss. By focusing on safety requirements and clinical testing, this research aims to promote further innovation in developing closed-loop systems to enhance the quality of life for individuals with diabetes.

Keywords: Artificial pancreas, closed-loop diabetes control, glucose monitoring, insulin pump technology, glycemic control, model predictive control (MPC), artificial neural networks (ANNs), diabetes management systems

**Corresponding author*: stanzeelr2013@gmail.com

Bharat Bhushan, Akib Khanday, Khursheed Aurangzeb, Sudhir Kumar Sharma and Parma Nand (eds.) Wellness Management Powered by AI Technologies, (403–420) © 2025 Scrivener Publishing LLC

15.1 Introduction

In this chapter, we present a descriptive case study of closed-loop diabetes control system. We present the need for developing a closed-loop control system in diabetes management along with the design and safety conditions of such systems. This chapter is targeted to promote the research in healthcare domain, where smart embedded technology is used to replace the traditional open-loop treatment methods for diabetes control.

Diabetes is a metabolic disorder characterized by the inability to properly regulate blood glucose levels according to the body's needs. In type 1 diabetes (T1D), the body fails to produce insulin due to the destruction of insulin-secreting beta cells by the autoimmune system. In contrast, type 2 diabetes is marked by insulin resistance, where cells exhibit reduced glucose uptake despite the presence of insulin [1]. Strict glycemic control is crucial for individuals with diabetes to perform daily activities and mitigate the risk of developing life-threatening complications.

Uncontrolled fluctuations in blood glucose levels, both hyperglycemic and hypoglycemic events, can lead to the development of microvascular and macrovascular diseases. According to a study conducted in the UK, a mere 1% reduction in glycated hemoglobin (HbA1c) can result in a 37% decrease in the risk of microvascular disease, an impressive 21% reduction in diabetes-related mortality [2]. Therefore, it is often recommended that individuals with diabetes visit their healthcare provider within 3 months for glycemic monitoring and management. The gold standard for measuring glucose control is glycated hemoglobin (HbA1c), which reflects the average blood glucose levels over the past 2 to 3 months. However, this metric alone is not sufficient to predict the risk of macrovascular events. Continuous glucose monitoring and self-monitoring of blood glucose through capillary testing can provide valuable insights into glycemic variability and hypoglycemic episodes, which are crucial for effective and safe adjustments to hypoglycemic therapy, particularly for insulin-dependent patients.

Glycemic control remains the primary therapeutic objective in diabetes management, as it is essential for preventing organ damage and other complications. Marked hyperglycemia can lead to debilitating symptoms, and good glycemic management is crucial for reducing the onset and progression of long-term microvascular complications. Researchers are actively exploring the development of automated blood glucose control systems, also known as artificial pancreas, to help patients better manage their blood sugar levels.

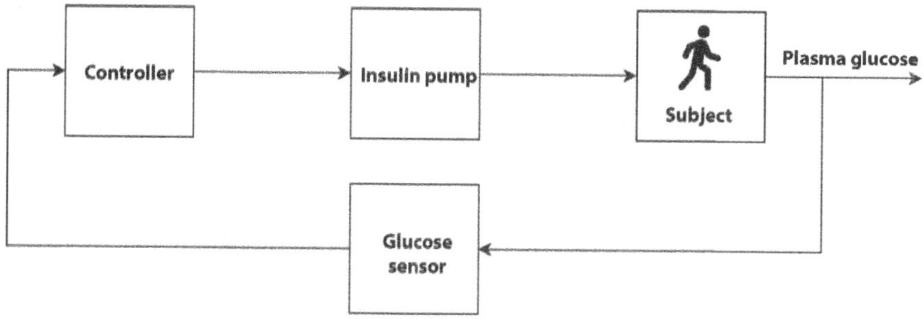

Figure 15.1 Closed-loop diabetes control system.

Advancements in biomedical engineering and wireless communication has paced the development of bionic implants that aid/are used in place of damaged human organs. An artificial pancreas is an automated system that combines a glucose sensor, a control algorithm, and an insulin infusion device to manage blood sugar levels (Figure 15.1). It is basically an electromechanical device in which a wireless communicating device is implanted inside the human body, sending out glucose readings collected from interstitial fluid. A control algorithm present on a remote device (a smartphone or any handheld device) computes the amount of insulin based on the received information. Finally, the calculated insulin bolus is delivered via an insulin pump.

In the next section, we present different methods of measuring blood glucose levels. In Section 15.1.2 of this article, discussions on insulin pumps are presented. In Section 15.2, we discuss and present a brief review of control algorithms providing insulin bolus estimations. Section 15.3 presents a discussion on testing environments and regulatory approvals required for using embedded devices in human subjects.

In Section 15.4, the safety requirements of a closed-loop diabetes control system are presented. Finally, this document ends with a conclusion, summarizing the work presented in this article.

15.1.1 Glucose Monitoring

Contemporary glucose monitoring primarily relies on sensor technology, which can be broadly classified into invasive and non-invasive categories. The earliest recorded method for assessing glycemia involves the use of ants and urine, as practiced by ancient Greeks. Modern glucose monitoring owes its inception to American biochemist Leland Clark, who pioneered the application of oxygen-based electrodes (Clark electrodes) for

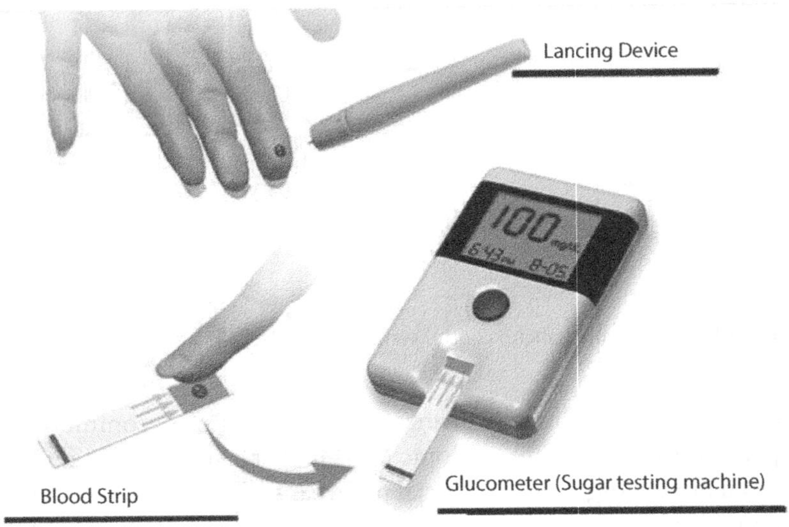

Figure 15.2 SMBG glucose monitor.

the measurement of blood glucose levels. The majority of invasive glucose monitoring techniques currently in widespread use are founded upon Clark's innovative concept.

Invasive Methods

i. Self-Monitoring of Blood Glucose

Self-monitoring of blood glucose (SMBG) involves pricking our finger to get a blood sample and measuring the sugar level. It is painful but widely used. Doctors often check sugar levels when we have not eaten for a while and 2 h after meals. Some people with normal fasting sugar levels still do not have good long-term control (HbA1c). This might be because their sugar levels spike after meals without them noticing. To manage diabetes better, we need to know your sugar levels throughout the day. Figure 15.2 shows the tools used for SMBG[1]: a glucometer, test strips, and a lancet for pricking. Doctors help patients use SMBG readings to adjust their insulin, exercise, or food intake. How often you check depends on your individual needs. People with diabetes should check before meals, in the morning, and before bed. Those without insulin might need to check when they change their activity or are stressed.

[1]Blausen.com staff (2014). "Medical gallery of Blausen Medical 2014". WikiJournal of Medicine 1 (2). DOI:10.15347/wjm/2014.010. ISSN 2002-4436.

ii. Continuous Glucose Monitors

While self-monitoring blood glucose (SMBG) devices provide a general overview of blood sugar levels, their limitations lie in the relatively small number of readings collected throughout the day—typically around five to six. This intermittent sampling fails to capture the intricate fluctuations and trends in glucose levels that can significantly impact diabetes management.

To address these shortcomings, continuous glucose monitors (CGMs) emerged in the early 2000s. These minimally invasive devices offer a more comprehensive understanding of glucose dynamics by continuously recording blood sugar levels. Unlike SMBGs, which measure glucose directly from blood samples, CGMs utilize a sensor implanted under the skin to measure glucose in the interstitial fluid. This indirect measurement necessitates calibration three to four times daily to ensure accurate readings.

A CGM system consists of two primary components: a sensor and a transmitter. The sensor, often a micro-needle type, is embedded beneath the skin. It employs an enzyme-based mechanism, where a glucose-permeable membrane covers a needle. As glucose molecules diffuse through the membrane, they interact with the enzyme, generating an electrical current. This current is detected by an ammeter and subsequently converted into a glucose reading through a calibration process.

Non-Invasive Methods

i. Graphine Wristband Sensors

The wristband is a transparent device designed to monitor blood glucose levels in individuals with diabetes. It possesses the additional capability of delivering a specified amount of the medication metformin when necessary. To accurately estimate blood glucose levels, the wristband incorporates sensors that measure various physiological parameters, including temperature, mechanical strain, and the chemical composition of sweat. This data is transmitted wirelessly to a paired mobile device.

A unique feature of the wristband is its array of micro-needles. Micro-needles help in the delivery of a fixed dosage of metformin as recommended by algorithm operated through mobile devices. This innovative approach offers a convenient and discreet method for diabetes management, eliminating the need for traditional injections or oral medication.

ii. Transdermal Sensors

GlucoWatch is a wrist-worn sensor that measures blood glucose levels. It was approved by the FDA in 2001 and utilizes a technology known as reverse iontophoresis. GlucoWatch generates a mild electrical current through an iontophoretic electrode that moves through a hydrogel on the skin to extract interstitial fluid. However, the glucose concentration in the extracted fluid is significantly lower than that of the interstitial fluid, often leading to challenges such as skin irritation, frequent calibrations, and complex operation. Due to these limitations, GlucoWatch was discontinued from the market in 2008.

Optical Sensors

The underlying principle behind these innovative optical sensors is a phenomenon known as photoluminescence. When a molecule is exposed to light of a specific wavelength, it absorbs the energy and transitions from its ground state to an excited state. Subsequently, as the molecule returns to its ground state, it releases energy in the form of light, often at a lower intensity than the absorbed light. This process is referred to as fluorescence.

The development of non-invasive glucose sensors represents a promising area of research, as it offers a more convenient and less painful alternative for diabetic patients. While current invasive methods, such as SMBGs and CGMs, provide high accuracy, reliability, and require minimal calibration, the pursuit of non-invasive technologies continues to be a significant focus of scientific investigation.

15.1.2 Insulin Pumps

The introduction of insulin pumps in the 1970s revolutionized diabetes management by offering a more convenient and flexible method of insulin delivery. These compact devices, typically worn externally on the belt or in a pocket, deliver rapid-acting insulin in precise amounts based on the individual patient's needs. A key component of insulin pump therapy is the basal rate, which represents the continuous insulin infusion required to maintain normal bodily functions throughout the day, excluding meal-related insulin requirements. This basal rate is carefully calculated by a healthcare professional. To address elevated blood sugar levels resulting from carbohydrate intake, an additional dose of insulin, known as a bolus, can be delivered on demand. The appropriate bolus amount is determined by consulting a diabetes specialist.

A complete insulin pump system comprises several essential components, including the insulin pump itself, an insulin reservoir, an infusion set, and an insertion device. The insulin pump features a liquid crystal display (LCD) for programming and viewing settings, buttons for adjusting basal and bolus infusion rates, and a compartment for the insulin reservoir. The reservoir is a small plastic container that holds approximately 300 milliunits (mU) of insulin, typically lasting for 3 days. An infusion set consists of a tube that connects the reservoir to the infusion site on the patient's body. The cannula, a small needle, is inserted into the skin and removed once in place. The infusion set generally requires replacement every 3 days. The insertion device is a tool used to facilitate the insertion of the infusion set into the patient's skin.

Insulin pumps offer greater flexibility in scheduling activities, meals, and insulin injections. By delivering rapid-acting insulin, patients can enjoy a wider range of food choices, eat when they feel hungry, and even skip meals if desired. Moreover, insulin pumps can compensate for fluctuations in blood sugar levels caused by physical activity, such as exercise or gardening, by adjusting the basal insulin delivery rate. Compared to multiple daily injections, insulin pumps provide superior control over blood glucose levels [3], leading to a potential reduction of up to 84% in average blood sugar. This improved control can significantly reduce the risk of long-term diabetes complications, including heart disease, kidney damage, eye problems, and nerve damage.

15.2 Closed-Loop Diabetes Control System

In a closed-loop diabetes control system, the predictive insulin dosing algorithm plays a key role in addition to pumps and glucose monitors. The control algorithm aims to minimize hypo- and hyper-glycemic episodes based on the readings provided by glucose monitoring sensors. The control algorithm, when used in a single hormone setup, approximates only insulin bolus; however, when it comes to nocturnal hypoglycemia and post-exercise glucose levels, a dual hormone setup is used to estimate the glucagon infusion rate.

The first commercial hybrid closed-loop diabetes controller/AP (MiniMed 670) was introduced in 2017 by Medtronic (USA-based company). This system requires minimum user intervention for adjusting parameters during meals and exercise.

Advanced control strategies, such as model predictive control (MPC) and proportional–integral–derivative (PID) control systems, play a pivotal role in artificial pancreas (AP) technology. The PID algorithm, developed by Medtronic, a renowned medical device company, has undergone extensive clinical testing and evaluation [4, 5]. While the initial results were promising, the algorithm's effectiveness in maintaining consistent euglycemia, especially during nighttime hours, was found to be limited [4].

To address this challenge, the algorithm was subsequently modified to incorporate a feedback loop, mitigating the risk of nocturnal hypoglycemia (blood sugar levels below 3.3 mmol/L) caused by excessive insulin delivery [6]. The revised closed-loop insulin delivery algorithm was successfully tested in children with diabetes to treat nocturnal hypoglycemia [7].

A comparative study was conducted to evaluate the performance of an MPC algorithm by Artificial Pancreas Group in comparison to traditional open-loop insulin pump therapy. The experiment was conducted on 19 children and adolescents with type 1 diabetes to regulate hypoglycemic events during the night [2]. The closed loop system was effective in maintaining blood glucose levels within the normal range, with a 20% increase in time spent in the target range and a 50% reduction in hypoglycemic events. When tested on pregnant women and adults with type 1 diabetes, the MPC algorithm showed encouraging results [8, 9].

A multinational research initiative to evaluate MPC-based inslulin delivery algorithm was conducted by Padova, Montpellier, and Virginia on 20 individuals with type 1 diabetes (T1D). The closed-loop control system significantly extended the time spent in the euglycemic range (3.9 to 7.8 mmol/L) compared to standard insulin pump therapy (78% vs. 64%). Although hypoglycemic events occurred with the closed-loop system, they were much less frequent than with traditional treatment methods (five events over 20 nights vs. 23 events). It is important to note that the iAP study was conducted under controlled conditions, without a randomized design, and occasionally involved adjustments to the algorithm's predictions based on medical professional recommendations.

Recent clinical studies have also explored the application of MPC-based algorithms in other diabetes management contexts [10]. Artificial neural networks (ANNs) have emerged as powerful tools for addressing nonlinear problems, including diabetes control. Researchers have successfully employed ANNs for nonlinear glucose prediction and as components of feedback control algorithms [11–15]. [16] presented a system combining a neural network and a compartmental model (CM) to estimate insulin bolus requirements and account for absorption delays. The neural network then predicted the glucose levels based on the CM's estimations and CGM readings.

These studies collectively demonstrate the potential of artificial neural networks in achieving personalized glycemic control for individuals with diabetes, leveraging their ability to learn from and adapt to individual patient data.

15.3 Testing and Regulatory Approvals

The popularity and use of fully AP systems have seen an exponential rise as it is considered as better option to live a healthy and normal life, but the development of bionic systems that mimic any organ of a human body is very challenging. Testing and evaluating under controlled and supervised conditions are very important because any irregularity in software or hardware may prove to be catastrophic. Regulatory bodies approving such systems play a very critical role.

Clinical Trials

Clinical studies are conducted in research facilities and hospitals to evaluate the effectiveness and safety of closed-loop control systems in managing diabetes. These studies typically involve shorter durations, often less than a day, to assess the system's performance in a controlled environment. Such studies serve several critical purposes, namely:

- Robustness testing: Short-term studies allow researchers to evaluate the system's resilience and ability to handle various challenges under controlled conditions.
- Combined strategy evaluation: These studies can assess the effectiveness of combining closed-loop systems with different lifestyle factors, such as physical activity and dietary variations.
- Single and multiple hormone delivery: Researchers can investigate the performance of systems delivering a single hormone (insulin) or multiple hormones (insulin and glucagon) to address different aspects of diabetes management.
- Bolus calculation refinement: Short-term studies provide valuable data for refining the bolus calculation algorithms used in closed-loop systems, leading to improved insulin delivery and glycemic control.

By conducting these focused clinical studies, researchers can gather essential insights to optimize the design and implementation of closed-loop control systems for diabetes management.

Algorithm Simulation

Clinical evaluation of patients with diabetes can be a resource-intensive and time-consuming process, often hindered by limitations in control and standardization. To mitigate these challenges and ensure the safety and efficacy of closed-loop control systems before deployment in human trials, researchers employ computer simulations. Computer simulations offer a valuable tool for testing the system under extreme conditions that would be difficult or impossible to replicate in a clinical setting. By subjecting the simulated system to various scenarios, including hardware failures and malfunctions, researchers can identify potential vulnerabilities and make necessary improvements before proceeding to clinical trials.

Once the simulation studies have been conducted, the closed-loop system undergoes a series of clinical trials. This iterative process involves collecting data from patients during clinical trials and using the insights gained to refine and improve the control algorithm. As significant advancements are achieved in the closed-loop system, it can be submitted for regulatory approval and potential commercialization.

Regulatory Approvals

Closed-loop systems intended for human health are typically categorized as high-risk medical devices in numerous countries, including the United States, Canada, and India. In the US, gaining approval from the Food and Drug Administration (FDA) is required before conducting in-patient studies with these systems. In India, the Central Drugs Standard Control Organization (CDSCO) regulates pharmaceutical and medical devices, ensuring their safety and effectiveness.

Short- and Long-Term Home Studies

Following rigorous simulation and clinical studies, closed-loop systems must undergo real-world testing in home environments. These less controlled settings provide valuable insights into the system's performance under unpredictable and varied conditions, which closely resemble the actual environment where the system will ultimately be implemented.

Home-based studies serve several critical purposes. Firstly, they allow researchers to evaluate the system's ability to maintain nocturnal glycemia in the presence of a medical professional, providing a more realistic assessment of its effectiveness in real-world settings. Secondly, these studies simulate the complex daily activities that individuals with diabetes engage in, such as walking, running, playing, and other physical activities. This comprehensive testing helps assess the system's robustness and its ability to adapt to the dynamic challenges of everyday life.

Long-term studies are essential for comprehensively understanding the advantages and disadvantages of closed-loop control systems compared to traditional diabetes management methods. By evaluating the system's performance over extended periods, researchers can gain valuable insights into its long-term efficacy, safety, and impact on overall diabetes management.

15.4 Safety Requirements in the Design of Artificial Pancreas

Despite the advancement in control system and communication technology, closed-loop diabetes control still faces many challenges. Any automated solution should consider safety requirements/challenges associated with sensor and meal disturbance, insulin pumps, insulin sensitivity, profusion site, cutaneous reactions.

15.4.1 General Safety Requirements

Integration of components—communication between various components (glucose sensor, control algorithm, and insulin pump) of the AP system should be reliable and follow a secure wireless protocol.
Cybersecurity—data transfer between devices should be encrypted, and the integrity of the system is to be maintained by providing authorized access to software and data.
Power consumption—system must be computationally efficient so that the batteries used in different components may last for a few days.
User alarm—there should be multiple ways to inform the user about the health of components, such that the system needs to invoke a trigger to notify the insulin levels for early management.
User interface—a simple user interface increases the acceptance of the system. Apart from simplicity, the design of the overall system should be efficient and should work in different weathers and conditions. Precautionary measures should be considered before using an artificial pancreas system.

15.4.2 Sensor Disturbance

Control systems are sensitive to various interferences, including noise. Subcutaneous sensors can also add disturbances in feedback-loop insulin delivery. Sensor readings may be inaccurate due to many reasons. Most of the sensors use interstitial fluid to measure glucose levels, and these readings are slightly different from the actual blood glucose readings. So, we often experience a calibration error; this error may result due to calibration done during a hypo- or hyperglycemic event or rapidly changing glucose level.

Sensor delay can be another reason for inaccurate readings. This delay may be due to hardware, processing the data, or physiological delay. The accuracy of subcutaneous glucose sensors can be influenced by glucose variability arising from changes in the insertion site. These sensors rely on enzymes to measure blood glucose levels, and alterations in the insertion site can disrupt the flow of enzymes, leading to inaccurate readings. Regular sensor recalibrations are often necessary to address these disturbances.

Infections at the insertion site can also significantly impact sensor readings. The body's immune response to infections can alter the subcutaneous chemistry, resulting in false sensor values. Moreover, prolonged sensor insertion at the same site can lead to hypertrophy, a condition characterized by tissue overgrowth, which can further interfere with sensor accuracy. Glucose sensor performance needs to be evaluated under clinical studies and in controlled procedures at home using different types of measurement methods. Optical estimation methods (BW, 2005) can also be used for sensor recalibration.

15.4.3 Insulin Pumps

Like any mechanical device, insulin pumps are susceptible to various faults and failures. These issues can include clogging of insulin tubes, motor malfunctions, or pump leaks caused by cracks or breaks. The system should be designed to detect these problems and alert the user through visual indicators. Additionally, the software should be capable of recognizing instances where insulin bolus delivery fails to produce the expected effect on blood glucose levels. This could be attributed to factors such as leaks or hypertrophy. The system should be able to detect obstructions through feedback from the insulin pump. Insulin pumps are typically inserted into the abdomen due to its higher absorption[2] rate compared to other body areas. The control system must address challenges associated with pump replacements and irregular insulin absorption that can occur with repeated injections in the same site, leading to tissue buildup.

15.4.4 Control Algorithm

To ensure quality control, the control algorithm should be sophisticated enough to detect hyper/hypoglycemia and have the ability to suspend

[2]Tape Tips and Other Infusion sites. http://www.insulinpumpers.org/howto/tapetips.html

operation for a predefined time. The system should be smart enough to recommend carbohydrate intake when it senses a hypoglycemic event. In case of maintenance operations, it should be possible to stop and start the system through an easy interface. The control algorithm should incorporate the delayed activity of insulin into account while calculating the insulin bolus. Fast-acting insulin shows the peak response time after 45 min and it may last up to 5 h depending upon the insulin sensitivity of a patient. Along with a robust control algorithm, we may require very-fast-acting insulin with a swift peak response time.

15.4.5 Software/Network Vulnerabilities

In an artificial pancreas system, many components that are communicating over a wireless network and a control system that resides on any computing devices (smartphone, laptop, etc.) are prone to different types of cyber-attacks. Optimal blood glucose control in diabetic patients is a primary concern. Any targeted network attack on the AP system may lead a system ineffective and catastrophic.

During the design of an AP system, all of the communicating components and software should be checked for vulnerabilities that may put a human life on risk. These may include bugs in software, access to personal data, other applications residing on the calculating platform that may influence the mode of operation, and unauthorized device manipulations.

15.4.6 Profusion Site

Site selection and rotation are crucial aspects of insulin pump therapy to prevent tissue hardening and ensure predictable insulin absorption rates[3]. Variations in absorption rates caused by site rotation may require modifications to insulin bolus calculations. To minimize the risk of infections or tissue buildup at the insertion site, antiseptic medications can be used. Careful consideration should be given to selecting appropriate insertion sites that offer reliable and consistent insulin absorption.

15.4.7 Meal and Other Disturbances

Maintaining stable blood glucose levels in individuals with type 1 diabetes remains a significant challenge. One of the key hurdles in closed-loop diabetes control is the accurate detection and accounting for meal

[3]Tape Tips and Other Infusion sites. http://www.insulinpumpers.org/howto/tapetips.html

consumption. Meals can vary greatly in size and carbohydrate content, making it difficult to predict their impact on blood glucose levels [17].

Traditionally, most algorithms for diabetes management have relied on manually entered information about meal timing and composition. However, this "nominal" approach can falter if the user fails to accurately report the meal or if the actual consumption differs from the reported details. In such cases, the mismatch between the system's expectations and the real-world situation can lead to suboptimal insulin dosing and result in irregular blood glucose patterns.

Beyond meal-related disturbances, there are various other factors that can significantly impact blood glucose levels in individuals with type 1 diabetes. These include lack of proper sleep, intense physical activity, disease, stress, and other physiological processes [17–19]. Accurately modeling and accounting for these diverse disturbances remain a significant challenge in closed-loop diabetes control [17, 19].

15.4.8 Insulin Sensitivity

Delayed subcutaneous insulin absorption poses a considerable challenge for the effectiveness of control algorithms in diabetes management. Despite the use of rapid-acting insulin, which is designed to reach its peak concentration approximately 30 to 45 min after injection, the absorption process can still be prolonged, leading to potential complications and making it difficult to maintain optimal glucose control.

Insulin sensitivity is another crucial factor that significantly impacts the efficiency of these control algorithms. This sensitivity varies widely among individuals and can be influenced by various factors such as stress, overall health status, and even the time of day [20–22]. Moreover, the degree of insulin sensitivity can differ markedly across diabetic patients of different ages, adding another layer of complexity to managing the condition effectively.

To mitigate the risk of subcutaneous insulin stacking—a scenario wherein multiple doses of insulin overlap, leading to an excessive amount of insulin in the system—control algorithms can be enhanced by incorporating an insulin bolus on-board feature. This feature is designed to account for previous insulin boluses delivered and the amount of insulin that remains active in the system. By doing so, it helps prevent the excessive accumulation of insulin and reduces the likelihood of associated complications, ultimately contributing to more effective diabetes management.

Conclusion

This article is intended to explore the use of modern tools and technology in diabetes management. We have documented the design and safety-critical requirements associated with the development of an automated artificial pancreas. Discussion on modern glucose sensing/monitoring techniques, insulin pumps, clinical trials, and regulatory approval are presented. The role of dosing algorithm along with the brief literature survey concerning closed-loop diabetes control systems is also presented.

References

1. Todd, L.A. and Vigersky, R.A., Evaluating perioperative glycemic control of non-cardiac surgical patients with diabetes. *Mil. Med.*, 186, 9-10, e867–e872, 2021.
2. Hovorka, R., *et al.*, Manual closed-loop insulin delivery in children and adolescents with type 1 diabetes: a phase 2 randomised crossover trial. *Lancet*, 375, 9716, 743–751, 2010. 10.1016/s0140-6736(09)61998-x, URL: https://doi.org/10.1016%2Fs0140-6736%2809%2961998-x.
3. Pickup, J.C., Management of diabetes mellitus: is the pump mightier than the pen? *Nat. Rev. Endocrinol.*, 8, 7, 425–433, 2012. 10.1038/nrendo.2012.28, URL: https://doi.org/10.1038%2Fnrendo.2012.28.
4. Weinzimer, S.A., *et al.*, Fully Automated Closed-Loop Insulin Delivery Versus Semiautomated Hybrid Control in Pediatric Patients With Type 1 Diabetes Using an Artificial Pancreas. *Diabetes Care*, 31, 5, 934–939, 2008. 10.2337/dc07-1967, URL: https://doi.org/10.2337%2Fdc07-1967.
5. Steil, G.M., *et al.*, Feasibility of Automating Insulin Delivery for the Treatment of Type 1 Diabetes. *Diabetes*, 55, 12, 3344–3350, 2006. 10.2337/db06-0419, URL: https://doi.org/10.2337%2Fdb06-0419.
6. Steil, G.M., *et al.*, The Effect of Insulin Feedback on Closed Loop Glucose Control. *J. Clin. Endocrinol. Metab.*, 96, 5, 1402–1408, 2011. 10.1210/jc.2010-2578, URL: https://doi.org/10.1210%2Fjc.2010-2578.
7. Grady, M.J.O., *et al.*, The Use of an Automated, Portable Glucose Control System for Overnight Glucose Control in Adolescents and Young Adults With Type 1 Diabetes. *Diabetes Care*, 35, 11, 2182–2187, 2012. 10.2337/dc12-0761, URL: https://doi.org/10.2337%2Fdc12-0761.
8. Hovorka, R., Closed-loop insulin delivery: from bench to clinical practice. *Nat. Rev. Endocrinol.*, 7, 7, 385–395, 2011. 10.1038/nrendo.2011.32, URL: https://doi.org/10.1038%2Fnrendo.2011.32.

9. Murphy, H.R., *et al.*, Closed-Loop Insulin Delivery During Pregnancy Complicated by Type 1 Diabetes. *Diabetes Care*, 34, 2, 406–411, 2011. 10.2337/dc10-1796, URL: https://doi.org/10.2337%2Fdc10-1796.
10. Breton, M., *et al.*, Fully Integrated Artificial Pancreas in Type 1 Diabetes: Modular Closed-Loop Glucose Control Maintains Near Normoglycemia. *Diabetes*, 61, 9, 2230–2237, 2012. 10.2337/db11-1445, URL: https://doi.org/10.2337%2Fdb11-1445.
11. Pappada, S.M., Cameron, B.D., Rosman, P.M., Bourey, R.E., Papadimos, T.J., *et al.*, Neural network-based real-time prediction of glucose in patients with insulin dependent diabetes. *Diabetes Technol. Ther.*, 2, 13, 135–141, 2011. 10.1089/dia.2010.0104.
12. Facchinetti, A., Sparacino, G., Trifoglio, E., Cobelli, C., A new index to optimally design and compare continuous glucose monitoring glucose prediction algorithms. *Diabetes Technol. Ther.*, 2, 13, 111–119, 2011. 10.1089/dia.2010.0151.
13. Robertson, G., Lehmann, E.D., Sandham, W., Hamilton, D., Blood glucose prediction using artificial neural networks trained with the AIDA diabetes simulator: a proof-of-concept pilot Study. *J. Electr. Comput. Eng.*, 2, 5, 1–11, 2011. 10.1155/2011/681786.
14. De Leiva-Hidalgo, A., de Leiva-Pz, A., BruguBrugu, E., From pancreatic extracts to artificial pancreas: history, science and controversies about the discovery of the pancreatic antidiabetic hormone. *Av. En Diabetolog*, 1, 27, 15–26, 2011.
15. Bhat, O. and Khan, D.A., Context-aware system for glycemic control in diabetic patients using neural networks. *Turk. J. Elec. Eng. & Comp. Sci.*, 28, 1, 153–166, 2020.
16. Mougiakakou, S.G., Prountzou, K., Nikita, K.S., A real time simulation model of glucose-insulin metabolism for type 1 diabetes patients, in: *IEEE 2005 Engineering in Medicine and Biology 27th Annual Conference*, Shanghai, China, vol. 1, 298-301, pp. 15–26, 2005, 10.1016/s1134-3230(11)70004-7.
17. Borle, N.C., Ryan, E.A., Greiner, R., *The Challenge of Predicting Meal-to-meal Blood Glucose Concentrations for Patients with Type I Diabetes*, 2019, arXiv preprint arXiv:1903.12347.
18. Hameed, H. and Kleinberg, S., Comparing machine learning techniques for blood glucose forecasting using free-living and patient generated data, in: *Machine Learning for Healthcare Conference*, PMLR, pp. 871–894, 2020, September.
19. Vehí, J., Contreras, I., Oviedo, S., Biagi, L., Bertachi, A., Prediction and prevention of hypoglycaemic events in type-1 diabetic patients using machine learning. *Health Inf. J.*, 26, 1, 703–718, 2020.
20. Hanaire, H., Continuous glucose monitoring and external insulin pump: towards a subcutaneous closed loop. *Diabetes Metab.*, 32, 5, 534–538, 2006. URL: https://doi.org/10.1016%2Fs1262-3636%2806%2972808-7.

21. Rabani, S.T., Khan, Q.R., Khanday, A.M.U.D., Quantifying suicidal ideation on social media using machine learning: a critical review. *Iraqi J. Sci.*, 62, 11, 4092–4100, 2021.
22. Rabani, S.T., Khan, Q.R., Khanday, A.M.U.D., Multi-class suicide risk prediction on twitter using machine learning techniques, in: *2020 2nd International Conference on Advances in Computing, Communication Control and Networking (ICACCCN)*, IEEE, pp. 128–134, 2020, December.

Index

Printed and bound by CPI Group (UK) Ltd, Croydon, CR0 4YY
17/09/2026
14964262-0005